Landscape with Two Saints

Landscape with Two Saints

*How Genovefa of Paris and
Brigit of Kildare Built Christianity
in Barbarian Europe*

LISA M. BITEL

OXFORD
UNIVERSITY PRESS
2009

OXFORD
UNIVERSITY PRESS

Oxford University Press, Inc., publishes works that further
Oxford University's objective of excellence
in research, scholarship, and education.

Oxford   New York
Auckland   Cape Town   Dar es Salaam   Hong Kong   Karachi
Kuala Lumpur   Madrid   Melbourne   Mexico City   Nairobi
New Delhi   Shanghai   Taipei   Toronto

With offices in
Argentina   Austria   Brazil   Chile   Czech Republic   France   Greece
Guatemala   Hungary   Italy   Japan   Poland   Portugal   Singapore
South Korea   Switzerland   Thailand   Turkey   Ukraine   Vietnam

Published by Oxford University Press, Inc.
198 Madison Avenue, New York, New York 10016

www.oup.com

Oxford is a registered trademark of Oxford University Press

Library of Congress Cataloging-in-Publication Data
Bitel, Lisa M., 1958–
Landscape with two saints : how Genovefa of Paris and Brigit of Kildare built
Christianity in barbarian Europe / by Lisa M. Bitel.
   p. cm.
Includes bibliographical references and index.
ISBN-13: 978-0-19-533652-8
1. Geneviève, Saint, ca. 420–ca. 500.   2. Paris (France)—Church history.
3. Brigid, of Ireland, Saint, ca. 453-ca. 524.   4. Kildare (Ireland)—Church
history.   I. Title.
BR1720.G37B58 2009
274'.02—dc22

9 8 7 6 5 4 3 2 1
Printed in the United States of America
on acid-free paper

For Lester and Elliott
whose cults I keep

Contents

List of Illustrations

Introduction

The Journey to Brigit's Well

On the road from Galway to the Cliffs of Moher on the west coast of Ireland, you might notice a nun in a telephone booth at Liscannor. If you are heading for the cliffs, one of the most spectacular sites of natural beauty on the island, you might not bother to stop. But if you visit the nun, you will see that she is small, lovely of face, and demurely draped in the black and white of a modern Benedictine. She gazes thoughtfully down the valley toward the ruins of a medieval monastery. This is no chatty sister, dialing up veiled colleagues around the county, but a statue of Saint Brigit of Kildare encased in glass. Just behind her is a low, dark entrance into a cave tucked beneath a hillside. Up the hill are gravestones. Inside the cave is a well. The effigy of Brigit guards her well.

Saint Brigit has many wells in Ireland and a few elsewhere. Her springs have bubbled, flowed, and leaked into streams, pools, and basins for millennia. The saint's waters must be gushing below the ground of Ireland with the volume and force of a geyser, for they burst through the surface from Ulster to Kerry, Mayo to Wexford. In this rain-soaked land surrounded by ocean, where water from the skies gathers in muddy fields and back gardens, pilgrims seek every drip and trickle from the saint. They duck into caves, clamber over fences, and slog through the rain to dip their fingertips in the holy waters. They bathe their eyes, their temples, their limbs. They collect water in bottles and jugs to take home and sprinkle on others. They come from small villages, whence parents and grandparents led them to Brigit's wells and explained the customs of the waters. They also come on airplanes, boats, and ponderous, road-blocking buses from foreign countries. They are led by nuns and parish priests, tour operators, Neo-Celtic webmasters, writers of guides and coffee-table books featuring dreamy images of the wells and shrines. Pilgrims leave behind photos of lost loved ones, discarded bandages and clooties tied to the trees, broken spectacles, plastic flowers and icons, or the occasional handwritten epistle to the saint.

The last time I visited Brigit's well I was seeking a cure for an obsession. I had become devoted, in my own academic way, to another early medieval holy woman, Saint Genovefa of Paris (ca. 420–509). I had read the earliest story of her life, composed by an anonymous monk about twenty years after she had died, and could not stop imagining its scenes of Genovefa's unlikely deeds: her childhood interview with traveling bishops, her efficient management of Parisian priests, her serenity when battling storms and monsters as she sailed the Seine. Genovefa defies the paradigms that historians of previous generations have constructed for female saints. Neither martyr nor nun, she was a charismatic Gaulish noblewoman who marched around the Parisian basin like a Roman commander, bidding kings, tribunes, bishops, and unruly neighbors to do God's will.

I was hoping that Brigit (ca. 452–524), a slightly more conventional saint, might distract me. I have followed Brigit's cult for twenty years or more. She has a well-argued early history and a much-studied set of medieval biographies, known by their Latin name of *vitae*. She also has a modern career as a nationalist icon. Irish girls are still named for her. Holy cards bearing her image are sold from Dublin to New Delhi. Her wells, her miracles, and her vitae are familiar to ordinary Catholics across the Irish diaspora, as well as to professional students of the fifth century, when she was supposedly born. Genovefa, by comparison, has had nothing like Brigit's publicity. Although she is the patroness of Paris and stands guard over a bridge to the Île Saint-Louis, her origins and early cult are obscure to everyone but specialists in the Gaulish fifth and sixth centuries, or historians of her cult's revival in the later Middle Ages. Few come to her shrines. She has no healing wells. No one has put her statue in a glass booth, although scenes of her life adorn the Panthéon in Paris.

Yet Genovefa and Brigit have much in common. They were born, according to their legends, in northern Europe in the age of barbarian migrations and Mediterranean missions to the pagan north. Both became saints while their countrymen and countrywomen were turning Christian. Both helped to convert others to the faith that was not yet dominant in Europe. They gained reputations for such holiness that learned men wrote their saintly biographies several times over. Both women became the focus of transregional cults that attracted pilgrims and sponsors from far beyond their local churches. While alive, they swayed bishops and kings. After death, they continued to perform miracles for devotees at shrines named after them. They inspired prayers, rituals, and architecture. Each gained a day in the calendar of saints, signifying recognition by bishops of Rome and other cities of Christendom.

Most intriguingly, as I realized at Brigit's well, they were the same kind of saints: peripatetic, influential women responsible for building prestigious churches. Genovefa raised the first basilica at Saint-Denis and was buried in the new shrine of the Holy Apostles in Paris, along with her king and queen. Brigit founded a monastery at Kildare and was later laid to rest in its new basilica, which also came to house deceased lords and ladies of Leinster, one of the four ancient overkingdoms of Ireland. Both saints' cults and their churches prospered throughout the Christian reforms of the central Middle Ages, although Brigit's Kildare dwindled before the Protestant Reformation. Both returned to popularity in the modern period, although Brigit became a more prominent patroness than Genovefa. Both acquired new profiles more typical of chaste, modest, motherly female saints in the Catholic revivals and nationalist movements of the nineteenth century.

The histories of their cults, rising and falling according to devotional trends and political shifts, are not unusual for medieval saints. However, the early careers of Genovefa and Brigit are unique in Christian history. Although both women gained reputations because of their inherent holiness and the usual repertoire of miracles, they also demonstrated their sanctity by means of travel and architecture. At the time, few women became bona fide saints by building churches. Although Italy, Britain, and Iberia produced some female travelers and some women sponsors of building projects, none of those regions produced traveling, building female saints in this period; nor did the empire that became Byzantium. Martyrdom was still the surest method for achieving sanctity. No convents existed in Genovefa's day, although vowed women may have lived together in private homes; only in Brigit's generation did women begin to earn recognition as abbesses of monasteries. At the same time, plenty of men built shrines and churches in the fifth and sixth centuries, but none won sanctity just for their architecture. Kings and patricians created religious monuments as acts of citizenship and public charity, rich men and women sponsored Christian mausolea for themselves and their families, and bishops built churches to house Christian ritual and saints' bodies.

Holy women rarely had enough resources or authority to sponsor building projects. In both Gaul and Ireland in the very early Middle Ages (roughly 400–800), women acquired wealth through marriage or inheritance but generally did not gain full control over its disposition. Women were rarely independent

sponsors, designers, builders, or owners of public architecture. No woman enjoyed unrestricted use of religious buildings or the public spaces attached to
them. By Genovefa's time, bishops had long ago forbidden women to preach or
teach Christianity in churches. Local councils as well as major synods of ecclesiastical men had begun to limit women's participation in liturgies. Christian
communities did not permit women to enter some areas of churches or to take
part at certain times of the day and season. Women could never command the
temporary sacral spaces of Christianity, such as the administrative circuits of
bishops with their official ceremonies of welcome by the Christian community,
or the brief sacred space of religious processions. Men ruled these places. Most
women of the very early Middle Ages, even saintly women, simply could not
move about as easily, regularly, or publicly as men. Men had as many reasons
for such rules as women did for colluding in restrictions on their mobility and
access. Nonetheless, in this historical context, the storied mobility of Brigit and
Genovefa is even more astonishing. That they actually inspired men to help
finance, design, and build religious architecture and were then celebrated for it
is nothing short of miraculous.

Alas, the nun in the phone booth did not cure my obsession but intensi-
fied it. Brigit imprisoned in glass seems an appropriately ironic symbol for the
book she has helped inspire. She is immobile now, but pilgrims continue to
travel to her wayside effigy, seeking supernatural solutions to problems of body
and soul. Her main shrine at Kildare, on the other side of Ireland, lost most
of its properties before 1600. The church there fell into ruin in the eighteenth
century; on the site today stands a faux-Gothic Church of Ireland raised from
Romanesque ruins, along with a patched-up round tower from the eleventh
century. Behind the church is a tumble of stones believed by many visitors to
be an ancient Celtic fire-house where pagan priestesses practiced sacrifices to
the goddess that Brigit replaced. Brigit's body is gone, although bits of it have
turned up in curious places around Europe—a bit of finger in Cologne, a skull
fragment in Lisbon.

Nothing is left of Genovefa's building project at Saint-Denis either, except
ancient foundation stones buried deep beneath the Gothic cathedral of Abbot
Suger. Genovefa's own shrine on Mont-Sainte-Geneviève was built and rebuilt
during the Middle Ages. Her monks and canons acquired lands throughout
the Parisian basin as well as prime real estate within the city itself. Her abbatial
church lasted until the eighteenth century. Louis XV commissioned the architect Soufflot to build a new one, but at the moment of its completion, in 1789,
the Parisians reclaimed Genovefa's place. Soufflot's church became a shrine to the
Republic, the Panthéon, and secular saints now occupy its crypt: Voltaire, Rous-
seau, Curie, Zola. Meanwhile, the church next door, Saint-Etienne-du-Mont, claims

to own a fragment of Genovefa's tomb. A single medieval tower of the Abbaye Sainte Geneviève rises above the roofs of the Lycée Henri IV.

Since neither Brigit nor Genovefa produced any writings of their own, religious men commemorated their lives. An anonymous monk composed the first stories of Genovefa about twenty years after her death, probably at the request of the Frankish queen Clothild. Brigit's first biographer, another monk called Cogitosus, wrote from Kildare in southeastern Ireland more than a century after the saint was supposedly buried there. In later decades, other hagiographers updated these early histories, adding new details and eliminating outdated data to suit changes at their shrines. Medieval histories, theology, laws, stories, and poems mentioned Brigit and Genovefa, too. We are left, then, with men's words and ruined churches as evidence for what these women accomplished—and, indeed, for the scanty proof that they even existed as breathing human beings. Medieval devotees, too, remembered them through both the words of their vitae and the stones of their churches. The saints' building projects attested to their inborn holy power, which medieval writers called *virtus*. Their churches provided both principal site and trusty measure of their cults for generations of believers. Through their bodies, Brigit and Genovefa continued to extend miraculous patronage to humble Christians who visited their sepulchers. The liturgies acted out in their shrines and the written descriptions of their miracles reinforced the truth of their histories. Holy women engineered the buildings, ordinary Christians worshiped within their architecture and visited their bodies, literate men explained the women's lives and projects. Brick and syllable, writer and supplicant, builder and architectural audience together created the two saints and their cults.

This book of words and images explains not only how Europeans came to venerate two women as saints but also how and where Europeans built Christianity at the start of the Middle Ages.[1] I use the unique histories of Genovefa and Brigit, set in contrast to other missionaries and saints, to explain the connections between religious change, landscapes, and gender over roughly four centuries. I rely on archaeological evidence to sketch what Parisians and the Irish of Kildare saw around them every day of their lives, and how Brigit and Genovefa shifted their views. I also interpret later stories of the saints' cults to chart the continuing conversion of their churches and territories. During four centuries of romanization and christianization, the people of Gaul and Ireland altered their landscapes, sometimes suddenly and purposefully, and at other times with slow, small negotiations and incidental decisions.[2] Thus they built themselves a new religion. Stories of Genovefa and Brigit inspired them to build, showed them how, and, in the hagiographers' versions of their saintly deeds and virtues, preserved the memory of Europe's conversion.

This history begins in Paris when the Romans invaded and moves, via Britain, to Ireland when it still lacked a Latin name. The story ends in Christian Europe, with its symbolic capital of Rome, at the moment when pagans became history. By then, around 800, the women and men who lived north of Rome had revised what it meant to be Roman and decided what it meant to be Christian.[3]

Grace and Gratitude

My own landscapes host many folks who have contributed to the production of this book, although its errors (material and symbolic) remain my own. I thank Pat Geary, Colum Hourihane, Jason Glenn, Felice Lifshitz, Gingy Scharff, Bill Tronzo, Greg Woolf, Don Worster, Ann Marie Yasin, and anonymous reviewers for *Speculum* and Oxford University Press for reading portions of the manuscript and providing precious criticism and suggestions. Useful tips also came via correspondence and discussion with Dale Kinney, Catherine McKenna, Jo Ann McNamara, Joszí Nagy, Carol Neuman de Vegvar, and Anabel Wharton. Participants in seminars funded by the Center for Religion and Civic Culture and the Center for Interdisciplinary Research, both at the University of Southern California, as well as audiences at Fordham, Princeton, the University of Kansas, and UCLA provided helpful discussion of my work. Sarah Blake assisted with the bibliography. The Center for Interdisciplinary Research (USC) and the Guggenheim Foundation funded research and travel crucial to the book's completion. Most important to the book and to me, Peter Mancall honored his lifelong commitment to love, honor, and edit. He and my children, Nick and Sophie, accompanied me on pilgrimage to the wells of Saint Brigit and the Paris of Saint Genovefa. Despite their complaints ("I've been to more churches than any other Jew in history!"), I thank them.

Landscape with Two Saints

Shrine, Liscannor, county Clare (photograph by author).

I

Paris before Genovefa

The Landscape Enters History

Although Genovefa's pious biographers made many claims about her, authorship was not one of them. She never recorded what she saw when she arrived in Paris around 435. She must have found the architecture lacking, though, because her life's passion apparently became to build another church there. Her first hagiographer, drafting his story of Genovefa almost a century later, did not try to guess about her impressions of the city. He had little to say about Paris's places except to recount how Genovefa changed them. He recalled the scenery of the saint's travels but not the city where she spent most of her life, except for a few offhand references to lodgings (*hospitium, cellula*) and churches. One episode in the saint's life featured a bridge across the Seine. Another important event took place in an unidentified plaza on the Île de la Cité. It was 451, and Huns were approaching Paris. Genovefa had just marshaled the city's matrons for prayerful vigils in the baptistery and was urging their husbands not to send property out of the city for safekeeping. The Parisians suspected a trick to defraud them and denounced Genovefa as a false prophet. A crowd had gathered near the river to decide whether to "kill her by stoning or by drowning her in the great eddies" of the Seine when, fortunately, a character witness arrived to save the saint.[1] The episode reveals few details of Genovefa's Paris: the island refuge at the city's center with its small open space for gathering; the baptistery, one of the oldest Christian buildings in any Roman town; the rocks (*lapides*) lying handy for stoning soothsayers.

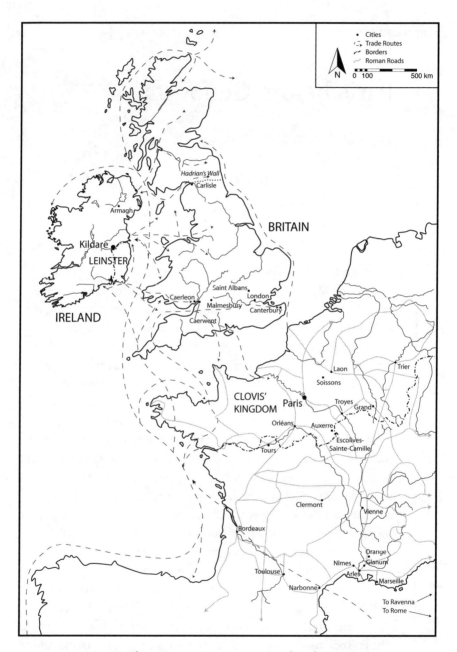

FIGURE I.I. Map: Northern Europe, ca. 500 C.E. (map by John Marston).

Every fifth-century resident had his or her own Paris, observed from points of stasis or passage and informed by particular places in the city.[2] Neighbors may have shared vocabularies of culture, history, and politics, which they used to define their town, but they did not take the same view. They just gazed in common directions. The Parisians who opened their gates to Genovefa had inherited conceptual models for working cities and their surrounding landscapes. We can only guess at the ways in which unlettered town dwellers understood Paris by studying what little remains of it. However, the documents of literate men of the time, including Genovefa's own biographer, emphasized four particular geographical discourses, or ways of looking at landscapes, dominant in the fifth century. Some citizens saw Paris in relation to other locations in the same administrative web of imperial territorial units. On this administrative landscape, whose center was in the Mediterranean south, Paris was a hinterland town of middling importance. Others looked upon a second, more mobile landscape stretched between Paris and the farms of its surrounding countryside. Wagons and boats bustled back and forth across this economic region, supplying Paris with all it needed to survive. Still others saw a third, sacral landscape with a foreground of churches set against a background of old temples and holy places. The Seine itself, curling around the town and protecting the islands in its midst, had once been sacred to Parisians.

Underlying and guiding these perspectives was a fourth view of Paris that encompassed all the others: looking back at the visible, legible, and tangible past of the city. Its citizens lived on a landscape of things left behind. Paris was already a pile of architecture when young Genovefa supposedly arrived. Before her, Stone Age settlers, Celtic wanderers, southern European invaders, Gallo-Roman indigenes, Christian missionaries, and Germanic émigrés had come to the place we now call Paris. Each generation had bequeathed to the next its homes, public buildings, gathering places, walls, and streets—whatever was left of them—among other detritus. Just as the Roman emperors had gathered the spoils of war to decorate their monuments of triumph, thrifty Parisians harvested the accrued layers of the past to maintain their city. They used history to bulwark town walls and adorn new churches. Just before Genovefa's arrival, they had begun to rearrange the ancient streets, neighborhoods, crumbling houses and shops, and even the old graveyards of Paris to accommodate new Christian ways of living and looking. At the time of her death, they were reordering the city once again to accommodate their latest ruler, Clovis, king of Franks, with his retinues and armies.

The useful, meaningful leftovers or *spolia* of Celtic, Roman, pagan Paris literally and figuratively provided building blocks for Genovefa's construction projects.[3] Genovefa was only one architect of change in a long history of urban renewal. Her story may have been unique among Christian saints, but it would have had little effect on her fellow Parisians had they not lived among other, older versions of Paris and its buildings. The story of Genovefa's Paris was really a tale of at least three cities—the Roman administrative center, the bustling cluster of neighborhoods and markets, and the jumble of religious architecture. Each of these Parises occupied a modest position on much larger landscapes of late imperial politics, economic networks, and sacral sites whose histories would converge in the life of Genovefa. But before that, Caesar had to conquer Gaul, and generations of Romans, Celtic Gauls, Gallo-Romans, and other assorted Parisians had to build, rebuild, and build again.

Roman Paris

In the 400s, while writers in southern Gaul were lamenting the end of Roman civilization, the people of Paris could still locate their city in an imperial territory with a Latin name. Modern historians have sympathized with the southerners and sorted the third, fourth, and fifth centuries into a series of invasions and crises for Gaul. There was the putative catastrophe of the 260s and 270s, when several different armies moved out of the Rhineland into imperial territory, and another series of so-called invasions at the dawn of the fifth century. Maps from the 1900s tracked barbarian armies and tribal migrations with complicated, crisscrossing lines that ended in the arrows of conquest and settlement, fixed by specific dates.[4] The threatening influx of non-Romans could hardly have been so obvious to fifth-century Parisians, though. For one thing, Gaul had recently been the stage for several internal wars among contenders for the empire who either came from Gaul or recruited troops there. So many Germanic and Gaulish fighters had joined the many Caesars' armies that, by the fourth century, whole cohorts of them ranged from Iberia to Persia. Even when war came to Paris, it did not include the dramatic confrontations or long-term sieges of written history but seasonal raids, sporadic banditry, and local destruction.[5] Armies never occupied Paris for long. No one expected a ruler and his army to settle down at a smallish island-town in the Seine, so Genovefa's generation could not have predicted that the former refuge of Celtic chieftains would become the capital of a Frankish king by 500.

The history and name of Paris were Roman; if the settlement had a previous designation, we do not know it. In the third century B.C.E., a second-tier Gaulish tribe had set up headquarters on both sides of the Seine. Latin writers called them Parisii. They had arrived over long centuries of the Bronze Age and Iron Age, in one of those many circulations of people, their ways, and their things that we now call Celtic. They built a fort (*oppidum*, according to the Romans) on an island within the protective marshes of the river. In imitation of communities farther south, they minted coins to proclaim their presence on the landscape, although the river really belonged to a mother goddess (Sequana in the Romans' Latin) whom they worshiped at shrines along its course. In the mid–first century B.C.E., the Parisii joined neighboring tribes in an alliance against Roman intrusion and Latinizing dominion. They burned their *oppidum* rather than surrender it to Julius Caesar. The Romans built a better fort on the south bank of the Seine and renamed the place Lutetia. The Parisii remained.[6]

The conquest that began with Caesar's demolition of the Parisii progressed through several centuries of construction. Government officials quickly organized Gaul into a hierarchy of provinces, each with its own administrative sub-units, linked by highways and aqueducts aimed ultimately at Rome. Gauls on the ground saw this tidy configuration take shape as forts, trading posts, ports, and towns at the center of *civitates*, or former tribal regions, all set on strategic sites along logical traffic routes. Paris grew up at a crossroads of roads and rivers that connected Mediterranean harbors with the northern European coast and with the Germanic interior. The city (sometimes called *civitas Parisiorum*, although *civitas* continued to mean a larger territory focused on a particular kind of urban center) spread quickly across a typical Roman grid, with a forum crowning the highest hill. Neighborhoods that collected around the edge of the central hill—sub-*urbes*—had their own public spaces, baths, and temples. The first serious architectural expansion of Paris lasted about 200 years. By the mid–third century, right before the attacks of the 260s, the city of the Parisii had become a complex collection of government buildings, residences, and places of business covering 370 acres and housing around 8,000 souls.[7]

Parisians dwelt in the discipline of the city's neighborhoods, monuments, and—probably after the mid-third-century attacks—walls. Everyone in town was affected by its periodic expansions, reductions, and rebuildings.[8] When wealthy families constructed fine homes adorned with mosaics or sponsored the construction of temples and monuments, local people yielded space and supplied labor, willingly or otherwise. Benefactors planted baths near the forum; two other bath complexes later appeared on the city's edge for neighborhoods growing there. The main complex still stands at the Musée de Cluny, with its remnants of plumbing and original vaults in the huge *frigidarium*, the room for cold baths. Once its great salons had been adorned with mosaics and murals, shrine niches of marble, and capitals carved as navy ships.[9] A theater for religious rituals completed the initial ring of architecture around the city center. An arena sat on the eastern slope of the main hill. Below it to the southeast and southwest, social elites lay their dead in privately constructed

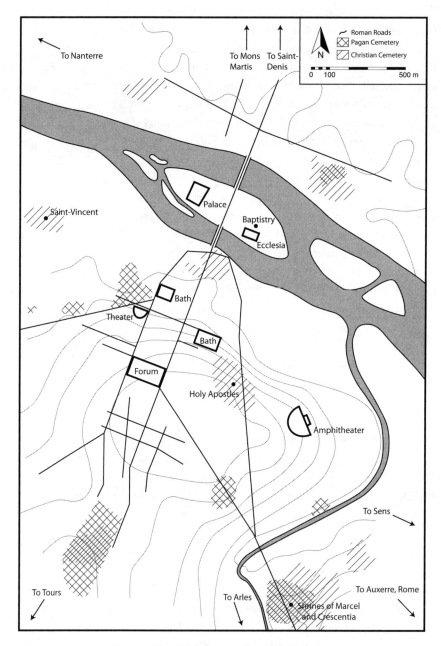

FIGURE I.2. Map: Paris in the fifth century (map by John Marston).

tombs outside the city's boundary, so that burials lined the roads from Paris.[10] Although cemeteries never violated city limits before the fourth century, other paths cut through the limits. An aqueduct drew water from the south along the now lost course of the Bièvre to baths, basins, and fountains at the hilltop imperial city center.[11]

Sometime after 260, during the dire wave of raids, townsmen and townswomen began a custom that has endured until today: they scavenged materials from ruined buildings of the city for use elsewhere. Faced with attack, they used these *spolia* of stone blocks, hewn by slaves in Gaulish quarries a century or more earlier, to fortify a newly defined, smaller city. Although they never completely abandoned the riverbanks, they hauled their blocks downhill and over water to the island in the Seine, where they built a walled refuge.[12] At least seventy other Gaulish cities raised walls of stone in the same period, recycling pavements, public buildings, funerary monuments, and housing materials to defend their communities.[13] Decorated columns and inscribed slabs, once rising vertically in the amphitheater and forum, now became foundations of a stouter, relocated, and condensed Paris.[14] The city then refocused on the island and hid behind its walls for hundreds of years.

Although the walls of almost all Gaulish towns followed directly upon the Germanic raids of the 260s and 270s, they were not the slipshod products of panic but conscientious investments in both durability and good looks. Most of them were at least ten feet thick, with enormous hewn blocks at the base and smaller concrete blocks above, some refaced so as to be smooth on the outside and decorated with triple bands of tiles. Many city walls also featured multiple stout towers.[15] Paris's defenses were so snug that when Flavius Claudius Julianus Augustus came to town a century later in 358, this grandson of Constantine the Great, future emperor, and fearless conqueror of Cologne and Strasbourg put his palace safely inside the walls of the Île de la Cité. His troops occupied Paris for three years while planning a Rhine campaign. They contributed to the enduring architecture of the city by building markets, quays, and government offices on the island.[16] It must have been a terrible disappointment, though, for the aristocratic citizens of the 360s to find that the only emperor to build a house in the city was an ascetic soldier-philosopher who disdained the trappings of Roman luxury.

Julius Caesar had once divided unconquered Gallia in three, but by Julian's time the Gallo-Romans maintained a more elaborate scheme for provincial government that had been in place for two centuries. The territorial hierarchy helped Parisians to learn their place, for when Roman officers had created Lutetia on the ashes of the Celtic *oppidum*, they had also created other cities for Parisians to look at and defer to. The settlement on the Seine was part of a system of regions, administrative centers, towns and villages of citizens and indigenes (*provinciae, civitates, municipia, vici*), suburbs, camps, and forts, each with its own particular functions. According to the *Notitia Galliarum*, a list of Gaulish cities and forts composed around 400, Julian's adored "little Lutetia" was among the lesser of seven cities in the province of Lugdunensis quarta (fourth Lyonnaise, also called Lugdunensis Senonia, after its capital at Sens).[17] The province stretched from the Marne to the Loire, bordered by the Saône in the east. Senlis, Meaux, and Paris clustered at its northern tip, Chartres and Troyes marked its sides, and Sens sat roughly at its center. All these other towns were also based on earlier Gaulish tribal centers, and all were at least as large as the *civitas* Parisiorum.[18] They spread out from Paris at an average distance of about sixty-six kilometers apart, linked by roads and rivers in a sensible Roman pattern.[19]

Bureaucrats in charge of keeping order and collecting taxes divided each *civitas* or urban region into smaller rural units, *pagi*, sometimes hundreds of them. Each *pagus* contained at least one population center, such as a village, estate, farm, or fort, and each maintined a distinct local identity. The great historian of France, Fernand Braudel, famously—although incorrectly—blamed the Roman parcelization of Gaul into provinces, *civitates*, and tiny *pagi* for the fractured national identity of modern Frenchmen.[20] Gallo-Romans distinguished cities from the other population centers of a *civitas*, though: cities were laid out, like Paris, in quarters and grids with recognizable Latin edifices, walls, and gates. They were not always the largest settlements in terms of acreage, and only a fraction of the Gaulish population lived in them, but they were the most densely settled points on the landscape.[21] Southern cities held up to 30,000 inhabitants, but Paris never grew so large.[22]

The internal order of each Gaulish *civitas* was topped by a fluidly class-based council (*curia*) of taxable men of means, some of whom held bureaucratic offices as *procuratores, defensores civitati,* or (by the fourth century) *episcopi,* that is, bishops.[23] These important men made decisions and rendered legal judgments. They also collected revenues for local and imperial government and sponsored civic life. They were middle-class merchants or landowning aristocrats, depending on the specific period, but always only men. The privilege of government was not cheap for concerned and wealthy citizens, who traditionally were supposed to spend much of the year living in town rather than on their rural estates, and much of their income on building projects, public diversions, and regional defense. They also had to maintain a network of clients—townsmen, managers, middlemen, servants, and, in the case of bishops, entire communities full of believers—who supported them in business and politics.[24] By the fifth century, responsibility for this complex administrative architecture belonged largely to local men, either of old Gallo-Roman stock or the emerging Germanic elite, rather than administrators sent from Rome or Ravenna.

The scribblers of administrative hierarchy tried to keep up with shifts in political bureaucracy and geography. They compiled and then regularly updated the late fourth-century *Notitia Dignitatum,* a comprehensive list of the offices of provincial government. In the first version, Gallia was one of four praetorian prefectures. It included the dioceses of Britain, Iberia, Aquitaine, and Gaul proper. The prefect of Gallia supposedly oversaw all judicial and financial aspects of its government, assisted by the governor of each diocese. The diocese of Gaul stretched over the two Belgiae, the two Germaniae, Sequania, the two Alpine provinces, and the four Lyonnaise provinces. A veritable army of officials worked for the governor of each diocese, from lowly accountants and messengers to high-ranking special agents of emperors. Yet this peacetime ideal was precarious in the fifth century, for the *Notitia* also included dozens of military officials attached to Paris, including a master of the navy; it seems unlikely that all these soldiers were simultaneously full-time residents, but at very least the document assumed that the city needed them. Whenever an army general or rising politician—usually the same man in the fourth or fifth century—used a town such as Paris for his base, he assumed responsibility for government, whether he came to defend that city or to rest before striking another. Armed commanders must have negotiated and squabbled with civil officials and local aristocrats about who was in charge, who made decisions, who enforced them, and who profited by them. It was hard to know who should supervise which places. One man's rebels were another observer's local gentry trying to reassert romanized order.[25] Ordinary town dwellers had to find the locus of political power so they could pay their taxes, lodge complaints, and secure armed protection.

Whose city was Paris? To a certain extent, the city itself answered when and if important men came to town. Even after Julian's departure and death, places like Paris remained recognizable administrative centers for periodic meetings and assemblies. They were also valuable prizes in struggles both local and imperial. Generals and Caesars fought over Gaulish towns in their battles for thrones elsewhere, while Germanic leaders and Gallo-Roman landed families manipulated cities in their attempts to gain regional prominence. Gratian (375–83) was the last emperor to visit Lutetia on one of his many trips to fight the Alamanni before meeting his end at the hands of the usurper Magnus Maximus at Lyon. Meanwhile, it was Arbogast, a Frankish general of Roman troops, who protected Gaulish cities and negotiated treaties with would-be Germanic invaders in 381.[26] Arbogast was a typical provincial general, fighting to preserve and control the existing political and administrative landscape, but also taking advantage of it for his own advancement.

Anyone with pretensions to empire needed cities. Nowhere else in Gaul could a man effectively advertise his leadership. Politicians and warriors, like bishops and saints, required the crowds, public spaces, defensive settlements, and markets of cities. As a result, purportedly barbarian Germanic leaders also preserved towns, for instance, when they allied with Roman-commanded troops in 451 against Attila. At other times, though, they attacked or destroyed cities in order to keep others from having them. In the first decades of the fifth century, Franks repeatedly sacked the "richest city of Gaul," imperial Trier, on their way west, thus making sure that western emperors did not return—they did not, however, raze the place or even prevent continued settlement.[27] When Aegidius, one of the last Gallo-Roman pretenders to empire in Gaul, wanted to set himself up as king (rex) of Gauls and Romans in the 460s, he waited until Childeric, the Germanic king of Soissons, was out of town. Later, when Childeric's son Clovis was ready to take back power, he marched directly to Soissons, chased out Aegidius's son and heir Syagrius, and plundered the town's churches to signal the change of regime.[28] Taking control of town—like raising a battle flag on a contested hill—was a public announcement of regional dominance.

Paris was vulnerable when the struggle was nearby but also when troops were diverted from the northern provinces to more distant theaters of empire. When legions moved elsewhere in the early fifth century, Gaulish cities called upon local military men and rural aristocrats to staff and fund their protection. Yet a single city could never muster enough technological and human resources for sustained defense. Town dwellers were not soldiers even when called upon to act as such. Towns needed professional fighters, weapons, supplies, and good walls for prolonged assaults. When towns in the most northerly province of empire, Britain, were under invasion in 423, their leaders sent pathetic requests for troops to Aetius, consul in Gaul; but Aetius was too busy defending Gaulish cities against troops of Franks, Alamanni, and Huns, all of whom kept switching sides.[29] Fifty years later, Bishop Sidonius wrote a less famous appeal from Clermont at the other end of Gaul, then caught in the Visigoths' expansion. He lamented, "We are not sure that the scorched face of our walls, or the decaying palisade of stakes, or the ramparts worn by the breasts of guards on constant watch will support our courage, so reckless and so dangerous."[30] Too often, citizens had no resort but to beg for defensive miracles from their saints.

When both local leaders and distant generals failed them, citizens turned to the only professionally trained, literate, aristocratic advocates left in cities, and the only universally recognized ambassadors among the factions and subgroups of their communities: Christian bishops.[31] Gaulish bishops redefined *civitates* as church-based communities with walls, offering both material and spiritual resources to support a concentrated population. They co-opted the administrative structure of the late empire and redirected the duties of its *curiales*, maintaining the system of dependent suburban and rural spaces and locating each town in the widening network of episcopal sees.[32] They maintained as long as they could the boundaries of provinces and the cities within. Although Genovefa's region, then the Fourth Lyonnaise, steadily lost efficacy as an administrative unit in the muddle of late fourth-century and early fifth-century northern politics, the metropolitan diocese of Sens grew within the province's bounds, governed by its bishop to whom the priests and bishop of Paris answered.[33] Within that larger episcopal territory, Paris remained a secondary town just as it had been a lesser city in the imperial province. Parisians could see far enough beyond Sens to know that Paris occupied a modest spot within the larger hierarchy of Gaulish episcopacies. When bishops of Paris, Sens, Orléans, and Troyes traveled to a synod at Arles in the fourth century and again in the fifth, they saw and felt the power of southern bishops from more elegant, ancient cities such as Narbonne and Lyon.[34]

Yet churchmen, too, squabbled over territories and boundaries, and argued about which cities took precedence within each administrative territory. Despite notable hagiographic exceptions—Martin of Tours, Severinus of Noricum— bishops of the period normally came from the same regional aristocracies that governed cities, so local families often took sides in their disputes.[35] In 428, the bishop of Rome complained to Gaulish colleagues because they were electing homegrown politicos with no clerical background to episcopal office. When Bishop Hilary of Arles started summoning councils in 439 and going from town to town to ordain other new bishops, military and civilian leaders supported him against other churchmen because he was one of their own. Likewise, Sidonius Apollinaris held political positions at home and in Rome—including that of prefect in Rome and, for one short year, son-in-law of the emperor—which complicated his later career as bishop of Clermont.[36] Often enough, the outcome of battles among bishops depended upon each man's ability to govern and defend his own community, as well as his reputation in other episcopal cities.

In the midst of such thick politicking, longtime residents of Paris knew that their security depended upon a collegial and efficient alliance of bishop, landowners, military commanders, and any other men of means left inside city walls. Such leaders were responsible for convincing even more powerful men who dwelt in more important places to protect—or, at least, not to damage— their little town. Parisians had only to glance outside the walls to recognize their relative unimportance in the scheme of empire. Except for the occasional army and traders moving on the river, not much traffic passed by. Signposts and milestones pointed the way to and from Paris, but no remarkable monument marked Caesar's defeat of brave Gallic defenders. Other cities had raised trophies to imperial victories, like the arches depicting chained and conquered Gauls at Glanum and Orange ordered by Augustus.[37] Paris's unadvertised structures were built for the use of Parisians, not the eyes of visitors.

It was hard for Parisians to convince distant rulers to take notice of their city, with the exception of Julian, who stayed only long enough to stabilize the Rhine frontier and gain the imperial crown. When lesser functionaries recorded their journeys through Gaul in the third and fourth centuries, they had hardly mentioned Paris. The *Antonine Itinerary*, a mid-third-century collection of lists of places en route to other places, put Lutetia on the way from Rouen via Petromantalum (near Guiry) and southward to Salioclitum (Saclay), hence to Chartres. Paris was a crossroads and stopping place—no more, no less.[38] Another road guide from the fourth century, now called the *Peutinger Table*, barely put Paris on the map. A sixteenth-century copy of the document spreads across 6.8 meters of parchment inked in black and red with the names of cities, forts, baths, inns, and important sights. Tiny towers and colonnaded courtyards marked buildings and places, signifying the spread of romanized settlement across 200,000 kilometers of empire and beyond, from Wales to China. Scholars and officials around the Mediterranean world read the *Table* and memorized the geographies of Britannia, Gallia, Italia, and Germania. Scribes made additions and copies throughout the fourth and fifth centuries, adding points to the route as they gained importance to travelers. Monks of the Middle Ages copied this guide to an earlier world, commemorating the footsteps of brave messengers from one boundary of lost empire to another.[39] For Paris, the chart has a single symbol: the word *Luteci[a]*. Paris was one point in a series of daylong journeys between more notable places. From Paris, the lines of those journeys passed over a horizon and vanished down the road to Rouen, Trier, or more often southward to Sens or Orléans and beyond.

Urbanites just a few inches closer to the right edge of the *Table*—a hundred miles nearer to the Mediterranean and Rome—barely noticed events so far north, if their written records are truthful. Political dramas in Byzantium or Rome loomed larger in their minds.[40] Southern authors who read and wrote history from the imperial point of view were wretchedly conscious of recent urban decline and the rupture of good government, punctuated by especially violent spells between the third-century crisis and early fifth-century invasions. The anonymous southern Gaulish chronicler of 452 was depressingly consistent in his reports of *civitates* (he meant territories rather than cities) "foully devastated" and "completely humiliated."[41] Even when the literati had personal experience of northern outposts, they preferred polemical tropes to rigorous analysis. Salvian, a refugee from Trier in the mid–fifth century who spent the rest of his life in and around Marseille, blamed selfish aristocrats and corrupt civil servants in Gallia and Germania for the repeated barbarian onslaughts of his city. For Salvian, as for the Roman historian Tacitus three centuries earlier, rebellious Northmen manifested a kind of fierce moral purity, whereas the decadent Roman bureaucrats of Germania deserved their destruction.[42] Yet, while men of letters lamented, Parisians and other northerners refocused and rebuilt their city centers again and again.

Along with late antique historians who bemoaned imperial decline and the bureaucrats who crafted itineraries, versifiers of the period also tended to ignore or misinterpret Paris. Refined men measured cities by the complexity of their government and the beauty of their civic monuments. As Ausonius of Bordeaux explained in about 390, three decades before Genovefa's birth, few provincial towns were able to transmit the magic of the Eternal City to the hinterland. Those closest to Rome were most successful. Arles earned a place in Ausonius's *Ranking of Cities* as a "little Gallic Rome." Trier, although a former seat of the western imperial court, attracted Ausonius's notice too but only because it was a military supply center, not an urban wonder. A generation before Salvian, Ausonius had enthused, "Long has Gaul, mighty in arms, yearned to be praised," because "[Trier] feeds . . . clothes and arms the forces of the Empire."[43] The "broad walls" of the city protected its people against menacing Germanic tribes (although not in Salvian's day). In Ausonius's eyes, Trier was an outpost in perilous territory. But Ausonius forgot even to mention Paris.

A city's reputation was another measure of its durability and Roman identity, no more mutable than the thickness of its walls, its location on the written itineraries of bureaucrats, or its position in the administrative hierarchies of provincial government. Like the dirt and stone barrier that Emperor Hadrian had built across second-century Britain to keep out northern savages, the physical and ideological ramparts of Gaulish cities held at bay barbarians, invaders, and *pagani* of all sorts. By the fifth century, Britons were desperate for sturdier ramparts that would exclude the violent newcomers who were settling their island. But they also wanted walls to encircle and preserve Latin speakers.[44] Borders, by their nature, kept things in as well as keeping them out; frontiers marked what must be preserved.[45] Once allowed inside, docile outsiders might possibly learn to share this symbolism made so visible in architecture and so urgent in literature. Bishop Sidonius, the fifth-century aesthete who sold his services to Euric the Visigoth, was optimistic about the potential of frontier cities to convert barbarians. He figured that the tenuous high culture of provincial centers such as Trier or Clermont could spruce up a Germanic warrior much like a good soak in a thermal bath. "You will find that people with learning are as much above simple folk as humans are above beasts," he advised a Frankish friend.[46]

For Sidonius and those who read him, the distance from Rome was mental. People were either cultured humans living in properly built settlements or illiterate animals. He was not referring to the lions and monsters of the desert but to the domesticated beasts roaming just outside of cities, of course: the cows of the farm, the pigs of the forest edge, and the rude immigrants who camped on other people's fields. Even more fearsome creatures such as the Huns would destroy a *civitas* capital, but those with the potential for cultural conversion could be improved if only they moved onto the administrative map. Once Germanic itinerants came through town gates, the city's built environment would cast its christianizing, romanizing spell upon the barbarians and make them human. This was the most lasting legacy of northern colonization by Mediterranean people: the notion of civilization as a process marked visibly by such outward signs as language, dress, and architecture. Christian organizers from Gaul to Galway would embrace this paradigm of cultural conversion.

But as Sidonius also admitted to his friend Syagrius, poet and great-grandson of a consul, conversion could work both ways. He warned Syagrius not to abandon Roman verses for Burgundian speech. Learn enough of the local Germanic dialect, he counseled, "so you will not be laughed at, and practice the other [Latin], so you may do the laughing."[47] In Sidonius's opinion both barbarians and civilized men could choose to improve themselves or lapse into beastliness simply by deciding whether and how to translate. By 435 Parisians capable of seeing beyond the local horizon were probably not chuckling at Germanic vernaculars but practicing Frankish tongues. They were watching the north with Syagrius but also scanning southern routes to Provence and Rome with Sidonius. Everyone was anxiously contemplating the limits of conversion, translation, and imperial administration.

Views of the Countryside

Although barbarism could easily permeate the fluid boundaries of cities, Romanness (*romanitas*) also flowed in the other direction from towns to the Gaulish countryside.[48] The line between urban center and rural territory had its own ideology, also culled from classical literature and architecture, complementary to the hierarchical ideology of cities and administrative territories. The Latin word *civitas* is instructive: it meant a city bound by the bustle of constant traffic to smaller towns, villages, and dispersed farmsteads. Parisians moved back and forth between city and country. Farmers hauled their products to town to sell or pay as taxes. Merchants traveled roads and rivers. Men of letters and politics divided their time between their rural estates and their business in Paris. Tools and more precious objects went from urban forges and craftshops to the villas of rural folk, although large farms also produced some of their own equipment. When the occasional horde of beastly foreigners arrived at the city walls, they had already passed by cultivated fields and marvelous villas attached to the town. Parisians were more directly invested in this daily landscape of economic and social connections than in the administrative itineraries of imperial government.

After the Franks took Paris, the movement of goods and people still linked town and country in a single landscape, even if some routes became difficult or particular sites of exchange shifted. After the mid–third century, the most successful merchants already had moved out of the old forum stalls to shops near the stone quays of the island. Some set up smaller markets outside the city walls. Production centers grew or diminished as demand fluctuated along with Paris's population, especially in times of war. Consumers changed places, too. No one was building new classically styled villas around Paris, as they were in some spots in the south of Gaul, or making new highways to town, or turning marginal land into fresh arable. But estate owners repaired roofs and raised barns after invaders had burned the crops and outbuildings, just as city dwellers fixed their walls after attack.[49]

It is hard to judge the density of rural population in fifth-century Gaul, since little remains of villas and even less of smaller or more traditional farms.[50] The land itself yields a few clues. Throughout the political and architectural changes of the fourth and fifth centuries, settlement of all kinds remained fairly stable, neither expanding nor dwindling suddenly. The total number of inhabited sites dipped in the third century but revived in the fourth.[51] Farms continued producing regularly. Woodland increased slightly after the fourth century, indicating some decrease in demand for timber but not necessarily a resurgence of wilderness or drastic depopulation.[52] Most of the land continued to be occupied by farmers and tenants who updated their houses with some sort of imported architectural feature—a rough mural, some wooden columns, a steam heating system—when they could afford it. When peaceable but hungry armies came near town, farmers and stock raisers took advantage. When raiders burned the crops and barns, everyone suffered.

In Genovefa's time, the landscapes of city and country were also bound together by shared pretensions to culture. Some farmers lived in more romanized style than others; *romanitas* in the countryside, as in the city, consisted of constant small efforts and daily choices about how to live and work. Not all the lands of Gaul had entered the imperial grids. Villas and estate-based agriculture were always most dense on the best lands near urban centers and along military routes. There were more of them in southern than in northern Gaul, although approximately one-quarter of rural settlements in the north had once been "villas" of some sort.[53] Rural Gauls also continued to farm and herd on more traditionally organized lands.[54] Yet in poetry—and, as we shall see, in Christian literature—*civitas* and *villa* remained complementary reservoirs of aristocratic power and culture. Late antique writers considered the country estate of a civilized man to be symbolic of his citizenship in empire. The fifth-century provincial Sidonius cherished some version of an ideal villa first celebrated by the poets Horace and Vergil: as a gentleman's island of refuge, a villa provided all the organic and intellectual elements of civilized life for the owner, his family, and his *familia* of tenants, servants, and slaves. His farm should produce olives, vines, apples, bees for honey and fish for supper, stock for meat and iron for tools, as well as an aesthetically pleasing and properly organized set of house, outbuildings, courtyards, well, and private shrines. In late antique Gaul, Sidonius's embattled estate was protected by a natural version of Hadrian's Wall, namely, the Loire; the river formed a frontier zone shielding the civilization of olive trees and grapevines from northern barbarians.[55]

When people had both the money and the desire to advertise themselves as romanized, they invested in objects that would tell this to their neighbors.[56] Ausonius recalled fine villas set along the Mosel at the end of the fourth century, in locations even more remote than Paris. Poetically following fish and noisy boatmen down the river, he rhapsodized about the "country seats" and "lordly halls" along its cliffs. The mansions, with their towers and pillars, their baths and soaring roofs, rose in profoundly provincial territory. Horace would hardly have recognized the towers and other defensive works that Ausonius took for granted, however. Likewise, Sidonius sang the pleasures of his villa near Clermont-Ferrand in the second half of the fifth century. His house had excellent plumbing but lacked nice wall paintings. He also adored the newly fortified villa of his friend Pontius Leontius in Aquitaine and Consentius's place near Narbonne, where they grew olives and grapes. Venantius Fortunatus, a sixth-century bishop and poet, described a few nice houses too, including the villa of Bishop Nicetius outside Trier, flourishing long after Salvian and his prefect had fled southward. Nicetius's estate was protected by turrets, which may explain its continuing prosperity; cautious owners of several other estates in northern Europe added bastions, towers, and ditches in the fourth and fifth centuries.[57]

Although the empire's economy began a slow downward slide in the third century, local trade and industries continued to accommodate the demand for symbolic luxury goods into the fifth century in some parts of Gaul.[58] For some wealthy farmers, it was enough to add a few Roman-style pillars or enhance their walls with murals on mythological subjects. Others tried to reorganize their traditional homes on villa-style plans as they rebuilt their houses every couple of generations.[59] A large main structure, a courtyard and garden, a shrine to the household divinities and baths to rinse off the dust—any and all of these manifested Latin culture to owners of estates and to those who worked and lived in their proximity.[60] Villa owners of declining wealth had to choose between shoring up walls or repairing paintings, maintaining the plumbing or funding public works in town, and building ditches and fences or fixing hypocausts. Sidonius and the other poets may have ignored the shabbiness of chipped mosaics and unused rooms, but their friends still tried to preserve the aesthetics, ideals, and economy of villa life, and the landscape showed it.[61]

In the fifth century, both Parisians and farmers had good reason to maintain economic connections. Even when enemies surrounded the city and controlled access, aristocratic landowners like Genovefa had to find ways to bring food from country barns to urban mouths. The empire's highways continued to bear transregional trade in the centuries before and after Genovefa sailed the Seine. The garbage of that exchange is today's museum treasure: a typical terracotta flagon, ring-shaped like the ancient vases of Corinth and abandoned beneath the Hôtel Dieu, came from an earlier century and a sunnier place. Before it became an artifact, someone had filled it with liquor, and the maker had inscribed it with a brief dialogue: "Hostess, fill my flagon with barley beer! Barkeep, do you have peppered wine?" "It's here!" "Fill 'er up!"[62] Wine arrived by riverboat in barrels, which were then hauled by wagon to rural tables.[63] Little bronze statues of Mercury and Jupiter, possibly cast in Parisian forges but more likely produced en masse in purpose-built industrial workshops of the larger southern cities, were available for purchase like today's tiny replicas of the Eiffel Tower for sale at tourist kiosks.

The countryside continued to supply building materials to Paris, too, although in smaller quantities than before. In more luxuriant years, Parisians had imported fine marbles for construction or interior decoration, for there were no major quarries around Paris, just local operations for rough-hewn stone and ordinary brick architecture. By the fifth century, when citizens had been reusing dressed blocks for at least a century, apparently no one was quarrying any kind of stone nearby. The ore for smelting must have come from mines outside the region and been forged locally, although Parisian artisans were no longer crafting the ostentatious torcs and shields of Celtic yesteryears.[64] Silver and gold coins recalling one emperor after another, lost or buried in Parisian foundations or tossed into the Seine, were minted in the imperial cities of Rome and Milan (and when provincial generals fancied themselves emperors, in Cologne or Trier).[65] Money came to Paris by the bag only to pay soldiers, victuallers, civil

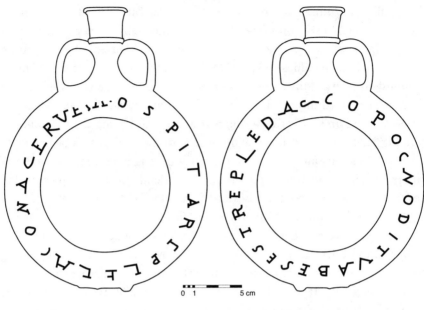

(H)OSPITA REPLE LAGONA(M) CERVESA   COPO CONDITU(M) (H)ABES
                                                    – EST – REPLE, DA!

FIGURE 1.3. Imported ceramic flagon, third or fourth century, found beneath
the Hôtel-Dieu in 1807 (John Marston after Duval). One side reads, "Hostess, fill
my flagon with barley beer!" while the other reads, "Barkeep, do you have peppered
wine?" "It's here!" "Fill 'er up!"

servants, and mercenaries, who then spent their money on the town or went to
their graves with it. Parisians returned the coins to Rome as tax surplus; they
were paying taxes with currency in the 430s, when Saint Germanus of Auxerre
finagled a tax break from the imperial government for his city, and in the 440s
when he did the same for the Armoricans.[66]

Like all towns, and even tiny *vici*, Parisians and their country neighbors
together produced much of the urban population's clothing, pottery, and iron
goods. High-living Parisians imported delicate glass vessels and embroidered
textiles when they could, but such fineries were of poorer quality and came less
frequently from the major workshops of Gaul after the third century.[67] Most
basic supplies arrived in boats from a few miles away. Parisians sent the finished products of their industry only short distances up- and downstream. The
nautae of Paris, boatmen and overland haulers who commanded the stretch
of the river in the territory of the Parisii, carried everything between the town
and its adjacent farms and industries.[68] They were local men, not long-distance
purveyors of exotic goods. Paris had its merchants (*negotiatores*) organized in

guilds (*collegia*) as in Trier or Lyon. Like traders elsewhere, they thanked the river goddess when she protected them with trinkets tossed into her waters and monuments on her banks. After the Seine had lost its navy in the fifth century and become less important as a conduit between northern and southern seas, rivermen were no less crucial to the provisioning of the city, but they either profited less or forgot to thank their patronesses, because they built no more monuments to Sequana. When they turned Christian, they began to thank Saint Genovefa instead.[69]

When the Franks occupied Paris and its environs in the mid–fifth century, noblemen and noblewomen continued to practice the same ancient commute between country estates and urban seats as had generations of local aristocracies. Peasants trekked their revenues and crops to town, as usual. Traders arrived and left at the quays. In Genovefa's time, merchants came carrying news from as far away as Syria.[70] Bishops went in and out of the city gates. Still, Paris and its environs were looking less and less like Provence or Latium. Although wealthy farmers outside town continued to inhabit and operate ancient villas, they tended to use the larger chambers for barns or stables. They may have dreamed of Roman style, but they constructed newfangled, Germanic post-built houses. They applied principles of classical architecture in religious buildings rather than private homes or halls of government.[71] Parisians were not leaving the landscape of the imperial *civitas*, but simply adapting to economic realities. The walls of Paris had always signified more than they contained.

When Parisians of the fourth and fifth centuries built, destroyed, and re-built, they were mindful of at least some of each site's previous uses and older meanings. When they strove to preserve the material environment of urban *romanitas*, Parisians demonstrated their conservative historical view of the political landscape. Meanwhile, common sense and the chance for a little profit gave them good reasons to maintain existing markets, trade networks, and patterns of landownership. The city's political and economic positions helped shape yet another version of Paris—the town of many religions. The cultural conservatism typical of provincial towns, the relative political and economic unimportance of Paris within the empire, and the rural base of its native aristocracy all influenced its residents' religious lives. Parisians who resisted changes to their administrative and economic environments took the same approach to the city's sacral landscapes, always seeking to conserve the existing spiritual resources of their environment, and always claiming that they only changed Paris to preserve it. Against this setting of age-old holy places and venerable religious architecture, the deeds of a very few individual Parisians influenced its religious history and contributed visibly to the shape of the city's religion. Genovefa was one of them.

2

Sacral Paris

In the fifth century, Paris had not belonged exclusively to native-born deities for a long time. The city's numinous protectors, including the river that nourished its islands and banks, had taken Latin names and opened their pantheon to newcomers. Their adherents attended them in many venues—natural springs, elegant temples, graves, cozy home shrines, and more secret places that we will never know about. The look and shape of these places altered after seismic historical shocks, such as conquest and conflagration, but also shifted with the constant small motions of individual believers. Whenever Parisians considered the orders of Caesar or the words of Christian preachers, they were standing about in plazas, sitting in someone's house, or working in the same old shops or fields. Religious conversion came into their ears as sounds but also arrived as changes in habit and place. The decision to begin catechism was no more or less momentous than an alteration of daily routes and destinations. It took both the words and the waters of baptism to make a Christian—words of a priest and waters of a pool or font built in a baptistery. No wonder it also took four or five centuries and at least three generations of determined saints to christianize Paris.

Since Romans had first established their conquerors' cults on the hill above the Seine, travelers and emigrants moving along the empire's highways had brought to Paris all sorts of odd beliefs and rituals with the rest of their baggage. They also lugged objects for worship and ideas about holy places. Christians had arrived to add their opinions and take up Parisian space in the third century or possibly the late second. There was enough shelter for a variety of religious practices. Roman administrators had never imposed religion beyond pro forma public participation in the imperial cult, but even that disappeared when emperors themselves turned Christian. Although Christian rulers passed laws about religious architecture, they did not force baptism on the Gallo-Romans as Charlemagne would upon his Saxon conquests several centuries later.

By the early fifth century, however, when the city was shrinking behind its defenses, its architecture no longer accommodated the assorted religious needs of its residents. In particular, its Christians had multiplied and now required larger, more visible places for worship, burial, and display. They also needed paths through the streets for processions from one sanctuary to another and to the graves clustered along the ancient highways. What is more, Christian leaders demanded that their holy places and buildings be segregated, or at least marked off, from the shrines and cemeteries of other religions. Throughout Gaul, bishops of old Roman provincial towns were urging pagans and half-hearted converts in their communities to abandon the outdated sanctuaries at the old heart of their cities, many of which stood neglected anyway beyond the newer defensive walls.

Among themselves, meanwhile, dedicated Christians argued about both buildings and beliefs. Debates about everything from the nature of Jesus, the proper jobs of vowed virgins, and the use of non-Christian monuments raged around the capitals of the Mediterranean world, thence to Paris. In clerical assemblies and personal correspondence, bishops and other learned men contended about which places were sacred, which most sacred, and what best to build there. Some of these struggles over how and where to build surfaced in other kinds of writings, such as the legends of martyrs who came from Rome to baptize Gallo-Romans, and the foundation myths that Christian historians produced for the new Jerusalems popping up from Gaulish soil.

It took a long time for a majority of Parisians to become Christian. What else could be expected of a town of many faiths and opinions that existed on so many political, economic, and social landscapes at once? In Genovefa's day, plenty of Gallo-Romans and Germanic newcomers to Gaul had not yet succumbed to the persuasion of the Gospels. Gaul had hosted many gods and goddesses by the time Christianity became an option, and early fifth-century Parisians could spot them all lurking about dark corners of imperial ruins and under the woodland shade. Some Parisians saw devils where other saw protective spirits; some could envision only tombs of the dead where others glimpsed the living saints. But all of them dwelt on the same sacral landscape with its age-old holy places, even though they interpreted those places in different and often conflicting ways. They shared a collective religious past, although they used its *spolia* to craft more personal and doctrinally specific histories.

The landscape and its history influenced where and how Parisians worshiped and thus how they built their religions. The presiding spirit of a holy place helped to designate a sacral site. A visit to a particular shrine constituted a significant individual interpretation. So did the decision to pray instead at home to a favorite god or saint. Someone always set the timing of a religious event, whether it occurred in an architecturally complex purpose-built basilica or the open streets of Paris, an old graveyard or the middle of a seemingly empty field. The precise operations of the landscape's influence, however, varied with other conditions of the local environment. Considerations of ethnicity, gender, and class guided the location, creation, and use of religious architecture as surely as the availability of sites and materials or the tenets of formal doctrine; all these issues helped, in turn, to shape the audience of a religious place. Every practitioner balanced social identity and political affiliations, the coincidence of his or her birth, and simple proximity when deciding whether and how to use a religious place.

In Saint Genovefa's Gaul, these considerations overlapped in historically specific ways. When it finally came time for Genovefa to travel and build, she was guided by three important principles. First, the residents of the Parisian basin had long distinguished between the uses of built urban shrines and less visible rural holy places. Second, they had an ancient habit of gendering particular kinds of sacred sites—some holy places were typically dedicated to feminine spirits or attended by female devotees. Finally, church leaders in Genovefa's time were beginning to make rules about who could and could not access their sanctuaries. Genovefa inherited religious terrain already shaped by countless generations of believers and continuously renegotiated by her fellow Christians.

Pagan Paris

Ancient sacrality lingered in the very names of places. The village of Nanterre, for instance, a satellite settlement about seven kilometers north of Paris, would become famous to Parisians as Saint Genovefa's birthplace, but in her childhood it was still Nemetodurum to Latin speakers.[1] *Durum* was merely the Celtic equivalent of *vicus*, a village, but *nemeto(n)*- charged it with numinous powers. The Latin cognate was *nemus*, but the word was old among peoples of the North Atlantic. In another Celtic dialect, Irish, the word *nemed* continued to mean "holy" or "sacral" throughout the Middle Ages, whether applied to people, texts, or the space of Christianity or other religions.[2] Nemetodurum was a sacred settlement, a holy village, long before its residents became Christian or Genovefa attended the Eucharist in its church. Settlements throughout Gaul had *nemeton*-names: Augustonemeton (Clermont-Ferrand), Nemausus (Nîmes), Nemetacum (Arras), Nemossus (Nemours), Vernemetum (Vernantes). Fortunatus, writing in the sixth century, explained Vernemetum as a place "which in the Gaulish language means the great shrine" or *fanum*.[3] How exactly sacrality manifested itself in places defined as *nemeton-*, as compared with other sacral sites, was not always clear to Parisians of Genovefa's day, though.

Legends of divinity haunted place-names as architectural remnants littered the landscapes of Gaul. Sites tagged with the name of Lug, a warrior god who also turned up in early medieval Irish literature, existed at Lugdunum (Lyon), Lugduninsis oppidum (Laon), and Lugdunum Convenarum (Saint-Bertrand-de-Comminges), among other spots.[4] Tribal names, such as the Sequani, contained references to tutelary deities (Sequana, the Seine). Indigenous words, unchanged by Latin speakers, recalled the oldest sacred sites.[5] Perhaps Genovefa and her hagiographer hardly noticed the sacral history available in a single word for a place; certainly, not every modern visitor to Paris pauses to reflect on the original derivation of Nanterre or Montmartre. But the sustained efforts of missionaries and builders in the generations surrounding her life suggest that Parisians were sensitive to the numinous powers of a place-name.

Before Christianity spread north with soldiers, merchants, and missionaries, Gallo-Romans had maintained a rich diversity of religious settings ranging from the grandly monumental to the secret unbuilt places of nameless, chthonic deities. When the Romans had first come, they sought privileged locations for their own important cults on their own map of Gaul: build a city, build a temple. But so long as native divinities remained at a polite distance, colonial officials did not bother to transform archaic holy places with new architecture.[6] Generations of Gallo-Romans sacrificed to indigenous deities, divinities recently imported from the south, assimilated gods and goddesses, and entirely new spirits in a dizzying variety of venues. At home, household idols ruled over hearths from private corners of villas and back rooms of houses. Small suburban shrines around every city drew circles of worshipers with shared interests; childbearing women might approach the house of one goddess for help with birthing, and another for aid in cursing evil neighbors or healing an abscess. Boatmen came ashore in midtrip to invoke the protectress of the river at the monument they had raised to her. A man from the country might visit the boundary shrine of his ancestral tribe but, when in Paris, help fund a monument for the protector of his chosen craft of, say, pottery. Meanwhile, landed noblemen attended rituals of the state cult—pagan or later Christian—when in town but kept private shrines to local gods or saints on their villas. Just as civic architecture advertised the Roman administrative past within a larger city and its history, the less-built edges of cities and suburbs recalled older divinities with Gaulish names. Most people probably never visited the major temples of a town or participated in collective worship on a large scale. Even public cults were exclusive as sanctuaries were screened and protected by architecture from observers milling outside.[7]

Gender was built into the land, helping to locate cults and shrines at particular kinds of sacral sites with permanent effects on the Gaulish landscape. In the city, goddesses and their cults tended to be subsidiary to gods originally from Rome or known by Roman epithets. Typically, a provincial city's grandest temples were dedicated to the emperor and his family and served by both priestesses and priests. Other major religious structures belonged to Apollo or Mercury, who sometimes took local goddesses for consorts. Temples and shrines to all sorts of deities, individually or in conjugal pairs, also stood as separate buildings, in baths, attached to fountains, or in the private houses of town.[8] However, significant shrines to indigenous goddesses more often stayed in the country, where they were less likely than gods to command major monuments or rich donations.

Like mortal ladies, the Gaulish goddesses did not normally travel far. Their cults rarely spread beyond regional boundaries, except for Epona, the horse goddess who became popular with the romanized military set. The others were local ladies lacking individual Roman identities. None of them acquired personal Latin names or Latinized epithets, as Apollo Granus did, that would allow for translation from their homelands. Virtually all existing inscriptions to goddesses in Gaul and Germania reveal simple native names. Nantosuelta, for instance, was a deity only among the Mediomatrici at Sarrebourg.[9] Her name meant "winding river," although her images reveal no aquatic associations; presumably her epithet referred to some fundamental attribute of fertility. Similarly, the goddess Rosmerta, whose statues stood at the Burgundian villa of Escolives-Sainte-Camille and Gissey-la-Vieil, was the "Great Provider" of the Gaulish tribe of Aedui.[10] Hundreds of other goddesses and ancestral mothers in Gaul, around the Rhine in lower Germany, and in Britain bore the simple title of Mother (*mater* or *matrona*) of a people or locality. *Matres* almost always appeared in threes or twos as if interchangeable or as if their strength in numbers made up for the weakness of their sex.[11]

The shrines of local goddesses were usually plainer and less durable than the temples of gods with more inclusive cults. Rural shrines and monuments belonged to the divine caretakers of small communities, single kin groups, and other special interest groups. Simple inscriptions carved on walls, plinths, and statues announced the presence of these goddesses. Their statues, which date mostly from the late second and early third centuries, were generally crude and small by classical artistic standards. Sometimes the goddesses appeared with male consorts, sometimes with babies. Often they sat serenely in their triads. Carved in stone or molded in pottery, they carried cornucopias, offered fruits, and were tended by dogs, crows, bears, or snakes. Their generic attributes, vague names, and intensely local presence made the goddesses confusing to classical commentators. (Julius Caesar famously translated all Gaulish goddesses into Minervas.)[12] Modern archaeologists also tend to essentialize indigenous goddesses as divine personifications of the Female expressed in a native tongue—as if Romans had no fertile mother goddesses or generic epithets for deities, or as if to take a Latin name specified an indigenous deity's attributes.[13]

In fact, the goddesses' worshipers chose how and where to recognize them. Believers responded to the will of the divinities themselves as well as gender ideologies and all the other motives for religious architecture mentioned earlier. Devotees purposefully crafted temples and statues of the *matres* and deliberately set them in country shrines. They chose for the divine mothers basic shelters housing uncomplicated images on the edges of towns and farms because that is where goddesses belonged. By Genovefa's time, those edges not only had become rural and female but also remained relatively un-christianized by comparison with episcopal cities. Fifth- and sixth-century men of letters, such as Sidonius Apollinaris, Gregory of Tours, and Caesarius of Arles, all measured virtue in terms of citification and rusticity: peasants labored on the Sabbath, country bumpkins relied on spells and omens rather than prayer, and rural patricians refused to come into town for paschal celebrations. All were bad Christians. The equation of rural territory with localized divinity and poorly built holy places was an inherited cliché voiced in a single word: *paganus*, from *pagus*, country region.[14]

The hierarchy of religious sites crossed the lines of Christian conversion. In both the written tradition of *romanitas* and the ruins of old holy places, urbanization aligned with architectural complexity, orthodoxy, and masculinity. Lack of settlement, monuments, and superstitious religion spoke of femininity. Christianized Gallo-Romans embraced this ancient dichotomy, recalling their classics to depict contemporary sites of worship. Latin writers had criticized the native religions of Celts and Germans by describing barbarian rituals enacted under tree boughs in sunless groves. Rude or nonexistent architecture—along with human sacrifice, decadent druids, and doctrines of metempsychosis— were signs of primitive peoples. Skewed gender relations among mortals and their native divinities were also signs of the uncivilized. Where goddesses had no distinct personality, and where women led warriors into battle or prophesied from the treetops, people lacked *romanitas*. Such customs had been predictable among unconquered provincials in the past and were also familiar among Germanic invaders of the late antique present.[15] Gallo-Romans of late antiquity believed that the agents of empire had brought better habits to Gaul, pegging tribes to identifiable regions, organizing clientage networks of territories with *civitas* capitals, renaming Gaulish divinities in Latin, building durable and aesthetically pleasing shrines, and reducing and assimilating pantheons.[16] When bishops began to assume management of cities in the fifth and sixth centuries, they applied this same gendered interpretation to Christian leadership and cult sites. The hierarchy of religious places and their control remained intact in Gaul long after ethnic distinctions between Roman and Gaulish had blurred and the deities themselves had given way to saints. In this sense, the decisions of first- or second-century women to honor their *matres* in the woods or on the riverbank, and the dedication of a forum's most important shrine to Apollo or Jupiter directly affected Genovefa's travels.

Although individuals and single events could inspire building or destruction, holy places were never static constructions of a single moment. Such sites were historical conglomerations of pious intentions and practical uses. In the first century, for instance, Roman administrators decided to shift a few important Gaulish tribal shrines nearer towns in order to reduce potential points of native resistance. They tried to manage local politics not by eliminating old gods, but by making the shrines more urban, more built, and more Roman. This shift also provided sites of worship for the rural population necessary to support the city. At Trier, for instance, pro-Roman city leaders constructed a major complex in traditional Gaulish form to local tutelary deities at the very moment that Emperor Augustus's troops occupied the town. As an act of accommodation to their conquerors, they amalgamated cults, joining different tribal groups, classes, and genders in worship at a single spot sponsored by the new state. Despite the aim of civic-minded builders, however, Trier's worshipers decided differently about the efficacy of the relocated cult. Although they visited the site, believers ignored the grand main temple. Instead, discrete groups marked by gender or occupation strewed tiny sanctuaries dedicated to their own favorite deities around the new temple complex. They built in combinations of Roman, indigenous, and more innovative forms. They also added kitchens for preparing sacrifices. In the second century, some zealot even paid for a theater. It is impossible to know which gods preceded the others, only that the site grew organically as the city of Trier itself did, mutating with each generation's needs.[17] The changing patterns of use and traffic, in turn, shaped the complex site's meanings. The logic of flux is less obvious at other sacral sites, where similar concerns about access, exclusion, and devotion more mysteriously shaped architectural development.

Even when celebrants united by ethnicity, neighborhood, or devotion to a single deity came together for seasonal festivals and parades, they used places differently depending on their status and gender. Healing waters attracted all sorts of pilgrims seeking cures, but craftsmen supplied special objects to be tossed in the waters (ex-votos) only for those with money to purchase them. Temple kitchens provided food only for the sacrifices of those who could pay.[18] Women making vows who could afford ex-votos probably purchased the ones shaped like wombs and breasts as part of their prayers for healing reproductive ailments, while both sexes might buy little metal feet or eyes. Similarly, the shrines of both Latin and local spirits called to wayfarers from crossroads and rivers, but only to those with the right vocations—merchants, sailors, or whoever else had raised pillars or other permanent markers of their visits. Aristocratic landowners, including some women, paid for familiar architectural forms—simple polygonal shrines called *fana* and little *cellae* housing images of the deity—on their own estates. They also sponsored little temples at sheltered spots around the countryside which they dedicated to members of the Latin pantheon, tutelary deities, and local spirits. Wealth paid for visibility, tangibility, and the illusion of permanent commemoration at privately owned sacral sites, allowing landowners more regular and intense participation in sacral architecture than those who occasionally visited shared shrines.

Before they became Christians, northern Gallo-Romans usually constructed rural shrines within a mile of roads or tracks but apart from dwelling places. They built in the woods, on riverbanks and at springs, on hillsides, and on territorial boundaries.[19] Many of these sites already had an astonishingly long history of human and divine interaction.[20] More than eighty known Gallo-Roman temples stood on cult sites that had been in use for centuries, some for half a millennium or more.[21] Something about the site at Gournay-sur-Aronde (Oise), for example, drew users for more than six centuries. Beginning in the third century B.C.E., locals raised a small wooden building surrounded by a rectangular ditch into which they pitched offerings of slain animals and broken weapons. The community tended the sanctuary for at least 300 years until it burned to the ground. Sometime during a subsequent 300-year hiatus in construction, the place returned to religious use. Twice during the fourth century C.E., inhabitants of the area rebuilt on the exact site of the earliest temple.[22] Elevation, water sources, or proximity to settlement may have been as important as supernatural signs in the decision to locate at Gournay. But something else lingered to distinguish the place and other similar indigenous sites, for no one ever built formal, classical, Roman temples there.

Places made their own arguments for appropriate use based on a local calculus of belief, access, and resources—both natural and numinous—that outlasted any single cult or political moment. A sanctuary might be merely a grotto, an earthen enclosure with posts and pit, or even just tracks that dead-ended at invisible markers.[23] Much depended upon regional tastes and resources, politics, the functions of a particular cult and its divinities, the ethnicity and gender of local sponsors, the class of its patrons, and the sanctuary's environmental context. Gallo-Roman religious structures were as diverse as their settings, their users, and their presiding spirits. They aged and changed, gaining authority with antiquity, adapting to new audiences and altered settlement patterns. Some sacral sites required less architectural investment and official government oversight than others. A major complex like that at Trier accrued a jumble of masonry and wood structures over time, along with baths, fountains, a theater with galleries, mosaics, ritual pits, statuary, crafts shops, taverns, and hostels. Other holy places, however, featured instead a single, simple monument inscribed to one god housed in a rude shelter. Across northern Gaul and Germania, pillars pronounced the name of Jupiter in a few towns but also on more lonesome sites, where private landowners raised them as statements of personal devotion.[24]

Humans initiated the creation of some sites of worship, but the divinities were responsible for the development of other shrines. Sanctuaries loomed on inaccessible heights or in isolated fields when the gods demanded. It was up to believers to find and exploit such holy places with monuments if they could and would. Worshipers who shared a doctrine or deity could repeat certain features of setting and architecture at different types of religious sites—a certain temple plan or iconographic element—but each holy place resulted from specific negotiations conducted sometimes over centuries by worshipers, deities, and the place itself. Just as places acquired or kept names that rehearsed a history of local belief, so they became and remained visible in site-specific ways.

Despite the persistence of sacral sites, the religious landscape of Gaul was changing noticeably in the period right before Genovefa arrived. By the later fourth century, Gallo-Romans had forsaken many grand classical temples when they had relocated city centers and dismantled buildings for their materials. Raiders from the east had destroyed many religious structures, too. Country shrines were easier to rebuild, which may explain why more rural than urban cult places persisted longer. At least 50 cult places (one-sixth of the 300 or so known for Gaul) originating in the first century or earlier were used, reused, rescued, visited, or kept up during the fourth or fifth century.[25] Country dwellers quit building new *fana* in the countryside, though, by the end of the third century after the first waves of Germanic attacks and initial invasions of

Christian missionaries. *Fana* did not become churches, although Christians did build on a few of the same sites.[26] At Grand, the healing spring of Grannus Apollo became the well of Saint Libaria (Libaire), a statue-bashing patrician virgin who was supposedly beheaded with her siblings at the order of Emperor Julian in 362. After her execution, according to her vita, she had carried her head to the holy pool at the center of the small sanctuary, dipping it in the waters and thus imparting Christian healing powers to the well. By the time Libaria's vita was written, the Christians of Grand had deliberately destroyed the pagan shrines of their settlement, but the waters of Apollo still marked the site after its users built a church on the spot. Christians continued to leave ex-votos at the saint's well into the nineteenth century.[27]

Some of these many ancient Gaulish cult places acquired new uses during the very early Middle Ages. Some became burial sites, not necessarily formal cemeteries with monuments but just safe places to keep the dead. At Escolives-Sainte-Camille, in Burgundy, a Gaulish farm was located on a site occupied since the Neolithic. In the Roman period, it had metamorphosed into a grand villa complete with a healing spring and an impressively decorated private shrine, where the Gaulish deities Rosmerta and Cernunnos, among others, demanded worship. Petitioners cast ex-votos into the spring before, during, and after owners expanded their house and outbuildings, added a few nice statues to the shrine, and adorned their house with frescoes, mosaics, and his-and-her baths. After its stylish family disappeared and the villa was burnt, probably in the late fourth century, local residents continued to live and work on the old estate. Even later, the ancient sacred site became the final home of several hundred Merovingian-era dead. Bodies went into the ground beneath the former courtyard, accompanied by Roman ex-votos fished from the sacred spring and pendants shaped as crude Christian crosses.[28] In the fourth and fifth centuries, such complex old shrines could offer both spiritual comfort and the physical protection of woods, isolation, and ruined buildings to travelers or beleaguered refugees. The sacral nature of these sites did not prevent them being useful, nor did their simple utility erase their holiness. But plenty of sacred sites probably also just disappeared, dissolving slowly back into the earth after an invasion or conversion, their protectors forgotten or left in disgrace.

Genovefa's Parisians inherited these many religious sites in various states of vitality, together with Christian monuments built during the fourth century. The bequest was more complicated for Christians than others because of an already hoary debate about the integration of new and ancient holy places that engaged their coreligionists. The conversation was political as well as doctrinal when converted emperors took part. Constantine was the first of many rulers to order the destruction of pagan statuary, probably at the urging of bishops in the early fourth century. But Constantine also took some nice pieces home to Constantinople with him.[29] Church leaders fretted about the least implication of paganism at built sites from Africa to Britain, but when holy places also featured signs of imperial authority, not to mention high-quality artwork, it was sometimes difficult to decide what to keep and what to discard. Church fathers Tertullian, Ambrose, and Augustine all protested the ubiquity of pagan symbols around their sophisticated towns yet complained, too, about how hard it was to distinguish objects of worship from mere decorations. One man's classically adorned salon was another woman's shrine. As Tertullian put it around 200, "The streets, the market, the baths, the taverns, even our houses are none of them altogether clear of idols. The whole world is filled with Satan and his angels."[30]

Ecclesiastics complained first about the most visibly obnoxious pagan monuments in major cities and then began a hunt for rural reservoirs of heathenism. Bishops meeting at Carthage in 401 demanded that temples in their region "in fields or in hidden locations" be demolished and all their contents obliterated.[31] Likewise, Saint Martin of Tours carried out campaigns of destruction across Gaul at the end of the fourth century, reflecting a growing sentiment among episcopal leaders around the old empire, as well as a perceptible shift in the larger transregional landscapes of Christianity. However, Martin's violent disgust was still rare in Gaul well into the fifth century. Perhaps bishops in the southern half of the empire were exposed to more pagan structures in their denser and more cosmopolitan cities. Perhaps the cult objects of northern temples were not as aesthetically pleasing to Christian collectors. More likely, the decrees of zealous bishops and propaganda of saints' lives reflected isolated campaigns, whereas most Gallo-Romans considered the material and spiritual resources of old holy places too useful to destroy. Also, in small towns such as Paris, citizens may not have felt the same attachment to venerable monuments as in major cities of the Mediterranean world, where emperors repeatedly forbade the dismantling of public works. Anyway, Gaulish bishops were too busy defending and governing their cities even to consider systematically erasing pagan architecture and cult objects.[32] Although some evidence of Christian destruction exists, for example, at the village of Grand, fourth-, fifth-, and sixth-century writers had nothing consistent to say about the conversion of pagan holy places and structures to Christianity.

The goal of northern church leaders, except Martin, was not to destroy old sacred sites but to reconceive both pagan and Christian places and their visible markers. Both architectural remains and written texts suggest that Parisians and their northern Gaulish neighbors constantly and creatively renegotiated their sacral sites and monuments. Agents of change could level a shrine and build nearby, revise old spaces for new religious uses, or reconfigure a place for nonreligious purposes, but recognizable religious meanings persisted at sacral sites. Christian writers of the fourth through sixth centuries revealed their pervasive anxiety about the influence of renegotiated sacral sites principally because it was so hard for everyone, believer or not, to interpret the whole range of built and natural markers of holiness, especially when these markers changed so often. The longer a site had been used, the more complex its meanings became and the harder it was to divest the place of old uses. Where saints' shrines replaced temples and *thermae* as at Grand, pilgrims continued to cast offerings into the ancient waters despite prohibitions like that issued by Gaulish bishops in 585.[33] Some folks insisted on hedging their bets, as the multifaith tokens tucked into coffins at Escolives betray. Christian writers of the very early Middle Ages regularly cautioned against such hybrid practice.

Continuing use of a place, the devotion of a particular group to the spot, or even specific devotional practices at ambiguous sites were no sure markers of a particular religion, either. Rituals changed meanings as the buildings themselves shifted purposes. When fifth-century visitors to a holy spot tossed coins or statuettes into a pit or a spring, they might have been offering sacrifices, supplications, or vows, or leaving cheerful souvenirs of their holidays, or just tossing away garbage.[34] Continuity of use did not necessarily signal an ancient meaning or a single intepretation. When modern archaeologists find potsherds in a ditch, they may have stumbled upon evidence of continuing libation to the gods, later pottery production at a former cult site, or signs of a clumsy vagrant.[35] If Christian villagers dove into the goddess's river to retrieve her pagan treasure, no one told. They may have gathered the ex-votos, as at Escolives, to use again. Or perhaps they willfully forgot the sunken trinkets. They could hardly have missed the ruined cult sites, though. It was no easier for Parisians in the fifth century to sort out the many layers of meaning at a sacred site than it is for modern diggers, even when its ancient users had shared a single religious doctrine.[36] That is precisely why previous use of a historical religious site compelled its continued use. The proof of a holy place was the place itself. Even its ruins were disturbing. To waste such a place was foolish; to ignore it could be disastrous.

Preparing the Way

When Genovefa traveled the Parisian basin, she followed the trail of Christian proselytizers and organizers who had preceded her over that densely sacral landscape. The popular story was that the second pope, Clement, had dispatched seven bishops to seven Gaulish cities. He sent the Greek Dionysius to Paris.[37] Gregory of Tours later listed the other six missionaries as Gatianus (Tours), Trophimus (Arles), Paul (Narbonne), Saturninus (Toulouse), Stremonius (or Austremonius, Clermont), and Martialis (Limoges).[38] But before Gregory wrote his Frankish history in the later sixth century, the keepers of Dionysius's tradition were neither efficient nor consistent. They were not even sure about which pope Clement was or when he had lived. Surviving accounts still do not agree on when Dionysius—called Denis in French or English—came to Paris or who ordered the persecution of Christians that killed him. Was it the emperor Diocletian, Aurelian, or Valerian? Actually, none of the persecutions much affected Gaul.

Even if the story had some truth, no one thought to write it down until Denis had been dead for years. The documentary tradition of Denis and his itinerary from Rome to Paris is reliable only from the sixth century.[39] Before that, the only known commemoration of Denis was in the liturgy of prayers performed in the churches of Paris, where priests invoked his name on the anniversary of his death. The written calendar of saints' feast days attributed to Saint Jerome included Denis and a few other Gaulish martyrs; assuming that this compilation reached Gaul on its way north to the Englishman Bede, who made a copy in the eighth century, we might suppose that Parisian worshipers prayed to Denis perhaps as early as 400. The Christians of Visigothic Spain celebrated his feast day from about 500.[40] Genovefa's hagiographer clearly knew about Denis, so the saint's legend was likely manufactured or substantially enhanced sometime between Genovefa's birth in the early fifth century and the composition of her vita; her purported discovery of his shrine probably inspired or coincided with a surge in Denis's cult and the need for a formal legend. Most of the written records for the other six missionaries in Denis's supposed team were likewise written to celebrate the (re)appearance of their corpses during the sixth century and their subsequent translation to new churches.[41] Full legends of these martyrs appeared only when local saints were becoming increasingly important to the residents of northern towns.

By the time Denis's grimly heroic story reached the written page, he had developed a simple strategy for proselytization: according to the legend, when he reached northern Gaul, Denis had headed straight into town. His six doomed colleagues had all done exactly the same. In the logic of imaginative sixth-century accounts, all missionaries targeted administratively complex and demographically dense urban centers. Early medieval hagiographers believed that pagan crowds ripe for converting had loitered about the public spaces of Gaul's ancient cities. However, these writers also understood that once upon a time cities had fostered christianization because complex architecture was

a prerequisite for religious conversion. According to legends, Denis and his colleagues had preached and died in town, after which grieving citizens had built
simple memorials to the martyrs in the existing cemeteries outside city walls.[42]
Although none of these shrines to the seven Gaulish martyrs were actually the
earliest churches built in their towns, still, the composers of legends were telling a kind of archaeological truth: their own contemporary sixth- and seventh-
century bishops—with the possible exception of the bishop of Paris—had all
recently located the tombs of these martyrs in old city necropolises and built
new basilicas to house them. In the same way, hagiographers created new-old
legends out of tidbits of history and their own convictions about how christianization should have happened so long ago.

Looking back through the centuries, early medieval writers tried to organize religious memory into a tidy teleology. Living by the written Word, they
also insisted that gospel words were the true heroes of christianization. In their
pages, heroic preachers had accomplished Gaul's conversion, not church builders. Even Genovefa's hagiographer invoked three famous missionary bishops
to northern Gaul who had preceded his patroness and prepared the Gallo-
Romans for her work. Each of these proselytizers had also offered a role model
for sanctity. In the first generation of Gaul's christianization, Saint Denis had
preached to hostile Parisian pagans and left his body for Genovefa to find. Saint
Martin of Tours destroyed pagan shrines at the end of the fourth century and
showed Genovefa how to exploit rural resources for the benefit of Christians
in the city. Finally, Saint Germanus of Auxerre had plucked Genovefa from
Nanterre and sent her to Paris. He had also taught her to govern her city and its
territory like an aristocratic bishop.

History, however, was not actually as neat as hagiographers wished it to be.
Genovefa had arrived in Paris at least seventy years before her hagiographer
had even thought up his tripartite scheme. She entered the city just as Christian entrepreneurs were rediscovering Gaul's martyrs and before the legend
of the seven Gaulish bishops had taken final shape. In the mid–fifth century,
her priests and neighbors still had only a spotty memory of their own apostle,
Denis, and his part in their city's past. In Genovefa's day, the best evidence
for the first Christians lay in the suburbs of the dead. Only the cemeteries
and mausolea outside Paris's walls commemorated the first phase of conversion. Meanwhile, the ruined forum, public baths, and temples continued to
argue for other religious customs, although these structures too stood outside
the living heart of the city. The wealthier residential population—people who
commissioned and paid for enduring architecture—had left these parts of the
old town to live inside the walls, or had fled to their estates. Deeper in the

countryside, Christian and pagan shrines mixed more erratically, depending on who was able to keep them in good repair.

Hidden in the archaeological remnants and also in the written words of those early medieval writers, such as Genovefa's chronicler, are hints of the decisions that Genovefa and her own generation made about how to live as Christians. Throughout the fourth and fifth centuries, members of growing Gaulish congregations had to choose how and where to build their religion on shifting terrain. They could try to slip their Christian spaces into existing shells, revising the monuments to suit Christian concepts about the afterlife. Thus, the earliest converts lowered baptized bodies into the ground of ancient pagan cemeteries. Alternatively, where Christians were plentiful and intolerant, their leaders could try to wipe out signs of the heathen past and conspicuously build anew, as Saint Martin supposedly did. They raised baptisteries and other churches wherever residents congregated, following them inside city walls where local markets and administrative buildings still stood. Or, third, Gallo-Romans could exploit the sacral *spolia* of their towns, purposely building Christian monuments on spiritually charged sites with materials selected from earlier religious structures.

Between 250 and 450, Gaulish builders chose all of these approaches at different times, altering architectural agendas according to local circumstances. In the third century Christians usually created only modest monuments, mostly baptisteries for new converts and gravestones or shrines for dead ones. To them it was most important to designate Christian bodies in life and death rather than create permanent sites for ongoing ritual. But as bishops of the fourth and early fifth centuries assumed greater responsibilities for civic life, they often used architecture more aggressively to establish Christian congregations in place of other religious communities, and to attach these congregations to cities. Beginning with Genovefa, Christian urban leaders would raise major shrines to their religious past and its historical founders, which hagiographers commemorated after the fact in written legends of ancient martyrs and, in one case only, the story of a Parisian holy woman who built churches.

The first missionaries to Gaul left no contemporary written records or stone monuments. Word of them trickled back to the record keepers of the eastern empire, though. The church historian Eusebius, writing around 312, described how Christians had invaded Gaul around 150 and then, in triumphant imitation of Caesar's conquest, had gradually worked their way north from the Mediterranean. "Other writers of history record the victories of war and trophies won from enemies," he sermonized, "but our narrative of the government of God will record in ineffaceable letters the most peaceful wars

waged in behalf of the peace of the soul."[43] The brave missionaries had hit a
hitch in Lyon, though, where lynch mobs had accused them of cannibalism
and incest. Soldiers arrested the Christians before a crowd at the forum, then
imprisoned and tortured them at the governor's order before executing them.
Survivors in Lyon and Vienne had supposedly sent an account of their trials
to coreligionists in Asia Minor. Although their letter vanished, Eusebius cir-
culated his version of the text; Latin paraphrases of his work probably did not
arrive back in northern Gaul until the fifth century.[44]

Other reports of Gaulish Christians also reached eastern church leaders at
the end of the second century. Tertullian (d. 230) and Cyprian (d. 258), both in
Carthage, mentioned communities of converts in Gaul, although they did not
name individual missionaries. Irenaeus, a Greek scholar who became second
bishop of Lyon (succeeding the one who died in the arena), left no information
about the christianization of his adopted city or about communities of converts
elsewhere in Gaul; instead, he spent his old age composing theological works
and antiheretical treatises until his death sometime after 200.[45] But records of
the first synod at Arles (314) listed sixteen Gaulish bishops at the international
gathering, thus proving a growing number of well-organized congregations.[46]

The visible history of Christian Gaul began with commemoration of the
most holy dead. Although preachers typically targeted town centers as Denis
supposedly did, seeking out open spaces and market crowds for their missions,
Christian architecture infiltrated cities in the other direction—from the built
edge toward the denser center. Christian gravestones appeared first in cemeteries outside city walls, followed by baptisteries built inside the town. In the fifth
century, Paris's most venerable Christian monuments lay among 400 years'
worth of limestone, marble, and human bones in a necropolis two kilometers
southwest of the city along the highway to Orléans. Stones from pagan Lutetia
probably greeted Genovefa on her way in and out of Paris with cheery saluta-
tions and melancholy advice so common in roadside epitaphs around the empire. One typical first-century slab lamented the demise of a young daughter
whose virtues could have come from the pen of Cicero: "eloquent, learned,
friendly, pious, chaste, modest" and "dead by the jealousy of fate."[47]

Such melancholy reminders of dead heathens mingled with newer slogans
and icons in the cemetery landscape as Parisians continued to bury their dead
in the same places over the centuries of christianization. Visitors to the necropolis must have realized that thousands of corpses were dissolving beneath their
feet, most only meagerly marked if memorialized at all. Was it lack of materials
or a stoic disregard for ephemeral bodies that led generations of Parisians to
open old graves, expose bones, and layer new dead atop long deceased?[48] Perhaps in the fresh dirt of a disturbed grave, the Christians of fifth-century Paris

stumbled across the signs of lost pagan souls: a coin left on each eye to pay the ferryman of Pluto, or a small votive statue now displayed in the museum at Cluny. Yet the living did not hesitate to disturb the dust and steal stones, sometimes for profane purposes. Around 310, servants of the eastern Caesar, Maximin Daia, carved over a lost epitaph to memorialize his brief reign and the extent of his imperial power, and to mark the distance to Paris.

The necropolis southeast of Paris became a sea of ambiguous religious symbols. On one slab from around 300, a woman named Ursina remembered her husband, a veteran of the Rhine campaigns named Ursinianus. She had a small palm carved into the bottom right corner of the stone. Was it a proud sign of imperial victory or remembrance of a Christian soul? The answer depended upon the viewer. On another stone, new in the late fifth century, Vitalis inscribed the name of his wife Barbara, buried at the age of twenty-three years, five months, and twenty-eight days. A chi-rho marked with the alpha and omega and two little doves holding each end of a broken vine decorated her epitaph.[49] Unlike Ursina, when Vitalis lay his spouse to rest, he made sure that the remains spoke in Christian iconography. But Vitalis may well have been reading the palm on Ursinianus's tomb as Christian, too. All these hints at belief simultaneously met the eyes of a visitor to the dead.

When users of the cemetery revised its monuments, they promoted christianization, but they also influenced patterns of settlement and traffic around Paris. Although the concentration of burials and monuments southeast of the city gained a reputation as the "Christian suburb" because of its shrines, the cemetery at Saint-Marcel was too far away from the condensed heart of Paris to be a useful burial place even before 300.[50] More graveyards grew within easier reach of funeral processions during the fourth century: one at the city's southwestern edge, another on the road to Sens, and yet another near the forum within the ancient town boundaries. In Paris, as in Rome, Christians had begun to visit their dead regularly, often in large groups. Although ritual traffic connected convenient cemeteries to the city center and opened dialogues between neighborhoods of dead and living, too-distant shrines quickly lost their use and became vulnerable to reinterpretation.[51] Gregory of Tours told a little story about the tomb of Crescentia near what was probably Paris's oldest church built on the city's periphery (*in vico Parisiorum*). Christians of an earlier generation had carved on her stone, "Here lies Crescentia, dedicated to God." But, Gregory added sadly, in his own time "no one could tell what her merit had been or what she had done in life."[52]

At the same time that Christians began commuting to the cemeteries and the dead began to move closer to the city center, church leaders began to co-opt different kinds of building sites inside Paris and other European cities. In the

MEMORIA(M)
FECIT URSINA
COIOGI SUO URSI
NIANO UETERANO
DE MENAPI(I)S
UIXX(T) ANNOS
[X]XXXXXV

FIGURE 2.1. Parisian funerary monument, late third or fourth century (John Marston after Duval). Originally used to commemorate a soldier named Ursinianus, a veteran of the Rhine frontier, by his wife, Ursina. The small palm frond carved on the bottom right corner could represent victory for the old soldier or his Christian persuasion—or it might have been added later, when the stone was moved and reused in the cemetery at Saint-Marcel during the Christianizing fifth century (courtesy of Musée Carnavalet, A I 82. 22).

mid–fourth century, Emperor Constantius closed down the pagan shrines of the empire; early in the fifth, Theodosius decreed that Christians could turn them into churches.[53] The first purpose-built church probably appeared in Paris's southeastern necropolis early in the third century (*ecclesia senior*, according to Gregory); the first church on the Île de la Cité (*ecclesia parisiaca*, church of the Parisians) rose sometime between the attacks of the 250s and 360, when bishops held a council there.[54] Both of these structures were so venerable by Gregory's time that they did not even boast famous martyrs or patron saints, for their erection had preceded the cult of saints.[55] Congregations began housing bodies in and near their churches or using burial shrines for regular congregational meetings only in the late fifth century, about the time that Genovefa came to town.[56]

As Christian communities grew and demanded more places of worship, thrifty Parisians scavenged the matériel of earlier Lutetia to build on familiar streets in existing neighborhoods, in traditional urban idioms. Early medieval writers described bishops who had demanded the donation of entire patrician houses for their urban congregations. These later writers imagined the instant conversion of banqueting rooms into sanctuaries for celebration of the Eucharist.[57] They did not, however, mention the laborious purification and redecoration of donated places—how builders repainted, altered mosaics, rearranged walls and rooms, destroyed statues, or gutted the houses to begin again with fresh space. We know that congregations elsewhere did so.[58] Each architect and his crew selected an appropriate combination of old and new elements in imperial, ecclesiastical, and more vernacular styles. Sometimes they ignored the original connotations of their materials, either willfully or because of cultural amnesia, simply using what was available; fine bits of carving or rare stones such as marble were too precious to waste. At other times, however, builders blatantly reused structural and decorative elements in imitation of a church's previous functions, for instance, reworking a pagan mausoleum into a martyr's shrine or claiming a late antique sarcophagus as an altar base.[59] Gaulish quarries were no longer producing so masons hauled blocks from semiabandoned public spaces of the older Paris to become the foundations of new basilicas.[60] Christianity literally rose from the ruins of Caesar's conquest.

Destruction and Rebuilding

Whoever got to them first—whether the martyrs of Lyon, the seven episcopal apostles, or many more anonymous carriers of the new Roman religion—the number of Gaulish Christians continued to grow during the fourth century. Congregations began to appear outside of major urban centers. In a reverse of imperial tactics of colonization, where bellicose soldiers had led the way for peaceable administrators, the first generation of passive-aggressive martyrs prepared Gaul for more ruthless warriors of the new faith. These men operated from urban bases but targeted rural communities for conversion, which brought new challenges for preachers, administrators, and church builders. Rural landscapes lacked plazas, halls of government, and large cemeteries, which were the most obvious sites of initial christianization in town. Traditional farming villages and prosperous villas brought populations together, but even the most flourishing fourth-century estate would not have supported as many souls as a small city. Both farms and sanctuaries might be scavenged for *spolia*, but not on the scale of city structures. With few exceptions, country temples were modest rural *fana* or private shrines. Other sacral sites outside town were ambiguously marked or even hidden. What is more, country people were hicks (*rustici*) without the complex architectural vocabulary of city people—at least, according to the hagiographers who recounted the adventures of Gaul's second generation of saints and stubborn rural pagans.

Gaul's most effective missionary, Saint Martin of Tours, was supposedly the first to bring Christianity to these locations between cities. He was suited to the job of converting yokels, as he made no claims to urban sophistication. Martin presented a controversial figure in Gaulish towns, whose citizens were used to well-dressed bishops with excellent hygiene and classy educations.[61] Born in what is now Hungary and raised in Pavia, he had trained in the imperial army before opting for an ascetic Christian life. After serving on the Rhine, he trained with Hilary of Poitiers, lived as a hermit on an island off Liguria, and eventually made his way to Ligugé, where he lived in solitude, thence to Tours. The townsfolk spontaneously elected him bishop in opposition to the local candidate. Throughout his tenure, he regularly withdrew to a monastery in the caves at Marmoutier, two miles from the city.[62]

Miracles of power and persuasion rather than philosophical terms or visions of martyrdom marked the story of Martin's sainthood written by his aristocratic admirer from the south, Sulpicius Severus, before the saint died around 397.[63] Martin became famous for his uncompromising approach to pagan resistance demonstrated in a series of remarkable conversions of peasants and their holy places, among other wonders. Once Martin was traveling through the countryside when he sighted a procession about a half mile distant. As Sulpicius explained to his readers, back then Gallic rustics used to parade cloth-covered images of their divinities around the fields. From the solemn pace of the marchers and the linen-draped figure they carried, the saint suspected that the peasants were practicing just such a "profane rite of sacrifice." He signed the cross in their direction whereupon the peasants were paralyzed. When they tried to march on, they began instead to jerk and whirl helplessly. Finally they had to set down their burden, which turned out to be a corpse destined for burial—the procession was a funeral, not an idol-worshiping parade. An unembarrassed and unapologetic Martin let them pick up their body and go on.[64]

In Sulpicius's estimation, Martin had made a predictable error of interpretation. The hagiographer knew what kinds of ritual movement through the countryside signaled Christianity, and what kinds of processions, in which venues, with which objects, meant pagan practice. To Martin's more naïve thinking, all suspicious processions in country or city were repugnantly pagan. Yet without buildings and other familiar cues to pagan practice, Martin misread this particular sacral landscape and its uses. Neither saint nor hagiographer precisely explained the ceremony, the destination of the peasants, or the kind of monument the mourners eventually chose to raise over the dead. Martin aimed to convert; whatever the peasants were doing with their body, it was not a Christian burial. Sulpicius, who came from Aquitaine, may have known better. He certainly learned from Martin's mistake, yet he also sympathized with the saint's intent and response.

More obvious pagan signposts marked the setting of Martin's second conversion episode, including an ancient temple, a high priest, a crowd of rowdy heathens, and a sacred tree. Martin tackled the temple first, then determined to chop down the tree. The crowd was not about to allow him near it; temples could be repaired, but sacred trees were hard to find. Martin read the situation just as classical writers had viewed pagan sacrifices in dim groves: the worship of a plant or animal was the most primitive form of religion known to Romans. Saint and hostile mob faced an impasse until one crafty pagan challenged Martin to stand under the tree while it was cut, hoping to solve the problem by squashing the ornery saint. Yet with a single gesture—his raised hand—Martin prevented the trunk from flattening him and instead sent it toppling near the crowd. All the heathens immediately clamored for baptism. Wherever there were sacred groves and pagan temples inhabited by idols, Martin raised churches and monasteries. Martin thus converted these simple folk from groves to church architecture as well as to Christianity.[65]

In the third episode, Martin destroyed two more temples. He set fire to one while protecting houses in the same settlement from burning. But in a settlement called Leprosum, worshipers again opposed the destruction of their temple, which Sulpicius described as a building rich with images and altars. The crowd beat Martin and ran him out of their village. He returned after three days of penitential fasting and prayer accompanied by two armed angels who bullied the crowd while he completed the job. He had biblical precedent for both the fasting and the angels; his acts invoked the destruction of Sodom and Gomorrah, as well as the prophets who purified themselves with self-denial before sacral acts.[66]

Martin practiced his architectural demolition in rural areas before crowds summoned for religious purposes, but he acted against the will of local people. Before anyone spoke a word, the saint interpreted buildings, locations, and processions as dangerously pagan. He shared with Gaulish farmers and herders a new concept of rural religious space and the range of actions that might occur within it. However, Martin evaluated the uses of sacral sites differently than did locals. He replaced the old, sometimes ambiguous markers of religion with undeniably Christian constructions. He taught his converts the functions of Christian buildings and places and, at the same time, converted the landscape's meanings. He left behind a visible geography of his proselytizing life at an assortment of formerly pagan *loca sancta* and new ecclesiastical establishments: the monastery at Ligugé, special spots in the cities of Amiens and Paris, and his own city of Tours, as well as rural sites in these regions.[67] Still, Sulpicius's account showed that in Martin's time even seemingly simple landscapes had posed problems of interpretation for Christian audiences. Martin's church at Tours celebrated his episcopal career, but his monastic retreat, hidden from his parishioners, offered a counterargument about spiritual priorities and the hierarchy of believers, and about who could use what kinds of religious space. Ordinary Christians knew about Martin's hermitage but were not allowed to visit it.

Sulpicius was writing from fond memory of Martin, but he also employed hagiographic bombast based on biblical dramas of avenging angels and fiery destruction to make his points.[68] One final example from Sulpicius's text revealed that Martin could, when he wished, use nuanced methods available only to saints in order to discern sacral space. In this chapter of the vita—tucked between Martin's work as bishop and the conversion episodes—the saint investigated a reputed shrine in the wilderness near his monastery. Tradition held that Christian martyrs were buried beneath it, but Martin was reluctant to accept recent accounts of the site's history because "no steady tradition respecting them had come down from antiquity." Was Martin looking for reliable oral testimony (*relatio*) or documented history (*lectio*)? Apparently neither was available. Nor did the site and its structures provide enough architectural clues; what is more, the devotions of easily deluded locals were entirely untrustworthy.

Once again, the saint was faced with several possible interpretations of a religious site. Once again, he made a choice to read the site in a particular way, but not so thoughtlessly as in the case of the pagan parade. Wary of destroying a legitimate Christian funerary chapel but, as Sulpicius wrote, "at the same time not lending his authority to the opinion of the multitude, lest a mere superstition should obtain a firmer footing," Martin visited the cemetery where the chapel was located and invoked the ghost of its occupant. The so-called martyr beneath the altar turned out to be a robber beheaded for his crimes. Unlike Genovefa, who found a lost martyr and built him a shrine, Martin had stumbled upon a misidentified body and a place wrongly commemorated.[69] Where local memory had disappeared, mere visual markers of a burial were confusing to both ordinary Christians and their saint. In the fourth century, no sure signs distinguished a Christian tomb.[70] Only once informed by a miraculous vision from the otherworld could Martin properly perceive the difference between unholy space and sacred place. Martin's dilemma occurred at the moment when Christian burials and their monuments were creeping back into towns from ancient necropolises in violation of a centuries-long habit of segregating the quick and the dead. Bishops of the late fourth century were just beginning to argue about where bodies belonged in relation to inhabited spaces, saints' burials, and religious structures. The debate played out in synodal decrees and canonical legislation, as well as in hagiography and architecture.[71]

Germanus among the Generations

Whereas Denis's only choice in the mid–third century had supposedly been to work and die within an urban milieu, and while Martin tackled the problem of ambiguous holy places in new contexts at the end of the fourth century, the third generation of evangelists worked in yet another idiom of landscapes and holy places. Saint Germanus of Auxerre (ca. 418–66) straddled the previous warrior generation and the following cohort of urban builders and relic keepers, which would include his slightly younger contemporary, Genovefa. His own body eventually became part of the whole argument over disposal of the most holy Christian dead. In life, though, he acted out an elegantly romanized version of Christianity in both urban and rural contexts. Like Martin, Germanus had trained as a soldier. Also like Martin, he was suddenly acclaimed bishop. Unlike the bishop of Tours, however, Germanus came from an excellent Gaulish family, was well educated in Gaul and Rome, and had taken his bishopric as a promotion from his previous position as military governor. In metaphors of construction, rather than battle, his biographer Constantius of Lyon (fl. 475–80) described Germanus's lifework as building "two roads to Christ." Again, like Martin, he continued to pursue a monastic existence while holding office: he "inhabited the desert while dwelling in the world," according to Constantius. He founded a monastery across the river from the town of Auxerre while running his diocese from within the city. He performed miraculous cures and exorcisms in public but tended his own soul in private, across the river. His reclusiveness brought him the reputation he desired, apparently, for after his death he was initially more celebrated outside Auxerre than at home.[72]

Germanus earned his fame by traveling father than Martin and Genovefa, taking correct Christian thought and practice not just into the countryside but to the northern frontier of civilization. Twice he went north to Britain to fight Pelagian heretics, where he preached mass "not only in the churches but at the crossroads, in the fields, and in the lanes." On his second trip, Germanus baptized pagans in a church "built of leafy branches . . . on the plan of a city church" in a military camp. This was a different countryside than the hostile territory encountered by Martin. Germanus had no need to destroy temples and idols. Instead, he created proper environments for orthodoxy and ortho-praxis. The elements of nature submitted to his architectural design. The very landscape aided him when under attack by savage armies, raining rocks on the enemy and drowning them in an otherwise calm river.[73]

When framing Germanus's history, Constantius contrasted the saint's ex-perience in distant British woods with his passage through civilized Gaulish territory. The bishop traveled Roman highways when visiting cities in Gaul and Italy. Instead of antagonistic heretics, he met welcoming crowds and ailing vil-lagers seeking cures and blessings. When he encountered supernatural oppo-nents on southern roads, they were neither unbelievers nor lost gods but pesky ghosts from the past. Early in his adventures, the bishop and his party stopped at a ruined villa for the night, choosing one "among a great many rooms" for his party to camp in. His companions, terrified of the "dangers and horrors" of the reputedly haunted house, preferred open fields, but Germanus insisted. Late in the night, after Germanus had nodded off, a specter arose. When Germanus had calmly confronted it, the shade confessed to being a criminal left unburied at the site. At Germanus's command, it led the way through the stormy night to its still-fettered bones. The next day Germanus watched while locals dug up the rubble and found the bodies of two criminals, which they wrapped in winding sheets and reburied with prayers. Afterward, as Constantius wrote, "the house lost all its terrors and was restored and regularly occupied" because Germanus had correctly interpreted and redirected the spirits of its pagan past.[74]

Germanus's last journey took him to Ravenna, a capital of the empire, and into the company of the empress Galla Placidia (395–450), who tried to lure him into staying. Most likely, the hagiographer was making the point that Germa-nus could have been buried in imperial Ravenna and housed in a mausoleum as elegant as that of the imperial family; Galla Placidia herself was a builder of churches. Nonetheless, Germanus remained loyal to his native region and his see of Auxerre. Two years before the empress died, his body took a final trip homeward. Clergy accompanied the corpse from one civilized point to another, chanting the liturgy. The people of each city carried it to the next stop, while the emperor provided the bier, the cart, and servants. Citizens hastened to re-pair bridges and fix up roads before the saint's remains arrived, so that even in death Germanus left his civilizing mark on the territory: a legacy of highway improvement and shrines commemorated his holy passage. Germanus neither destroyed nor built during his life, but wherever he traveled he stabilized the countryside in preparation for future construction. He was both harbinger of a new medieval generation of builders and the last of the warrior saints.

Each generation of christianizers in northern Gaul developed tactics in relation to the missionary and administrative efforts of previous generations.

When it came time to commemorate these religious pioneers, the hagiographers and cult keepers of each city tried to place their saintly patrons in the existing history of Gaul's conversion. It was essential to Genovefa's hagiographer that a single familiar road lead from Rome to Denis's tomb, via Martin's Tours, Germanus's Auxerre, and finally Genovefa's Paris. Martin's biographer Sulpicius inspired Germanus's hagiographer Constantius, who, in turn, provided a model for Genovefa's hagiographer. Denis had operated in an urban setting, not even attempting to build in rural areas. Martin had destroyed the countryside and built anew. Germanus had fixed up the wilderness between cities, restoring the infrastructure of the empire, repairing roads and graves on a landscape that became more intensely built as it stretched southward. Genovefa did all these things and more.

For, despite the best efforts of the saints, other religions still flourished in the fields and woods outside sixth-century Paris. Construction of Gallo-Roman temples had stopped during the fourth century because of destruction from invasion, abandonment in favor of other holy places, or the emperor Theodosius's decree of 391–92 closing down pagan cult sites.[75] But people still attended the old places, especially in rural areas. By Genovefa's time, crowds were no longer flocking to the great temple complex at the source of the Seine, to spend a night in the presence of Sequana and seek her help in recovering from illness and injury; nonetheless, the power of the river persisted, and shrines to the goddess still existed. Martin had put his monastery at the site of one such healing spring, so that now the saint's holy waters cured the blind, the lame, the paralyzed, and the crazed.[76] But not every patient or penitent sought out Martin. What is more, more and more new sorts of pagans had been coming to Gaul from Germania, bringing their own ideas about holy places. Much work remained for a new generation of proselytizers. Even when saints could tame the inherent sacrality of a place, the powers of such a famous pagan site could deceive more vulnerable humans.

When Christian leaders could locate and exploit existing sacral resources by reading the symbols of a place and then converting it, they did so. In hagiographic accounts, when missionaries could not transform a pagan place, they tried to destroy or abandon it. Martin had harassed a presbyter who chose to live at an abandoned temple; the man appreciated the fine marble architecture, adorned with towers, which "preserved the superstition of the place by the majesty of the work." When the presbyter protested that a whole army let alone a couple of clerical weaklings could not tumble such a temple, Martin spent a resolute night praying for a storm to destroy it.[77] Over the next couple of generations, proselytizers in other parts of the former empire used the same tactics of destruction or avoidance. Saint Benedict (480–547), before building his monastery on the hill above Cassino, objected to a temple on the site where locals sacrificed to Apollo. He smashed the idol, toppled the altar, and set fire to the surrounding woods. Then he built an oratory to Saint Martin on the spot.[78] By contrast, the Irish Saint Columbanus, stumbling through the mountainous forests of the southern Alps in the late sixth century, found only ruins of Roman temples where he built monastic communities.[79]

Each missionary adapted to his or her environment depending upon resources and the natives' collective memories of place, as well as local political and economic circumstances. The historical evidence of their trials usually reminds us of triumphs by building rather than subversive pagan practice or any genuine negotiation of sacrality. However, the purposeful architectural revision implied by stories of Martin and Benedict, based on the supposition of continuing ritual use of classical pagan temples, was more a medieval authorial figment than historical reality in the sixth century; Jonas's story of Columbanus was probably more realistic than tales of Benedict. In most areas, some lapse occurred between the active use of pagan sites and their revision as Christian venues. Although excavations have revealed churches built from the foundations of Gallo-Roman temples, and many pagan sites with Christian churches or mausoleums atop, almost none of these sites were actually in use as pagan places of worship when they were converted.[80] By the sixth century, only memory and ruins lived at many former religious places.

Nonetheless, each generation of a community needed to reinterpret for itself the existing markers of historic sacral landscapes, and then to rehearse changes in the meaning of those markers. In Martin's time, a grave outside of Tours could be pagan or Christian. Converters and converted agreed on the existence and utility of sites imbued with the numinous, but they also argued about which sites were holy and how best to exploit them. Even Martin did not evacuate pagan communities from older sites of worship—he just demolished temples. The places he violated remained places, often holy places. As missionaries accomplished Christianity, first in cities and then in smaller *vici*, tiny farming villages, villas, and even more remote sites, they faced new challenges posed by the landscape. How to convert architecture that no longer stood, or monuments that had never been built? How to revise an unwritten, barely remembered history of a sacred place? Some spiritually powerful places had obscure, deceptive, or even invisible markers. Ecclesiastics such as Martin and authors such as Sulpicius suspected that rural devotees of local deities—turned demons, criminals, and ghosts in Christian accounts—had secret signs that they refused to share with proselytizers or outsiders.

Each Christian builder had to learn the local landscape and its history, then negotiate his or her response to it with multiple audiences: scions of senatorial nobility as well as barbarian kings and queens; women as well as men; farmers as well as urban laborers; self-identified Franks, Alamanni, and Goths as well as professed citizens of the empire. If local people hid sacred places or resisted architectural revision, the builder had to wait. If they disputed the history of a site, its advocates had to demonstrate its sacrality. The missionary first had to achieve, one way or another, consensus with his or her neighbors about the meanings and uses of places. Denis never managed such consensus, so he ended as a martyr. Martin fasted in the forest until the angels could help him raze a temple. Germanus, more diplomatic, made basilicas in leafy bowers and inspired bridge repair. Following them, Genovefa heralded a new generation of builders and audiences who learned from their ancestors and devised environmentally appropriate techniques.

3

Genovefa's Territory

Genovefa's Paris vanished long ago. The alleys she walked and the
houses she visited have given way to broader avenues and more
recent constructions. The island in the Seine has grown vertically
and horizontally since she knew it. The marshes that protected
the island have disappeared along with the river called Bièvre. The
forum that crowned the southern heights is a memory kept only by
antiquarians and tourists. Parisians long ago demolished the church
over Genovefa's tomb, as well as the basilica she founded north of
town, and built on the ruins. Her landscapes are lost forever beneath
modern Paris, except for a few bits that have risen to the surface and
lodged in museums. Still, buried evidence may be the most appropriate testimony to the sacral landscapes of earliest medieval Gaul. Even
in the fifth century, architectural monuments were clues to riches
beneath the earth's visible surface—bodies, spirits, remnants of
previous religions.

The sixth-century *Life* of Genovefa preserved a memory of the
lost monuments and already antique limits of her fifth-century Paris,
sketching what the saint herself had seen a few generations before her
hagiographer wrote. The story of Genovefa reminds us of the constant small shifts in every late antique city even in times of peace and
stability. It also suggests the diverse and sometimes incompatible
principles by which women and men arranged religious sites and the
routes that connected them. Parisians had not only different views of
their surroundings but also different ideas about how to manage

their environment. Only a few individuals had enough power and wealth to impose their notions upon others. Birth, gender, and ethnicity as well as religious identity affected the ability of Parisians to organize religion and its places. The physical environment of the Seine basin and its available resources also guided them when choosing where to practice and worship and what to build there. Believers struggled to find sacrality, as they sought out water or timber, and to live near it, harness, and harvest it. But only exceptional leaders of the Parisians who were both intimate with the native landscape and wise in the politics of religion could engineer large-scale exploitation of the city's holy resources to everyone's satisfaction.

When an anonymous monk wrote his account of Genovefa's life around 529, Paris belonged to a Frankish king and queen. However, the hagiographer depicted an earlier time when a cadre of imperial military men, aristocrats from old local families, and Christian bishops had governed Gallo-Roman towns. In the hagiographer's view, this well-born and explicitly male elite had controlled the city's material and spiritual resources and sponsored Christian architecture before Genovefa came to town. Then she had arrived to wrest Parisian landscapes and *spolia* from both imperial and priestly control. She accomplished this by traveling constantly around the Parisian basin, demonstrating with miracles her knowledge of the land and its resources. Whereas her saintly role model, Martin of Tours, had misunderstood pagan rituals and demolished old heathen places, Genovefa rescued and refashioned the abandoned landmarks of ancient Lutetia and its countryside. Like her mentor, Saint Germanus of Auxerre, she worked within imperial administrative hierarchies and the urban economy. She put *spolia* to good Christian purpose. Genovefa showed Parisians how to restore the sacral resources of their native environment—not by smashing an idol or issuing a doctrinal decree but by seeking out and properly housing the body of Paris's apostolic first bishop, Saint Denis. As Christ's heavenly kingdom supplanted all earthly empires, Genovefa's territory improved upon an existing landscape and its governments.

Genovefa's hagiographer, looking back across a century, framed the saint's life as an arduous route leading from her childhood home in the village of Nanterre, to Paris and the basilica she built for Saint Denis, and ultimately to her own tomb on Mont-Sainte-Geneviève. Christian teleology and hagiographic convention helped direct his version of Genovefa's journey. A missionary imperative drove his understanding of Parisian history and architecture. Genovefa's whole life was a comment on the proper roles of gender, politics, and Christian history, and specifically on the relative unimportance of Paris's early medieval bishops. Her anonymous vita commemorated debates raging across Christendom in the fifth and sixth centuries about how to mark and exploit sacral sites, particularly the shrines and tombs of saints' cults, and what roles women might play in this process. Her miraculous deeds, travels, and building projects helped other Christians define sainthood and practice saintly cult. Denis's magnificent new basilica stood as undeniable evidence of Genovefa's heroic role in the initial christianization and continuing romanization of her city. After her death, Genovefa's own body and shrine finished the city's conversion, thus readying it to become the Christian capital of the new Frankish kingdom.

Genovefa's Generation

Genovefa arrived early in her generation of church builders. She was the first female among them—if other women built shrines in Gaul, no one wrote about it. Genovefa apparently looked upon her territory with a single-mindedly Christian perspective, untroubled by interpretative doubt about past landscapes or their relation to the present. We cannot know what she saw of Sequana in the Seine, or Mars, Mercury, and the Matronae in the architecture of Gaulish cities, because she left no record of her views. None of the holy places around her hometown of Nanterre have survived the almost sixteen centuries since her birth. The routes she traveled later in life passed riverside shrines, like the one at Meaux, but Genovefa's hagiographer recounted no encounters with explicitly pagan places or cult objects. Her Gaul was not that of Martin, who never met an offensive idol that he did not stop to topple. She did not face the trials of earlier female saints who had resisted lascivious pagans and refused to enter their temples. Even Genovefa's younger contemporary Saint Brigit had to deal with bloodthirsty heathens caught in ritual acts.[1] Yet Genovefa never had to fend off a pagan. She may have avoided the old places and their practices, or perhaps she averted her eyes as she approached a shrine where the lame and diseased hopefully cast their ex-votos. Or maybe the pagans had disappeared from her neighborhood with no ghostly traces. Bishop Caesarius still fulminated against them in Arles during the first half of the sixth century, although in clichéd terms of idols and groves; Byzantine councils legislated against minor pagan infractions as late as 692, but maybe Paris had got rid of them for the time being.[2] The hagiographer who wrote Genovefa's life did not mention ancient religious structures and their man-made contents.

Although the hagiographer arranged Genovefa's vita as a long journey to Paris, she got off to a slow start. Like Denis's body, hidden for many years, Genovefa's saintly power remained buried until other saints discovered it. Until she was about nine years old, Genovefa never traveled beyond the village

of Nanterre, where she lived with her parents. The family of three was among
a crowd of locals (*vulgus*) milling in front of the church on the day that news arrived of two approaching bishops.[3] The church was splendid enough to host a
royal baptism in the mid-sixth century, suggesting both serious wealth in the
area and a sizable population.[4] In saints' lives and Christian histories, crowds
appeared outside major churches to witness crucial comings and goings. These
were the same audiences that awaited the formal ritual entry (*adventus*) and
official welcome (*occursus*) of governors and kings at city gates and before the
palaces of major towns.[5] A mob had gathered to eject Martin when he tried to
destroy their shrines, and a similar gathering of citizens had acclaimed him
bishop in Tours. *Vulgus* was the word Gregory of Tours used more than a century later for the urban crowds that elected subsequent bishops of Tours and
Paris, gaped at miracles and the translations of saints' relics, and expelled heretics. Crowds would also welcome the adult Genovefa to Laon, Tours, Orléans,
and Troyes.[6]

On the day that Genovefa watched with her parents, Bishops Germanus
of Auxerre and Lupus of Troyes were supposedly headed north to the Channel
and thence to Britain, where they planned to chastise Pelagian heretics. They
stopped in Nanterre although it was not on the most direct path.[7] Even if the
hagiographer, a man of Tours, did not know it, his Parisian informants must
have realized that this route forced the bishops out of their way and across the
Seine twice just west of the settlement. Nanterre was really on the highway only
to Nanterre. The hagiographer was suggesting that Genovefa drew the bishops,
for Germanus and Lupus "sensed from a distance" the girl's intense holy presence. Upon their arrival Germanus immediately asked for her to be brought
to him, thus beginning a long-lasting sponsorship of his new protégé, while
Lupus faded quietly into the background of Genovefa's life. Germanus publicly
proclaimed the child's greatness before God and asked her whether she secretly wished to take an ascetic vow. She admitted that it was the very thing she
longed for. "Be brave!" Germanus advised her—literally, "Act manfully!" (*Age
viriliter!*), echoing Psalm 31: "Be of good courage, and he shall strengthen your
heart, all ye that hope in the Lord."

Then the bishops took Genovefa through a series of ritual steps, playing
out a liturgical drama before the crowd. Everyone entered the church for celebration of the hours and the Eucharist. During the liturgy, Germanus kept
his benedictive hand on the girl's head. Afterward, he commanded her father
Severus to stay the night in town so that at dawn he might conduct a private
audience with Genovefa in the hospice. The next morning, Genovefa repeated
her vow. The bishop finished the ceremonial process by plucking a coin from
the dust of the hospice and ordering Genovefa to have it pierced to wear as

a reminder of him. Like a devotee casting tokens into the river, Genovefa sealed her promise of good behavior with a bit of stamped metal, which hung from her neck for the rest of her days. She was too young to take the veil, but the entire two-day drama foreshadowed her official consecration as a professed virgin a few years later. The bishops predicted Genovefa's saintly potential through a precisely choreographed set of social interactions and ritual reminders in specially selected spaces.[8]

But after Germanus and Lupus departed for Britain, the girl went home with her father. She was still too young to leave without permission, and her parents refused to understand that she had "made a vow to St. Germanus." Events soon made manifest their blindness, however, especially that of Genovefa's stubborn mother, Gerontia. When Gerontia refused to take Genovefa again to church—perhaps because she feared another public demonstration—the girl threatened to "haunt the threshold of the church" until allowed to honor her vow. Gerontia slapped her and was instantly struck blind, a motif of parental punishment common in the vitae of child-saints. Only after more than two years of blindness did Gerontia think to try healing waters, although not those of Sequana. She asked her daughter to fetch water from their well. In the Bible's

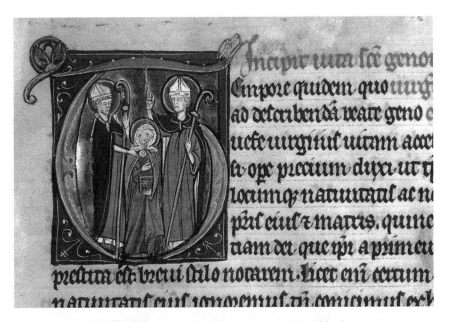

FIGURE 3.1. Genovefa with Bishops Germanus and Lupus (Bibliothèque Sainte-Geneviève, ms 1283, f. 4, fourteenth century, courtesy of Bibliothèque Sainte-Geneviève). Germanus gestures toward the coin hanging around Genovefa's neck, which has become a medallion inscribed with a cross, while Lupus blesses her.

Israel, women (Hagar, Rebecca, the Samaritan woman of John 4) had carried water to parched men, always with beneficial results. Gerontia's tearful, guilty child signed the dipper with the cross and brought it to her mother. Gerontia gestured to heaven, rather than tossing an ex-voto into the waters like a pagan, thus signaling her faith in the Christian God, his agent, and his instruments. When she dabbed her eyes with the water, she began to see a little. She repeated the gesture two or three times until she completely recovered her sight. Once her blindness was cured, Gerontia saw that she must let Genovefa go with two older girls to Bourges, where Bishop Vilicius could veil them. Gerontia and her husband disappeared from the vita at this point. Vilicius, however, improvised a ceremony in recognition of Genovefa's special status, ordering her to lead the other girls in procession to the altar even though she was youngest and ought, by custom, to go last.[9] Thus the hagiographer imbued every step and gesture of Genovefa's life with extraordinary meaning.

Soon after Genovefa's veiling, she went to Paris. Her godmother took her in and then also disappeared from the vita, leaving a house for Genovefa's city residence (hospitium). Like other characters in the story, the godmother remained nameless. In fact, the hagiographer rendered few details of Paris or the Parisians. The city itself served as an architecturally vague setting for the saint's deeds, its principle points including only Genovefa's private cell, a couple of churches where she prayed, and large open spaces where the predictable mobs gathered. The anonymous Parisians appeared mostly as an unfriendly crew of backbiters and malcontents. Genovefa's arrival somehow provoked them. They spread "malicious slander" about Genovefa and held "blind prejudices" that the hagiographer, too, refused to reveal fully.[10] If she had no family or ecclesiastical sponsor in Paris, it is easy to see why the citizens were suspicious of a self-proclaimed vowess from somewhere else who immediately sought public attention and claimed spiritual authority. The hagiographer's report is the only evidence for a godmother, a bequest, and Genovefa's reputation.

Eventually, Genovefa was able to expose her antagonists' secrets and win their hearts, but first she had to prove her worth. The hagiographer proved Genovefa's credentials in several ways. First, she made a visionary journey to heaven while suffering a fever. A century and a half earlier, Saint Martin had undergone a similar physical breakdown, vision, and recovery preparatory to converting rural Gaul.[11] Confident in her personal revelation, Genovefa set out to establish herself as prophet to the Parisians. Second, Bishop Germanus intervened twice more to attest to Genovefa's sanctity. His second visit occurred while he was on another supposed voyage to Britain. He stopped in Paris to see Genovefa and argue with her detractors, seeking out her hospice where she had sought refuge and conversing with her. He found her prone and weeping in prayer.[12] Once again he helped the passive saint reveal her worth to the crowd, this time leading a tour of Parisians to Genovefa's private cell so that they might see her intense piety in action. He pointed out the floor made muddy with her tears. He recited Genovefa's personal history, just as simpler clerics rehearsed saints' vitae in sermons on church feast days. After his hagiographic performance, Germanus returned to the road. Thus three ritual passages prepared Genovefa to become the protector of Paris: her move to the city, her out-of-body journey, and Germanus's ceremonial second arrival in her life.

Ready finally to prove herself publicly, Genovefa had her chance when the Huns threatened attack in 451. She organized the Parisian defense, arguing with men who wanted to flee with their possessions and rounding up the ladies to pray. The hagiographer compared her to Esther and Judith, but the panicked and fickle Parisians turned on her, accusing her of false prophecy. They were trying to decide whether to stone her or toss her into the Seine when a messenger from Auxerre fortuitously arrived with Germanus's final intervention. He had died in 448, but his archdeacon sought the Parisian mob at its usual haunt (loca conventicola) in order to recite the "magnificent testimony" to Genovefa's sanctity that he had composed before his death. The crowd gave up their evil plan—good thing, too, as the hagiographer pointed out, for Genovefa's prayers kept the Huns away. The writer compared her to Martin and Anianus, bishop-saints who had defended their own episcopal cities, one by making treaties and the other by miraculously aiding the troops. "Aren't the same honors due to Genovefa," the hagiographer demanded of any lingering antagonists, "who drove away the same army by her prayers so that it wouldn't surround Paris?"[13] Genovefa was clearly superior both to heroines of Old Testament and to episcopal administrators responsible for civil defense, for the Huns never even came within sight of Paris.

Genovefa's trials among the Parisians and her hagiographer's explicit demands for recognition of her *virtus* reveal the writer's defensive assumptions. Some readers must still have doubted the saint. It had been hard for even the holiest woman to establish her civic authority in fifth-century Gaul. God shed his grace on women and men, but public command required manliness, acquired by birth or through family, marriage, imitation, or patronage. Holy women had no formal ecclesiastical roles beyond vowing chastity, praying privately on behalf of others, marrying bishops, or patronizing Christian men, as the lady Paula did Saint Jerome. Without the training and status of a bishop, even though she enjoyed the unfailing support of a famous bishop, Genovefa had to build her reputation with a combination of tactics: typical demonstrations of feminine humility and piety, imitation of male leadership, economic self-sufficiency, and sponsorship by an important man. With the exception of

Empresses Helena and Galla Placidia, no female rulers offered useful paradigms for exercising power. Without access to throne or priesthood, without the options of martyrdom or a formal convent, Genovefa could display and establish her God-given authority only by emulating other local leaders. The hagiographer consistently represented Genovefa as bishoplike, exercising all the duties and accepting the privileges of the episcopacy and enjoying the collusion of bishops from other places.

The hagiographer wrote of a saint who practiced the job of holiness. Like Martin and his models, the desert fathers, Genovefa prepared herself by self-denial for the work of sharing God's bounty. Asceticism was an appropriate behavior for Christian ladies if not taken too far. According to the hagiographer, Genovefa was a severe dieter from the age of fifteen, eating only barley bread and beans with a little oil twice weekly for thirty-five years. When some unspecified bishops finally urged her to eat fish and milk—she must have been at least fifty years old by then—she obeyed because to contradict them was sacrilege.[14] Yet her regimen, which also had liturgical connotations, had revealed her sanctity to those who could neither understand nor imitate it.[15] Ritual fasting also sharpened her vision, reducing her to ecstatic tears during her penitential exercises. "She is believed," wrote the hagiographer, "to have seen the heavens open and our Lord Jesus Christ standing at the right hand of God . . . for the Lord made no idle promise when He said, Blessed are the pure in heart for they shall see God." She kept company with the twelve spiritual virgins, whose names the hagiographer retrieved from the second-century mystical tract, the *Shepherd* of Hermas: Faith, Abstinence, Patience, and the rest without whom "neither virgin nor penitent could inhabit Jerusalem which is built as our city" (Ps. 121:3).[16] The rigors of fasting and ecstasy prepared her for a more important revelation—the lost resting place of Saint Denis—and the building of another metaphorical Jerusalem, which would provide the ultimate proof of Genovefa's worth.

Genovefa alone knew where Denis lay. He was harder for other Christians to find, possibly because no one had written his vita by Genovefa's time. Even the hagiographer may not have known the full story of Denis's martyrdom, although a few lines of Genovefa's vita explained who Denis was and what happened to him. But someone else jotted these words between the lines of Genovefa's life during the eighth century, claiming that it came from "the tradition (*tradicionem*) of authorities or the telling (*relatio*) of [Denis's] Passion."[17] Those ancient traditions and tellings were also recorded in a brief sixth-century history of Denis called the *Gloriosae*. According to both *Gloriosae* and the interpolation into Genovefa's vita, Denis had arrived in Gaul during an imperial persecution, been beheaded by colonial officials, and was buried between four and six Roman miles outside of Paris.[18] The *Gloriosae* and later versions of Denis's Passion gave the saint two companions, the priest Eleutherius and the deacon Rusticus.[19] In all versions, Denis and his head ended up in the Seine. According to the *Gloriosae*, a pious matron named Catulla fished the body parts out of the river and buried them north of the town; but Catulla was probably a creation from the place-name Catulliacus, site of Denis's fifth-century shrine as well as earlier graveyards.[20] Medieval devotees of Denis at his monastery of Saint-Denis elaborated the tale in other directions. According to Hilduin, abbot in the ninth century, the saint and his companions had actually met their end atop Montmartre (which he understood as "mount of the martyrs," or Mons Martyrum), after which Denis had picked up his head and carried it two miles north before finally expiring. The saint usually showed up in medieval illuminations and sculpture with his head quite literally in his hands.[21]

Genovefa knew some version of Denis's story, at any rate, even if his legend got jumbled in the tumultuous two centuries between the Decian persecution and her building project. The site of his grave may have been lost or just disregarded.[22] Like so many saintly burials miraculously found and reported by bishops in the sixth century, Denis's tomb lay in a suburban cemetery awaiting rediscovery. Genovefa knew exactly where it was not because she saw it with her eyes but because she experienced an unbelievable love and veneration for the site where the saint had been hidden in the *vicus* of Catulliacus, an old rest stop on the Roman highway.[23] Other saints needed verification when they sought the graves of their missionary predecessors; whereas Martin had to call up a ghost to check the validity of a holy site, Genovefa knew instinctively, undoubtingly. The hagiographer never told how and when she had first come to the place, only that she determined to build a basilica there in Denis's honor. Like other late antique matrons who built monuments for their favorite dead bishops, Genovefa determined to commemorate Denis. However, her job involved much more than the usual tasks of a patroness who ordered carpenters and paid for stonemasons.[24] She lacked sufficient wherewithal—*virtus*, as the hagiographer wrote, which suggested wealth as well as influence and power.[25] Other evidence in her vita (the inherited house and a later episode concerning estates to the east) suggests that Genovefa was a noblewoman of some means but apparently not enough to single-handedly sponsor a building project.

Without the funds or authority to raise them, Genovefa waited undeterred until two priests, one unnamed and the other called Genesius, made a regular visit to her cell. She begged them to take up a special collection for the project.[26] "Let a basilica be built in honor of St. Denis," she urged, "for there is no doubt this site is terrible and awesome [*Nam terribilem esse et metuendum locum ipsum, nulli habetur ambicuum*]." "Terrible" and "awesome" were words for deserted but holy places like the biblical Bethel where the patriarch Jacob had dreamed his ladder (Gen. 28): "How awesome is this place (*terribilis . . . locus*)! This is none other than the house of God; this is the gate of heaven."[27] As Jacob properly deduced, "Surely the Lord is in this place and I was not aware of it." Jacob had marked the spot with a pillar. For Genovefa, too, the obvious qualities of the site demanded a religious monument. However, the priests, less clear-sighted or biblically sensitive than Genovefa, disagreed about the wisdom of construction at place both *terribilem* and *metuendum*.

The question concerned Christian theorists and administrators throughout the early medieval centuries. Ausonius and his fellow poets preserved nostalgia for the countryside and its serene retreats, but they never praised wasteland. Classical aesthetics helped them distinguish well-built from rudely built or unbuilt landscapes and led them to prefer well-managed, architecturally enhanced places.[28] Patristic theologians preached that humans left an orderly Eden for lonely desert only when forced. Their heaven was a gleaming city surrounded by gardens more formally beautiful than anything built by Caesar. Rather than the modern dichotomy of civilization and wilderness, then, late antique and early medieval texts proposed a tripartite landscape of human-built civilization, God-given wilderness, and perfect places of the afterlife. Desert wasteland lured hermits precisely because it was the antithesis of civilization and harbored such enemies of Christianity as demons, monsters, and ghosts. Stout men of God, such as Germanus and Martin, tested themselves in the wilderness in imitation of Christ, but they always returned reluctantly to their urban bastions of civil and ecclesiastical authority.[29]

Genovefa's hagiographer described the wilderness north of Paris in these traditional terms. In his eyes, Genovefa surpassed part-time hermits who took their personal struggles to the desert, for she aimed to turn waste into landscape. As protector of the Parisians, she would enter the wilderness to harvest its spiritual and material resources on behalf of her people. Paris's priests were poor administrators unable to use God's nature efficiently. Genovefa knew exactly how to exploit the desert productively, and her face shone as a sign to Genesius as she explained in simplest terms (*claro vultu, manifestum eloquium*). To know what she knew, to see what she saw, they had to travel as she had between country and city. She commanded them to enter the wilderness. "Go outside and walk over the city bridge and report back to me what you hear," she told them.[30]

The hagiographer described the priests' adventure as yet another ritualistic tour. First they crossed a bridge, probably to the right bank, where they loitered uncertainly and eavesdropped on two pigkeepers. One swineherd said, "While I was following some pigs wandering toward their pasture, I found a huge lime kiln." The other replied, "And I found a tree in the forest uprooted by the wind. Under the roots there was a similar furnace which looks as though no one has stripped anything from it." Craftier Parisians had not yet found these precious resources. The city priests had never thought to look. These bumpkin swineherds could not properly interpret what they found, but priests and herders pooled their knowledge under Genovefa's direction. The clerics followed the herders to the kilns, then rushed back to report to the saint, who, of course, already knew. As she gently pointed out to the priests, if God could provide the lime, the ecclesiastical officials of Paris could certainly conduct a fund-raising campaign to finance the basilica. A paragraph later, Genovefa was out in the woods, supervising the lumbering for her church and miraculously supplying drink for the thirsty laborers. She had them bring the empty butt to her and then knelt on the ground, making contact with the earth that would supply her resources, watering it with her tears. She prayed, signed the cross over the butt, and filled it to the brim with a never-ending supply.

The hagiographer told so much in such a simple anecdote of pigs and limekilns: the building boom of first- and second-century Paris, the decline of settlement and its structures after third-century invasions, the loss of technology, the ruralization and poverty of the fifth century, and the fearsome landscape with its hidden bodies and buried buildings, all expressed in a story of unimaginative priests and two pigkeepers stumbling through the woods. The urban clerics, like us, must have wondered how Genovefa had known about the antique but fully functioning kilns hidden in the pasture and the woods. Who built them? Who left them? Why were these valuable resources discarded among the grasses and vines of the forest floor? The hagiographer interpreted the limekilns as leftovers of empire, but more likely they belonged to a recent generation of *spolia* burners turning old stones into new cement on the edge of Paris.[31] Others must have known of the kilns or glimpsed the existing Gallo-Roman site that Genovefa chose for her discovery and translation project. She would lay her foundations atop an old cemetery and possibly even over an earlier Christian shrine.[32] When workers laid out the walls, they cut through existing graves.[33] The building crew used decorated masonry blocks from an earlier structure to create a basilica of approximately twenty by twenty meters, with an interior half as wide. These proportions help confirm Denis's shrine as a fifth-century construction. Seventh- and eighth-century expansions of the basilica relied on the same design and orientation as Genovefa's original church and retained the same focus on a particular burial at one end of the basilica, which suggests that both initial builders and medieval remodelers regarded the tomb as Denis's. Merovingian royalty certainly thought so, because after about 500 they began to lay their dead near the central tomb.[34]

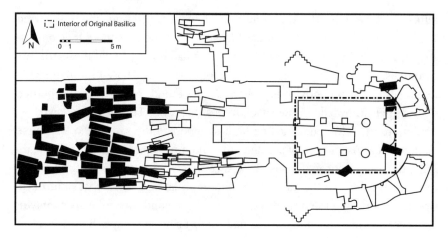

FIGURE 3.2. Design for original basilica at Saint-Denis (John Marston after Fleury).

Genovefa had finally become the choreographer of her own story. The shrine at the end of this road proved her sanctity visibly and permanently to her fellow Parisians. Like imperial administrators who had encouraged the creation of indigenous cult places along the edges of their new towns, Genovefa located the shrine of Denis in a spot belonging to no particular constituency but at the farthest imaginable edge of the city. The route of discovery that she designed for the priests and pigkeepers prefigured early medieval ritual processions between Paris's island and Denis's basilica. In subsequent chapters of the vita, Genovefa expanded the daily travel of her fellow Christians to this new boundary of the town. She took vowed sisters to Saint Denis to keep vigils. When storms and floods at the *locus terribilis* doused the sisters' candles on stormy nights, Genovefa wondrously relit them without a flint. She led laypeople in procession to the basilica, too. Once her city neighbors brought twelve demoniacs to her for exorcism, tugging them as they floated along in the air like balloons. Genovefa brought them down to earth, had them bound, and marched them solemnly to the basilica. Throwing herself on the pavement before Denis's tomb, assisted by an audience of angels, martyrs, and saints as well as Parisians, she cast out the evil spirits. Every bystander who had processed to the church caught a whiff of the foul stench of departing demons. Each restored madman proved that Genovefa could see as easily into the depths of human souls as beneath the earth.[35] As she had translated Saint Denis from obscurity to renown by building his shrine and his cult, so she transported both virtuous and unclean Parisians up the path to his basilica. It became the road to salvation.

Bishops, not ladies, usually led ritual processions from church to church in their cities. Some decades after Genovefa's death, Gregory of Tours recounted stories of impostors who tried to preempt this typical episcopal duty. One time a foreign cleric turned up in Tours dressed in holy man's clothes of tunic and linen mantle and carrying a cross hung with vials of holy oil—or so people said. He burst in on Gregory at the crack of dawn and boasted of having high-class relics. When the bishop was slow to react, his putative colleague stalked off to Gregory's own sanctuary to recite the morning liturgy. Then he did the same in Paris, attracting a low crowd that he paraded from church to church. The bishop of Paris was quicker than Gregory; he had the man locked up and examined his relic collection only to find that instead of saints' bones, the fake bishop carried a big bag full of roots, moles' teeth, mouse bones, and bear claws. Gregory eventually encountered the charlatan curled up in the corner of a little Paris church, stinking of wine and sewers and sleeping soundly through the daily office. The man turned out to be a runaway slave and one of "quite a number of these people who go in for impostures of this sort and keep on leading the common folk astray."[36] Gregory and his fellow bishops may have seen through the ruffian, but the people of major cities did not. As far as they were concerned, a man with decent clothes, a cross, a bag of bones, and some Latin prayers was a bishop. Gregory's tales suggest the possible reaction of Paris's bishop—who remained invisible to Genovefa's hagiographer—to Genovefa's assumption of episcopal authority.

Genovefa, too, repeatedly demonstrated her authority with processions and ritual journeys. Throughout her vita, the author sketched a series of routes traveled by his holy woman that marked the extent of her territory. Rather than priestly liturgy, however, she used other rituals to sacralize these boundaries and confirm her rule over them. More than once Genovefa co-opted baptisteries and churches for night vigils even though ecclesiastical leaders in Rome and Byzantium had begun forbidding women from participating in vigils for fear of licentious behavior in dark corners. The beneficial results—deflecting the Huns, miraculously producing illumination—justified her unorthodox actions.[37]

Parisians learned to respond to her exactly as they did to beloved bishops. She passed in and out of the city, enjoying the same ritual entries and welcoming crowds as bishops (*occursus* and *adventus*), performing prayers and cures in public, receiving supplicants wherever she stayed and prayed. Like Germanus and Martin, Genovefa advertised her authority with displays of personal asceticism and healing. Unlike other bishops, she was not an official participant in city government, but she did collect taxes from her estates east of Paris to support the city, and she had, after all, defended it from attackers.[38] She also practiced old-time evergetism, the responsibility of raising funds for civic buildings that normally fell to wealthy men and their wives. The city's bishop and other civic leaders should have assigned their assistants to collect revenues for Denis's basilica, but instead Genovefa ordered the priests to do it.[39] The discovery and translation of a saint and the building of a basilica to house his relics was yet another usual method whereby bishops reinforced their authority, as well as the prestige of their cities.[40] Genovefa seized the job for herself as Denis's episcopal heir. She, not a bishop, raised her city to the status of Arles or Tours by commemorating its Christian origins.

It is no coincidence that her hagiographer never mentioned any bishops of Paris but Denis, not even Saint Marcel, whose reign ended just before Genovefa first arrived. Bishops in Gaul held power to rival that of generals and governors. Many of them came from venerable senatorial families, as Gregory of Tours would, and inherited their sees as they did villas from male relations. These aristocrats knew well their value as cultural middlemen and political players in a declining Roman world. At their best they might, like Germanus, use their romanized savvy to win tax relief and other privileges from rulers. At worst, bishops squabbled and competed among themselves, tyrannized Christian populations with petty politics, and prevented charismats such as Genovefa from gaining the recognition and authority they deserved.[41]

Genovefa defied the norm and actually gained prestige from her patronage of Paris's first bishop, in spite of Paris's living bishops, but with the approval and help of bishops from other cities. She posed no formal threat to any bishop in his own see. She never competed directly for administrative power over the town of Paris, the diocese of Sens, or the larger system of Gaulish churches. Nonetheless, except on the matter of diet, Genovefa submitted to no episcopal authority. Her obvious sanctity, once established by prophecies and prayers, allowed her to escape the restrictions that kept other women in one place or prevented them from entering and using men's spaces. She could cross boundaries from city to terrible wilderness because she was at home everywhere. No one ordered her to stop traveling or tried to prevent her digging up Denis, or kept her from supervising the project. Although Germanus had found her in Nanterre, she never appealed to him or other episcopal leaders for recognition—they came to her. Bishops, kings, and saints voluntarily acknowledged her *virtus*. Even Saint Simon Stylite, the Syrian misogynist who lived on a towering pillar for forty years to avoid the temptations of womanly flesh, called down to passing merchants to ask about Genovefa and sent his admiring greetings to Paris with a request for her prayers.[42] Genovefa operated from an episcopal city yet without the restraints of episcopal office, deriving her political authority from her multiple identities as charismatic holy woman, surrogate bishop, urban dweller, and expert on Paris's past.

Genovefa's Territory

Once she had established her guardianship of Paris by the traditional means of conquest (her defense of the city against Huns) and the charitable construction of public architecture (Denis's basilica), Genovefa began to colonize a larger territory. As the bishop of Paris ought, she continued to protect her citizens by representing them to the larger world of northern Gaul. She traveled in and out of town, touring the entire diocese of Sens and visiting its major cities but only venturing beyond the diocese a few significant times. Genovefa's travels created enduring links between Paris and these other *civitates* in the diocese and also connected her region to Tours, the city of Saint Martin. Her travels furthered her fame and advertised the new basilica of Saint Denis, for she performed public miracles everywhere she went. Genovefa thus shaped a dynamic ecclesiastical hierarchy distinct from the official diocesan structures based at Sens and Tours. The hagiographer's record of her journeys defined this new hierarchy and its geography similar to the way imperial itineraries had once imagined the extent and workings of provincial government.

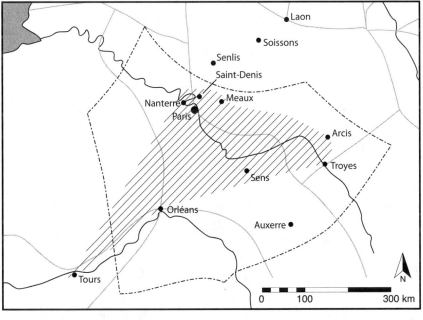

FIGURE 3.3. Map: Genovefa's territory (John Marston).

The city of Sens (*civitas Senonum*) had been the administrative center of the region since the late fourth century. Although Paris had hosted emperors and would later become a home to the Frankish king Clovis, Sens was chief of the seven episcopal cities in the diocese. Sidonius called its fifth-century bishop Agroecius "head of Senonia" and "head of the province" (*Senoniae caput, provinciae caput*).[43] Its metropolitan (chief bishop of the diocese) governed Paris as well as Troyes, Orléans, and other lesser episcopal cities, all of whose bishops appeared in fourth- and fifth-century conciliar lists. Only two living bishops commanded more authority in fifth-century Gaul, on account of their personal accomplishments rather than the importance of their home cities: Genovefa's comrades Lupus of Troyes, called "bishop of bishops" by Sidonius, and Germanus, who had negotiated with English heretics, Armorican rebels, barbarian leaders, and the imperial government.[44] Genovefa visited towns and villages managed by these bishops, although she never got to Sens itself. According to the vita, Genovefa's first trip was to Laon, just over the northern boundary of her diocese, in the jurisdiction of Reims. Next she went to Meaux, Arcis, Troyes, and Orléans. She crossed the southern border of the Senonian diocese to visit Tours, returned to Meaux with stops at Paris and Saint-Denis in between, and finished finally in Paris.

Everywhere Genovefa went, including her returns to Paris, the public welcomed her at the gate or conducted her in procession to the church, or both. As the hagiographer put it, everyone "honored her in her comings and goings."[45] Crowds gathered in anticipation of her arrival and the miracles she would perform. Victricius of Rouen described such a welcome ceremony for celebrities— in this case relics representing once-living saints—in a sermon written shortly before 400: "Every open space would at once be bright with garlands, matrons would fill the rooftops, the gates would pour forth a surge of people, every age, divided in its enthusiasm, would sing of glory and warlike deeds."[46] The farther the meeting point was from the city center, the lengthier and more prestigious the welcome. Sometimes the crowd accompanied Genovefa to private homes where she performed wonders, as in Laon, where she prayed over a paralytic in bed, or in Arcis, where city elders escorted her to a tribune's house so that she might cure his wife.[47] Witnesses prevented these marvels from being private and also conveyed them to the hagiographer, thereby enlarging Genovefa's welcoming crowd to include many generations of readers.

Elsewhere, the saint performed publicly in open spaces. At Troyes, a crowd met her bearing ill and diseased supplicants. While she healed her patients, the rest of the faithful snatched bits of fringe off her clothes to keep as protective talismans.[48] In Orléans, a matron sought Genovefa in the basilica of Saint Anianus, begging the saint to save her ailing daughter.[49] At Tours, a swarm of the possessed greeted her at the town gates and processed with her back to the basilica, where she out-Martined Martin by healing demoniacs in his own church. The next day, in the midst of celebrating Martin's feast in the same church, she intervened to save a crazed psalm singer who was mauling himself.[50]

The settings of Genovefa's miracles reinforced her extraordinary sanctity, even though the deeds were imitative of other saints. Fifth-century Christians were not much interested in unusual wonders, preferring instead the proof of recognizable miracles. Genovefa's hagiographer was influenced by Sulpicius Severus and hence cast Genovefa's healings at Tours in the same language as those of Saint Martin. The exorcism of the demented psalm singer mirrored Martin's cleansing of a possessed cook.[51] However, location changed the meaning of these cures. Genovefa was working wonders in the basilicas and baptisteries of other clerics and saints and in cities other than her own, helping those whom their own patrons could not. The basilica in Tours was new, raised between 458 and 459 by Bishop Perpetuus to celebrate Martin's growing cult. His psalm singer came down with a demon when pilgrims from all over Tours were thronging the new basilica in celebration. On that day, when men of the cloth gathered to sing Martin's praises, only Genovefa could see the demon lurking behind the sanctuary railing, although she was hiding modestly in a corner of the nave with the other women.[52] In this and similar episodes, Genovefa came to town and taught lessons in sanctity even as clerics and bishops advertised their own ecclesiastical office.

Other bishops' churches served as stages for Genovefa's miraculous performances, as her powers observed no predictable administrative limits. Her expeditions to cities around the greater diocese of Sens linked its towns and people together under her saintly patronage. She also beat new paths from these outposts of Christian civilization to wilder places, thus mapping together both built and unbuilt lands in her territory. On one occasion, as she cruised the river to Arcis, she passed through a rapids where ships regularly foundered. Genovefa ordered her shipmen to bank their boat so that she might investigate. She had them chop down a partially submerged tree while she quietly prayed. The sailors soon found two colorful, smelly monsters tangled in the tree roots. The beasts wrangled for two hours, tormenting the sailors "with intolerable blasts of fetid stench."[53] The odor signaled demons and hinted at the river's history of divinity, but neither Genovefa nor her hagiographer identified the monsters as devilish.[54] Yet she alone spied the malicious beasts that had claimed so many Christians. Only she understood the history of this dangerous site and how to make it safe. The creatures shoved off, and no ships were ever wrecked there again. Like any number of bishops and early popes who drove off serpents or dragons, Genovefa cleansed her landscape and made it fit for human use.[55]

Genovefa was particularly good with waters, which not only were familiar sites of healing but also were explicitly symbolic of rebirth and purification in Christian art and literature.[56] Like Jesus, the saint scanned the skies for the destructive forces of rain and wind and averted storms.[57] Outside Meaux she stretched herself in the dirt to weep and pray and thus halt crop-destroying torrents; she used the same penitential posture with which she had demonstrated her personal humility to the Parisians long before, and which she also employed for cures.[58] She had used well water to cure her mother's blindness. She also revived a boy who had tumbled into a well and drowned.[59] On the way home from Arcis, while leading eleven grain-laden ships back to Paris—a miracle in itself during war and famine—her fleet was buffeted by gales and driven upon the rocks. The boats took on water. Genovefa stretched her hands to heaven and prayed for succor. The wind abated, the ship's priest praised her miracles, and the sailors sang canticles to the bosun's beat all the way home.[60]

Genovefa fasted and prayed with the best of them, but her God-given talent was vision. She could look out beyond her city to empty lands, into moving waters, and up into the roiling air. She could see inside and outside, from the dark stillness of her private cell or in transit and sunshine upon the rivers of Gaul. Walls, trees, water, or earth never hindered her scrutiny. Through the soil she had seen the bones of Denis and spotted the forgotten limekilns. At a distance she had watched the Huns approach Paris. Through the flesh she found demons buried deep within human bodies, and under water she had tracked monsters that she might cast them out. She alone could view at once natural and built, living and past landscapes. Her vision encompassed past, present, and future. In theological terms, she bypassed illusory creation and sensed transcendent reality, seeing God's Creation for what it really was.[61] By strategic traveling, Genovefa extended her visionary ability beyond Paris to help Christians in other cities and denizens of the desert. Her mobility and vision together facilitated her unique dynamic relationship with her physical environment, allowing her to control all its untamed forces and extraordinary creatures, including the forces of disease and even the aristocratic bishops of Gaulish cities.

Still, Genovefa's greatest miracle was to win public religious authority in fifth- and sixth-century Paris and environs. Other holy women inspired stories of their virtue but left nothing to show for themselves after lives spent in retreat. Some few built tombs or shrines for saintly men but did not themselves achieve the title of saint or the power of bishops. Other women ruled, as the Empress Helena had, but only in men's names. Galla Placidia could not even persuade Saint Germanus to remain with her in Ravenna. Jerome's friends Melania and Paula had excelled at learning and created household monasteries in Jerusalem, but they built no great basilicas, discovered no lost saints, and commanded no territories. A few famous tourists journeyed farther than Genovefa but only to view historic landscapes, not to manipulate and monumentalize sacral resources. Women were simply less mobile and less in command of the landscape than men.[62] These matrons of the old empire had no opportunity to move into the Christian leadership or out of christianized cities because they dwelt within the limits of approved Christian roles for women, subject to men's administration and geographies.

Genovefa's relationship with her landscapes defied gender limits. She was at home in the natural world, yet she shared no particular affinity with nature in its divine feminine guises. She was not personally fruitful, although she brought grain to Paris. Neither text nor icon identified her as a sacred mother or a fertility figure, nor associated her with the crows, dogs, or horses of the Gaulish Matronae. She traveled the river and commanded its beasts but did not dwell at its source. At the same time, she was an urban woman untempted by the bucolic gardens of gentlemen's poetry or the deserts of male ascetics. Her Creation was the postlapsarian wilderness of Genesis, which could only regain perfection in the shape of a city inhabited by sinless women and men. She saw clearly the flaws of Gaul's post-Roman, christianizing landscapes—the wasted resources, perils, ruins, and empty spaces. Genovefa's job was to map and improve Nature as part of the civilizing project of late antique religious conversion. Finding materials allowed her to build. Building churches enhanced cities, and Christian cities were a great leap forward in the teleological march to transcendence: from Nature to Paris, Paris to Rome, Rome to Jerusalem, thence to the heavenly city.

Civilization had rarely been a woman's job until Genovefa took it on, but then Genovefa only occasionally observed the norms of gendered custom and space. In Paris, she lived with other vowed women in a kind of household fairly new to Gaul.[63] In this women's place she worked feminized wonders, like rekindling the candles when darkness frightened the girls. She did not close her community to men, for Germanus apparently felt free to bring the neighbors over to witness her penitential exercises. She abided by gendered divisions of church space, as at Tours, but crossed those boundaries when needed. She cured women in their own homes when asked, but she did not remain in women's spaces or minister primarily to women, or even treat all women in private. She never attended pregnant or birthing women. Fathers as often as mothers presented children to her for healing. Her virtues of chastity and humility, her company with virgins both human and symbolic, and her constant weeping identified her as a woman, but she was never a saint for women or their problems exclusively. Even when she worked with women, she used tools more properly reserved for clerical spaces, such as the consecrated oil that she used to anoint and exorcise women.[64] As her hagiographer told it, Genovefa did not work the kind of homely girlish miracles that would make Saint Brigit famous. Her only food-related miracles demonstrated her episcopal authority (she used imperial transport and collected taxes) and landed wealth (she prayed to halt rain over her estates).[65]

Her miracles proclaimed her utter access to all corners of all cities. When the saint organized the matrons of Paris to carry on night vigils, she not only occupied a baptistery but broke rules about its gendered use. The hagiographer remembered this radical use of Christian architecture as a dangerous challenge that provoked the mob. When Genovefa performed exorcisms in the churches of Martin and other bishops, she diminished their authority and episcopal office and simultaneously regendered those clerical spaces. Another time, Genovefa protected a refugee's virginity by locking the girl and herself in the baptistery at Meaux.[66] When she processed through the gates of other towns, joyously accompanied by supplicants, she displayed her access to the ritual routes of bishops and even kings. In one strange episode, she even invaded the judicial space of the pagan conqueror of Paris, Childeric. The king hurriedly left the city to execute some hostages beyond its walls, ordering the gate to be locked behind him so that Genovefa could not follow him and beg for the prisoners' release. Parisians were then amazed to see the saint unlock the gate without a key, pursue the king, and persuade him not to behead the prisoners.[67] Childeric knew he had to leave town to exercise his barbarian justice, but he should also have realized that the walls of Paris obeyed Genovefa, not him. She determined who left the city and who found refuge within. Other saints persuaded kings to release hostages and prisoners, but no other woman told Childeric what to do in the town he had conquered.

Germanus had advised her to act manfully, and so she did. She ruled cities and churches as effectively as men armed with weapons of war or written words of gospel. Who best knew the suburban edges and deep countryside where terms of command and ritual lost force, and where conversion meant visionary changes in the land and its uses? Who could discover the land's hidden treasures? Not a bishop, stuck in his city. Who could deter water monsters and shape safe paths between urban center and the desert outside? A local woman born to intercede. Who could best transform the formerly Roman, still unchristian wilderness into sanctuaries for Christian pilgrims? Only a saint who could speak in both feminine and masculine dialects, who could see what lay beneath the land and could envision what might be built above it. Out there, in the terrible awesome places where ancient saints and smelly demons still hid, building came naturally to a holy woman. Because she was a saint, she could take the place of a man, Paris's bishop. Because she acted as a bishop, she was able to build.

Even if the marvelous Genovefa of the written vita was a figment of hagiographic imagining, the living woman left tangible evidence of her accomplishments. Parisians gave her credit for building the fifth-century shrine of Saint Denis whose foundations still exist under the city.[68] They honored her tomb from the moment of her burial and mentioned her own shrine repeatedly in medieval documents. Thanks to the hagiographer, though, Genovefa's strategies for christianization became famous. He placed her firmly in the tradition of proselytizers and church leaders. Like Martin before her, she had worked to christianize the Gauls. Like Germanus—and as Carolingian reformers would in subsequent centuries—she reformed ecclesiastical administration. She preserved Paris's Roman heritage and was herself the last of the Roman saints of Gaul.

As death approached Genovefa, she continued to serve as Paris's bishop, thoughtfully and miraculously refilling a jar of consecrated oil that would keep the lamps of Paris's churches burning. After she died, miraculous cures occurred at her grave, reassuring Parisians that she would continue to protect them. Although Genovefa had been a wanderer for most of her life, she had come home to her city and its basilicas, suburban villages, roads, rivers, and fields. She moved one final time to her new sepulcher on the highest hill in old Lutetia, near the ruined forum. Clovis, by then Paris's king, honored Genovefa on that site with a lofty basilica.[69]

Clovis did not need to search for her body in the wilderness, for the saint obligingly left her remains in a public place. He did not name his church for Genovefa but after apostles buried far away in Rome, thus glorifying Rome's apostle to Paris, Denis, as well as the woman who had built his cult. The Basilica of the Holy Apostles sat at the meeting place of old highways, on itineraries that had once passed Paris for other Roman cities. The northward axis of the old Roman grid now led from Genovefa's hill to the Île de la Cité, where the king dwelt and where his son would build another magnificent basilica to Saint Stephen. That same highway continued across the Seine, past the suburban edge of Paris to Saint-Denis. Southward, the *cardo* still aimed at Rome and its bishop. Eastern and western roads led to regions that already belonged, or would soon fall, to Clovis and his sons. A new axis reached vertically up from Genovefa's tomb to the heavenly Jerusalem. Genovefa occupied the dead center of the historical grid.

4

Paris after Genovefa

Even as the hagiographer was composing a reputation for Genovefa in the 520s, her Paris was giving way to yet another new version of the city. The hill where she was buried had long been a vantage point for scanning Gaul. Now, for the first time, all Gaul was looking back at the Parisians. Their city was no longer a mere outpost on a secondary itinerary, perched somewhere between the edge of the world and the source of imperial Christianity. It had become the base camp of an energetic king who had expanded his rule westward to the ocean and southward through Burgundian territory to the Mediterranean shore. From her tomb on the heights, Genovefa guarded the now-royal city just as she had once defended the *civitas* against Huns and Clovis's own father. The hagiographer caught both versions of the city in his story of Genovefa: the end of Genovefa's Paris and the new Paris of Clovis's Christian kingdom.

For Clovis, the gates of Paris opened to an imperial past. As other ecclesiastical authors later told the legend, Clovis had embraced the role of the emperor Constantine, whose conversion from paganism in the early fourth century had already become the foundation myth of Christian Europe. Like Constantine, Clovis had a God-sent vision on the night before a crucial battle. Constantine chose a new Christian capital at Constantinople; Clovis settled for Lutetia. Clovis, clad in the cloak of Roman generals (*chlamys*), assumed the imperial titles of *consul* and *augustus*.[1] At the end of his career, he began to build the church of the Holy Apostles, named after Constantine's own mausoleum.[2] When the Frankish king lay down his crown after thirty years, he rested in the basilica that he had founded upon the hill above his capital city, where Genovefa also lay. The hagiographer claimed that the king built "in [Genovefa's] honor" but never specified whether Clovis chose the site for Genovefa because she was already there.

The hagiographer had no doubt that Clovis built to please Genovefa. The last paragraphs of the vita made clear that her patronage was essential for this newcomer squatting in Parisian buildings and trying to construct a new kingdom out of old Roman bricks. Genovefa had created the Christian Paris where Clovis played out his imperial drama. She was Helena, dowager empress and Christian pilgrim, to his Constantine. Helena had dug up the True Cross for her son. She had enshrined the Holy Sepulcher in order to help convert an entire empire to Christianity. Likewise, Genovefa had found the body of Gaul's own apostle and built Saint-Denis for Paris. Although Clovis's wife had persuaded him to convert and a bishop had baptized the king, Clovis must have planned Holy Apostles as Genovefa's shrine.

Yet the chronology of Holy Apostles' construction was not quite as straightforward as the hagiographer suggested, nor were Clovis's motives so selfless. Both king and saint disappeared into history before Holy Apostles was finished. It fell to Clovis's widow, Clothild, to continue building the crucial landmarks of Genovefa's cult and Clovis's Christian kingdom. Clothild most likely commissioned the vita of Genovefa, which promoted the association of Genovefa, Clovis's family, and the queen's church. In the early sixth century, when Genovefa's hagiographer wrote and the paint was still fresh on the new basilica, Holy Apostles advertised the treaty between Genovefa, saint of the Roman city, and her Merovingian allies. A new cohort of Gaulish-Frankish Christians flocked to meet Genovefa in the royal shrine rising among the Roman ruins. Noble families that had been too cheap to pay for Denis's shrine bore precious offerings to the church built by Clothild. Bishops hastened respectfully from other cities to Genovefa's hill, searching for the saint's tomb as Germanus and Lupus had sought the child herself long ago at Nanterre. When Clothild had her husband, her children, and herself buried at Holy Apostles, other aristocrats ordered tombs there.

Clothild died around 544. Genovefa's hagiographer never revealed—or perhaps did not live to realize—that Genovefa's authority would begin to diminish as soon as Clothild joined her in Holy Apostles. When Gregory of Tours wrote some forty or so years later, he hardly noted the collaboration between saint, king, and queen. He mentioned that the queen had finished the church and that Genovefa was buried in it, but he was much more interested in Clovis's vicious politics and Clothild's fertility.[3] The Merovingian kingdom was secure enough that the building projects of Clothild and Genovefa were no longer crucial to its early history. Although Holy Apostles gained property and prestige throughout the Middle Ages, its position at Paris's ancient symbolic center did not mean much while the city remained on its defended island. By the time Paris outgrew its water-bound refuge, other shrines and churches on both river-banks had become more important than Holy Apostles.

In the meantime, Parisians accumulated other saints. They constantly made new decisions about which patrons and holy places to attend. They used and interpreted religious buildings to suit themselves. They chose whether to visit Genovefa in her church and whether to carry her relics in procession—or not. The hagiographer's job had been to convince early medieval Parisians that Genovefa, better than any bishop or king, should be the foremost patron of their city and the kingdom won by Clovis. But sometime between Clothild's widow-hood and the reign of her great-great-grandson Dagobert (d. 639), the moment had passed for traveling church builders, and the hagiographer failed to per-suade. Paris's rulers looked away from the tombs on the southern hill to the little basilica at Catulliacus. Saint Denis won the glory, and the church that Genovefa had built for him became the royal resting place for the next twelve centuries.

It was not entirely the hagiographer's fault. It was hard to promote a saint who did not fit any familiar hagiographic models. Genovefa was neither martyr, queen, abbess, nor, above all, a male ecclesiastic in an age of bish-ops. She moved between periods of Christian history, refusing to settle in either pagan antiquity or the new age of European kings. She remained an im-portant saint and even became official patroness of Paris, but Parisians admired and honored other holy women. The French eventually chose an adolescent warrior as their favorite. Genovefa's churchmen and monks became rich and influential among the community of Paris's churches. But Genovefa's vita and tomb served to support other, newer devotions. Genovefa's territory, although rich with historical meaning for the first Merovingian rulers, was never the main instrument by which the Christians of Paris measured their city and its place in the cosmos.

Clovis in Paris

Sometime before 500, Clovis (Latin for Germanic Clodovech) and his wife, the Burgundian princess Clothild (Chrotechild), chose Genovefa as their Christian patron and Paris as their home. In general, Frankish royalty was not used to pre-siding over old Roman cities as were Clovis's rivals, the more southerly Visigoths, who had occupied parts of Aquitania and Hispania for many decades. Still,

Clovis's warriors were hardly ignorant of *romanitas*. Cohorts of Salian Franks, Clovis's people, had been fighting on behalf of the empire for a century, at least. By the fifth century, it was hard to distinguish between Germanic generals and imperial officials anywhere in Gaul.[4] Clovis's father, Childeric, had allied with the Gallo-Roman general Aegidius against the Visigoths and had gone to his grave wearing Roman ornaments. Frankish leaders quickly grasped the architectural and strategic attractions of modest northern *civitas* capitals such as Paris. But the Franks were not yet innovative urban planners. When they settled in a city, their options for enduring architectural impact were limited to preservation or destruction.

Like each generation of Roman or romanized rulers before them, the cadre of Franks that arrived in the 480s or 490s rearranged Paris's spaces. They probably did not significantly displace its permanent residents. For one thing, there were not enough outsiders to cause a major shift in settlement. Even if Paris could boast a couple thousand citizens in the later fifth century—which is doubtful—and even if the city attracted a disproportionate number of permanent Germanic settlers between 450 and 500, newcomers to town could not have numbered more than a few hundred scattered over a couple of generations.[5] Archaeologists who dig deep beneath Parisian streets today have never found pervasive levels of ash in the soil to prove fire or demolition. No violated burials or broken effigies remain to indicate widespread destruction in the mid–fifth century, as had occurred throughout Gaul in the mid–third. Contemporary writers, such as Genovefa's hagiographer, depicted discrete bands and armies of Franks led by militarized chieftains who attacked Gaulish towns primarily in order to enter and own them. Invaders wanted the goods stockpiled in cities as well as control over productive citizens, urban-based administrative structures, and symbols of civilization.

The Franks before and after Clovis had other capitals besides Paris. Clovis's father, Childeric, who had assaulted Paris during Genovefa's lifetime, was never fully at home there, although he knew the value of both the city and its patroness. During his siege of Paris, he allowed her to leave town in order to collect food for starving citizens. The hagiographer claimed that "the pagan king Childeric, king of the Franks, loved [Genovefa] with a veneration that I cannot express."[6] Clovis, however, made Paris his city. He had already become "fearful king" of Gaul "by right of war," having beaten back the Visigoths at Vouillé, 200 miles to the southwest near Poitiers. He had sent troops to Narbonne and Arles, had wintered in Visigothic territory at Bordeaux, and had sacked their capital of Toulouse. Yet, like Julian, he chose to live in modest Lutetia.

Despite what the hagiographer implied, the new king of the Franks had many good motives for spending time in Paris. He certainly valued its proximity

to both Frankish homelands to the northeast and his newly conquered southern territories. He must have grasped its strategic location on the Seine. He
had already worked with ecclesiastical leaders of other towns in the region to
establish his government, notably Reims, where he was baptized, and Tours,
where he was crowned.[7] Paris was a good place from which to view the many
kingdoms of his *imperium* and manage its regions. He must have prized the
city's markets and its place on the crossroads of trade, as well as the belt of rich
farmland that encircled it and kept it fed.[8] He may also have welcomed the
refuge of its walled island, where either he or his sons (or grandsons) built (or
rebuilt) a palace.[9] But according to Genovefa's vita, Clovis came to Paris primarily to honor the saint and build a church. As Childeric had freed hostages for
Genovefa, so did Clovis, although he did so willingly and often.[10] Clovis's grasp
of protocol was important to Genovefa's hagiographer. Clovis became a civilized city dweller not when he crowned himself with Roman titles or even when
he accepted baptism but when he settled down to cooperate with the existing
aristocracy and its urban-based government.

Clovis was an improvement over other barbarian city managers. The hagiographer understood that some invaders, such as the Huns, burned down
everything in their way. Other foreigners used urban spaces improperly, like
Childeric trying to judge and execute hostages outside city courts and gates.
The hagiographer's assumption that architectural *romanitas* lured barbarians
into town was typical of the early medieval literati, who could not always understand how new kings used old cities. This attitude may reflect the dismay of
long-term urban residents who were negotiating with their rulers about particular monuments or areas of their cities. Even well-intentioned renovations of
living neighborhoods caused disruption, especially in towns where citizens had
repeatedly mined disused homes and public buildings. One venerable neighborhood could remain viable only at the expense of another.[11] In towns across
the former empire, the same set of needs drove the development of similar
architectural elements—the creation of new ruling elites and their palaces, defensive walls, cemeteries, and markets—but with completely different results,
sometimes even within a single city. In early medieval Carthage, as in Britain
in the same centuries, city walls defended former urban centers but did little
to maintain their vitality, while undefended suburban neighborhoods and markets rose and fell independently of the core.[12]

Back in Rome, by comparison, the Ostrogothic king Theodoric (454–526)
must have demolished entire neighborhoods when he sponsored an old-
fashioned amphitheater in grand Roman tradition. He also took marbles from
Rome to restore Ravenna, earning praise as a collector of *spolia*, "a lover of
building and restorer of cities." Theodoric claimed somewhat defensively that

he wished "to build new edifices without despoiling the old."[13] More than fifty years later, Clovis's grandson Chilperic did the same thing in Paris and Soissons. He razed sites to raise circuses in 577, very possibly within city boundaries.[14] Beginning in the fourth century, eastern emperors had issued law after law against dismantling public edifices and thereby degrading both the beauty and heritage of cities, but lawmakers wrote for looters of *spolia* who recognized imperial authority, not Germanic rulers shifting ordinary houses and shops in order to set up royal palaces and circuses.[15] At least Theodoric and Chilperic rebuilt in imperial idiom, making decisions about urban spaces that were relatively explicable to their subjects if not always universally acceptable. By contrast, Lombard troops invading Italy a generation after Theodoric's rule selected particular quarters of conquered cities for barracks, crowding together in one militarized zone expropriated from previous residents. Like the Franks, they were not used to complex towns and classical architecture; they broke up the spacious painted rooms of city villas to create compact billets for their soldiers.[16]

While historians have characterized the revision of early medieval towns as either barbarian decline or urban renewal, it was really a constant series of debates between rulers and ruled about where to live, work, govern, and worship within a town. Some decisions were instant and personal, but others took generations, as did the Merovingian revision of Paris. Kings and their nobles did not always have the final say. According to Gregory of Tours, arrogant warriors of the fifth and early sixth centuries who disregarded the proper Christian meanings of buildings paid for their sins. When they insisted on using church courtyards for stables or despoiling shrines, saintly protectors of cities punished them with injury or death.[17]

Clovis and Clothild seem to have kept most of Paris intact. With the possible exception of the palace on the island and the new mausoleum, they built nothing so far as we know. Clovis may have needed to fix up the road that connected the emperor Julian's walled "little town" to its older Roman city center. Not many Parisians would have been inconvenienced. Few lived near the construction site on the left bank, although the hill was not entirely evacuated. An area just to the west of the forum had become a cemetery.[18] At least Clovis's new church stood by the ancient east-west axis of the city (*decumanus*) and was much closer to the city center than older shrines in the suburban necropolis at Saint Marcel. And there were plenty of available building materials around the old Roman neighborhood in the stones of the forum and the nearby baths.[19]

Nonetheless, the creation of Holy Apostles was more complicated, according to the single piece of contemporary written evidence, than the miraculous building of Denis's basilica. Genovefa's hagiographer described three stages of negotiation among Parisians and the royal couple, only two of which occurred in Clovis's lifetime. First, immediately after Genovefa's death around 502 and before any foundations were sunk, Parisians began spontaneously to visit the saint's grave. They came to mourn but also to pray for her intervention. The hagiographer recounted two miracles that occurred at the grave between Genovefa's death and Clovis's decision to create a basilica. In the first story, a young man with the Gallo-Roman name of Prudens came to her tomb (*sepulchrum*, *tumulum*) to beg a cure for kidney stones, which plagued him so terribly that his parents feared for his life. His mother and father accompanied him to pray and cry at the site. Prudens was cured. In the second miracle, a captive Goth who worked on the Sabbath in violation of church rules suddenly lost use of both hands. He spent the night praying to Genovefa in "the wooden oratory over the tomb" (*oratorio super sepulcrum de lingo contextum*) and left the next day completely healed. Apparently, Genovefa listened impartially to all Parisians, whether Gallo-Romans, enslaved and probably Arian Goths, or recently baptized Frankish rulers.[20]

Parisians knew where Genovefa lay and believed that, as a consequence, the place was sacred. What is more, they were willing to climb the hill to meet her. Supplicants could invoke the saint at her grave just as they used to seek her out in her cell or at the city gates. Prudens attended the tomb specifically because of his "reverence for the place" (*pro reverentia loci*). He felt the same attachment to the hill that Genovefa had felt (*amor, veneratio*) for the site of Denis's burial. Similarly inspired, someone else had already provided a rudimentary wooden shelter on the spot. It was customary in the late Roman world for wealthy women to sponsor family shrines and memorials to the most holy dead, so perhaps Clothild or Genovefa's sisters in religion had ordered the oratory to be built.[21] Maybe the owners of the plot had paid for it. Someone had contributed the real estate for Genovefa's new place; families normally bought and maintained burial property for their many generations. Others had labored with hammer and nails to build the wooden walls and roof of the oratory—perhaps the Goth slave. The oratory was not necessarily meant as a temporary structure. Church builders often located their wooden structures among the *spolia* of existing graveyards.[22] Most early Merovingian churches were wooden or constructed from a combination of wood and stone. Only important shrines were built originally in stone or replaced by masonry, as was the oratory of Saint Martin in Paris. Thus, whereas Genovefa had been concerned to find both a site and construction materials imbued with historic Christian meaning, it was sufficient for these builders of Genovefa's first shrine to find a convenient spot in company of the ancient urban dead where they might put a wooden shelter.

In the second stage of cult construction, however, increasing numbers of visitors to the site of Genovefa's grave negotiated with the owners, the sponsors, the builders of the original oratory, and the rulers of Paris about its use. Parisians like Prudens and the Goth gathered beneath the oratory's roof to pray. The place was big enough to accommodate a patient, his supporters, and witnesses spending a night of intense prayer and needy dreams near the saint's remains. As the visitors who periodically used and occupied this sacral space multiplied, the oratory's users must have required more room. Genovefa's discovery of Denis's putative tomb illustrated the same process of cult expansion, although with a significant hiatus between first and second buildings.[23]

The demands of pilgrims to Genovefa's tomb and its location in an existing cemetery—where at least two previous bishops of Paris were also buried—helped Clovis choose the site for a mausoleum.[24] It is certainly possible that king or queen was already among the devotees at Genovefa's tomb, although the hagiographer did not mention any history of interaction between Genovefa and the royal couple beyond Clovis's release of hostages. Gregory later wrote that Clovis was impressed by miracles at churches elsewhere, so he may have been open to the benefits of local pilgrimage.[25] Whether or not Clovis built in honor of Genovefa's merits, as the hagiographer claimed, the location in an existing cemetery with an energetic cult was perfect for a mausoleum. Clovis probably funded the basilica in which most of his family was eventually interred. Half a century later, Gregory of Tours called the church variously "the basilica of St. Peter" and "Holy Apostles" and added that Clothild had built it.[26] Only much later would the Parisians begin to call it Saint Genovefa's church.

Clothild's Church

Clovis died soon after building began, so Clothild oversaw the third phase of design and construction. The place would honor saint and king together. From its commanding position on the hill, the basilica proclaimed in style and decoration the status of its occupants. Imperial families of Rome, Ravenna, and Milan had always been buried in impressive chapels. Nearer to Paris and closer to Clothild's time, one of the Visigothic leaders who held southwest Gaul sometime in the fifth century—before Clovis invaded it—went to rest in just such a Roman-style mausoleum at Toulouse. Its mosaics expressed the faith of its ruler, who happened to be an Arian Christian; thus its scenes of the Epiphany from Saint Matthew's Gospel, the infancy and childhood of Jesus, and the Magi emphasized the humanity of Christ rather than his divinity. Old Testament scenes of deliverance—from the fiery furnace, from the Flood, from Egypt—proclaimed the building's funerary purpose, as at other mausoleums (Santa Constanza in Rome and Centcelles near Tarragona).[27] Inside and out, the Visigothic shrine invoked its king's heritage as heir to western emperors and his position as a Christian ruler.

Clothild likewise sought to invoke the Christian *imperium* of Clovis and his descendants by her design of Holy Apostles. The shrine was a rectangular basilica typical of orthodox northern Gaulish saints' shrines. Based on the basilicas where emperors and their officials sat in judgment, it stood near the site of the forum and an earlier basilica. Clothild ordered a lofty roof that rose far above believers, like the roofs of grand public buildings from Gaul's past. Such vaults were typical features of major burial shrines and much admired by Gregory of Tours for their classical workmanship.[28] Clothild also commemorated the Merovingians' *romanitas* with a traditional triple portico over the basilica's entrance.[29] She covered the interior walls of the porticoes with narrative scenes meant to inspire and guide worshipers. These were not simple Bible stories or pictures selected to promote a heterodox version of Christianity, as in the Arian mausoleum at Toulouse. They were "images of Patriarchs and Prophets, Martyrs and Confessors to the faith in ancient times drawn from pages of history books."[30] An entire chronology of orthodox christianization was visible in the entry to this Parisian mausoleum, beginning with biblical fathers, passing through the years of imperial persecution of Christians, and finishing with the missionaries and scholars of late antiquity.

Within the church, altar and tombs preserved a parallel history of conversion in the sanctuary, beginning with the altar dedicated to the apostles Peter and Paul, which later contained relics of those saints—hair from each of them and a bit of cloak from Paul. Genovefa, who had rescued Denis, preserved Paris's *romanitas*, and accomplished the final christianization of both the city and its king, lay near (or under) the altar. Clovis, ultimate source of the Christian Frankish dynasty, rested there too.[31] Clothild and her offspring would later join the ranks of the commemorated. Although earlier bishops of Paris were later brought into the sanctuary from nearby graves, for the moment no churchmen or others saints entered this teleological scheme.

While Clothild may have drawn inspiration from Genovefa's example as a builder, she may also have looked to other women of wealth and influence for her learned decorative program. The wife of Namatius, bishop of Clermont-Ferrand, had built and decorated a church for her city almost a hundred years before. Gregory wrote about the projects of Namatius (d. ca. 462) and his unnamed wife. As soon as Namatius was elected, he began to fulfill his duty and sponsor public architecture. He raised a massive cross-shaped structure with a fifty-foot ceiling, seventy columns, and eight doorways, adorned with imported marble and relics. The building's forty-two windows gave viewers the sensation, as Gregory put it, of "the fear of God and of a great brightness." This was

no low-ceilinged hall of barbarian conquerors but the dwelling place of the empire's saints. Nature did not obtain within the church, for what was normally
dark and enclosed was instead illuminated.[32]

The bishop's wife also built a shrine.[33] To complement Namatius's architectural wonders within the city walls, she sponsored a little basilica for Saint
Stephen in the suburbs, presumably in an old cemetery. There she brought
history back to life with frescoes based on her reading of "stories of events
long ago." She actively embraced the duty of patronage, not only ordering the
painting but sitting in the church with her book on her lap, keeping an eye
on the artists.[34] Her project was not as splendid or public, but it was certainly
as theologically informed, orthodox, and aesthetically pleasing as that of Namatius. Each had a particular purpose in building, suitable to his or her gender
and office; while Namatius raised the episcopal church, his wife sponsored a
memoria in the city's suburbs. After her husband died, she buried him in her
shrine and may also have ended up there herself.[35] Namatius's successor also
constructed a monastery and churches in other neighborhoods. These shrines
accumulated upon the Christian grid of Clermont, connecting its center to its
peripheries across a complex early medieval landscape of worship.

Clothild's project was on a different scale from all of these shrines, as befit
the royal wife of a new Constantine and the mother of a dynasty. Her monument
commemorated at once her husband's conversion and her kingdom's future,
symbolized in the tomb of a miracle worker from the romanized Christian past.
Other Christians had raised funerary monuments to religious virgins, but no
one else built a shrine to the enduring relationship between a converted dynast
and a female saint—what is more, a saint who represented the entire span of
Gaulish christianization in her relationship to Saint Denis. Like the well-trained
episcopa (bishop's wife) of Clermont, Clothild played a properly gendered supporting role in this great Christian establishment. The purpose of memory
keepers such as Clothild and Namatius's wife was to build something other
than episcopal churches and to promote cults other than those favored by bishops and rulers. Namatius's wife, like Genovefa, also built to honor an ancient
apostle who lay neglected in the suburbs.[36] In Clothild's Paris, another woman
had already recovered the apostle while the bishop kept his church on the walled
island. In this historical and geographical context, Clothild's hilltop basilica
dominated the southern horizon of the city like a defensive citadel, preserving
Genovefa's cult and Francia's first family against approaching enemies.[37]

For Gregory, Clothild's building was just one of her duties as queen. He
never mentioned the queen's later building projects, though other authors did.
In Gregory's telling, Holy Apostles enhanced Clothild's royal prestige, but it
was not nearly as crucial to the Merovingian dynastic agenda as the queen's

part in Clovis's personal conversion. She had borne and baptized children, she had invited Bishop Remigius of Reims to baptize Clovis, and, finally, she had ordered the construction of Clovis's tomb and had sanctified it with the relics of Genovefa. She had rebirthed her husband in baptism and afterward deposited him and the rest of her family, one by one, in the shrine she had completed. Clovis went to his rest in 511; their daughter Clothild followed in 531, and two grandsons shortly after. Clothild herself was buried in Holy Apostles in 544, possibly in a specially constructed funerary chapel.[38] Clothild was the architect of Clovis's conversion and the keeper of his memory. Her life after Clovis and her building projects were merely additional details in the central narrative of Gregory's written history.[39]

Neither Gregory nor Genovefa's hagiographer revealed a relationship between Clothild and the saint. Later Carolingian writers celebrated their collaboration, though. "How fitting," the author of Clothild's own ninth-century vita remarked, "that the church dedicated in the name of the Holy Apostle should be adorned by the body of that virgin and the limbs of so glorious a queen, so devout a widow, mother of Roman Emperors, and the genetrix of the King of the Franks."[40] In life, Genovefa had dealt with kings and bishops but no queens.[41] Clothild's name appeared only once in Genovefa's vita when the queen finished the church. For his part, Gregory showed Clothild working more closely with clerics of Tours than with vowed women. He recalled that the queen retired to live "as a religious" in Martin's city—which was, of course, his own episcopal seat—and made only periodic trips to Paris. The Carolingian hagiographer of Clothild described her continuing involvement in both royal and religious politics, taking sides in her sons' battle for succession and strategically endowing churches and monasteries.[42]

In the estimation of both the sixth-century bishop Gregory and the ninth-century Carolingian writer, Clothild's asceticism and charity in widowhood balanced her early career as a royal childbearer, making her as good as a saint. Indeed, the Carolingian writer celebrated Clothild's patient suffering and self-deprivation, casting her as an abbess manqué similar to queens of the late sixth and seventh centuries who became nuns (whose vitae were written much earlier than Clothild's). Like Genovefa, she had subsisted on bread and legumes and mortified her body with ascetic penances. The writer of her vita pointed out that the queen had been anguished by the murder of her father and mother, her grandchildren, the early death of her daughter, her sister's exile, and "her own marriage to a pagan king."[43] "None would have thought," he intoned, "that this holy woman . . . who sprang from stock royal in this world and rose to the highest place in the realm, suffered pain and torment in this life." Clothild's marriage to Clovis was ordeal enough to merit sainthood.

The Carolingian hagiographer celebrated Clothild's involvement with architecture, but not primarily as a builder and decorator of Holy Apostles. He listed monasteries she had endowed in Tours, Rouen, and Laon, and her funding of the expansion of a church at Reims. It was she, according to this vita, who had advised Clovis to build the shrine in Paris, although not on Genovefa's account. "If you wish, Lord King," she supposedly argued, "to expand your kingdom on earth and to reign with Christ in his celestial kingdom, build in this place a church in honor of Saint Peter, Prince of the Apostles, that, with his help you will succeed in subjugating the Arian peoples to yourself."[44] Of course, this vita also claimed that Clovis lived out his days like a monk, spending his entire wealth on monasteries. Yet Clothild's ninth-century hagiographer clearly read her building projects as religious acts in imitation of Genovefa, for while overseeing the construction of the monastery near Tours, Clothild miraculously supplied drink for her builders as Genovefa had done in the woods outside Paris. The queen transformed spring water into wine for her laborers.[45]

For the Carolingian writer, the real clue to Clothild's life lay in her travels between Tours and Paris, two sites of royal and sacral power. Clovis had taken his crown in Saint Martin's church at Tours—the same church (or its replacement) where Genovefa had cured demoniacs. Clothild lived in Tours after Clovis's death. It was there that an angel alerted the queen to her own imminent passing. Her sons hastened to hear her last words of wisdom before she expired thirty days later. Yet after she died—filling her house with light and fragrance as befits a saint's departure for the next world—her sons bore her back to Holy Apostles in Paris. There the "mother of Roman emperors and the genetrix of the king of the Franks" lay with her husband and her sister in architecture, Genovefa, under the protection of Saints Peter and Paul, Denis to the north, and now Martin to the southwest. Long before, Genovefa had constructed a series of similar links among the cities of the diocese of Sens. By her travels, she had created a historical connection between the old Roman administrative province and Christian Paris. Then she had invited in the Franks to govern this territory. In the same way, Clothild made space for the kings of Francia in Genovefa's basilica; and she joined Martin with Genovefa and Denis as patrons of the emerging dynasty. It was years before Clothild, collaborator with Clovis and builder of the dynastic monument, gave way to Clothild, wifely martyr.

Paris Renegotiated

In the sixth century, Holy Apostles and Saint-Denis were only two among Paris's glorious collection of chapels, oratories, and churches paid for by nobles and royalty and dedicated to Stephen, the Virgin Mary, John the Baptist, Denis, Martin, Marcel, Christopher, Vincent, Julian, Symphorien, Bacchus, Severin, Laurence, Gervasius and Protasius, Germanus of Auxerre, Columba, Victor, Médard, Medericus, and the Holy Innocents, among other unnamed patrons, as well as Peter and Paul.[46] The unnamed baptistery where Genovefa observed vigils before the onslaught of Huns was probably a fourth-century structure near medieval Nôtre Dame; later a chapel dedicated to John the Baptist marked the spot. The cathedral (or simply *ecclesia* as Gregory called it) where Paris's bishops preached was nearby, along with their residence and an oratory where they prayed privately. Shrines to Marcel and possibly to Crescentia rose in the cemeteries southwest of town. One of them may have been the *ecclesia senior*, or oldest church in Paris, but Genovefa's hagiographer did not notice.[47]

For the hagiographer, Parisian geography was simple. Holy Apostles was the most important building, Saint-Denis the second. A straight line of religious processions connected the two points. The hagiographer did not mention other shrines. He did not name the local priests, bishops, or city officials, except the priest Genesius. He did not specify neighborhoods or identify existing landmarks in his vita of Genovefa but referred only vaguely to Paris and its places. He was probably not a Parisian but may have come from Tours with Clothild. As a result of his ignorance and partiality, the hagiographer did not reveal how the builders, users, and keepers of Holy Apostles fit the new shrine into the existing network of Parisian holy places. He could not have known that the appearance, meanings, functions, and even the name of Holy Apostles would shift in years to come. No one else described the visitors to Genovefa's tomb or the clergy who tended Holy Apostles in those first decades after it was built either. We have only Gregory of Tours's stories of other churches and the detritus of excavations with which to rebuild the sixth-century history of Genovefa's shrine.

Bodies and coffins tell part of the tale. Excavations carried out under Napoleon in 1807, before the demolition of the medieval church, brought to light thirty-two Merovingian sarcophagi. None was exactly contemporary to Genovefa, but all were probably in their original positions clustered close to her supposed burial site.[48] Crosses were carved on many of these trapezoidal stone boxes in a style similar to those found elsewhere around Merovingian Paris. High-ranking Parisian Christians apparently sought burial *ad sanctos*, near the holy dead, and *ad reges*, close to royal corpses. The Napoleonic archaeologists believed they had actually even found the tombs of Clovis and Clothild, for two of the sarcophagi were more highly decorated than the rest. A statue of Clovis discovered near them seemed to confirm the identification. Two smaller coffins appeared to contain the children of Chlodomir, Clothild's grandchildren.[49] But the excavators were mistaken. The statue of Clovis was Gothic; it now lies with the other royalty of France in Saint-Denis. The tombs of Clovis and his queen had disappeared in the many rebuildings of Holy Apostles long before the antiquarians sought them.

By then Genovefa had already moved too. Her grave had originally dominated the apse, probably marked by a cenotaph before the altar. Saint Eligius (Éloi, ca. 588–660), treasurer and craftsman to King Dagobert, had redecorated her sepulcher with gold and gems, according to his seventh-century vita.[50] The precious monument must have been above ground for the wonderment of pilgrims. When a proper crypt was built below the choir, Genovefa's official tomb took its place underground at the head of its coffin-clad crowd of Merovingian admirers, where it remained through the eleventh century.[51] But her bones did not stay at home—she came out when Vikings threatened, and she processed in a reliquary whenever her neighbors needed her protection. In the thirteenth century, she went into a finer reliquary. Her original sarcophagus eventually disappeared in one of the rearrangements of her basilica. [52]

Before that, though, many bishops and other saints had joined Genovefa and Merovingian royalty in the nave. Some had been translated from the necropolis near the church, which had grown to be one of the largest in medieval Paris. Saint Perpetuus and Saint Eusoz moved inside probably in the sixth century.[53] Saint Ceraunus, another bishop, was laid in the sanctuary in 614 when he died at a council held in the church.[54] By the mid–sixth century, if not earlier, the nave had acquired at least one funerary chapel or *sacrarium* on the north side of the apse where Clothild was apparently laid. The basilica gained both space and architectural flourishes as it acquired bodies. The original church had about the same dimensions as Saint-Denis: the interior was nine meters across, although almost twice that on the outside, and double that in length.[55] Gregory of Tours mentioned the addition of another oratory (*secretarium*). By the Carolingian period, the church ceiling was carved wood.[56] Where Genovefa's hagiographer had described a triple portico, a Carolingian reviser of Genovefa's vita boasted of plural porticoes and vestibules (*atria*) or side chambers off the apse.[57]

Like other churches of the sixth century, Holy Apostles must also have gained ritual functions as it grew. It began as a mausoleum, dynastic monument, and one saint's shrine. However, the basilica also became a council hall in the sixth century. It was large and important enough to host prestigious meetings of decision-making bodies of clerics. Bishops met there in 573 and 577 (no one significant enough to mention had dropped dead during these meetings). Eighty men signed the canons of the 614 council that met in Holy Apostles, and the king was there too.[58] From the start, of course, the shrine was also a pilgrimage destination. Gregory mentioned that Genovefa rewarded petitioners at her tomb, and that sufferers of fever and chills could be cured there.[59] The feast-day liturgies of Holy Apostles must have expanded to include special days and prayers for the saints who followed Genovefa into the sanctuary. By the mid–eighth century, Genovefa's church had acquired a hospice to accommodate pilgrims and monks to tend them.[60]

Holy Apostles also served as political propaganda beyond its initial purpose as a Merovingian monument. It helped advertise the place of Paris within a Christian polity much larger and more powerful than Genovefa's territory. Holy Apostles' dedication to Peter and Paul linked the basilica to other buildings in the Parisian basin named for these saints, and to similar structures in more distant Frankish episcopal towns. Writers of the eighth century interpreted the identification of all these apostolic churches with Rome and its earliest pope as part of a campaign against Arianism; Clothild waged war with meaningful architecture while her husband deployed actual armies against the heretics, and bishops hurled theological refutations at them. At least three of Clothild's other projects were called after Saint Peter to emphasize her family's doctrinal alliance with orthodox Frankish clerics and with the Roman see.[61] Likewise, the triple portico of Holy Apostles recalled the portico of Old Saint Peter's in Rome, stating a theological position in stone. A net of ecclesiastical sites named for the apostles thus bound Paris to Rome, reminding all believers in both cities of the orthodoxy of Frankish bishops and kings. The anti-Arian program of Holy Apostles disappeared, of course, when the Arians did, and the basilica's symbolic links to the orthodoxy of Rome became less urgent.

Although it remained a burial shrine, Holy Apostles never accumulated generations of kings as Saint-Denis later did because Clovis's sons built their own mausoleums dedicated to other patrons. When Childebert I (d. 558) brought the tunic of Saint Vincent back from his campaign against the Visigoths in Iberia, he had himself buried in a new shrine dedicated to Vincent. The church also housed a fragment of the True Cross, according to Fortunatus, as well as the body of Saint Germanus of Paris (d. 576), after whom a monastic community at the site was named.[62] Chilperic (d. 584), son of Chlotar, who had christened his son Theodebert in Genovefa's baptistery, buried that child a year later in Saint-Vincent.[63] When Chilperic was murdered in Chelles the next year, his body was brought secretly back to Saint-Vincent, and just one year later, the body of his son Chlodovecus was laid beside him. Still another of Chilperic's sons was reburied there soon after. His queen, Fredegund (d. 597), was also entombed there, followed by several other members of the royal family in the following century.[64]

Chlothar I (d. 561), however, chose Saint-Medard in Soissons, although during his life he had patronized Martin's church at Tours.[65] His queen, Radegund

(d. 587), built herself a convent at Poitiers and decreed in a letter to Frankish bishops that she should be laid to rest in the nuns' church "whether that church is finished or not. If anyone wishes or attempts anything to the contrary," she added, "may he incur the wrath of God."[66] Beginning in the sixth century, others of the royal family also went to rest in Saint-Denis. Aregund, wife of Clothar I, went there in the 560s (supposedly with all the ornaments and buckles now so proudly displayed in the Louvre as hers). She was followed by a steady succession of her descendants.[67] By Dagobert's time, beginning in the 620s, Saint-Denis had acquired a community of the living to care for the saint's grave, as had Saint-Vincent (which became Saint-Germain des Près), and multiple estates to support them. Royal wealth followed royal bodies, whether as revenue or as burial treasure. Holy Apostles, too, acquired properties and monastic attendants but no longer flourished as a royal mausoleum or the principal church of the ruling family.

The demand for cult places grew intense during the sixth century as Merovingian nobility collaborated with church leaders and christianization continued. Demand led to argument about who could create and control shrines. The same problem of authenticating a sacral site that had plagued Martin, Germanus, and Genovefa offered opportunities to enterprising cult builders. When bishops found bodies in the basement, it was in their interest to establish shrines where devotees might come to pray, process, and even seek sanctuary, since grateful users of churches brought gifts to the saints and their keepers. Bishops collected traditions of local missionaries and martyrs, and even sent to Rome for proper written vitae that might reinforce the value of suddenly revealed relics. Gregory complained that the untutored—which is to say, ordinary Christians—preferred bodies with verifiable pedigrees rather than otherwise undocumented remains promoted by bishops. At Troyes, the keeper of Patroclus's tiny shrine received guests who, wondrously but fortuitously, brought with them a vita of that martyr. At first the local bishop resisted the text, calling it a forgery and accusing the shrine's guardian of trying to manufacture a cult. Only when a second recension of the vita also reached Troyes did the bishop relent, build a new church to replace the shrine, and declare an annual feast day.[68] Likewise, Genovefa's hagiographer produced a text to supplement the evidence of her body at Holy Apostles and to authenticate Clothild's construction project. Each time the church was subsequently rebuilt, someone rewrote the story of Genovefa's life and miracles to celebrate. At least five different versions appeared between 520 and 870.

When users of a church supported the cause of a resident saint against the wishes of their clergy and secular rulers, they had to make a different kind of argument for authenticity, however, without benefit of history books or hagiography. In the town of Dijon, country folk came to pray at what they thought was the tomb of Benignus. Clerics and sophisticated city dwellers resisted the shrine because of its magnificent Roman sarcophagus, which knowledgeable citizens figured for a pagan coffin. However, when the city residents noticed that their country cousins were receiving miraculous responses to their prayers, the church gained customers.[69] Similarly, although no clergy appeared in the life of Genovefa to urge the building of either Saint-Denis or Holy Apostles, wonders at both sites validated their sacral potential, overwhelming users such as Genovefa and Prudens with love for those places, who then persuaded churchmen.

Believers also clashed with clergy over the proper uses of sacred space. The line between congregational and funerary sites had already begun to blur in the third century when burial shrines had begun to host the Eucharistic liturgy. Increasingly the crowds that attended liturgy on feast days also visited saints' tombs on other occasions in smaller groups or individually.[70] Early medieval saints' lives frequently featured scenes where a man or woman prayed privately in the nave or crypt of a church. The presence of holy bodies sacralized not only the space of the church but whatever events took place within it, hence rendering prayer more efficacious.[71] As one result, Christians also used their churches as legal arenas where hostile parties conducted treaty negotiations and criminals sought sanctuary under the protective eyes of the saints.[72] Some of Gregory of Tours's tales suggest that clergy, lay communities, and saints together determined the extent to which religious and legal functions overlapped in sixth-century shrines. In the 560s, one Parisian father went to Saint-Denis to defend his daughter accused of adultery. Witnesses from his family and the kin of his son-in-law gathered around the tomb of Denis in the church that Genovefa had built. They met in the sanctuary to swear oaths over the relics of the saint, because Denis would monitor their behavior, and reverence for the saint would prevent an outbreak of violence. Yet when the father raised his hand over the tomb and altar to swear his daughter's innocence, the family of her husband drew their swords to attack the man and his assembled kin. As Gregory of Tours put it baldly, "The holy church was spattered with human blood."[73] Denis worked no punitive miracles; the king simply ordered both families to pay fines to the church keepers for violating the sanctuary. He also sent the alleged adulteress to secular trial, but she hanged herself before royal officials could haul her to court.

Secular and ecclesiastical law designated shrines and churches as places of refuge, but as Gregory's stories indicated, the limits of sanctuary were commonly contested when users disagreed about the qualities of sacral space.[74] Consensus was crucial to the functions and efficacy of church architecture.

When Count Leudast of Tours sought to ask pardon for his many crimes, he first approached Gregory at his episcopal residence, then sought King Chilperic in his military camp at Melun, and finally confronted Chilperic and his queen Fredegund as they attended mass at the cathedral in Paris. Everyone knew the royal couple would be in church along with a large audience of witnesses. At that moment, Chilperic, Fredegund, and Leudast agreed with the crowd that space within the church was sacred and safe. So did the soldiers who ambushed and captured Leudast among the market stalls after he was ejected from the church, so that the queen could have him tortured and killed elsewhere.[75]

Clergy and laity battled over access to sacred space and thus control over its functions and qualities. Saintly remains were one site of the contest. Bishops kept their churches and crypts locked. They moved the bodies of holy men and women, replacing them with cenotaphs as at Holy Apostles. They constructed railings around apses to separate visitors from saints. Such barriers segregated the ordained keepers of shrines from the merely prayerful. Clerics and other powerful Christians also collected and secreted stashes of relics. Queen Radegund, wife of Clothild's son Chlotar, became a famous collector after she retired to a convent. Gregory of Tours kept spares in cupboards and trunks. When he sponsored the rebuilding of a church dedicated to Saint Stephen near Tours, he had his workmen reposition the altar and was astonished to find no relics underneath, despite local tradition about a buried saint. Luckily, he kept extra bones in a locked and sealed reliquary back at Tours where no one without a key—or a miracle—could touch them.[76]

Ordinary believers rejected restrictions on their access to the saints, though. They broke into crypts and sneaked into sanctuaries at night. Saintly assistants magically sprang locked doors for them. Hagiographers revealed the saints' sympathy with the trespassers, for many of the intruders gained religious visions denied to the priests who moved freely through the sacred spaces by day.[77] At Bordeaux, an old lady who regularly brought oil for lamps in the crypt of Saint Peter's was accidentally locked inside one night after the clerics left. The priests could not hear her calling. Around midnight, though, the doors opened, and a troop of men entered in a blaze of light. They were complaining about the deacon Stephen, who was late for prayers. The tardy deacon arrived soaking wet and explained that he had been helping sailors at sea. After the clerics left again, the old lady sopped up water from the damp Saint Stephen with her hanky. When she showed her prize to Bishop Bertramn the next day, after her liberation from the crypt, he grabbed it and kept it for healing the ill. In fact, he used to snip bits off the handkerchief to bestow upon other churches.[78] The devoted old lady had been privileged to receive the vision because she ignorantly broke the rules of access, to everyone's benefit.

Still, the clergy were wise to protect their churches, as Gregory's many stories of thefts and violations demonstrated. In times of peace and plenty, churchmen let the saints guard objects of value. Some actually belonged to the most holy dead, like the gold and silver reliquary of Genovefa crafted by Eligius. A wave of rebuilding and redecoration swept through royally sponsored basilicas and chapels during the later sixth and seventh centuries, enriching the shrines with precious ornaments. Besides Genovefa's shrine, Saint Eligius the goldsmith also wrought reliquaries of precious metals and gems for Germanus, Severinus, Quentin, Lucian, Columba, Maximian, and Julian, among many other saints of Paris. According to Eligius's hagiographer, Dado of Rouen (d. 680s), he wrought even more elaborate shrines for Martin at Tours and Denis, north of Paris, which substantiates the slip in Genovefa's status. At Saint-Denis, Eligius fabricated a marble ciborium encrusted with jewels and adorned with golden baubles, along with plenty of other treasures to impress visitors to the tomb.[79] As church leaders segregated saints from believers, their reliquaries gleamed remotely for those who might see but not touch.

Even when saints, builders, and users of shrines agreed on the sacrality of certain built spaces, enhanced by all the beauty that royal riches could buy, a few naysayers still refused to acknowledge the power of such places. It was not long before thieves were after Eligius's handiwork. Eligius himself blamed the saints for sloppy protection of their own tombs, according to his hagiographer. When one Parisian shrine was robbed, Eligius prayed to the virgin buried there: "Listen, St. Columba. . . . My Redeemer knows that unless you restore those stolen ornaments speedily to the tabernacle, I will have the entrance sown over with thorny plants so that veneration will never be offered to you again in this place." Given the difficulty that believers had in identifying legitimate shrines, this was no idle threat. Columba responded swiftly with the miraculous restitution of her stolen property.[80]

Elsewhere, the holy dead were less helpful, though, which taught clerics to be on guard. When Sigibert (great-grandson of Clovis, d. 575) attacked Paris in his bid for kingship and burned its suburbs, one of his fighters stormed Saint-Denis. The doors were unlocked, and no one was watching—so far as the intruder could tell, anyway. He snatched a bejeweled silk coverlet off the tomb and escaped in a boat with his servant, who carried off 200 pieces of gold. The servant fell out of the boat and drowned; the thief lived to return the shroud to the tomb. Even so, he died on the first anniversary of his crime. Another would-be burglar climbed up the "tower" or pitched roof (turritus) of Denis's tomb to reach for a golden dove ornamenting the shrine. He fell first on the tower, crushing his testicles, and then impaled himself on his own spear. As Gregory pointed out, no one could doubt that this happened "not by chance but by the judgment of God."[81] But Gregory did not explain why some saints were more vigilant and punitive than others, or why kings chose to load some shrines with gifts and endowments while letting others battle brambles and decay.

Tales told by writers of Gregory's generation, along with hard evidence of expanded churches and accrued burials, chronicled the religious choices of Parisian Christians a generation or two after Genovefa's hagiographer had written. The hagiographer had not explained Holy Apostles' place among the city's churches but had only claimed its preeminence. Other evidence, especially stories of church users and abusers, shows how sixth-century Parisians and other Franks chose their holy places. Among the Merovingian propaganda and clerical scheming that cluttered his chapters, Gregory of Tours spoke of churches in relation to other churches, traffic among sacral sites, and constant negotiation among clerics and laypeople about whom, where, and how to worship. Users decided what to do in church. Sometimes they agreed with their ecclesiastical and royal leaders, sometimes they did not. Devotees shifted allegiances. The pious divided their attention among the many saintly patrons of Paris. Bishops and other shrine keepers competed for devotion, constructing cults as they built shrines, recovering bodies and texts to promote their own holy places. Constantly, new histories replaced old stories about the landmarks of christianization.

Saint Denis's Paris

As the medieval keepers of Genovefa's reputation and modern historians have both acknowledged, Parisians have always had a logic for choosing their patrons and holy places.[82] History and personal politics influenced them, as when Clovis and Clothild allied with Genovefa. In moments of crisis, however, devotees sought the most powerful saint for a particular job of protection, whether it be against fever or fire or yet another disaster. In general, the more saints and churches a city boasted, the more secure it was. The churchmen of Paris built cults to Denis and Marcel, the apostles Peter and Paul, Saint Stephen, and all the other holy men whose living administration and bodily fragments reinforced the numinous powers of the city's many churches. Bishops all over Francia imported wonder-working relics from Rome and farther east to bulk up their urban defenses. "Behold!" exclaimed Bishop Victricius of Rouen close to the year 400, when his new relic collection arrived in town, "the greater part of the celestial army deigns to visit our city . . . let those who want shield themselves with a weapon; as for us, your battle line and your insignia will protect us."[83]

Many things made a saint more or less appropriate as a protector.[84] In the early seventh century, Dagobert, great-great-grandson of Clovis, needed a new patron. He had returned to Paris to rule Neustria, the western half of the Frankish kingdom. He needed a saint who could, at once, advertise his place in the dynastic past of the Frankish west and demonstrate divine support of his reign. From the available candidates—Remigius, who had baptized Clovis; Martin the proselytizer; Marcel, who had battled a dragon; Genovefa; and Denis—he selected the first bishop of Gaul. Remigius and Martin, despite their ties to the Merovingians, were bishops of other cities. While Frankish royalty continued to honor Genovefa, they no longer needed a nurturer and civilizer of dynasty. Instead, the kings of Francia wanted someone with an official rank in the saintly hierarchy, to help them govern a kingdom.[85] Dagobert decided that the martyr and bishop Denis best represented the might and authority of Neustria's kings.

Clovis's offspring had already expanded Denis's church and littered it with objects of nearly obscene value. The first documentary evidence of Saint-Denis's riches was a charter of 620 issued by Clothar II, Dagobert's father, confirming a gift to Abbot Dodo of goods, lands, houses, and tenants. In fact, all but one of the earliest forty-six charters now kept in the Archives Nationales record gifts to Saint-Denis, including donations and endowments from Dagobert himself.[86] In 630, Dagobert also decreed the right of the monastic community to hold an annual fair for four weeks each year, beginning every ninth of October on Denis's feast day, on the road to Paris. The monks earned fees from every trader who took part, especially the foreigners, who had to pay a dozen deniers for each cartload of merchandise. The king enhanced the monastery's income by giving it more property, but he assured its perpetual wealth with the fair and tax breaks. His successors saw fit to renew the charter repeatedly.[87]

Dagobert also ensured the status of Saint-Denis by enlarging the basilica and lavishly decorating it with the handiwork of Saint Eligius, turning the humble basilica into a mausoleum fit for a king—himself.[88] Although royalty already occupied niches in the sanctuary, Dagobert was the first king to take eternal rest near Saint Denis's tomb. Before he expired, though, Dagobert had his builders enlarge the church, adding north and south side aisles and a semicircular apse. They extended the nave about twenty-eight meters to the west, where a vestibule sheltered the new main doors. The interior spaces of the church were rearranged and visually revised. With railings and doors, builders separated the sanctuary from the nave and the saint's grave from the altar. Dagobert paid for a new altar under a marvelous ciborium, added a throne, a gilded balustrade or chancel around the altar, complete with silver lectern and silver doors, and all the rest of the precious paraphernalia listed in the life of

Eligius.[89] In fact, Dagobert lavished so much money and interest upon Saint-Denis, and thus so thoroughly changed the scope and face of Genovefa's project, that his ninth-century biographer celebrated him as the original builder of Saint-Denis.[90] By the eleventh century, if not earlier, keepers of Saint-Denis had invented a new myth of consecration, which involved Dagobert, a leper, hosts of angels and saints, and Jesus Christ, but not Genovefa.[91]

In the 620s, Genovefa's building project was neither as visible nor as memorable as it had once been. The rulers of Francia had completed her job of transforming that once terrible and awesome site into the land's premier monastic establishment and making its almost-forgotten martyr the premier saint of the kingdom. Saint-Denis became an even greater edifice in the ninth century when Abbot Hilduin carried out another building campaign and composed a vita for Denis. In the twelfth century, Abbot Suger brought Saint-Denis up to date with his newfangled cathedral and his treatise on its architecture. His collaborators in building Saint-Denis's reputation, the twentieth-century art historians Erwin Panofsky and Sumner McKnight Crosby, located the new church permanently in the canon of Western architecture.[92] Together they managed to bury most of what Genovefa had achieved in the fifth century.

The hagiographer is our only authority for Genovefa's original importance at Saint-Denis. The remains of her first project, like the foundations of Holy Apostles, are scanty precisely because Parisians constantly renegotiated the uses of shrines and the status of saints. In life—according to her hagiographer—Genovefa had performed publicly as a thaumaturge and bishop, literally reaching out to people everywhere she went, whether they sought her or not. After her death, though, the saint became at once more passive and more intimate with her devotees, who sought her in church through prayer. Her continuing presence, manifested as a decorated box of bones, occupied Parisian landscapes differently than had the living saint. She withdrew from society as effectively as the holy cloistered abbesses of the later sixth century. The time when women could win sanctity by building churches and landscapes was over.

In the decades after Dagobert, Genovefa's keepers rebuilt her church and revised her vita to suit the times, as did the attendants of rival saints' cults in Paris and elsewhere.[93] Vikings burned her funerary basilica, now known as Saint Genovefa's, in 857. The reconstruction inspired one of her canons to record new miracles at her tomb in the rededicated church. In the eighth and ninth centuries, at least four writers reworked the first hagiographer's composition, rearranging the details of Genovefa's travels, abbreviating the text, and sending their versions to monastic communities around Francia. These authors studiously discarded outdated place-names and translated the old Roman measures of distance into terms that contemporaries could understand. By their revision,

FIGURE 4.1. Blind devotees healed by Genovefa's relics (Bibliothèque Sainte-Geneviève ms. 1283, f. 21, fourteenth century).

they unintentionally erased the very *spolia* of *romanitas* that Genovefa's first hagiographer had labored so hard to emphasize in his vita.[94]

Still, thanks to the rewritten lives and the rebuilt shrine, Genovefa remained in the hearts and minds of Parisians even if she was no longer as visible or available. On feast days and in crisis, when the citizens cried out for her protection, faithful servants carried her glittering reliquary into the streets in solemn procession. Meanwhile, her canons gained ground, quite literally, in the urban real estate granted them by grateful suppliants. They accumulated considerable holdings outside Paris, as well.[95] With revenues and donations flowing to her church, Genovefa's shrine on the hill continued to function as an elaborately adorned theater for contact with the sacred, as well as a venue for ecclesiastical politics and a site for the continuous rebuilding of religion. During the Middle Ages, Genovefa's cult prospered precisely because it was one among many in Paris. Genovefa herself no longer threatened to rearrange the city or control the Parisian basin. The moment for peripatetic female builder saints continued elsewhere—in Kildare on Europe's Atlantic fringes—but not in Gaul.

5

Crossings and Conversions

Around 650, just a few years after Dagobert was buried at Saint-Denis, the Irishman Cogitosus wrote the story of Brigit of Kildare using the same formula that had made Genovefa famous. Cogitosus praised a woman who had traveled to gather the bounty of her lands and from this harvest had built Christianity. But the story of a builder saint necessarily took different shape in Ireland, where Brigit's monastery squatted on the fertile farmland of the Liffey plain, than it had taken in the streets of Paris. Ireland's christianization must have begun sometime late in the fourth century, long after Saint Denis had supposedly preached in the Lutetian forum and been tossed off the Mons Martis. Saint Martin was probably busy tumbling pagan temples in Gaul when converts first arrived in Irish harbors. At first they came as slaves, visitors, merchants, or returning natives. Then in the fifth century, while Genovefa revised a Parisian geography of burials and shrines already two centuries old, missionary men landed to preach and baptize in Ireland. Only in the next generation of church organizers, with Brigit, would Irish believers and their leaders build permanent architecture and a hierarchical infrastructure for their communities. In Cogitosus's account, then, Brigit's career capped a long history of Ireland's conversion. In some ways, his tale was true.

The mission to Ireland differed from Genovefa's conversion of Paris, for one reason, because Ireland had no towns as Romans knew them. In fact, Ireland had no Romans to speak of.[1] There were no forums, basilicas, temples, forgotten saints' graves, or any other familiar venues for the drama of christianization. No urban mobs existed to embrace or assault missionary bishops. No monuments to the Roman past challenged converts with *spolia*. Ireland lacked enduring public architecture except for sacral enclosures perched on the heights and stark tombs that often mimicked natural features of the landscape. Buildings were flimsy, ephemeral houses and huts dispersed among farmsteads, linked by rivers and unpaved tracks. Irish technologies were relatively simple; the economy was based on herding and agriculture, and cows were the standard medium of exchange.

Although Ireland's surfaces were mutable, its places were ancient. Natural features broke the small island into intimate landscapes, each with its own ancestral holy places. Some hilltops were famous across the island as ritual sites where semidivine kings had built grand forts. Long after the so-called forts had collapsed and royal heroes had disappeared from the earth, people still knew their locations. Communities also kept track of rivers and springs that harbored spirits and burial mounds where an unsuspecting mortal might encounter folk from the *síd*—a word that meant both a mound and the otherworld into which it was a portal. For such sites and their numinous powers, communities developed schedules of ritual gatherings and offerings but no complex architecture. They loyally tended the same places for centuries, building their houses and burying their dead nearby. They kept traditional geographies with little bearing on living politics, inventing new myths when necessary to justify ancient toponymies.

Meanwhile, tribal divisions rendered Irish territories unstable and boundaries shifty. The Irish organized themselves into political units that historians have called both tribes and kingdoms, but which they themselves called *túatha* (sg. *túath*) or—once they learned Latin—*plebes*. A *túath* was not a piece of ground; it was a group of people more or less attached to a region but not permanently anchored. Each *túath* had a *rí*, or king, who was typically a client of a mightier king (or kings). Some of these clientage relationships existed for generations between faithful overlords and underkings, whereas others lasted only as long as two war leaders found each other useful. If Christian missionaries arrived in Ireland hoping to convert the island by baptizing a few kings, they were disappointed. No *rí*, no matter how skillful a leader, directly governed any tribe except his own. In Brigit's time, two or three tribal confederations—the Uí Máil, Uí Dúnlainge, and Uí Cheinselaig—fought for overlordship of her province of Leinster. The Uí Máil lost importance at the end of the sixth century, but the other two remained under constant attack from below, by their supposed client kingdoms; internally by their own factions; and from outside, by other tribal confederations. By Cogitosus's time, tribes of the Uí Néill, especially the Clann Cholmáin, were expanding their political boundaries from mid-Ireland southward into what had once been Leinster.

Ireland thus posed problems that proselytizers would not face again until they penetrated the interior of Germania. The Irish had come to know of, and even desire, Christian *romanitas* and its objects. Yet they had no recognizable places or proper *spolia* from which to build an inherently romanized religion. Their conversion was complicated by a mobile politics and by local attachment to historic sacral sites and hidden pagan places. Even Saint Martin—that masterful detective of hidden heathenism—would have been puzzled about how to transform Irish places of worship into churches. Even Genovefa might have stumbled when treading ground so seemingly boundless and unprepared by imperial colonization. Bishops had nowhere to go.

Indeed, the shock of *romanitas* proved too great for the Irish to absorb immediately in all its Christian forms. They acquired new religion in three long periods. In the first stage, they learned how to desire foreign exotica from imperial territories and what to do with the stuff once they got it home. In the century or so before Brigit's supposed birth around 450, the traffic and trade between her southeastern province of Leinster and the west coast of Britain were especially dense.[2] There, at the edge of Ireland closest to empire, the circulation of rare goods and alien ideas fueled an increasing demand for the new religion. In the second period, bishops and other preachers marketed the words and goods of Christianity across Ireland. They organized congregations and then began to locate them on properties. A legion of harbingers labored to adapt Christian organizational concepts to Irish politics, society, and landscapes and thus to ready the land for the permanent establishment of romanized religion. Finally, in the third phase of Ireland's christianization, Brigit's cohort could begin to build churches, ecclesiastical territories, and monasteries recognizable to Christians coming from the former empire. Merchants and consumers prepared the way for Bible-toters, community organizers, landscape architects, and eventually builders.

The Traffic in *Romanitas*

Before 400, the Irish glimpsed Rome in the treasures brought by traders and returning adventurers. Some travelers carried Gaulish and Mediterranean pottery or weapons forged in Britain. Others brought home a familiarity with the Latin alphabet and an inspiration to carve it on stone monuments.[3] Still others lugged soldier's pay in ingots and coins, hauled wine in jugs and barrels, wore jewelry twisted into Mediterranean snake shapes, or toted the occasional bit of glass. They brought slaves, too, although before 400 more slaves probably left Ireland than arrived there.[4] In exchange, the Irish exported dogs, furs, metals, wool, and mercenaries to Continental markets via British and Gaulish ports.[5] Local demand shaped this traffic in portable goods. Distinctive bits of gold hair ornaments hammered at the Shannon estuary, for instance, turned up on the east coast and traveled thence from Leinster to northern Wales. Together, the entire assemblage of imported bits and pieces suggests a regular pattern of contact between Ireland and the empire.[6] Demand, volume, and specific routes shifted, but the trade continued for many centuries.

Foreign merchants of imperial exotica knew how to get to Ireland even if they had never read their classical geographers. The Greeks had written of mineral resources in the islands. Mediterranean sailors had been heading up the Iberian coast, aiming for Hibernia since the Bronze Age. Latin speakers had strayed into Ireland well before the time Roman troops invaded the larger island. Britons fleeing the legions ended up in Ireland. On Lambay Island in Dublin Bay, someone buried a few bodies with Romano-British jewelry and weapons in the first century B.C.E., not long after Caesar had landed at Kent.[7] Romans from Britain—or Romano-Britons, romanized Britons, or other imperial citizens coming from Britain, however we might designate them—may even have built a trading post or two in eastern Ireland.[8] In the first century, Gnaeus Julius Agricola, conqueror of Wales, had actually gathered intelligence from merchants intimate with Irish harbors in preparation for conquest. The invasion never happened, but traffic across the bounds of empire continued.[9] In the late fourth century and the fifth century, the safest route to Ireland from the Continent was still through western Britain.[10]

The problem was not how to find Ireland, but what to do after arriving. When a ship put into an Irish port, it did not find the mile-long wharves of London or the quays of Paris's island but likely just safe waters near a familiar beach or cliff. After unloading, most of the goods probably changed hands near the shore; without city markets or regular fairs, the only major sites for exchange were the fortified residences of royalty and nobles. It was hard to move anything but small items along Irish roads, so most trade would have followed rivers from the coast. Since the Irish typically paid in bulk goods that had to be transported to the coast, it could not have been profitable to trade in merchandise from abroad. Only rare items were worth the effort, and only a few prizes could have trickled through a series of local exchanges from the sea to the lords of inland kingdoms. The ceramic jars and amphorae that commonly transported wine or oil to imperial markets from Carthage to southern Britain simply did not arrive in Ireland before the fifth century, and then only a small number of containers reached a very few places.[11]

Irish women and men familiar with the world beyond their own waters were not always sure what to do with their fancy goods when they got home.

Imports from Britain and Gaul had meanings that could not cross the sea.[12] Money, for instance, had no place in the exchange economy of Ireland except as fetish. Pilgrims to the ancient tomb complex at Newgrange in the Boyne Valley deposited Roman currency in holes there, marking their tourism to a native sacred place that was much older than the Romans' Eternal City.[13] Whether visitors to the Bronze Age necropolis were foreigners paying respect to local cults or Irish using rare trinkets to perform a familiar rite, they chose Newgrange as the right place to do it. The deed was no less thoughtful than Germanus's plucking of a metal disk from the dust at Nanterre to hang on a cord around Genovefa's neck. For both Irish pilgrim and Gaulish bishop, coins had the value of Rome. Rather than re-creating the cultural and economic context that had produced the money, the Irish adapted their prizes to traditional rituals and spatial habits. Coins were easier to interpret, though, than other objects such as the ape's skull found buried at Emain Macha (Navan, county Armagh). Emain, one of the great royal enclosures of ancient Ireland, was 2,500 kilometers away from the ape's natural habitat.[14] Yet one day, in the early centuries of the first millennium, someone buried the skull there. Was it pet or meat? The skull may point to long-distance trade and Roman influence, but it could also have been a serendipitous, macabre souvenir. At any rate, the presence of a simian skull suggests that a complex logic beyond simple profit drove consumers and carriers along the paths of trade. The sorts of Irish men and women able to obtain new objects and promote foreign styles not only had to be wealthy enough to acquire them and of sufficient reputation to attract the attention of entrepreneurs seeking customers, but imaginative enough to want such things.[15]

New religion must have come to Ireland as other trade goods did, beginning as curious bits and pieces that made little sense. Fragments of soggy wood found last century in Irish wetlands at Lisnacrogher in county Antrim might once have been a crannog or artificial island habitation site, but they might also have been part of a timber platform where Iron Age devotees of a now unknown deity tossed a massive collection of fine metalwork into the water. Weapons and decorated scabbards lay undisturbed in the water for hundreds of years, but no domestic remains have turned up at the site. Water deposits were common in northern Gaul and western Britain, and plenty of valuable items have been found in Irish lakes and rivers, but no other ritual bridge or jetty has turned up in Ireland, although wooden causeways crossed many bogs.[16] If the custom of ritual deposits arrived from abroad, and if one Irish community decided to build a platform from which to pitch offerings, and if the timber at Lisnacrogher represents such a structure, the whole business never gained popularity. Without other examples or native testimony, it is hard to prove that the reputed timber bits had any religious significance. As excavators warn us, we find what is left, not what existed, and from the remnants we construct our own symbolic systems.[17] Modern interpreters have a tendency to impute religious importance to seemingly unique or bizarre archaeological finds.

However, when it comes to understanding how new religion arrived in a place, we moderns also often ignore religious meaning in the movement of ordinary objects. It is crucial to understand the investment in interpretation that both new goods and new ideas required in a place like fourth- or fifth-century Ireland, and the ways that trade in exotica directly prepared the Irish to take Christianity home. While rumor and fad might inspire demand, consumers always wanted to make sense of their acquisitions for the neighbors. An exotic possession, even if it tucked into a pocket or the fold of a cloak, brought heavy baggage: the long history of cultural intercourse around the Irish Sea, the network of carriers who had brought the thing, the knowledge of traditional landing places and trade routes, and the landmarks of those routes. The item arrived because a few privileged Irish had a habit of acquisition and interpretation. As part of this constant but limited circulation of shared goods and translated knowledges, Christianity arrived in Ireland just like every other item of trade. It came in the form of ordinary purchases and glamorous new objects as well as words. New goods rarely arrived without language to help locate them in local cultural contexts. Some items, like coins or ceramics, were easier than others, such as an ape's skull or a gospel text, to reinvent in Irish terms.

Most imports, including Christianity, came to Ireland as secondary trade goods through Britain from farther away. Irish from the east coast had colonized parts of the Welsh west coast. People and objects moved regularly through familiar corridors across the Irish Sea.[18] Before the mid-fifth century, Saint Patrick would leave his homeland on the northern border of Wales to spend his youth in captivity in Ireland. The first missionaries to southeastern Ireland also probably came via Wales from Gaul. Britons on this northwestern frontier of imperial administration not only knew of Rome, Romans, and romanization but had built and lived *romanitas* in their own region. They had cities—not many, and not large, but with walls, the occasional bit of monumental architecture, highways, and harbors that would have looked familiar, if modest, to anyone in the empire.[19] At Caerwent and Caerleon, short miles across the Irish Sea, fifth-century citizens still used coins for exchange rather than dropping them into the dirt of tombs. Even when Britons dismantled basilicas for barns and forges, let their quays fall to ruin, or turned their port cities into shore forts, they continued living in and around their towns.[20]

Unlike Ireland, then, Britons had both a partially romanized, urbanized landscape and a ready cultural context for Christianity. Britain also had Christians by 200, half a century before Denis supposedly reached Paris.[21] In the fourth century British converts tried, at least, to behave and look like Christians elsewhere. They ordained bishops and created episcopal territories to match the administrative units—*civitates*—of imperial government. They sent representatives to Continental councils.[22] In the fifth century, British leaders even issued a doctrinal challenge to bishops abroad, who then sent Germanus of Auxerre not once but twice to correct the Britons' mistaken notions about free will. The rebel behind this heretical cause was Pelagius, called a "porridge-eating Scot" by Saint Jerome but probably a British native.[23]

Although the British channeled exotic trade goods to Ireland and although Christians left Welsh ports for Leinster and Ulster, British Christians could not bring churches over the Irish Sea. They had no exportable ecclesiastical architecture. They must have congregated somewhere to celebrate Eucharists and baptisms in their towns and on their villas, but there is little evidence to show where. If they built churches of wood, these have long since disappeared. Christian Britons surely created cemeteries for their dead, but rarely with lasting monuments to their faith.[24] They left behind a surprising number of lead baptismal tanks and silver liturgical instruments, but they do not seem to have made permanent Christian landscapes even where they used stone and brick for other sorts of structures.[25] Certainly the conditions that had allowed earlier generations of Britons to develop a distinct Romano-British style of shrines to their latinized gods and goddesses had drastically changed by the end of the fourth century. Urban populations were moving outside of old city centers and using their towns in innovative ways; meanwhile, the occupants of grand old villas were purposely preserving some distinctively Continental technologies, such as steam heating systems, while discarding others, such as decorative mosaics.[26] We cannot fathom why British Christians did not build more, build permanently, or build on a Continental model. We only know that, despite having towns, an already long Christian history, and even a few martyrs—Alban at Verulamium (Saint-Albans), Julius and Aaron at Venta Silurum (Caerleon)— the Britons did not consistently turn their urban *spolia* into churches or their churches into arguments for sanctity.[27] No one even bothered to pull down pagan sacral sites or turn them into churches.[28] There was simply no historical moment for British Christians to build their religion in a Roman monumental vocabulary.[29]

Of the many romanizations that occurred in Britain, then, none resembled the christianization of Paris and its neighboring cities through architectural revision, so expertly engineered by Gaulish church builders and hagiographers. No native Genovefa appeared to root out martyred bodies and raise splendid structures over them. When the Christian princess Bertha came from Gaul to marry the still-pagan Aethelbehrt of Kent at the end of the sixth century, she supposedly worshiped in an old chapel east of Canterbury. The site has yielded Roman-style bricks from the third or fourth century but no identifiable chapel.[30] Still, neither Bertha nor any other woman in sub-Roman Britain won sainthood, or even achieved any lasting historical significance, for building or rebuilding a Christian church.[31] No one inspired a pious queen or king to raise a Christian shrine until 600 or so.[32]

British Christianity in the fifth century was no more or less typical than northern Gaulish Christianity or than Irish Christianity would turn out to be. Christians in Britain built their religion less densely and permanently than Gaulish Christians, but their religious habitus was more infused with imperial culture than Irish Christianity could ever be. Both British and Gaulish micro-Christianities served as models and sources for the Irish, but neither made much sense on Irish landscapes. Nonetheless, during the fourth and fifth centuries, while town dwellers in Britain were manning defenses against Germanic invaders, the Irish began to demand Christianity from their trading partners. Although the merchants of *romanitas* responded to Irish desires with new kinds of goods—complex religious practices and symbolic theology, to begin with, not to mention written Latin—they could not supply the materials or the expertise for building the new religion on Irish lands. The Irish had to develop an architectural idiom for Christianity from local resources on traditional landscapes, with only portable exotica and the Latin words of scripture to guide them. It took some time.

The Trade in Words

In 431, Christians in Ireland sent for a bishop. Some of them understood Latin, and they had learned enough about the organization of Continental churches to know how and where to write. They wanted a Roman, so they appealed to that city's bishop for a translator fluent in *romanitas* who might create and organize Christian communities in Ireland. Prosper of Aquitaine, far to the south of Kildare, took time from recording Gaulish events to write that "Palladius was ordained by Pope Celestine and sent to the Irish believers in Christ as their first bishop." This was probably the same deacon Palladius who had brokered Germanus's errand to Britain. In fact, Palladius may have been leading a similar mission to Ireland in order to prevent British Pelagianism from spreading across the Irish Sea to fledgling congregations in Leinster. But Palladius disappeared from written records after his elevation to episcopacy and departure for Ireland. Centuries later, medieval hagiographers and chroniclers were still wondering where he was. They felt compelled to reconcile Irish ecclesiastical history, by then under Saint Patrick's dominion, with Continental sources that recalled his predecessor.[33]

Palladius may have completed his Irish mission. Other Christian men had reached Ireland with or before Palladius but left even fewer tracks across the historical and archaeological records. Place-names of the early Middle Ages recorded some vague memory of preachers who landed in the southeast and built churches at Killashee (Cell Auxili), Dunshaughlin (Domnach Sechnaill), Kilcullen (Cell Chuilind), and Aghade (Ath Fithboth).[34] Their founders, Auxilius, Secundinus, Iserninus, and Benignus, made only cameo appearances in other saints' vitae. From the seventh century on, Irish authors cast these men as bishops and disciples of the Briton Patrick, who had worked the northern half of the island, but the tricky evidence of place-names suggests rather that the earlier missionaries had come from Gaul to cover the south. They aimed for Leinster, the province most heavily involved in the sea trade.[35] Some other early monastic sites in Leinster were named for Welsh or British proselytizers: Cell na mBretan in County Kildare was "Church of the Britons," although when those particular Britons arrived remains unclear.[36] Whether or not the origins stories of southern churches were authentic to the fourth or fifth century, or manufactured much later, at least the memory of ancient Christian settlement lasted long enough to be commemorated by both legend and architecture. There were probably more congregations that left no trace at all for archaeologists or philologists.[37]

The British bishop Patricius was the first to describe Ireland in the process of christianization. Patrick never wrote about churches. Ireland was not ready for them, nor was he interested, apparently, in teaching new Christians how to prepare for architectural conversion. Instead he brought portable Christianity and achieved fame with words. He justified his mission in a *Confessio* addressed to British episcopal colleagues sometime after 450. Every syllable we have from fifth-century Ireland came from the pen of the man who called himself "Patrick the most unlearned sinner" (*Patricius peccator rusticissimus*). Besides his testament or confession, he produced only one other document, a letter scolding a British warlord for taking Christian captives as Patrick himself had once been taken.

No other nameable author wrote from Ireland or described Irish Christians before the end of the sixth century, when the self-exiled Saint Columbanus posted letters to Rome from the southern edge of Gaul. Columban did not mention Patrick.[38] Irish clerics may have been keeping records of dates and events in between, in order to calculate liturgical cycles, but they never noted the precise details of Patrick's career. Irish bishops gathered probably between 550 and 600 to generate a set of written guidelines for Christian practice and behavior. Later writers gave Patrick credit for summoning the synod, which is unlikely.[39] A century or two after Patrick's death, annalists were jotting down multiple dates for his mission to Ireland that differed by thirty years (432–61 or 461–93).[40] His saintly biographies did not appear until the end of the seventh century, after Cogitosus wrote the life of Brigit. The only eyewitness to Patrick's Irish landscapes remains Patrick himself.

Yet for his whole life, Patrick looked at Ireland with the eyes of a foreigner.[41] At the end, while writing his own history, he would have preferred to go home to Britain and visit the brethren in Gaul.[42] He had been born in the *vicus* of Bannavem Taberniae, probably somewhere near Carlisle.[43] His father was a decurion and a deacon (*decurion, diaconus*), and his grandfather a priest or some other official in the Christian community (*presbyter*). *Decurion* was the term for a landed man who took part in city government. It was a well-bred family of *cives*—men loyal to their land and to Roman ways—who held an estate (*villula*, literally a small villa) and owned slaves, although they were not aristocrats in the cultivated style of Germanus or even in the same suburban class as Genovefa.[44] Patrick learned Latin but did not grow up speaking it. He claimed to have no proper training in either laws or sacred texts, although he learned his Bible and wielded it in prose with visionary charisma.[45]

From this particularly west British, mildly romanized, somewhat urbanized context of simply built Christianity, Patrick was seized at age sixteen by Irish raiders.[46] He later recalled no specific itinerary. He charted his life's journey by his personal interactions with Christians, would-be Christians, and recalcitrant pagans rather than by visual markers of named landscapes. Scholars still argue about where, exactly, he went in Ireland and whether he spent a few years, many years, or no years on the Continent. His seventh-century hagiographers claimed that he had trained with Germanus in Auxerre and had visited Rome, but Patrick mentioned nothing of it.[47] He told only how, on arrival in Ireland, he looked after sheep in the woods or on the mountain "in snow and frost and rain," 200 miles from the nearest harbor with ships to Britain. Perhaps he was in Mayo.[48] After six years of slavery he escaped and, surviving a shipwreck and short detour possibly through Gaul, went home.[49] His parents begged him to settle down, but he dreamed of an angel named Victoricus who brought him letters from Ireland. He heard the Voice of the Irish crying to him from the Wood of Voclut "near the western sea," pleading with him to return to them, and so he did. He spent the rest of his life evangelizing in Ulster and Connacht.

The confessedly unlettered Patrick dreamt his mandate as a text rather than as images of people or places familiar from his earlier life.[50] The converts of Ireland were to him the words of scripture made flesh. Ireland was the "land of our captivity" (2 Chron. 6:38), a biblical territory where he was bound on pilgrimage as surely as he was traveling to heaven.[51] Later, Patrick wrote, he wandered constantly around the island. He never named locations. He depicted himself as a peripatetic visionary, footloose as Jesus in Judea, who found eager converts everywhere. He wrote home to boast of baptizing thousands and, in particular, of consecrating women to lives of Christian chastity. "How," he demanded, "has it lately come about in Ireland that those who never had any knowledge or God but, up till now always worshipped idols and abominations [*idola et immunda*], are now called the people of the Lord and the sons of God?" He urged his British colleagues to approve both his mission and his tactics on account of the great demand among the Irish for clergy to "baptize and preach to the needy and expectant masses."[52] Patrick never revealed, though, where these crowds of converts lived, met, or worshiped, nor who ministered to them after he had baptized them. The dense symbolism of his letters made geography irrelevant. To the question quoted by Saint Augustine—"Do walls then make the Christian?"—Patrick would have answered: No, nor do places.[53]

Patrick purposely phrased his memoirs as a journey to the boundary of civilization. His geography was so scant that he might have imagined Ireland. Even as an old man he was a sojourner and refugee (*proselitus et profuga*) who paid no attention to his surroundings.[54] His utter silence about baptisteries, shrines, or churches suggested both his missionary ideology and his lack of concern for the physical environment of his work. He saw himself as bringing only scriptural words to this unbuilt country, leaving Irish converts to translate gospel into a material context for daily life. If anyone created special shelters for Christian worship, Patrick—whose eyes had been trained to recognize the kind of religion constructed in western Britain—did not see them.

Patrick himself never rested from the moment raiders caught him at his father's *villula*. Unlike Genovefa, who circled Paris but settled there for life and death, Patrick did not choose a place to remain with companions and neighbors. According to his own confession, converts trailed after him like the retinues that followed kings from fort to fort. Suppliants could not seek his place of prayerful retreat in order to approach him. It was difficult for medieval devotees to admit that the saint had never named his final resting place or chosen his main church among the many Christian communities that he supposedly founded.[55] Even after his death, according to the medieval biographers who elaborated his career, he could not lie still because disputing disciples from rival monasteries quarreled over the destination of his body. Later, the clerics of Armagh would claim his apostolate and the monks of Downpatrick (Dún Lethglaise) his remains, but in the fifth century, Patrick had no place of his own.[56]

Ordinary believers, less impelled by the spirit, could not abide upon such a visionary landscape. People who had no angel to guide them, no voices calling to them from afar, required stable religion. Theology was cold comfort. They wanted shelters where they could gather and practice, and where they might keep their holy things. They needed daily routes and boundaries for the practice of Christian habits. Presumably, the earliest communities made do with houses, for they were unprepared to build. By the late fourth and fifth centuries, European churches consisted of more than a humble roof. *Ecclesiae* and *basilicae* were too architecturally sophisticated and symbolically charged for immediate translation outside the empire, even an empire in its last effective days. This was partly why Britons lacked churches. They had lost the monumentally situated ritual functions of their cities and villas at precisely the time when, elsewhere, public administrators were sponsoring urban oratories and basilicas. Without Christian evergetism, urban leftovers, or even a memory of towns that once were, the Irish had only rumors of buildings and a scripture full of urbanized settings. What were they to make of cities heavenly and historical, or the grand temples of pagans and Israelites? They could not build churches without words, nor could they build religion with words alone.

Legendary Landscapes

Once the Irish obtained the language of Christianity, they had to figure out how to take it home and use it as the dialect of everyday life. They needed places to keep it. Although they had no pagan Roman cities where they might build religion, they kept an extensive collection of ancient legends about the ritual places and political centers of their island. Whereas church builders in Gaul entered into architectural dialogue with pagan temples and Roman governmental structures, Irish proselytizers contended with the barely visible history of a much subtler landscape. Proselytizers and converts engaged material paganisms utterly unlike the hybrid cults of Gaul or Britain. Instead of temples, they had hilltop sacral sites capped with wooden palisades, ditches, and ruins of earlier occupations. Instead of imperial provinces and barbarian kingdoms, they had mobile tribal territories juxtaposed with well-defined family properties kept intact for generations.

As soon as the Irish became literate, they tried to make written sense of these many landscapes. The earliest Irish documents thus explained how previous generations had christianized their places. Writers described the simultaneous extermination of pagan places explicitly in hagiographic tales of saints battling druids. But in the legends of ancient migrations, kingdom-building, and constant warfare they also broached the more complex problem of how their ancestors had located Christianity and arranged Christian territories in a land covered with unmarked pagan sanctuaries yet lacking recognizable states and cities. Scholars of the seventh and eighth centuries composed genealogies and heroic tales that put ancient tribal migrations, pagan sacral sites, political territories of their own day, and ecclesiastical communities all on the same map.[57]

No one knows now, if anyone knew then, whether these antiquarian medieval tales about the origins of ancient kingdoms recalled actual prehistoric events.[58] Antiquarians and nationalist historians of the nineteenth and twentieth centuries tried to tag each myth to a particular population movement, and to date the migrations. They were encouraged by archaeological excavations at ancient sites mentioned in the written lore. Legends of very early medieval writers claimed to capture a much earlier era and explained a traditional geography just recently transformed by christianization. Not all of these dynastic histories were genuinely ancient, but some certainly preserved originally oral content predating writing. It is reasonable to believe that the circulation of historic legends of origins—kept locally, if not exactly accurately in scholarly terms—helped prepare Brigit's cohort of church builders for their tasks, just as Gallo-Roman and Frankish consciousness of recent Roman centuries shaped Christian Paris.

These stories of building on the edge of the world usually began with the Irish looking across the seas. In several medieval myths, the first rulers of Ireland had come from elsewhere to create kingdoms and raise royal forts.[59] The earlier a tribe had supposedly arrived to claim its place, the greater its prestige among other tribes in the region and the more expansive its claims to territory. The people of Brigit's province of Leinster (the Laigen) maintained that bloodthirsty kings had led their ancient fathers along ocean routes from Gaul and Britain to the southeast coast. Leinster poets of the seventh and eighth centuries recalled superwarriors who had reached the island before the folk of any other province, thus gaining rule over all Ireland.[60] Each early dynastic group of the Laigen claimed descent from a different branch of the original invading tribes, and each produced its own legendary homeland and capital fort.[61]

Some of the Leinster people's earliest stories of themselves featured a king named Labraid Loingsech ("the Exile"), who was banished out of Ireland to Gaul, where, according to one genealogical poet, he conquered the province and visited the Alps.[62] He returned in vengeance to seize the kingdom of Leinster.[63] Labraid made his capital at Dind Ríg (Fort of the Kings), in southern Leinster on the Barrow River—at least, until he himself burnt it over the head of the king of Ireland. Medieval monks who kept yearly annals placed Labraid's career in the fourth century B.C.E.[64] One tribe of his supposed descendants, the Uí Cheinselaig, continued to rule much of Leinster in the seventh century.

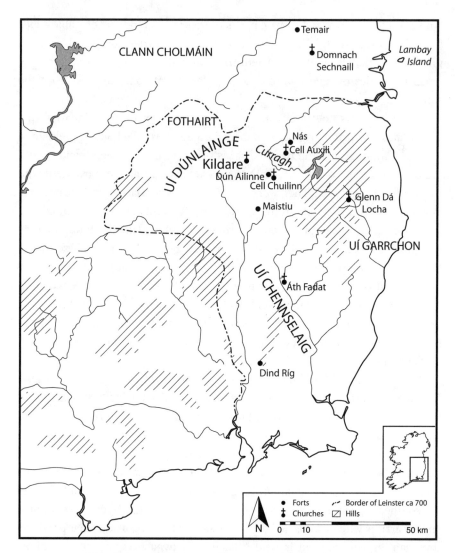

FIGURE 5.1. Map: Leinster in the seventh century (John Marston).

Another tribe of reputed offspring, the Uí Dúnlainge, took control of the northern half of the province by the end of same century, keeping their own ancestral forts at Maistiu (Mullaghmast, south of Kildare) and Nás (Naas, just northeast of Kildare). Their tribal historians revised existing royal genealogies and dynastic epics of the primeval past to reflect this more recent Uí Dúnlainge dominance.

An even earlier contender for symbolic capital of the Laigen, however, was Dún Ailinne, once ruled by the Dál Messin Corb who had supposedly built it. The site became part of Uí Dúnlainge territory sometime near the end of

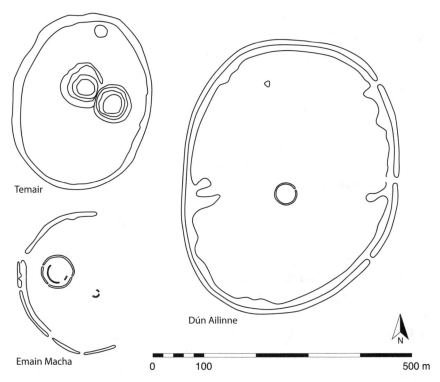

Temair

Dún Ailinne

Emain Macha

0   100   500 m

FIGURE 5.2. Dún Ailinne, Emain Macha, and Temair (John Marston after Wailes, Waterman, Lynn, et al.).

Cogitosus's lifetime and featured in several pieces of antiquarian literature from the period. Like the enclosures of Dind Ríg, Maistiu, and Nás, the latest structures at Dún Ailinne were a result of population expansion very early in the Iron Age (after about 600 B.C.E.). But the site had been used since the Neolithic and by Brigit's time was thus at least 2,000 years old. It crowned a hilltop 180 meters above sea level. Its fortifications had once enclosed thirteen hectares of land.[65] Surrounded by ditches, earthen ramparts, and sometimes timber walls, Dún Ailinne was easily visible from territory below and strategically set to command expansive views from above. To the west of the site, bogs marked the ancient borderland between Laigen and the province of Mide. Eastward stretched the Curragh, a 2,000-hectare pastureland where the ancient Irish raced horses and their kings met in battle; and beyond the Curragh, the Wicklow Mountains fell away in limestone plains to the sea.[66] The ruins of Dún Ailinne thus sat on a slightly inconvenient but still accessible hill above more fertile land.[67] Fighters, farmers, and slaves dwelt under the guard of Dún Ailinne, in less elaborate enclosures set upon well-drained lower slopes, nearer good fields and pastures.[68]

Such complex hilltop structures were only for occasional occupation and ritual use in the display of kingly powers. Their builders relied on site type rather than distinctive architecture to mark these symbolic places.[69] Only one other place in Ireland had a design, situation, and layout similar to those of Dún Ailinne: Emain Macha (Navan), capital of the ancient Ulstermen. Emain was part of a complex of two "fort" sites that began as large enclosures associated with small lakes or pools for ritual deposits. Both Dún Ailinne and Emain were first built in the late Neolithic. During the Iron Age, each featured a large hilltop ditch and rampart, continuously repaired, replaced, and revised over centuries. At both places, as well as at one other inaugural site called Rath na Ríogh (Fort of the Kings at modern Tara), ramparts circled an interior ditch. A more practical arrangement for keeping out animals and raiders would have been a wall with exterior ditch, but at these three enclosures the ditches were meant to contain something—the sacrality of the place, perhaps. Laborers at Dún Ailinne and Emain raised successive concentric timber structures, possibly henges or houses, within the earthen enclosures. At Emain Macha after about 100 B.C.E., workers cleared some small existing figure-eight structures from the site and hauled farmed timber from miles away to construct an enormous round structure about forty meters in diameter. At the center, a massive post rose skyward; a ritual walkway led from the building's western entrance to the ridgepole. Later, laborers surrounded the wooden structure with limestone boulders, fired the outer timbers, and covered the whole thing with sods so that it became a hollow mound, similar to a giant burial site from much earlier times. Dún Ailinne also gained a forty-meter structure in this same period, possibly a ring with a wooden tower or a hall inside. Either construction would have required an impressive investment in human sweat and building materials. Both Dún Ailinne and Emain could have accommodated major crowds. The concentric theme of the enclosures, the ritual entrances, and the central poles together suggest a hierarchy of spaces focused inward on a ritual core. Emain, at least, was initially laid out in a wheel diagram, with lines radiating from the central pole to the circular walls.[70]

At the same historical moment, both sites became tribal centers on a scale found nowhere else in Ireland, marked by unique, innovative architecture. Like temples of the state cult and the open forum found in every Roman town, these Irish monuments drew audiences. Few visitors, however, must have gained entrance to the small inner sanctum.[71] Other royal forts boasted complex earthworks, as at Temair (Tara) and Rath Crúachain (Rathcroghan in county Roscommon), although no one there planned timber monuments of the same complexity or centralized the layouts of these sites. However, only these four places, spread across the island, were reconfigured on the same scale in the same century. Other, smaller forts, even when associated with megalithic tomb sites, were smaller and more cluttered with overlapping generations of barrows and dwellings.[72] By comparison, no signs of consistent occupation or regular burials were left at Dún Ailinne and Emain, although the Iron Age lords of Dún Ailinne strewed garbage from great feasts in its ditches.

Those who possessed Emain, Dún Ailinne, Temair, and Rath Crúachain were purposely using the *spolia* of much earlier burial sites and other religious construction to create new kinds of ritual centers. Whether they thought of themselves as reviving or re-creating ancient custom, they gathered enough followers, dependent laborers, and wealth to erect grandly impressive monuments where their people might act out shared political and religious ideologies. When these lords lost influence and thus their ability to command crowds, their tribal centers also lost purpose. Excavations suggest that both enclosures were systematically destroyed by fire, possibly as part of their intended ritual use. Some sporadic activity continued at Emain in the early medieval centuries. Dún Ailinne's timber circles disappeared in the later fourth century c.e.[73]

Although the forts lost (or changed) religious use in the century or two before serious christianizers arrived in Ireland, they did not lose place in the religious memory of those who lived in view of them. Families that gathered at night in their houses far from Dún Ailinne or Emain heard tales of the forts for many generations after. Today readers can still ponder genealogical verses composed for Leinster kings in the same period as Brigit's early vitae, between the mid-seventh century and early eighth century, celebrating the mysterious enclosures upon the hills. Poems praised the hero Art Mes(s)-Telmann who had supposedly built Dún Ailinne and become first ruler of the entire province.[74] The paeans reflected ongoing efforts of Leinster dynasts who used the hillforts and their legendary builders as symbolic capital while they competed for regional supremacy.

Scholars crafted written territorial histories even as contenders for overlordship were building the territories. One poem celebrated the abandoned Dún Ailinne and its princely hero Mes-Telmann, "who has reached the realms of the dead, the noble son of Sétnae, laid waste the vales of the Fomoire under the worlds of men. From the heights of Ailenn, the powerful tribune [*trebun*], great in dominions, Mess-Telmann of the Fir Domnann, slew the mighty of the earth."[75] Although his deeds were set in the prehistoric centuries of the Iron Age, nonetheless Mes-Telmann was clad in the authority of a Roman title (Irish *trebun*, borrowed from Latin *tribunus*). The poet-historian who wrote this verse probably came from a wealthy monastic community in north Leinster. He cleverly drew on Isidore of Seville and Bible stories as well as local folklore for his models of migratory heroes. He linked the first ancestors of the Leinstermen with Noah's descendants, the most ancient travelers of all. Thus the genealogist synthesized scriptural history and dynastic tradition to justify the continuing visibility of Mes-Telmann's ancient, pagan place in Christian times, on converted landscapes.[76] Other tales told how Mes-Telmann's son Nuadu had killed the king of Ireland at Dún Ailinne; and how Nuadu's great-grandson became yet another legendary lord of the fort while his brothers ruled the rival strongholds of Rath Crúachain and Temair.[77]

Long after its Iron Age ramparts had disappeared, Dún Ailinne remained a focal point on the sacral landscape of north Leinster. It dominated the region's political geography.[78] Kings still came to Dún Ailinne, and rivals still aimed for its possession. When troops from another province wanted to declare their invasion of north Leinster, they headed for what was left of the fort and occupied it. When Leinster dynasts announced a bid for tribal leadership, they staged battles at Dún Ailinne. In 727, for instance, Faelán mac Brain defeated his brother Murchad in a battle for Uí Dúnlainge leadership at Dún Ailinne.[79] The skirmishes and feuds of Irish lords and kings were mostly about movable wealth and control of clientage networks rather than territory. Tribal kings never owned their kingdoms, as English kings came to do. Winners of border wars were not interested in expelling their victims or expropriating their lands, but in driving off cattle and slaves, and collecting revenues acknowledging their overlordship.

Thus poets and genealogists may have claimed that Dún Ailinne represented all Leinster, but by Brigit's day it stood for a dynastic group already losing a grip on the provincial overlordship; and by the time Faelán subdued his brother, victory at Dún Ailinne brought him only leadership of the lords of northern Leinster, if that. Other regional kings had their own ritual capitals and political claims. Southern Leinstermen reveled in the legends of a place called Dind Ríg, so that poets could speak of the seventh-century rivalry between Uí Dúnlainge northerners and Uí Cheinselaig southerners as a clash of the two forts. Poets outside of Leinster kept similar traditions of forts and ancestral migrations that helped them argue for historical stewardship of their own provinces or even the entire island. The possessors of Temair, capital of the midlands, were in constant struggle with those who held Cruachain to its west in Connacht as well as Dún Ailinne to the south. Leinstermen responded to the claims of these rulers with aggressive propaganda and outright warfare. One regnal poem about Dún Ailinne spoke of Cruachain and Temair as "citadels magnificent among strongholds, fortresses which an illustrious, powerful, spear-wielding royal host would smash."[80] The verses evoked ancient rivalries but also revealed the increasing threat of incursions by subgroups of the Uí Néill tribal confederation over the northern boundaries of Leinster during the sixth and seventh centuries. In this way, poets and other writers anchored fractured contemporary politics firmly to Ireland's venerable but still powerful symbolic geography.

Even the violence of constant raids and pitched battles—the bloody death and mortal hurt, burnt houses and trampled crops, stolen cattle and women— took symbolic form in the written legends. Some early medieval tales of historical politics were called simply *togala* (destructions). In legendary Ireland, the most powerful kings had marked their ascent by firing buildings and ravaging landscapes rather than building new proofs of their power. "Every Monday he waged a bloody battle against Fergus," chanted a seventh-century poet of Leinster kings, "every Wednesday he razed a wood, every Saturday he laid waste a bog."[81] Likewise, the early medieval annals were full of historic destructions both effective and symbolic: quick raids to level a couple of borderland farms, steal some girls or cows, and fell a symbolic tree (*bile*) or demolish the frontier outpost of a neighboring dynast.[82] To take territory, a king had to destroy the landscape. Even after Christian establishment, kings never won the same fame for sponsoring the building of churches and mausoleums as Clovis did, but only for granting and protecting the property of those who wished to build.

Yet clever kings and Christian leaders must quickly have realized the political benefits of collaboration. The words brought by Patrick's generation of missionaries were more durable than orally kept memories of forts and dead kings. Literate men could not only maintain and publicize a tribe's heritage of destruction but also manipulate the past by revising genealogies and rewriting the lyrics of legends. We know that from first writing, genealogists added or erased ancestors to reflect updated politics. When any family lost influence and territory, it disappeared from legends of ancestral turf.[83] The Uí Garrchon, for instance, had once controlled lands around the place where Brigit would settle. Yet by the time Cogitosus wrote, less than two centuries later, they had become known as a *fortúath*, a clan of low-status immigrants. They were actually natives whose only historical migration was exile from western Leinster to the poor soils east of the mountains after they lost lordship.[84] Theirs was a particularly melancholy and elliptical legend of passage.

Other tribes disappeared entirely from both landscape and genealogical literature but turned up as bit players in early saints' lives; although politics had passed them by, they retained forever the gratitude of hagiographers for religious endowments made far in the past. We know something about the Uí Garrchon because Brigit's bishop Conláed, buried next to her in Kildare's church, descended from a subtribe called the Dál Messin Corb, which vanished altogether from later medieval literature. In a few references to Conláed and his tomb lay the entire history of a tribe and kingdom that had once flourished.[85]

The saints' infiltration of the political past, accomplished by the seventh century, was an effective way for Christian leaders to shape their religion for the Irish landscape. Within a couple hundred years between the first plea for a bishop and Cogitosus's story of Kildare, churchmen and religious women had conquered the volatile political geography of Ireland at its symbolic centers. All the major regnal sites in Ireland eventually attracted ecclesiastical settlement.[86] At least a century after its purposeful dismantling, Dún Ailinne and its history drew Christian builders to settle nearby at Kildare, and monastic poets to recall its fall. Around 800, the monk Óengus mac Óengobann wrote of this deliberate juxtaposition of religio-political sites in his martyrology, casting the process in historical terms of dynastic rivalry and royal succession. Temair's fort had fallen with its princes, he declared, but Patrick's fame was always growing. He meant that Ard Macha (Armagh), by then the most influential community dedicated to the saint, was strategically allied with the current possessors of the ancient inaugural site of Temair (Tara). Ties that had nothing to do with natural features but everything to do with landscape and politics bound the two places eternally.[87] Emain, much nearer to Armagh, had been irrelevant to island politics for several centuries, so the keepers of Patrick's church had chosen more influential dynastic partners. Meanwhile, Ráth Crúachain had faded away, Óengus also wrote, yet nearby Cluain Moccu Nois, the monastery of Saint Ciarán, flourished on the Shannon's banks. Likewise, Kildare had subdued and exploited Dún Ailinne:

> Ailenn's proud fort
> Has perished along with its warlike host;
> Great is victorious Brigit;
> Fair is her crowded cemetery . . .
> The old cities of the pagans,
> Kept and held since ancient times,
> Are laid waste without ritual . . .
> The places were taken over
> By pairs and by trios [of missionaries],
> They have become little Romes [*alt.* cemeteries] crowded
> With hundreds, with thousands of people.[88]

Spolia of a glorious Leinster past were less obvious and less tangible but no less influential than the broken blocks of a forum or temple to Apollo. Dynastic legends about ancient places shaped the development of Irish Christian landscapes in the same way that the imperial past had inspired fifth- and sixth-century Gaulish church builders. In Óengus's version of Leinster history,

Dún Ailinne had never disappeared. Its existence made possible the triumph of Kildare. By comparison to the royal fort's ruin, Brigit's cemetery—her *ruam*— housed and signposted the bodies of thousands of baptized Irish. The word *ruam* had come to mean at once the preeminent place of the holy dead, Rome itself, as well as any great ecclesiastical settlement or its cemetery. The sacral sites of Ireland were micro-Romes, replicating the Christian city just as forums across the ancient empire had re-created the architectural center of Rome and thus extended its sway. For Óengus, the tombs of the romanized dead had replaced the tombs of the pagan kings; what was below on the plains now commanded the hilltop, but the same place was sacred in the same old way.

Christian poets used the metaphor of conquest for the conversion of landscapes, praising saints as invaders and war leaders. One of Brigit's bishops at Kildare composed a hymn in the early ninth century that reflected back on the settlement's fifth-century foundation as a political victory:

> Sit safely enthroned, victorious Brigit,
> On Liffey plain as far as the sea's shore:
> You are the sovereign with legion bands
> Who rules the children of Catháir Mór [ancestor of the Laigen] . . .

> Illustrious Aileann—dear the lore—
> Many princes are beneath its face . . .

> Your [Brigit's] fame has surpassed the king's fame—
> You transcend them all.

> You share sovereignty with the king
> Except for the land where your sanctuary is.
> Grandchild of Bresal, son of Dian,
> Sit safely enthroned, victorious Brigit![89]

In this poet's conceit, Brigit had led the religious community at Kildare to usurp the kingship of Dún Ailinne. She had gone on to set up a permanent capital where she would reign forever. The saint's rivals had been royalty rather than pagans per se. In this land where mobile territories were profoundly masculine and no woman could rule independently as queen, Brigit had surpassed both dead and living kings of Leinster. She was supreme secular and sacral power. The king himself no longer ruled Ailenn as his ancestors had, nor did he have any jurisdiction over Brigit's well-marked sanctuary of Kildare. What is more, the phrase about sharing sovereignty deliberately invoked a mythology of territorial goddesses who granted their bodies and lands to men whom they chose to govern.[90]

Brigit's hymnist celebrated, in the voice of a dynastic poet, a sacral geography that eventually emerged from and, in turn, replaced an even more ancient symbolic landscape by the seventh century. Between Patrick's account of his wanderings and Cogitosus's account of Brigit's life in Leinster, no document captured Irish landscapes. Yet the changes must have begun by her lifetime, or else Brigit could not have traveled and built. Only hagiographers and others who wrote about saints, such as Óengus, included women in what were normally men-only stories. Women had never penetrated the legends of ancient forts, except for a few notable warrior queens from Connacht and Ulster.[91] The earliest royal genealogies generally treated female ancestors as minor characters, if at all. Women shuffled through the background of dynastic history. In the relatively textless time between Patrick's *Confessio* and Cogitosus's vita, Christians had begun revising not only the Irish landscape and its political history but also the gender of its places.

Signs of Paganism

Practical leaders of congregations contended with mundane geographies and priorities when they chose sites for Christian buildings. Medieval hagiographers tended to claim that divine inspiration drove holy men and women through the Irish wilderness until an angel or a sign from the clouds led them to good real estate.[92] But too many monasteries and their churches occupied strategic positions on good agricultural land, major trade routes, fords, or the mutable marchlands of tribal kingdoms to be the result of merely miracle. Church builders settled near historically important sites and with an eye to tribal politics, but they also aimed for existing settlements and plentiful natural resources. Like Continental proselytizers, they often chose spots with previous cult associations. What is more, both those who needed and those who gave property for churches and religious communities were probably already residents of the neighborhood.

The process of Christian settlement involved two distinct kinds of site preparation typical of church builders everywhere in Europe: the acquisition of places from spiritual forces and the acquisition of property from human possessors. Gaulish hagiographies, organized into bounded and documented territories with urban capitals and romanized property laws, provided no useful models for these strategic encounters on Irish turf. The Irish were very fond of Martin and his vita, but Martin had worked in a Gallo-Roman legal context where temples were collectively owned and architecturally signed; when he tried to identify heathen sites by reading human behavior, he made mistakes.

Genovefa, likewise, had relied on administrative maps generated by the laws and limits of urban and provincial government to define her territory. In Ireland, neither property laws nor recognizable temples advertised the places where idols were likely to lurk and where proselytizers might directly contend with symbols of old religion. What is more, since there were no shrines to destroy or statuary to smash, there were also no fragments of religious building for modern archaeologists to excavate. As a result, most of the evidence for the religious conversion of Irish pagans and their sanctuaries comes from Christian-authored, early medieval documents.

When Cogitosus wrote in the 650s or so, he considered christianization to be complete. Pagans hardly figured in his tales of Brigit's fifth-century adventures. However, Irish bishops gathered in synod around the same time and produced written decrees, which offered some specific advice about interactions between Christians and unbelievers. They advised Christians not to behave like or do business with the unbaptized. The bishops prohibited only a few heathen religious practices: swearing oaths before a diviner (*aruspex*) and professing belief in a *lamia* or *striga*—words later translated as "vampire" and "witch." But the synod did not consider any problematic pagan places and referred only vaguely to churches. The bishops warned priests not to celebrate the Eucharist in a church (*aecclesia*) that had not been consecrated by bishops, nor to build churches without episcopal permission. It was not enough to secure the permission of a layman, meaning either the owner of an appropriate property or a tribal leader.[93]

Seventh-century saints' lives told more detailed stories of believers and places, but by then authors were describing an already historical pagan landscape. Tírechán and Muirchú, who wrote a few decades after Cogitosus, included in their narratives several dramatic confrontations between Saint Patrick and pagan magicians. They also described his exorcism of pagan influences from potential building sites. Scenes from Patrick's vitae became normative histories of paganism's extinction, whereas Brigit's interactions with her landscape, as we will see in the next chapter, were more about building Christian territories and a romanized church. Brigit had only one direct encounter with practicing pagans, whereas the Patrick of hagiographic legend repeatedly vanquished malicious recusants. Patrick's hagiographers suggested that the purification of a place had to precede its legal acquisition as property. Their Patrick also purposely targeted the unbuilt or barely built places where pagans gathered: wells and springs, burial places, and seasonal assemblies. Seventh-century saints' lives may not have reliably reported incidents of the fifth century, but the texts did suggest, at the very least, challenges that had faced ecclesiastical leaders and church builders up to the hagiographers' time and the continuing need to neutralize traditional ritual places.

Wells were both social sites and holy places in Ireland, as in Gaul. Patrick had found crowds of converts in rivers and at springs, according to his hagiographers, which was convenient for baptism. Sacrality was already in the water when it bubbled out of the earth. Once Christian leaders purified it, they could use the water as they wished, baptizing with it, blessing lakes to yield fish or cursing them dry, causing springs to erupt spontaneously, and even moving entire bodies of water to suit their needs.[94] Tírechán wrote a story about Patrick's exorcism of a heathen well called Slán (good health) by the natives. It was square with a squared stone lid and reinforced ducts for the outflow of water (*fons uero quadratus fuit et petra quadrata erat in ore fontis et ueniebat aqua super petram.i. est per glutinationes*). Patrick encountered the usual crowd at the well. People were talking about the "wise man" who had chosen to die and leave his soul in the well waters because he feared the flames of the afterlife. Druids (*magi*) called the place "King of the Waters" (*aquarum rex*) and worshiped its occupant as a god. According to Tírechán's story, Patrick approached his audience of pagan priests and locals, informed them brusquely that the gold and silver deposits in the spring were "wicked sacrifices" (*de auro et argento . . . reprobis immolationibus*), and then heaved the lid off the well. Yet Patrick and onlookers found no bones and no gold.[95] In this story, intentionally reminiscent of Saint Martin's feats of destruction, the shrine was not a shrine at all, nor even a site of genuine ritual deposits. It was just a well. Wells were just places where housewives drew water for baths and the washing-up. Some old pagans had clearly chosen the wrong place to worship. Like a bad translation, the well of Slán had misled gullible unbelievers who hung around it because they secretly longed for the properly built religion of Christianity.

Burials presented a trickier target for the first missionaries because they were harder to find unless mourners were visiting. The Irish had never devised a reliable system for marking the places of their dead. In the Bronze Age, high-status corpses or cremations had been stowed inside chambered tombs built of giant stones, adorned with carved symbols and often covered over with earth to mimic natural features. Only rarely, the tombs clustered together in necropolises.[96] By the Iron Age, burials were more diverse. If they featured dolmens, the stones were smaller, although still concealed beneath artificial mounds. Families buried their dead at ancient cemeteries but also in new ringed enclosures. Sometimes bodies crouched singly but sometimes in groups.[97] Cemeteries were not fenced or signposted. By the age of church builders, most of the recent deceased lay in low mounds or covered pits hard for an untrained eye to detect.

Only a few burials in coastal regions had any kind of manufactured monument. A fashion for pillars, slabs, or smaller boulders inscribed with personal names spread between southwestern Ireland and the Welsh coast beginning in the fourth century.[98] Carvers wrote in Ogham, a system of slashes and dots, in purposeful imitation of Roman-style memorials. Only a few stood in the vicinity of Kildare. At Colbinstown, about seventeen miles southeast of the place where Brigit would build, seven stones now commemorate seven men. MAQIDDEC[CEDA] MAQI MARIN, reads one. But it is impossible to tell when Mac Deichet and the others lived and who memorialized them, or even where the stones and their dead originally lay—that is, if they actually marked graves. Ogham monuments never caught on in other parts of Ireland but remained confined to regions near coasts where sea traffic was common.[99]

According to seventh-century hagiographers, then, nothing helped Christians see unfamiliar graves. Any potential building site might harbor the unbaptized dead. Christians needed to find the bodies and subdue the malign spirits of heathen places; they also wanted to commemorate the graves of baptized women and men from former times. Tírechán assumed that pagan bodies had been disposed differently than Christian bodies.[100] In one episode of Patrick's vita, Loegaire Ua Néill, king of Tara (Temair), refused to be baptized because he had promised his tribesmen to be buried pagan style. The king wanted to be interred in standing position in a pit within the ridges of Tara, his ritual capital. He would spend eternity armed and facing his enemies in Leinster, for, according to the hagiographer, it was the custom that "the pagans, armed in their tombs, have their weapons ready" for combat with the enemy. Perhaps Tírechán knew of late Iron Age burials in which the dead crouched.

Short of digging up bodies, however, church builders might have identified pagan burials and cemeteries by elements of place-names. *Fertae* (alt. *fert*) signified an old burial mound. Patrick supposedly ordained a man and founded a church at a place called the *Fert* of Fíacc's Men.[101] In another story, Tírechán laid out a step-by-step guide for transforming a *fertae* into a properly identified Christian burial.[102] Patrick had successfully converted King Loegaire's two daughters, who then immediately expired and went to heaven. Their bodies were placed in a ditch-ringed mound near a well, according to the hagiographer, "after the manner of a *ferta,* because this is what the heathen Irish used to do, but we call it a *relic,* that is, the remains [*residuae*] of the maidens." Tírechán showed how Christians quoted older, unchristian burials but gave cemeteries new names and uses. Both Loegaire and his daughters were buried in mounds, but the disposition of the bodies and their monuments were different. While Loegaire crouched impotently below his outmoded royal capital, the virgins stretched modestly in their tomb, which, by virtue of their sacrifice, became a Christian shrine. What is more, the owners of land around the *relic* donated it to Patrick and his ecclesiastical heirs, so Patrick built an earthen church atop

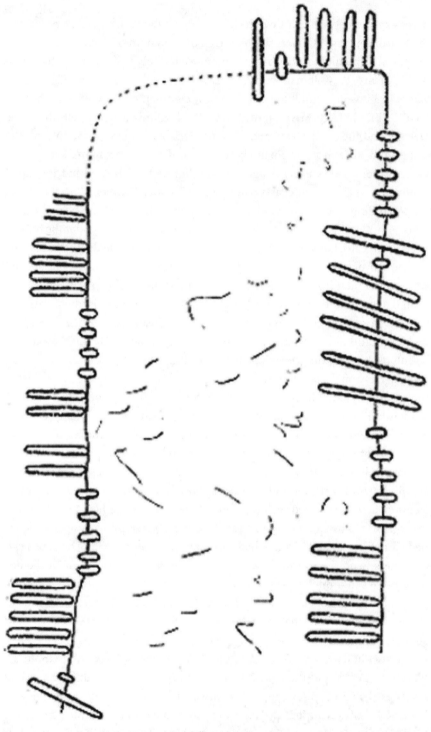

FIGURE 5.3. Ogham stone, fifth through seventh century, Colbinstown, county Kildare. The symbols read, according to R. A. S. Macalister: MAQI-DDEC[CEDA] MAQI MARIN.

the mound (*aecclesiam terrena*) that would, presumably, host memorial liturgies for the virgins in Tírechán's own time.[103] Relics replaced bodies while memorial shrine succeeded pagan burial site. Tírechán's story set the virgins' shrine in relation to Loegaire's burial in the same way that Óengus and Leinster hymnists would link churches in relation to the barrows of kings.[104] Thus Tírechán explained the history of his landscape's conversion and how pagan sites had been prepared for Christian construction.[105]

Like the Gallo-Romans, then, the Irish sought to christianize cemeteries and other pagan sites but had trouble reading the landscape without architectural clues or textual records. However, in Ireland proselytizers were dealing with many more unstable sites based on far older spatial practices than in Roman Gaul. Tírechán was responding in the late seventh century to the continuing problem of unidentified pagan places when he wrote his guide to missionary history. Saintly proselytizers, he was arguing, could tell whether a lump on the horizon was a famous political center, a sanctuary for pagan bodies, or just an abandoned farm. To ordinary Christians, though, one mound, cairn, or unlettered boulder looked just like another unless the viewer knew its past. The ancient tomb builders had purposely invoked organic forms and cleverly disguised their mounds as features of the natural landscape. Christians had to be sharp-eyed to find obnoxious holy places. They needed expert scouts familiar with the territory's history who could translate what lay below into visible landscapes above. Saints made careers of such translation.

Another set of seventh-century Patrician tales showed how crucial the ability to spot a holy place remained even after communities had begun to sign sacral sites with Christian symbols. Tírechán recounted how Patrick and his retinue had come across an enormous burial (*sepulcrum*) marked with an ordinary rock. Patrick raised the gigantic dead man from the ground just long enough to ascertain his identity as a pagan. Then the saint baptized him and laid him back in the grave. In the following episode, however, told in two different versions by Tírechán and the contemporaneous hagiographer Muirchú, Patrick found a pair of new graves. Only one was marked with a cross. When Patrick demanded to know who was buried beneath the cross, a voice from below ground admitted that the body was pagan. The dead man explained that someone had mistakenly placed the cross over him—either a mother blinded by grief (Muirchú) or a stupid and foolish man (Tírechán). In Muirchú's telling, Patrick had not even been able to see the cross at first "because it stood on the burial site of a pagan." A veil of unbelief, rather than any built monument, blocked his view.

In Tírechán's version, though, Patrick hurtled out of his chariot, wrenched the cross from the ground, and replanted it on the Christian's grave. As they drove away, his charioteer asked why Patrick had not simply baptized the dead pagan as he had baptized and reburied the giant of the earlier episode. Patrick did not answer. Both the charioteer and the writer of the story remained puzzled. Tírechán suggested, "I think he left the man because God did not want to save him." Perhaps, too, the hagiographer was casting Patrick as Martin, who had performed a similar discovery when he debunked the shrine containing a robber's grave. Still, the hagiographer could not disguise his anxiety about Patrick's inexplicable behavior.[106] Why would a saint leave pagans moldering in sanctified Christian earth? Tírechán still could not tell a baptized from a heathen burial, and felt that it was not sufficient just to mark the good graves. Patrick should have christianized the entire spot.

A proper Christian ritual place required a body, a marker such as a cross or church, and people to recognize the signs. Tírechán recalled yet another episode about a well-marked but neglected Christian burial. One dead monk haunted another monk's dream, complaining that "I loathe my death because I am alone in a solitary church, deserted and empty, no priests offer beside me." Eventually the living brother took an iron shovel to the burial mound (*sepulcri fossam fodiuit*) and translated the bones to his own monastery.[107] His desecration was justified because the site was deserted and its shrine untended, like old Iron Age mounds and Bronze Age dolmens. The place had all the right signs but no one to see them. Church leaders were clearly still working out the geography of burials in the seventh century.

Use was key to the identification of a sacral site on this mobile landscape. Some of the most important pagan rituals apparently took place at seasonal or impromptu gatherings where temporal location was more crucial than spatial location. Brigit's one encounter with hostile pagans occurred at a completely nondescript location on the open road. She only realized that she had stumbled on a savage ritual when she heard a group of men shouting oaths of a "godless and diabolical superstition." Cogitosus never explained what the men were doing, beyond swearing vows, or why they chose the spot.[108] Patrick also dueled with spell-casting druids in open-air gatherings at traditional royal sites. Muirchú described an annual "ceremony with many spells and conjurings and other idolatries" that unbelievers of the fifth century had celebrated at Tara. He was referring to a traditional inaugural ritual that other writers called the Feis Temra, or Feast of Tara. In Muirchú's version, kings, warriors, "druids, magicians, soothsayers, clairvoyants and teachers of every art and skill" gathered at the regnal site for "heathen worship." The hagiographer could not translate the encounter into hagiographic terms without imagining the hill of Tara as an Irish city of Babylon. The local Nebuchadnezzar—King Loegaire—had the right to kindle the first fire of the new year in his house (but there were no permanent houses at Tara), and anyone who lit a flame before him was put to death. Patrick, of course, found the highest hill visible from Tara and lit up. The druids predicted with horror that "the fire that we see, which has been lit tonight before the fire was kindled in your house: Unless it is extinguished on this same night in which it was lit, it will not be put out forever."[109] Loegaire, now compared to Herod, set in motion a series of magical contests between his druids and the saint, similar to those between Moses and Pharaoh's magicians, which ended badly for the druids. Meanwhile, the king lolled gloomily on a couch drinking wine like a classical sybarite.[110] Muirchú knew, as he penned these lines, that rituals at Tara had been celebrated for the last time more than a hundred years earlier, in 560.[111]

Paganism was all the more dangerous for having places and times but not dedicated permanent structures. It might hide anywhere; it lurked everywhere. To seventh-century Christians reading or hearing the vitae, Patrick and Brigit represented the powers of the first generations of holy men and women to divine and control unmarked paganism. They could spot it deep in wells and graves, on the road, in shouted words, or in plain sight yearly at Tara. Hagiography, with its records of heathen encounters, provided a counterhistory to the royal legends of pagan places. It offered new guides to sacral landscapes for those not savvy enough to read the sparse visual markers. Seventh-century stories proved that Christian founders had been superb judges of real estate. They were able to neutralize powerful pagan places and turn them into choice locations for Christian building. Patrick, his hagiographer recalled, had twice climbed a mountain to view the lay of the land and select sites for churches.[112]

Another major difference between historic pagan landscapes and the still emerging Christian maps of Ireland, as the story of the lonely monk made clear, was that Christian sacral sites were in constant use. The living came only occasionally to old pagan places. No one dwelt at wells but pagan deities. Tombs were homes of the dead. Assembly places existed only so long as the holiday lasted and the crowds remained. No mortal owned these places, although communities may have tended them. When Christian leaders chose building sites, they wanted places where peopled lived and worked. That meant negotiating with the mortal owners of property. Patrick the Briton had been comfortable enough on the move, but every other saint in Irish hagiography searched for a place to settle, build, and be buried.

Christian Property

Although the first generation of preachers had prepared Irish souls and soil for christianization, it took several more generations for Christians to get around to building and the formation of administrative networks based on well-defined territories. Ireland was ripe with possibilites for churches but initially lacked a civic-minded aristocratic class willing to sponsor religious architecture. Elites were rich in cattle, clients, and the occasional imported trinket, not in cash, land, or buildings. According to the saints' lives, some offered property to Christian leaders or, more likely, to their kin who became ecclesiastics, but they saw no reason to pay for buildings. Patrick recalled noblewomen who chucked their jewelry at him, but those ladies did not sponsor new basilicas as proper Roman matrons or Merovingian queens did. Everywhere else in Christendom bishops had territories, estates, civic duties, and even palaces. Even when they disagreed about whose episcopal see was superior or where the diocesan limits lay, they could refer to existing cities and polities to argue their claims.

In Ireland, bishops had to reinvent their jurisdictions to match shifting kingdoms and occasional pagan places before they planted congregations. Missionaries and Christian organizers must have known that kin-based properties were the most durable, reliable units of land. Besides megalithic tombs, the earliest permanent structures on the island were stone fences that enclosed networks of small fields at Neolithic coastal settlements such as Céide Fields in county Mayo.[113] Fences and farms were more numerous than tombs. Clusters of farms occupied the same choice spots, year after year. The last major clearance of forest in Ireland had taken place in the second and third centuries, perhaps a little later in Leinster.[114] Since then, occupation had remained fairly stable throughout Ireland. There was no major shift in settlement or population decline until the pandemic of the mid–sixth century.[115] Patrick's vague geography ignored the hedges and ditches of long-established farmsteads, but by Brigit's time every tract of land from the tops of mountains to the depths of boggy wastes, even if uninhabited, had already been identified, possessed, valued, and argued over by farmers and herders. Every useful place was settled and owned.[116] If a gang of raiders drove a family off, the names of owners changed but the farms themselves remained in place. By the sixth century, there was so little true desert left in Ireland that aspiring hermits had to go abroad.

When literate men came, in the seventh or eighth century, to record the customs by which their ancestors had parceled out property, they had little to say about kingdoms but a great deal to tell about the boundaries of farms and pastures, orchards, forests, fisheries, and mills. The organizing principle behind their laws was *dúthchas*, heredity and collectively recalled, generally acknowledged right.[117] Communities collectively kept histories of their lands along with the memory of its varied uses, occupants, and methods for preserving ownership. *Dofet rand ime,* advised one medieval legal text: division precedes fences. No place existed without other places; fences always defined a group relative to other families and their histories.[118] The phrase served as a metaphor, too, for the way that legal writers looked back upon the traditional establishment of local field divisions which had long preceded the inked lines of recorded property laws.

However, to make more evident the ancient limits separating one family's ground from the land of another, legal writers obliged neighbors to maintain fences and ditches of earth, wood, wattle, blackthorn hedge, or stone. The early medieval legal tract dedicated to trespass laws, *Bretha Comaithcesa,* showed how to apply collective memory to the environmental reality of properties.[119] The law laid down how deep, how high, how wide, and how impenetrable barriers were to be. Different kinds of land demanded different limits; rocky territory had stone fences, whereas ditches and banks or hedges surrounded fields on good agricultural land. A flimsy marker was fine for forestland, but a three-banded rod fence was more suitable for keeping intruding piglets out of the garden. The legal text called the *Heptads* mentioned an especially stout fence called *tórandaile* for boundaries between the holdings of different families.[120] Landowners who neglected their fences were liable to heavy fines.

As laws about the making of fences and hedges also demonstrated, however, property boundaries were both breachable and mutable in practice. Legal lines were concise, but property constantly needed redefining in mundane situations. Heirs divided farms among themselves after a landholder died. Farmers bought, sold, and traded parcels. Neighbors and kinfolk renegotiated property boundaries after someone laid claim to a neglected patch of land. Each group strove to find mutually agreeable boundaries and then to advertise them with familiar markers such as fences.[121] Contested property sometimes changed shape. The early medieval tract on legal entry, *Din Techtugad,* explained the official means by which a claimant to land could cross a property line and stake his or her claim against that of the current occupants, thus, if successful, adding land to his own property.[122]

But boundary crossings were legally and ideologically problematic. Marauding warleaders made their careers by charging over territorial lines, but ordinary farmers worked hard to keep out the most peaceful invaders. *Bretha Comaithcesa* listed many kinds of trespass over boundaries by humans and animals and the legal fines these infractions occasioned. Penalties varied by the kind of land, the type of fence, the season, the identity and motive of the trespasser (Cow driven by man or dog? Swine determined to root up the garden? Man bent on poaching timber?) and the resulting visible damage. Particularly reprehensible was the case of the dog that wandered through a fence and deposited a pile of excrement on a neighbor's property. In reparation, the hound's owner was to pay the landowner a volume of butter, curds, and bread dough equal to three times the volume of *conluain* or excrement. How such a thing was to be measured was, amazingly, not specified in the text. Even empty land demanded regulation. The most difficult cases for medieval legalists concerned the maintenance of fences along an abandoned property, such as a farm well marked but emptied of its original purpose for boundaries. The abandoned land remained a space defined only by memory of its possession, just like the ruined forts of dead kings.

Legal writers recognized some kind of conceptual link between suppos-edly stable property boundaries and shifting political territories, based on the vulnerability of both kinds of limits to trespass. Kin groups with political power were generally composed of the wealthiest farmers and herders, and leaders of prominent families were usually noble warriors, too—the kinds of men who suffered most damage from trespass. The man who made his reputation by leading fighters over political boundaries also strove to keep his own family's property inviolate. Kings—basically heads of families and lords of lords—had the responsibility of maintaining the limits of everyone's properties and pre-venting trespass.[123] The king was legally in charge of the "measurement by poles . . . marking out [fresh] boundaries, planting of stakes, the law as to points [of stakes], partition among co-heirs, summoning of neighbors, stone pillars of contest, fighters who fasten [title]." In other words, his authority enforced the division and marking of family lands. He ensured the fence-building and creation of inscribed stone boundary markers (which helped settle disputes, hence the "fighters"). In addition, the king was to protect all boundaries from "stealthy penetration, stealthy intrusion . . . blocking tracks" and trespass by any number of creatures, "sudden breaches across a road, stampeding across holdings, similarly [over] strands . . . [and] final responsibility for trespass."[124]

The stability of family properties and the rules by which communities organized their lands and limits had direct effects on ecclesiastical travelers and builders. Conversion and church-building happened in Ireland as else-where in the early medieval world, one negotiation at a time. But any larger pattern remains obscure: Did church builders take advantage of the existing rules about boundaries and their violation to occupy contestable property, or did church builders' need for reliable boundaries spur the development of written laws of property? On the one hand, indigenous law limited how much property a family could give away to people not related to them by blood. The expectations of the next generation of owners constrained pious donors.[125] On the other hand, every church builder (except Patrick) was a member of an Irish family with property. Every Christian professional—except for the odd Gaul or Welshman—already had neighbors who might be persuaded to shift the boundaries, or not.

The question of how christianization initially influenced property ownership in Ireland, or vice versa, has no clear answer because no one wrote about
it until almost 700. Patrick certainly did not consider it. For succeeding generations of Christian founders, though, the question was more properly about
translation: Which existing properties, political landscapes, and sacral sites
most easily translated into sites for churches? Which territories could best be
adapted to episcopal administration? Besides places purified of pagan influences, Christian organizers also needed stable and uncontested properties
with visible boundaries. At first religious leaders required only enough land
for humble churches or burial shrines with, perhaps, a small graveyard. But
as they realized the need for serious architecture to accommodate growing
congregations and orthodox liturgies, and as the bodies of the Christian dead
required ever more space, builders needed considerable endowments of land
and revenues to support construction, equipment, and personnel.[126] Beginning
in the fifth or sixth century, communities of ascetics also appeared, demanding property to endow settlements dedicated to prayer and the veneration of
saints.

The result had to be displacement. Under early medieval Irish laws, the
acquisition of ecclesiastical property required complex negotiations among
several kin groups or even entire communities, not just the charitable impulse
of individuals. Even when the builder of a church or monastery came from a
local family, someone lost land. When kings and queens gave ancestral properties to hungry saints, as they did in so many hagiographic tales, the outcome
was predictable: one heir lost out to another. Lands long associated with particular families gained new names of saints and their settlements.[127] The prospect
of alienating property to churches continued to trouble donors, recipients, and
the writers of saints' lives along with jurists, canonists, and poets throughout
the medieval centuries. Especially problematic were women's donations, since
daughters could not officially inherit kin's land. The number of women who
could sponsor Christian architecture in Ireland must have been pitiful.[128]

The balance of fixed and shifting boundaries, the juxtaposition of working
farms with ancient ritual centers, and the trade in *romanitas* all helped prepare
the land for Brigit's career of church-building. One more feature of the legal
landscape was crucial, however, to the history of Brigit the builder and saint.
Property, like the rest of the landscape, was gendered. Ownership, boundary
markers, and uses of property were different for men and women. Although
kingdoms, laws, family properties, and the very shape of the land itself were
profoundly different in Ireland than in Gaul, only a woman of extraordinary
influence could have created and ruled a religious territory in either context—
and, in fact, a woman did exactly that in each.

Gender in the Land

The legal landscape of early medieval Ireland lives on in laws recorded in the seventh and later centuries. According to these laws, Irish women moved across, possessed, and fenced land with effects and implications different from those of men's actions. Women could dwell upon land and manage it, but they only inherited the usufruct or occupation of property, or kept bits of property that had accrued to their mothers through gift or purchase.[129] They lived in the households of men. Women's daily labors were more likely to keep them near the house and farmyard while men moved more freely around or beyond family lands. Men marked and owned the land upon which women worked. Men owned the ground where they buried their dead and the places where people worshiped. Women could not read the arcane legal tracts containing these rules, or react to them publicly and officially in legal disputes. Women were liable for trespass and for helping with the responsibility of keeping property boundaries, but they could not decide who crossed and who did not.

Thus, even while leaders and literati pondered the continuing difficulties of christianizing landscapes and acquiring properties, gender complicated the problem. The crossing of boundaries was a gendered act. Although the early medieval laws dealt with all kinds of trespass by human or beast, legal writers treated cases of changing and crossing boundaries involving women as exceptional. Women operated under different rules, for instance, in cases where the movable property of debtors or legal opponents was impounded. In some instances, a creditor could enter a debtor's property without prior notice in order to seize stock in the amount due, then drive the animals to a corral on his own land.[130] However, a woman could not enter without notice. The jurist who recorded these customs around the eighth century thought it improper or dangerous for women to move aggressively across boundaries into another person's property.

Another early medieval legal tract, *Din Techtugad*, emphasized the unique legal character of female boundary crossing. Both men and women were able to perform legal entries onto disputed land, accompanied by their stock animals and human witnesses, which set in motion a formal claim to the property. But women's legal entry required different witnesses, different animals, and equipment to mark possession of lands, and it took place within a different time frame from men's legal entry. In a legendary story that used prehistoric events to explain this complex process, a famous lawgiver named Sencha insisted that the process of legal entry be identical for men and women. He was instantly punished by supernatural forces for this misjudgment by the appearance of blisters on his cheeks (a common cosmic penalty in Irish literature for damaging or negative speech acts). A woman judge named Brig then reiterated the difference between male and female legal entry, and Sencha was cured of his deformity. In the story, only a woman could judge the nature of women's movement. The assumption of this literature was that women's travel across boundaries had always been both symbolically and legally distinct from that of men, with discrete ramifications for property and its owners.

Laws of trespass put women in the same legal class as children, beasts, and slaves. Writers of laws not only imagined every inch of land enclosed and contained but also distinguished between living beings "outside" the fenced property and those "inside." Animals ought to be confined every night; cows should go into their enclosure, swine in a sty, horses in a stable, and sheep in a fold. Since trespass at night incurred a worse fine for man or beast than trespass by day, the implication was that humans ought to be inside after dark, too. Disenfranchised humans, like land and its animals, must be surrounded and enclosed. Men of land and standing were responsible for all those who had no right to wander: children, women, slaves, imbeciles, and animals.[131] Whether this tendency toward enclosure was a traditional feature of Irish attitudes about the domestic landscape or a motif borrowed from classical literatures of women's claustration, the aim of laws was to keep everything but men within boundaries.

At the same time, jurists and their clients admitted the reality of trespass during the early medieval centuries. They knew that women crossed legal, geographical, social, and political boundaries both regularly and at particular points in their life cycles. Formal marriage was patrilocal, so that women in such unions left natal homes to wed, as marriage and divorce laws acknowledged. If the ladies were noble, they might make a considerable journey across many political and property boundaries before finding new homes with their husbands from other important kin groups. Women of the highest status might even marry and divorce repeatedly, moving from one bed to another, one house to another, one set of affines to a new set, and crossing from one chiefdom to another—all the while maintaining their own loyalties to blood kin in another place altogether.[132] According to laws of sexual union, some contracts allowed women to stay put and let men visit them for reproductive sex. In unions by elopement or abduction, however, women moved in yet other ways across all sorts of territorial and social limits.[133] Even once married, some farm women annually left their homes and settlements to lead their animals up to higher ground in the summer. Although the community below might own the pastures above, women formed their own summer settlements within men's boundaries once each year.[134] Women and men both left home and sometimes natal territory to go on short pilgrimages or to join religious settlements permanently.[135]

Despite the opinions of legal writers, then, women constantly crossed boundaries not only between properties but also between families, communities, and even kingdoms, and may have done so more regularly than men, who were tied more firmly to patrilocal lands.[136]

Most women and men probably abided by and within the legal boundaries. But no woman helped to make or write about them. Despite legends about the jurist Brig, no real woman created or monitored the rules that kept the lines clear and the fences up. Legal boundaries were not as relevant to women's movements, nor were women's border crossings as important under the law. The map of legal properties, which seems so simple and transparent when noted down in seventh or eighth-century texts, officially tracked the places, boundaries, and movements of men but hid a second, buried map of the wanderings of women. The written laws reflected an enduring social principle: Gender, kinship, and boundaries were mutually influential upon the landscape. Gender directly affected women's uses of family properties, as well as their ability to move over land, gain, and give it. All writers and audiences knew that women had always been disenfranchised, had limited property rights, and could not travel as freely and visibly as men. Women crossed the lines that men drew between the physical and social spaces of families, political units, and territories.

Gender had been built into the Irish landscape long before Christians arrived. Land belong to men, but much of the landscape belonged to women—or, at least, to female entities. Legal properties and secure boundaries were gendered male, but mutable political territories and ambiguous sacral sites had feminine connotations. A long tradition of territorial goddesses persisted in the names and legends of natural features of the environment. The Boyne River, which wound through one of the island's greatest prehistoric necropolises, bore the name of the goddess Bóann. Emain Macha, the famous ritual complex, surmounted a hill named after the triple goddess Macha. Two hills of Kerry were named for the breasts of the protectress Anu. In some of the oldest vernacular legends of Ireland, supernatural mistresses from the otherworld decreed which warrior kings would build kingdoms and dynasties. Aspiring monarchs mated with these divinities to prove their virile right to rule historical territories. Even the annual festival at Tara supposedly involved the ritual coupling of a king and a goddess.[137]

While royal forts such as Dún Ailinne reminded Leinster folk of ancient kings and symbolized contemporary kingdoms, then, specific natural features also evoked the folklore of goddesses. Tombs and necropolises also called to mind pagan goddesses, because mounds offered entry to the otherworld. Bóann and her consorts still dwelt at the necropolis of the Boyne valley, where those pilgrims had dropped their Roman coins. On the unbuilt soil of Irish stories,

warriors wandered in eternal pursuit of rootless feuds, pausing only tempo-
rarily within the shelter of ephemeral walled enclosures where properly behaved women waited for them; but out on the land lurked equally ancient and
far more dangerous females. Men commanded settled places while females
haunted uninhabited spaces—wells, tombs, and abandoned forts.

Gender influenced both the theory and the practice of Irish religious landscapes. Early medieval writers used femaleness to represent the crossing and
transgression of boundaries, lost or inaccessible landscapes, and degenerate,
dangerous environments—that is, the land's most pagan places. Female characters moved through and took control of environments in ways that the real
women of early medieval Ireland never could. The goddess figures and other-
worldly women of story, for example, seem to have represented fickle eruptions
of nature that led to social or political chaos but not for everyone—only for
those men who had betrayed them.[138] In various early medieval texts, Mother
Ireland and Roisín Dubh did not welcome all their sons; they played favorites.[139]
The discursive landscapes of early Irish literature were neither negatively nor
positively female, nor even consistently female. The land was a woman when
it misdirected or harmed men. Survival depended on reading the landscape for
its fixed points and visible limits. Boundaries moved, people rearranged and
crossed them, and landmarks deceived because they were essentially female.

The first church builders were haunted by dead kings and feminine spirits.
Yet the gender of natural places offered builders and writers a comprehensible
sacral geography ripe for conversion. The division of places into live or dead,
Christian or pagan, male or female helped church builders situate themselves
when other landmarks did not suffice. The Irish read or heard of these ancient
geographical principles in legends and dynastic verses, as well as in hagiography and laws, but they also lived in constant sight of them. Dún Ailinne
and the other ancestral forts symbolized the ritual aspect of political power derived directly from the bodies of previous kings supposedly buried beneath the
monuments. Already in the fifth century, Dún Ailinne was a territorial relic, as
unreal as romances of protective goddesses. Church builders completed what
the ancients had begun, just as New Testament finished Old, and Christ's covenant replaced that of Moses. Christian builders made better use of the political
symbols, the spiritual resources, and the gendered meanings of the land than
had goddesses, ancient kings, or dynastic poets. At least, that is how the laws
and legends of early medieval writers remembered it.

In telling stories about the first cadres of Christian missionaries, authors
of the seventh and eighth centuries explicated the history connecting Christian
settlements and much older religious sites. New genres of Irish written memory, such as dynastic poems, monastic annals, and hagiography synthesized the

histories of kings and saints. Writers loaded regnal sites, family properties, and Christian settlements into one symbolic geography. The concept of powerfully gendered places was also potentially useful to enterprising architects of Christian landscapes. The new religion offered another set of markers and boundaries by which to judge and gender trespassers and control the land's willfulness. Proselytizers roamed Ireland's territories like warriors and migrants in predictable, customary ways. They were by vocation transgressors of boundaries and takers of properties. Like women, church builders had a natural right to trespass if their crossings had positive consequences. Their disruptions led to more stable settlement and the establishment of Christian territories visibly fixed by permanent landmarks. Christian men and even a few persuasive Christian women could justify their travel along well-signposted roads from one fixed ecclesiastical point to another by the doctrinal imperatives of conversion and pilgrimage.

The gendered implications of property, borders, and landscapes were boon and curse for Christian organizers. Patrick had mentioned slave girls who fled their owners in order to convert. Tírechán told of virgins who crossed over to heaven, using their bodies to transform pagan places into Christian burials. By the seventh century, when Cogitosus celebrated Brigit's long career of travel and building, plenty of women and men were Christians. A considerable number of them were living as vowed professionals in religious settlements; either they had left home or they had given their family property over to Christian purpose. Indigenous gender practices, which emphasized the stasis and the legal inferiority of women, continued to make possible and yet to complicate the creation and use of exclusively female religious space. The organizers of parishes and monasteries constantly wondered where to put female Christians. Who owned Christian space? Who set its limits? Should women worship where men did? Could holy women create boundaries and designate ritual space in the same ways, to the same extent, as missionaries and saintly men? Did Christianity trump gender and traditional law? Or were the boundary crossings of female travelers and builders always transgressive, no matter what religion set the limits? Was there something immutably feminine about non-Christian places and a bit of paganism in every woman?

Certainly in the seventh century, when Irish hagiographers worked, and probably in the late fifth, when Brigit supposedly came to Kildare, Irish communities were sorting out these problems everywhere that indigenous traditions met Christian *romanitas*. It had happened in Gaul and would happen again in Anglo-Saxon Britain and later in Germany. In Ireland, where population and settlement remained stable but territories did not, Christian practice collided with traditionally gendered interpretations of property and boundaries.

The delicate balance of stable but unmarked ritual sites, shifting political land-scapes, and hereditary properties needed only a little nudging to collapse. Instead it received an earthquake of change in the shape of christianization and the desire for Rome. New kinds of territories and properties, new sacral sites, and new architecture required women to move upon and use the landscape in distinctly unwomanly ways.

Brigit arrived in the middle of the quake, after the introduction of *romani-tas* but before its absorption into the Irish landscape, at the moment when the goddesses were sinking below the earth's surface forever. Unlike Patrick, she chose a place for herself. Her community at Kildare and the historical record of her life begun by Cogitosus offered an alternative solution to the vexed problems of where to put churches and how to include women in Christianity. It was neither the solution that Patrick's hagiographers proposed nor the answer eventually favored by the medieval ecclesiastical establishment, but it always remained an option. While Patrick's job, according to his own *Confessio*, had been to convert placeless souls, Brigit's aim, according to her seventh-century vita by Cogitosus, was to create a new kind of uniquely Irish ecclesiastical territory and cover it with *ruama*—little Romes.

6

Ekphrasis at Kildare

In the later fifth century, when Brigit had supposedly walked Ireland, Christian holy places were still in the making.[1] Preachers were still hauling their religious merchandise up rivers and down well-trodden tracks to farmsteads and kings' houses. Christianity was only slowly becoming a native manufacture. Bishops produced converts, some of whom became priests who then produced more converts. And yet for the next century and more, the Irish remained unsure about how Christians should behave and what Christianity should look like. From Brigit's time through Cogitosus's day, believers negotiated with clergy, scholars, and rulers about crucial issues of religious space and identity. Church organizers continued to legislate about how Christians should live their religion.[2] Meanwhile, devotees of the most holy dead crafted new definitions of sanctity to suit Ireland. They argued over which founder of churches was most deserving of veneration and whose congregation was the richest, most politically powerful, and divinely favored. At the same time, experts in theology and cosmology calculated lunar cycles and the passage of years, fabricating a calendar to parallel an older pastoral rhythm of seasons and holidays.

In the seventh century, when Kildare flourished, the Irish were arguing over the date of Easter and the identity of saints, but they had learned which places in Ireland were most holy and how to build and use them. Tírechán might betray some anxiety about the insidious influence of pagan places, but Brigit's settlement was proud proof of how much rearranging Irish Christians had already accomplished since Patrick's mission. Brigit's body lay honorably enshrined and crowned inside the great church (*basilica maxima*) at Kildare, one of the island's largest and wealthiest monasteries for women and men and the seat of important bishops. In about 650, when Cogitosus wrote the first extant vita of Saint Brigit, Kildare headed a confederation (*paruchia*) of religious settlements that stretched in all directions across the limits of any single tribal kingdom and even beyond Leinster's provincial borders. This network of churches and monasteries rivaled in prestige and wealth the organizations of Saint Patrick at Ard Macha (Armagh), Coemgen at neighboring Glenn Da Locha (Kevin, Glendalough), Comgall at Bennchor (Bangor), and Columcille on Í (Columba, Iona). No other woman's foundation or women's community came to command such an extensive network of dependent foundations.

Like Genovefa, Brigit had gained a reputation for proselytizing by miracle, movement, and construction rather than by martyrdom or asceticism. In the seventh century, she was the only Irish woman famous for traveling and building, although there were hints of others, and more builders would follow. Brigit had become the same kind of saint as Genovefa in a similar sort of historical moment, that is, when change in religious habit made it possible for a woman to express unusual authority visually and materially. But Brigit followed routes uniquely Irish and built something appropriate only for Irish Christians. Whereas Genovefa had assumed authority over an ancient city and an imperial territory by circling and confirming existing boundaries, Brigit took control by transgressing political and property boundaries made by men. By comparison, Patrick had confessed little interest in a territorial diocese, although he came to be celebrated for founding an episcopal hierarchy modeled on existing tribal kingdoms. Instead, Brigit built a monastic city, laid down roads to it, and made the land around it safe for all good pilgrims who would follow her there. Then she set other women to do the same all across Ireland.

We know nothing about Brigit before Cogitosus wrote, and nothing sure about him except that he recorded the travels and miracles of Brigit. The span between his life and hers was almost two centuries, compared with the mere twenty years or so separating Genovefa's death and her hagiographer's text. Cogitosus recalled a Brigit no more familiar to him than Patrick was to Tírechán and Muirchú. The latter two hagiographers had Patrick's *Confessio* as evidence, along with traditions kept by Patrick's devotees at many northern churches. Cogitosus had two written sources, now lost, and whatever churchmen and churchwomen of Kildare could tell him. But he also had Brigit's own settlement, founded by her as home, whereas Patrick had never been abbot or bishop of a particular place. She was a native. He was not. What is more, Patrick's burial site was disputed and his relics scattered. Kildare was Brigit's chosen resting place. The body was there for all to see. For Christian followers of Brigit, other aspiring hagiographers, and cult builders, Cogitosus offered a uniquely reliable resource. Kildare, in all its built glory, was proof for everything he wrote.

Cogitosus's vita propelled Brigit from fifth-century obscurity to her visible resting place in the renowned seventh-century church of Kildare. Devotees would praise Brigit for commanding nature and healing the faithful, but Cogitosus intended her as a saint who accomplished changes in the land and successfully redirected the views of the Leinster Irish across the southern sea. The hagiographer revealed every meaningful step of Brigit's journey from birth, across the threshold of death, to the Christian afterlife. He showed how Brigit offered refuge to Irish women and men desperate for shelter in the wilderness. For those who did not know the way to Rome, or who longed to see little Romes on the hills and plains of Ireland, Brigit revealed paths. According to her vita, Brigit circled Ireland, gathering the faithful to her, but always returned to her province of Leinster and its Christian heart at Kildare. Brigit marked her tracks, according to Cogitosus, with architecture built in the universal language of Christian pilgrimage. Her greatest contribution to the landscape of Irish Christianity was the fixed point of her church and city.

Cogitosus chose to commemorate Brigit in a new genre of architectural hagiography, providing at once a saintly legend of traffic, a history of ecclesiastical building, and a map for his own generation of Christian travelers. He combined a narrative of the saint's life from birth to death with an Irish version of classical *ekphrasis*, the vivid rhetorical, symbolic, and even fictive description of a visual scene or physical objects—in this case, the architecture and decor of the seventh-century church at Kildare. Unlike the panegyrical *ekphrasis* of ancient writers, Cogitosus's text did not have any formal aesthetic aim beyond impressing audiences with the grandeur of Brigit's church and tomb. But, as in contemporary Byzantine *ekphrasis*, Cogitosus intended his text to parallel and evoke a work of architecture rather than illuminating its physical reality.[3] Like a medieval Baedeker, his description was packed with practical visual cues for those ignorant of Rome but desirous of it, and who sought it in Brigit's city. Together in one vita, Brigit's life narrative and Kildare's architectural description guided readers and pilgrims through the landscapes of Ireland to Brigit's body, which in Cogitosus's mind marked the most sacred, most Christian, most romanized place on the island.

Text, tomb, and ritual were as inseparable to Cogitosus as were event and symbol, image and word, saint's life and saint's body, or biblical past and Christian present. The church described in such detail by the hagiographer evoked events that continuously occurred there—the harmonious hymns, the chanted prayers, the processions lit by candles and performed in honor of the holy woman Brigit who presided from her tomb. Cogitosus's description of the church and tomb also recalled other shrines, other times, and other sacred cities. Traveling with Brigit and Cogitosus puts us purposefully on a map of early medieval architecture, pilgrimage, literature, and ritual that stretched from Jerusalem and Constantinople through the Rome of Old Saint Peter's, past the episcopal towns of Gaul to Kildare and Saint Brigit.

Cogitosus's Aims and Audiences

Not all of Cogitosus's audiences would have readily understood his Christian *ekphrasis* or connected Brigit's deeds with the architecture of Kildare. Cogitosus came of a literate elite conversant with patristics, Continental hagiography, the rules and laws of Christianity, grammar, and even rarer sciences. For the most sensitive and intimate devotees, an incident in Brigit's childhood may have echoed the details of her shrine, its placement in the church, and the kinds of rituals conducted around it. For less informed audiences, Cogitosus built these conceptual links episode by episode, relying on literary structures and themes already traditional in hagiography by 650. He presented an argument for Brigit's *virtus* or saintly power. He recounted the history of Brigit and Kildare and offered information about the practice and meaning of her cult. He provided biblical and theological lessons. Cogitosus wrote for all of them: the educated clerics who would appreciate his literary tricks, the ecclesiastical colleagues at Armagh and the secular chieftains inside and outside of Leinster who listened for Kildare's political aspirations, and pious foreigners unfamiliar with Brigit and Ireland. None of these was his target audience, though. Cogitosus wrote principally for the congregants and pilgrims who visited—or might someday visit—Brigit at her shrine. He told the life of the saint but at the same time explained to audiences where to find Brigit and what to do when they entered the awesome presence of the holy dead.

When Cogitosus wrote, the religious settlement at Kildare had probably existed for close to two centuries. His vita, like the two seventh-century lives of Patrick, suggests an Ireland littered with small religious settlements organized in networks called *paruchiae* (sg. *paruchia*), much like tribal confederations and, indeed, overlapping them. Patrick's *paruchia* partnered with tribes of the Uí Néill and Brigit's with several leading tribes of Leinster. Cogitosus addressed the vita of Brigit to his fellow monks (*fratres*) at Kildare and to the religious professionals who tended the client churches of Kildare's confederation. Brigit's *paruchia*, according to Cogitosus, extended over Ireland from sea

to sea and was jointly ruled by an abbess "whom all the abbesses of the Irish revere" and an "archbishop of the bishops of Ireland."[4] Cogitosus meant that the
settlement at Kildare, besides having monks, included nuns, priests, at least
one bishop, and an abbess. He also referred to laypeople occupying outlying
properties at Kildare (*suburbana*), thus emphasizing the community's size and
wealth, and implying an audience for the annual reading of Brigit's vita.[5]

Cogitosus began with the usual apology for literary ineptitude. He also
warned readers in both introduction and conclusion that he had carefully
crafted his history of Brigit's deeds. He had rearranged and edited his unnamed
sources, rejected a normative life-to-death narrative, and left out information
about some of the saint's multitudinous wonders.[6] His story proper began with
Brigit's parentage. She was born a saint in the first chapter, foreknown by God
and, as Cogitosus wrote, "predestined according to his own image." By the end
of chapter 2, she had chosen a life of chastity and religion over marriage. In
subsequent passages Brigit continued to work homely miracles for reapers and
bishops, sheep and pregnant women, poor wanderers and blind men. Cogitosus
included some thirty episodes concerning Brigit's miracles and travels around
Ireland, arranged to make thematic points rather than to chronicle the years of
the saint's earthly life. After a brief mention of the saint's death, he described
posthumous miracles that he himself had witnessed at Kildare. He finished the
vita with a detailed description, unique in early Irish hagiography, of the main
church at Kildare and an account of the celebrations of Brigit's feast day there.
His last words were a pious plea: "Pray for me, Cogitosus, sinful descendant of
Áed" ("Orate pro me Cogitoso nepote culpabili Aedo").[7]

Although Cogitosus structured the vita after familiar saintly models, all of
which were male, he created in Brigit a distinctively Irish holy woman.[8] He had
no female Irish exemplars, for this was the first native-born vita. His saint could
not claim hagiographic descent from the educated cosmopolitans of Jerome's
fifth-century world. Genovefa provided no explicit example; her deeds resonated with those of Brigit only because the saints shared gendered constraints
on travel, building, and Christian preaching. Although one Frankish clerk is
known to have been in Ireland right before Cogitosus wrote, and though he
even became bishop of Paris shortly after, no manuscripts of Genovefa's life
reached Kildare, so far as we know.[9] Nor did other Frankish female saints provide any explicit sources for Cogitosus. Brigit was not a royal politico, like her
contemporary Saint Radegund, celebrated by Bishop Venantius and the nun
Baudonivia.[10] To foreign and native readers alike, the simple phrase *in Scotia
orta* (born in Ireland) would have signified Brigit's unique provincial origins
beyond the reach of Rome and its established hagiographic models for women.
Her domestic miracles of feeding, providing, and herding did not necessarily

mark her as a female saint but placed her in a rural barbarian milieu. Her background in the fields and kitchens of her parents typed her as *rustica,* an illiterate of peasant stock only recently christianized. To all Cogitosus's readers, Brigit belonged on the farm, but Irish audiences would also have recognized the relative unimportance of Brigit's "Christian but noble" descent from the Fothairt, a tribe occupying what is now modern county Louth.[11] Brigit's arenas were remote pastures and isolated houses, not episcopal cities, royal palaces, or the provincial retreats of romanized Europeans.

Cogitosus structured the Life of Brigit as an *iter,* or pilgrimage from her birthplace to her death-place, and from obscurity to fame. He sent Brigit on her life's journey in order to establish Kildare's authority among churches in Leinster and the community's influence in other Irish provinces beyond its immediate territorial possessions. Brigit's circuits through Ireland, to Patrick's Armagh and churches of other provinces, had blatant political implications, underscoring the explicit claims made by Cogitosus to the transregional jurisdiction of Brigit's abbatial and episcopal successors. In the hagiographer's time, Irish ecclesiastics were debating some key organizational and liturgical matters. Cogitosus was one of many scholars scattered in Irish monasteries who seem to have been familiar with the debate over the computus (the science of harmonizing lunar and solar calendars) and standardization of the liturgical calendar, the regulation of sacral spaces, and questions of episcopal authority. The clergy of Kildare were not even invited to one particularly important discussion of the liturgical calendar, probably because they had already chosen to follow Rome's lead in Christendom's arguments about the date of Easter.[12] Irish church leaders of the seventh century were trying to establish a hierarchical organization and to define their relations to Rome and Continental churches.[13]

Still, Cogitosus was not interested in the extent of Brigit's territory or Kildare's place in the hierarchy so much as her cult's architectural and ritual capital. While he claimed an expansive *paruchia* for Kildare and directly raised the issue of *romanitas*—intentional Romanness or romanization—in both his narrative and his *ekphrasis,* he never mentioned specific churches established by the saint beyond Kildare. Rather than place Brigit in the episcopal debates of the seventh century or imbue her with the by-now stereotypical traits of Continental women saints, Cogitosus established her place in a larger, civilized Christendom in two other ways. First, he emphasized her *imitatio Christi* and her similarity to biblical prophets. Second, he built for her, by his words, a church of marvelously romanizing pretensions, thus putting Kildare and its saint on the Christian map. What mattered to Cogitosus was not how many miles separated Kildare from Rome but how close an approximation Brigit's followers could make of Rome at home.

The hagiographer revealed Brigit's expanding influence paragraph by paragraph, step by step, as she journeyed through her vita to Kildare. At the same time, more and more characters in the vita moved in the opposite direction, toward the saint. In the first scenes of the text Brigit acted alone or with a few others in domestic space.[14] But soon individual paupers and pilgrims, and then whole "droves" were "flocking to her from all sides attracted by the enormous renown of her miracles and of her lavish generosity." In a land where most houses were tiny mud and stick huts, and where the Romans had built no cities for medieval Christians to ruin or rehabilitate, Cogitosus imagined the saint meeting her flock in large, open spaces.[15] Like the peripatetic Jesus of John's gospel who had no permanent venue, she came to them outside farmhouses and on hillsides. When the crowds got larger, Brigit sought other sorts of public sites, such as the hilltops where legendary warriors had traditionally inaugurated their kings, or the plains where they gathered for "fairs" (óenaig) and other pagan ritual events. By this point in the vita, the saint was driving by chariot to major assemblies, one of which was with a "multitude" at the king's house (*palatium*), another at an unspecified gathering place.[16] At the same time, the crowds came from farther away; her acquaintances had come to include not just local or provincial countrymen but a man "from a distant province" (*delongens veniens provincia*). Brigit's clientele, her fame, and her dominion grew simultaneously. Even as Cogitosus described the saint's increasing reputation, he himself contributed to it with a vita that labeled her deeds "amazing and worthy of admiration," performed in "imitation of the person of God like the Saviour" and otherwise "famous," "admired," and shedding "lustre" on the saint.[17] All she needed to accommodate her followers was a home with large, accessible spaces, especially after she died and her charismatic presence became less visible.

The author, who must have been intimate with the country surrounding Kildare, chose not to substantiate the settings of most of the vita. Yet Brigit's miracles demonstrated her special ability to convert landscapes from wild to safe, hostile to habitable, ill-defined to specifically Christian. Cogitosus's audiences would have understood Brigit's journey to her tomb at Kildare as a sacralizing progress through an imperfect natural world full of pain, illness, hunger, and injustice. Like many early saints she was a weathermaster and commander of animals. She tamed a fox, halted a wild boar, caught a duck in her arms, prevented rain, and hung her cloak on a sunbeam.[18] When the land and its beasts did not produce enough, she increased their fertility, as when she caused a cow to give milk three times in one day, or was led by bees to hidden honey.[19] She transformed basic elements of the earth into nourishment, changing stone to salt and water to ale.[20] She rescued humans from illnesses and defects that were predictably natural, sparing one woman an unwanted pregnancy and restoring sight, speech, and movement to other sufferers.[21] She guided cattle, horses, pigs, and humans that lost their way in the wilderness.[22] Twice, she shifted the river boundaries of landscapes, once in order to protect her livestock and once to help her kinsmen.[23] She never contended with sinners or druids for territory, as Patrick did in his earliest vitae, although she did deny use of her mill (and thus sustenance) to a druid.[24] Nor, as in her later vitae, did she actually consecrate space with formal Christian rituals. Yet, like Moses, she witnessed wood burnt but not consumed and, like her Saviour, she multiplied food and fed the multitudes.[25]

Brigit's mere presence imparted a quality of sanctity to the land. In one story, when a chaste woman escaped from a lustful nobleman who schemed to enslave her, the victim "fled for safety to saint Brigit as to the safest city of refuge" ("quasi ad civitatem refugii tutissimam").[26] In each episode of her journey Brigit transformed its setting so that, as Cogitosus put it, "from all this it can be clearly understood that the whole of nature, beasts, cattle and birds, was subjected to her power," as well, apparently, as wicked men.[27] The untamed, unyielding Ireland of the past had given way to Brigit's prosperous sanctuary. In the context of Cogitosus's inexact settings, Brigit's ability to transform landscapes created a historical and physical distance between the saint and her audiences, similar to the screens and grilles dividing pilgrims from saintly tombs; they could approach but never touch. Her body, placed in a reliquary-tomb at Kildare, continued to infuse the landscape and its human settlement with numinous efficacy.[28]

Cogitosus anchored Brigit to an identifiable site only after her spiritual departure from the flesh, purposefully contrasting the mostly anonymous countryside traveled by the living saint with the settlement at Kildare. He gave no account of the founding of Kildare and made just a brief notice of her death ("she laid down the burden of her flesh"), mentioning that her miracles continued where "her venerable body" rested, in locales that could be visited and revisited. By the time readers finished Brigit's journey and reached these last chapters, then, the landscapes of the vita had become identifiable and even tangible. What is more, Cogitosus's proofs for Brigit's *virtus* became increasingly solid. In the final chapters of the vita, Cogitosus relied not on hearsay, which he had used for evidence in most of the vita, but on visible evidence of particular spots in or near Kildare that he had "not only heard of but seen with [his] own eyes."[29]

The vita gathered narrative momentum toward the end, propelling readers to Cogitosus's home and Brigit's ultimate destination, Kildare. After chronicling many events in small, nameless houses and churches, Cogitosus lingered in his final chapter over the description of Brigit's greatest contribution: her shrine and church (*basilica maxima*) within her monastic city. None of the other events of the vita elicited such topographical or architectural specificity. Kildare was only the only "real" place in the hagiographer's cosmos and the only accessible site on Brigit's life itinerary.[30] Brigit's tomb was the focus of Cogitosus's geographic strategy. His literary method was to combine vita with architectural description. His targets were resident nuns and clerics, pilgrims, congregants, and all other visitors to Saint Brigit's body. Some were ready to appreciate his alignment of Brigit's personal past with the past of Old Testament and Gospels, his explications of her *virtus* via the transformation of landscapes, and his political messages about territorial politics. To instruct his readers and keep their attention, he offered a stunning and memorable explication of the saint's final earthly abode.

Ekphrasis at Kildare

Kildare was a marvel of romanizing and urbanizing architecture in the mid–seventh century, unique in Ireland when Cogitosus described it—or so his text claimed. The church was not the only site but was certainly the main sight to see in the *civitas* (city) of Kildare. "City is the right word for it," Cogitosus wrote. "That so many people are living there justifies the title," claimed the Irishman from an island with no experience of cities or of Continental architecture, and no memory of Roman presence. Nonetheless, he enthused over the settlement in terms laden with purposeful *romanitas*.[31] Kildare was a *maxima metropolitana* (great episcopal town), within whose sanctified boundaries no enemies were feared. It was a "refuge among all the towns of the whole land of the Irish, with all their fugitives." It was a place where kings kept treasure, where everything was "reckoned to be supreme in good order" ("et decorati culminis excellentissima esse videntur"). The crowds were already flocking there as they had to the living saint, Cogitosus assured his readers, for festivals, for people-watching, and to bring donations to Brigit, "who on the First of February, falling asleep, safely laid down the burden of her flesh and followed the Lamb of God into the heavenly mansions" (*coelestibus mansionibus*). Likewise, readers of the vita followed the pilgrims' track to Kildare.

If Cogitosus's description of the church was accurate, the building deserved his boasts. Most Irish churches of the period were small, rectangular structures of wood surrounded by ditches or walls of a larger circular enclosure.[32] Even the biggest buildings were meant as focal points of clerical ceremony or monastic practice rather than as shelters for large congregational gatherings. They sometimes housed bones or secondary relics, but the Irish more commonly lay their saints outside church, in special slab-lined graves or exterior shrines in cemeteries.[33] Not all churches were lucky enough to have the bodies of their founders as did Kildare. Although the names of these other churches and shrines appear in hagiography, annals, and other documents, and many still exist as modern place-names, few descriptions of their design remain. The hagiographic material closest in date to Cogitosus's work—the life of Patrick by Muirchú and itinerary by Tírechán, and Adomnán's Life of Columcille—mention far simpler churches.[34] Tírechán referred in his *Collectanea* of Patrick to rectangular churches (*aecclesias quadratas*) and "a square earthen church of clay." He also named a *basilica sanctorum*, implying a foreign-style church founded by foreigners, but the hagiographer never described the building; he may have regarded it as a place-name. The *Liber Angeli* also referred interchangeably to a "southern" basilica or church (*aeclessia*) at Armagh where only bishops, priests, and monks held services. Eventually, Armagh's main church was a different structure dedicated to Patrick at the city's center.[35] Tírechán's contemporary Muirchú understood the word *basilica* to mean *regularis domus* or *regnum*: that is, a king's house or the kingdom itself. Likewise, Irish canonists of the eighth century used the word for a royal graveyard.[36]

Only one other seventh-century Irish writer described a church in any detail. The poetic primer *Hisperica Famina* contains fourteen lines about a square wooden church with towers, a central altar, portico, and "innumerable objects" of decoration (*innumera plasmamina*), although with only a single door.[37] None of these texts suggested visual or textual models for Cogitosus, however, or romanizing influence. In his eyes, Brigit's church was no typical Irish *domnach* or *cell* (although the settlement itself was Cell Dara, "church of the oak tree"), no humble wooden chapel in the "Irish fashion," in Bede's slighting reference.[38] Like his *iter* of Brigit, his elaborate explication of Kildare and its structures was innovative in Ireland, although not in other Christian contexts of the period.

Cogitosus placed his architectural description immediately after Brigit's demise. He led his readers down a verbal path from the saint's death to the entrance of her church, bridging the chasm between carnal life and saintly afterlife with his text. His narrative described the route of the very pilgrims who came—as the previous chapters of the vita hopefully suggested—from increasingly afar to approach the saint's tomb and church. He intended the events that followed Brigit's obituary to demonstrate the saint's continuing powers among the living at Kildare but, more important, to prepare the hagiographic site for details of church and settlement. He ended the text with a detailed, physical, and symbolic description of paths, buildings, and spaces at Kildare. He wrote of sanctity and cult in the language of built environments and interior design, employing a nuanced architectural vocabulary clearly acquired from non-Irish sources. Cogitosus may never have seen a church better than the church at

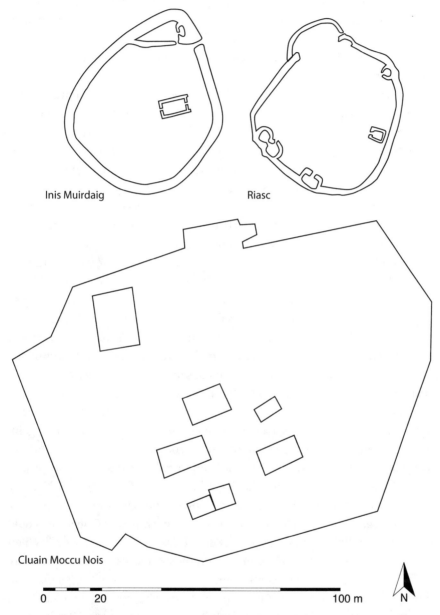

Inis Muirdaig

Riasc

Cluain Moccu Nois

0   20   100 m   N

FIGURE 6.1. Irish ecclesiastical communities: Inis Muiredaig, Riasc, Cluain Moccu Nóis (John Marston after Herity and Evans).

Kildare, but he had probably read of them in the panegyrics and church histories of Continental writers and heard of them from Irish travelers. (He never directly quoted foreign architectural descriptions, but then, he never quoted the vitae of Martin or Benedict, although he used them as hagiographic models for his saint.) His rendering of the church at Kildare was his contribution to an already ancient tradition of Christian *ekphrasis*, but set in an innovative, Irish, hagiographic context.

Cogitosus's architectural passages began with the tale of a miraculously found and transported millstone, which the saint had helped Kildare's prior and stonecutters to move. The men had selected a huge stone atop a rocky mountain, carving it on site. Neither men nor oxen could bring the finished stone down, though, so they heaved it off the summit while "invoking the name and power of the most revered saint Brigit."[39] Brigit guided the millstone past other rocks, marshy ground, and all other hindrances to the mill below. In case the saint's devotees could not recognize the wondrous nature of this event, Cogitosus pointed out that the millstone also refused to grind a druid's grain. Because of the stone's miraculous origins and history, the leaders of Kildare eventually moved it to the gate of the walls around Brigit's sanctuary.

From hilltop, where the stone was found, down the rocky summit, across bogs to the mill site, then into the settlement of Kildare and to the courtyard walls surrounding Brigit's own church, Cogitosus's readers followed that stone. In the hagiographer's own time, a touch of the millstone healed pilgrims of disease. But this was not just another miraculous detail. Cogitosus was instructing visitors to Kildare in the ritual of entering the courtyard of the church. The ill or physically flawed, Cogitosus's text explained, were to pause at the entrance to the inner courtyard to seek a cure. Whole and wholly Christian once again, they could enter the sanctuary and rejoin the congregation. Cogitosus thus allowed his audience to reenact a miracle from Brigit's posthumous past. He also showed them how to enact the theological hierarchy of believers practiced by other Christians, which prevented catechumens, sinners, and the chronically ill from entering the most important spaces within churches. Only Brigit could disclose the religion's most important mysteries to those excluded.[40] When healthy pilgrims saw the stone, they too remembered its miraculous history and thanked Brigit for their membership in the community of Christians. Visitors to Kildare and readers of Cogitosus could visualize this external feature of Kildare's architecture and mentally link it in space and time to Brigit's past, current liturgical practice, and theology.[41] Journey, entry, and the crossing of boundaries were central themes in the iconography of Brigit and her church.

After the miracle of the stone, Cogitosus lured readers inside the surrounding walls to the church door. From the bright sun outside, the pilgrim stepped into an interior lit by the church's windows and lamps, his or her fuddled gaze moving immediately to the illuminated spectacle partially visible through yet another set of openings at the far eastern end of the church. There,

> the glorious bodies of both—namely Archbishop Conleth and our most flourishing virgin Brigit—are laid on the right and left of the ornate altar and rest in tombs adorned with a refined profusion of gold, silver, gems and precious stones with gold and silver chandeliers hanging from above and different images presenting a variety of carving and colors.[42]

Cogitosus, having chaperoned readers inside, laid out the church: its spacious floor, its high roof, its three separate areas (*oratoria*) partitioned with walls and hangings. The building was cut lengthwise (east to west) by a screen or wall that divided it effectively into two naves. Toward the eastern end, another decorated partition or *iconostasis* ran crosswise (north to south), creating a kind of chapel for the altar and tombs. Internal openings in the shorter cross-wall allowed abbess, nuns, bishop, and monks to enter the sanctuary where the saints reposed. Textiles hung in these openings. A southern external door allowed priests and laymen into one of the larger naves, while the northern door opened the other nave to virgins and other women. "And so, in one great basilica," Cogitosus wrote, "a large number of people, arranged by rank and sex, in orderly division separated by partitions, offers prayers with a single spirit to the almighty Lord." Joining their voices in prayer and hymn, ecclesiastics, pilgrims, and congregants observed an order implied by architectural design.

Cogitosus's *ekphrasis* was full of learned references to other built Christian spaces. He drew on several sources for his visual rhetoric, including the evidence of his own eyes at Kildare and an architectural idiom shared with near neighbors in Gaul and Britain. Some of his references were to existing buildings, some to symbolic interpretations of structures elsewhere, and still others to the lessons of his own narrative of Brigit's life. But all combined to form one intricate theology of display. What is more, Cogitosus probably wrote to commemorate the translation of the saint's remains and the rebuilding of Brigit's church, the latter process described in his last chapter. Translation and rebuilding were traditional inspirations for Christian *ekphrasis*.[43] Kildare's leadership, sometime between Brigit's death around 524 and Cogitosus's vita written around 650, must have decided to enhance their city and bulwark Brigit's cult with a pilgrimage center and more elaborate shrine. In this effort, Kildare was unique in Ireland but not among the edifices of other Christian landscapes.[44] The fifth and sixth centuries had been periods of intense church-building for

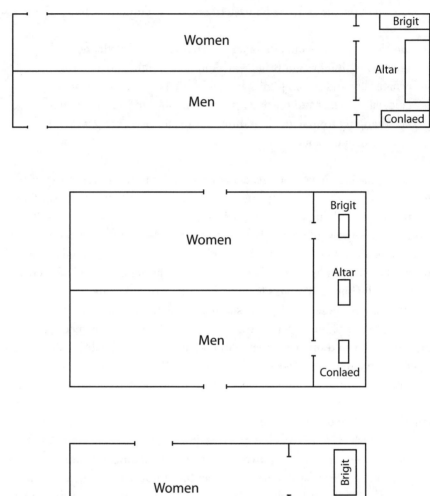

FIGURE 6.2. Modern designs for original basilica at Kildare (John Marston, after Macalister, Thomas, and Neuman de Vegvar).

new Christian congregations in the provinces, as well as the recovery of crumbling churches and decaying martyred bodies. Contemporary sources from
other places around the Continent besides Paris record the revamping of existing buildings. The *Liber Pontificalis*, for example, a running history of the
popes written and redacted around the mid–sixth century, listed the constant
expansion and redecorating projects sponsored by more than two centuries of
pontiffs.[45]

Cogitosus considered his project to be part of a larger process of rebuilding saints' cults with basilicas, even if Kildare's church resembled nothing
constructed between Sicily and Brittany. Other builders throughout formerly
Roman territory also called their memorial shrines to the saintly dead *basilicae*,
as Genovefa referred to Denis's shrine, though they also named them *ecclesiae*,
oratoria, *martyria*, and *mausolea*. Sometimes such churches had small chambers (*exedrae*) or apses projecting from the nave for special reliquaries or the
thrones of bishops, as Holy Apostles had. Even English clerics built churches
on such a plan at Monkwearmouth, Jarrow, and Malmesbury during the later
seventh century, at least one of which was called a *basilica*.[46] When Cogitosus
described walls and screens in his church, he envisioned complex, multipur-
pose, multichambered churches.[47] When he wrote of Kildare's numerous windows, he had in mind the luminous basilicas at Rome and Tours, where the
fifth-century building featured 120 columns and fifty-two windows.[48] Whatever
the actual appearance of the church at Kildare, Cogitosus saw before him a sub-
stantial structure for Christian congregational worship that paid homage to native saints and Roman forms.[49] His label for it—*basilica maxima*—encouraged
readers to imagine Kildare as one in a chain of churches stretching to Rome.
He was well aware that no other Irish church formed a link in the chain.

Kildare's *basilica* also offered a material reminder of Brigit's sanctity, her
place in the worldwide company of the saintly dead, and her leadership of a
Christian community. Brigit and her bishop Conláed lay, like companionable
episcopal partners, at the heart of the settlement, deep inside the larger *civitas*
of Kildare, at the end of the pilgrim's track. The builders of Kildare had flanked
the sanctuary altar with Brigit on the more honorable right side, facing the
nave, and Conláed on the left, thus reinforcing Conláed's minor role in Brigit's
life and ecclesiastical organization. Their placement signified the administrative status of the abbess-saint who, with her attending bishop, had founded the
"feminine and episcopal see" of Kildare. The layout of the great church and the
position of Brigit and Conláed put the saint and her first bishop in the midst of
all ceremonies, along with the living abbess and bishop who performed them.
The saint presided at every mass. Her presence inspired later hagiographers,
who represented her as the only female bishop of early Christendom, uniquely

episcopal among female saints and uniquely feminine among the Christian leaders of early medieval Ireland.[50] In addition, the geography of the two saints' burials mirrored the social and moral hierarchy of Brigit's parishioners and Christian communities generally. In the sixth century, only founding saints and bishops lay inside the church walls, while even kings lay with other believers *extra muros*, beyond the sacred interior.[51]

But Cogitosus relied on more than the evidence of his own eyes to describe Kildare. In addition to the author's familiarity with architecture and burial practices at episcopal churches elsewhere, his *ekphrasis* intentionally recalled other writers' descriptions of churches in other regions of Christendom. Cogitosus never named his literary sources, but his description of Kildare's church and its contents resonated with other ceremonial descriptions of churches from the sixth and seventh centuries. Gregory of Tours wrote of several churches, including that at Clermont-Ferrand, which had so many grand windows, mosaics, and varieties of marble that believers inside it had to employ more than one sense: they were simultaneously "conscious of the fear of God and of a great brightness," as well as a "most sweet and aromatic odor."[52] Gregory's words enabled readers to relive the environment of his shrine but also to think beyond it, to the indescribable, extrasensory experience of communing with God. Just as every saint negotiated between believers and God, so architecture and its description lifted pilgrims beyond the visual to the spiritual.[53]

Cogitosus's orderly description functioned in the same way as the *tituli* or inscriptions carved and painted onto the walls of English and Continental churches. Both kinds of text taught worshipers how to move through the church while understanding its design and decor. Labels on the frescoes in Martin's churches at Tours and Marmoutiers helped pilgrims interpret the symbolism of what they saw, just as modern museum labels do for today's tourists. "As you enter the church lift your eyes upward," read one epigraph, "a deep faith recognizes the lofty entrances." By the painted scenes of apostles and images of the Sepulcher at Jerusalem, another *titulus* ordered,

> You who have knelt on the ground, lowered your face to the dust,
> and pressed your moist eyes to the compacted ground,
> lift your eyes and with a trembling gaze look at the miracles
> and entrust your cause to the distinguished patron.
> No page can embrace such miracles.
> Even though the very blocks and stones are engraved with these
>   inscriptions,
> a terrestrial building does not enclose what the royal palace of
>   heaven

acknowledges and the stars inscribe in glittering jewels.
If you seek Martin's assistance, rise beyond the stars
and touch the heavens.[54]

These lines integrated the pilgrim's act, his or her sensory environment, and the many possible interpretations of things and spaces around him or her. The words themselves became part of the pilgrimage experience. Afterward, they became another kind of text, recorded in a manuscript appended to stories of Martin that allowed readers elsewhere to enter the shrine of the saint. Other writers did the same for other saints. Paulinus of Périgueux wrote such *tituli*, or dedicatory inscriptions descriptive of churches, as did Venantius Fortunatus, who evoked an entire landscape of Christian architecture at poetic length in his *Carmina*.[55]

Like basilica architecture and hagiographic models, the tradition of architectural description and instruction spread across the sea routes to Britain and Ireland, where Cogitosus and other writers composed *ekphrases*. Christians had returned to Britain (or returned to daylight) in the century or so before Cogitosus wrote. Aldhelm, abbot of Malmesbury and bishop of Sherbourne (d. 709), composed poems for a mixed community of religious men and women. In fact, Cogitosus may have inspired Aldhelm, who read Irish religious works, whose own writings were copied in Ireland, and who composed for female audiences and patrons as well as for men.[56] Aldhelm's poem in dedication of Saint Mary's church near Malmesbury for the abbess Bugge (ca. 675) combined material and symbolic description of the building with an account of rituals performed there by a community of nuns and monks. His verses about the new construction are similar in structure and vocabulary to Cogitosus's description of Kildare, thus helping us to interpret the more elliptical phrasing of the Irishman.[57]

Saint Mary's was a "lofty structure" (*praecelsa mole*) with an altar in the apse dedicated to the Virgin Mary, and twelve other dedications of altars or niches to the apostles. The interior glowed with sunshine through its glass windows, filling the rectangular nave with light. A golden cloth covered its altar. A jeweled chalice and silver paten set atop the altar reflected light like the stars of heaven, a motif common in the *tituli*. A precious cross and embossed thurible, dangling over the altar, completed the decorative ensemble. Aldhelm elaborated an iconography of heavenly light that inflamed the reader's and viewer's spirits, leading them to an internal as well as aesthetic appreciation of the sacred space. "Let bright glory" be offered to the Father, Son, and Holy Spirit, he exclaimed.

Like Cogitosus's *ekphrasis*, Aldhelm's poem set images in motion, locating them in time as well as space. His references to the liturgical cycle reminded readers of Rome, seat of apostles, and Jerusalem, scene of Christ's Passion. Mention of the liturgy also impelled readers into imaginative movement through the spaces of the church. When Aldhelm described the congregation's singing and praying, he placed people and ritual at precise points, looking at particular objects or scenes. For instance, he mentioned the dialogue of women and men in "twin choirs," taking turns at singing and reading scripture, thus emphasizing the presence of both sexes and their segregation within the church.[58] The experience became even more vivid for readers when Aldhelm evoked the sounds and smells of the Christian ritual, recalling the fragrance of incense drifting from the thurible in the apse. His readers thus not only shared Aldhelm's vision of the church but also participated in the feelings and movements of clerics and congregants from different places within the church. Aldhelm may have intended this and his other poems to become part of the architecture when carved into the walls as *tituli*.[59]

Cogitosus shared a visual rhetoric of sanctity with Gallo-Roman and British writers. He employed motifs common in literary descriptions that preceded and followed his own, using architectural description to elucidate living rituals in the church. Like the poems of Aldhelm or the *tituli* of Martin's church, Cogitosus's vita operated on a simple visual level as well as at a symbolic level, just as Cogitosus imagined the church building itself to function.[60] According to the vita, the most undeniable proof of Brigit's *virtus*, and the manifestation of saintly principles enacted during her lifetime, was the space built around her. The church glorified her body while her body made possible Kildare. The *basilica* was comprehensible only through a combination of seeing and reading, of pilgrimage and hagiography. Just as particular episodes in her life illustrated certain Christian themes, so the written details of the church's construction, decor, and subspaces taught distinct lessons about Brigit's cult, resonant with lessons from her life.

Cogitosus described a church organized for specific liturgies performed by men and women, professionals and laity, neighbors and visitors. In Brigit's vita, the saint's miracles transformed Irish people and landscapes into a Christian civilization. Likewise, the last chapters of the vita organized and located congregants at Brigit's body, within her episcopal and monastic center. Inside the church, the remains of Brigit and Bishop Conláed, set near the altar and screened from the nave, were emphatically signposted by the decorative lamps, called crowns (*corona*), suspended above.[61] The lamps spotlighted the saint and her bishop, glimpsed by congregants through curtained arches or over the painted screen that divided the church. Only Brigit's ordained successors could move within the altar area. Most believers could see the light but not the saint, whereas the saint could observe all.[62]

Cogitosus wrote that worshipers were organized "by rank and sex," with separate spaces and entrances for each group, as in the church of Bugge and Aldhelm, and bisected or double-naved churches elsewhere in Christendom.[63] The geography of Kildare placed women to the north but allowed both male and female officials of Kildare into the sanctuary, rhyming visually with the placement of Brigit on the north side of the sanctuary and Conláed to her south. The segregation of females on the north from males to the south was not uncommon in Christian churches, and it theologically echoed other dualities: Old Testament and New, dark and light, moon and sun. Mosaics and paintings to the north were normally of female saints, including the Virgin Mary, while southern walls featured male saints. Women, like the Virgin in scripture and art, sat at the right hand of Jesus, assuming that he stood at the altar facing the congregation.[64]

Cogitosus's divisions operated in time as well as space, in liturgy as well as architecture. The "Lord's sacrifice" (*Dominica sacrificia*) conducted by the bishop occurred in the chapel, while "prayer" took placed in the nave. Cogitosus meant that vowed women and men entered the chapel for the Eucharist ("the banquet of the body and blood of Jesus Christ," *conuiuio corporis et sanguinis*). The larger congregation, which included laypeople, entered the church for other rituals such as celebration of the saint's day and reading of her vita, baptisms, and prayers.

Thus while the division of the nave repeated the gendered division of the chapel and of the ecclesiastical hierarchy generally, the arrangement of the congregation also mimicked the ideal political and social order of Irish Christendom depicted in Cogitosus's hagiographic episodes. In stories of Brigit's life, the saint herself humbly outshone clerics, who in turn outranked even kings of the laity; good kings ruled noblemen and noblewomen, peasants, and slaves, and at the bottom of the order languished lepers, druids, other pagans, and sinners. Beyond the church walls, dynastic warriors battled over shifting boundaries, mercenaries and marauders roamed from one settlement to another, beasts and thieves prowled the wilderness. No enemies dared broach Kildare's borders, according to Cogitosus, just as non-Christians could never enter the church nor laypeople invade the sanctuary during the Eucharist. Inside Kildare's cathedral everyone entered and exited where ordered, kept to their subspaces, participated in appropriate Christian ritual, and submitted to Brigit and her companion in harmonious hierarchy. Screens and partitions, decorated with didactic scenes recalling Christian history and hierarchy, reinforced the congregation's geography. Nun and bishop, woman and man, cleric and laic, these were the fundaments of order within the sacred space, which set the goal for the rest of the world. And, of course, this arrangement repeated the layout of the "heavenly mansions" where Brigit's soul resided with God and his other saints, angels, the virgin mother, and her son.

Cogitosus's *ekphrasis* stretched beyond the church itself, beyond even the numinous boundaries of Brigit's city to include pilgrims. The interior design of the church, according to Cogitosus's description, guided the traffic patterns of visitors. The crowns that illuminated tombs also drew pilgrims' attention to the bodies. Doors and dividing walls channeled visitors into the building, then—if they were sufficiently important—deeper into the sanctuary, circulating around the tomb with perhaps a touch of, or a prayer to, the saint, and then led them out of the sanctuary and church again. In other churches, where visitors lacked instruction, architecture made the job of pilgrims more difficult. Saints' bodies in some Continental shrines lay behind bars or under altars, remote to the touch of venerators. In other churches, where martyrs were originally buried in crypts or catacombs and churches later constructed above, the saints lay at the end of dark tunnels and long stairways.[65] At Hexham and Ripon, pilgrims approached subterranean crypts through a dim, descending passage that brought them, dramatically, to the brightly lit presence of the saints.[66] In Ireland, with Kildare's exception, builders had not devised a systematic shrine architecture, and even major saints lay unattainable in their graves. At Downpatrick in the seventh century, Patrick's remains languished under a solid cubit of earth beneath the church floor to prevent anyone making off with them (as Ulster clerics later snatched Brigit's body). This was a poor strategy for attracting pilgrims who needed to be able to view and feel the saint.[67] Armagh's securing of Continental relics in the seventh century addressed the same issue of pilgrims' access stressed by Cogitosus.

Cogitosus referred to the bodies at Kildare as *in monumentis posita*, which meant above-the-ground monuments, whether reliquaries containing body parts or coffins holding entire bodies. This was the tradition in Anglo-Saxon churches and Columban monasteries on the Continent, too; at the same time, Frankish churchmen were busy translating their own saints from hidden coffins to above-ground monuments centrally placed in sanctuaries.[68] The *monumenta* at Kildare were "decorated with variegated gold and silver and precious stones," as was the portable art in Bugge's church. They were also adorned with "different images presenting a variety of carvings and colours." Worshipers must have been directed close enough to appreciate such artistry and to read the images. The tombs at Kildare were colored too, either painted on stone or marble, or perhaps of wood featuring hammered metal and enamel panels so typical of early medieval Irish art and later Irish reliquaries. One page of the Book of Kells (ca. 800) depicts what is probably a church-shaped metal reliquary, intricately colored and inscribed with typically Irish designs. The structure is rectangular and features the peculiar crossed roof beams at either end derived from Irish wooden churches. The manuscript illumination at once suggests the identification of shrines with church buildings and the ideal biblical house of God—the temple at Jerusalem—upon which all tabernacles were modeled.[69]

Cogitosus integrated historical advertisements for Brigit's cult with cues for pilgrims' use and interpretation of the shrine. In the midst of his discussion of the church's interior, the author inserted a story of miraculous rebuilding and prayerful incubation in the shrine. Builders at Kildare, he explained, had to expand the church to accommodate its increasing number of pilgrims. The old northern door turned out to be too small for its frame. Workmen argued over whether to add a piece to the door or make a new one. The chief craftsmen suggested that a night of prayer at the foot of Brigit's tomb might bring an answer. He spent the night with the saint, "praying by the glorious tomb of Brigit." In the morning, he had the old door rehung and found it to be a perfect fit after all. As a result of the miracle and Cogitosus's rehearsal of it, "all who see this doorway and door" understood the powers of the saint. Cogitosus thus located the entrance to Brigit's shrine in recent Christian time as well as in a specific architectural space. Readers learned the historical significance, and pilgrims were visually reminded of the miracle every time they entered the door, just as visitors to Martin's shrine at Tours took cues from *tituli* on the walls. Indeed, visitors relived the miracle when they passed through the door, just as the gate to the church healed them and reminded them of the millstone miracle. Both were passages of pilgrimage. Whereas the millstone had sorted Christians from outsiders and reunited flawed believers with the whole, this doorway taught a lesson to Christian adepts about the rewards of personal prayer and devotion to the saint. In fact, the hagiographer's focus on entrances may reflect a series of rituals enacted first outside, then inside the church, and finally in the sanctuary.[70] Simultaneously, visual cues, issues of access and traffic through the sacred space, and the decorated tombs all reinforced the logic of the vita for its many audiences, linking the saint's past with that of the savior, but also with the pilgrims' ritual present. Devotees could hope eventually to pass, as Brigit had, to heavenly mansions. Meanwhile, the entire vita—life narrative and *ekphrasis*—came to occupy space in Christian teleology when it was read aloud during Brigit's feast day to the crowds of pilgrims attending her tomb. Then and there, Cogitosus's actual audiences, arranged appropriately according to vocation, sex, and rank, shared the diverse, simultaneous meanings of the vita.[71]

From Kildare to Rome

Nothing is left of Kildare's foundations to support Cogitosus's claims for the church, just as nothing of the saint remains to support her dossier begun by the hagiographer. Historians and archaeologists have complained of Cogitosus's vague phrasing in these last passages, which makes it so difficult to make a visual plan or virtual reconstruction of the church.[72] Such attempts to visualize the church make another kind of claim for its reality and the authenticity of Cogitosus's description. But why should we accept his account of the church literally when we would never read Brigit's life events in the same uncritical way? Cogitosus's aim was not to describe but to evoke and invoke, not to rebuild the church but to re-create an experience. He wielded a precise rhetorical tool in the last two chapters of the vita, arguing for Brigit's *virtus* in terms that complemented the finely crafted narrative of the vita's first thirty chapters.

Cogitosus's carefully selected words recalled both visual memories and written evidence from across Christendom during the sixth and seventh centuries. Irish scholars and missionaries went back and forth to Britain, passing by Roman remnants as well as more recent basilicas, and visiting English monasteries. Irish pilgrims to Gaul either sailed the Seine past Genovefa's Paris or traveled inland on the Loire, where they stopped at Tours, resting place of the ever-popular Saint Martin. Saint Columban certainly stopped at Tours on his hasty way out of Gaul. Tourists to Martin's shrine and the churches mentioned by Paulinus and Venantius must have read the *tituli* painted on the church walls and later copied down in the *Martillenus*. They may also have traveled through Auxerre, city of Saint Germanus, as Patrick supposedly did.[73] We know that they went to Rome. According to the Irish bishop Cummian, in a letter of 632, a council convened at Mag Léne in 630 had sent an embassy to Rome to investigate the question of the dating of Easter. There the pilgrims had lodged in the precinct of Old Saint Peter's (*in aecclesia sancti Petri*) with others from the eastern Christian world. Cummian failed to say whether the pilgrims inspected the sights of the holy city, but Cummian's pilgrims certainly saw Saint Peter's basilica and other major churches of the city inventoried in the *Liber Pontificalis*. They observed Continental liturgy, and, as the bishop put it, "they saw all things just as they had heard about them, but they found them more certain inasmuch as they were seen rather than heard."[74]

What is more, Irish pilgrims brought home souvenirs. British clerics, too, lugged home manuscripts and relics every time they went abroad. Armagh clerics began collecting in Rome soon after Cogitosus wrote, if not before, in order to bolster the position of Patrick's church as Ireland's own apostolic city.

The *Liber Angeli*, written at the end of the seventh century by Armagh clerics to bulwark their claim for their bishop's supremacy in Ireland, boasted a collection of Roman relics "of Peter and Paul, of Stephen, Lawrence and others."[75] In a similar bid, perhaps, Cogitosus mentioned Bishop Conláed's "foreign vestments from overseas," which Brigit, in all her saintly generosity, gave away and miraculously replaced. Whether or not Conláed's original garments included an archbishop's *pallium*, someone had to fetch them from abroad.[76] In addition, high crosses at Kildare and Monasterboice show biblical motifs adapted from carving programs on Roman sarcophagi. Irish pilgrims may even have brought home hairstyles from frescoes in Rome.[77]

Finally, and most important, travelers brought home to Ireland an enriched vocabulary of *romanitas* to adorn Cogitosus's hagiography and Kildare's architecture. For Cogitosus, this was the most precious import to an island lacking any historical connection to the civilized center of the western Christian world. With his Continental idiom he translated Brigit's church into a *basilica maxima*, drawing on the concept if not the form of the imperial seat of judgment, revised as a Christian place of worship. He transformed the saint's settlement into a *civitas*, the usual domain of an *episcopus* such as Conláed, Brigit's first partner. He created a *maxima metropolitana*, the geographically complex region based on old imperial divisions, ruled by a metropolitan bishop in charge of other bishops and their flocks.[78] The properties around Kildare were *suburbana*, less urbanized districts than the city itself. In a previous age and more thoroughly romanized region, *suburbium* was where the citizens of late antiquity had buried their dead and built funerary monuments, not where one located the main *ecclesia* of a congregation. Denis had lain in a *suburbium*. Genovefa's own shrine, for all her hagiographers' arguments about its centrality, was on a suburban hill south of the Parisian island. But Brigit built her church first and then surrounded it with a city, ringed with *suburbia*.

This symbolic architectural vocabulary put Kildare, alone of all Irish churches, on the route to Rome and beyond. Cogitosus relied on ideal, textual models as well as visual examples and reports of churches elsewhere to convey the significance of his *basilica*, its shrine, and its saint. For him, as for late antique pilgrims to the Holy Land, pilgrimage was an act of sensory engagement, particularly of the eyes.[79] Scripture provided him with architectural prototypes and parallels just as Old and New Testaments offered exemplars for Brigit's saintly behavior. The very concept of *terra sancta* derived from biblical usage identifying the land of Israel as specially holy territory.[80] Kildare, which needed no physical walls or ditches to protect it, was a "city of refuge" and a "center of pilgrimage" full of treasures, like Rome, which echoed Constantinople, which referred to Jerusalem. The *suburbana* of Kildare were also the fields of biblical cities in Numbers and other chapters.[81] If we knew the dimensions of the basilica at Kildare, we might even be able to calculate its architectural ratios in the manner of 1 Kings and 2 Chronicles.[82] Again, Cogitosus was practicing a rhetoric common to Christian writers and Christian architects of the very early Middle Ages, who cast their sanctuaries as New Covenant replacements of Solomon's temple and post-Constantinian versions of the Holy Sepulcher.[83] Perhaps in the gold and silver tombs at Kildare, set below their crowns *a dextris et a sinistris altaris decorati*, there was an echo of the silver pillars that flanked the ark in the *sanctum sanctorum* of the temple as well as the precious ornaments of late antique Roman churches. Or maybe Cogitosus had just heard a rumor of the works of Saint Eligius.[84]

Although Irish writers of the generation after Cogitosus also employed the language of biblical layout and Christian topography to articulate theological principles, they never integrated verbal and visual clues as thoroughly as he did. The artist of spatial diagrams in the Book of Armagh was probably articulating concepts from the Apocalypse. Adomnán drew inspiration for exegesis from Arculf, the windblown pilgrim who washed up at Iona at the end of the seventh century and gave reports of buildings in Jerusalem.[85] On the same biblical landscape, by contrast, Muirchú described the royal site of Temair (Tara) as a pagan structure of testamental design: the *palatio Temoriae* (palace of Tara) was the new Babylon, with a mystical flame burning in its pagan center.[86] In late seventh-century Christian discourse, every text resonated visually, and every vision was focused on the Bible. Every vita retold the Christian story from creation to salvation.

But Cogitosus took the integration of text and image to a higher level, creating an iconography that linked architecture, space, congregational ritual, and pilgrimage. According to Cogitosus, Brigit's life journey had prepared the site for her church by expunging any pagan remnants from the landscape; now, as text, that same "Life" led and instructed visitors to her body in its tomb. She lay as a permanent, visible reminder of Kildare's connections to the centers of Christian history and civilization. Her physical presence allowed pilgrims to walk the path of Moses and to follow the footsteps of Christ. Her church located every visitor to her tomb in the larger landscapes of Christendom and the teleological drama of death and resurrection.

Cogitosus's church and city, with its romanized architectural idiom and sacred boundaries, set an impossible standard for later interpretations of Brigit by other writers. Without Brigit's body, no church could compete for her cult in the same way. The authors of the slightly later *Vita Prima* and *Bethu Brigte* had to make a different case for the saint's veneration in other vocabularies of landscape, territoriality, and dynastic legend.[87] *Vita Prima* also linked Brigit's clerics to Rome with stories of recovered liturgies and bells, and other hints at connections to the Continent, just as Armagh's propagandists made claims based on Roman relics.

Meanwhile, back at Kildare, architecture rarely appeared in texts composed after Cogitosus's vita. Monastic annalists had no reason to practice *ekphrasis*. They mentioned a simple *dairthech* (wooden structure) at Kildare in 762 and 836. They referred to the *altair* and *crocaingel* (chancel?) of the church also in 762. A *tech mor* (literally "big house") and *dairthech* appeared in the entry for 964. In 1050 there was a *daimliacc* (stone church) at Kildare, and in 1067 a *teampull*. By the eleventh century, Kildare's *basilica* had given way to the usual motley collection of cramped church buildings. By the time Gerald of Wales and his Cambro-Norman cousins got there in the 1170s, the body was gone and the church not nearly so interesting to Gerald as the wicker enclosure surrounding an eternal flame of pagan origins, or the fields left unplowed for the ancient saint. The landscape of Brigit had become more important than her built shrine or lost body. It seems that the basilica's messages existed in a more historically limited and less biblical span than Cogitosus had proposed after all.[88]

In the seventh century, though, the saint was alive in her vita and immanent in her body. She dwelt within her ornamented tomb, lit by the magnificence of a royal crown suspended above her head, even while she resided with God and his other saints above. As Cogitosus pointed out at the start of the vita, it was only from this on-site vantage point that Brigit could have "made provision in every detail for the souls of her people according to the rule . . . over the churches attached to her in many provinces." She had called Bishop Conláed to her side, first to consecrate other monasteries that she herself founded and then to preside beside her in her sanctuary. As Cogitosus put it, in an organic landscape simile, "Their episcopal and conventual see spread on all sides like a fruitful vine with its growing branches and struck root in the whole island of Ireland."[89] In a reverse of Eden, where divine order was ruined by a pair of impetuous humans who were then set to wandering the earth, Brigit and her bishop had come to build Kildare. But it was Cogitosus who led Christians to Brigit's church and located them in the history and geography of Christendom.

7

Brigit Goes to Ground

Cogitosus wrote for posterity, but his text celebrated only a single historical moment in the long life of Brigit's cult. He wrote when Kildare flourished. Brigit's church was newly rebuilt. Women and men of the Leinster royalty governed the monastery. Its abbess of abbesses purported to rule all the province's monasteries and all Irish communities of holy women in the name of Brigit. But in earlier years Kildare had been a humbler place and Brigit less commanding. Her journeys had supposedly taken her to settlements and churches around Ireland whose inhabitants also venerated Brigit. They too helped to maintain her memory beyond Kildare, supplying material for Cogitosus but also keeping their own recollections of the saint. Her cult survived in many places beyond Kildare and was commemorated by other hagiographers at many other moments.

Although Cogitosus's rendering of Brigit was so popular that it spread from one copyist to another across the Continent, a second Irish hagiographer from another monastery wrote a much longer account of the saint's life less than half a century later, followed soon after by more versions in Latin and Irish. Hagiographers of Saint Brigit shared some material among themselves and with chroniclers of other saints, but each author emphasized different attributes of his subject, making a unique case for the superior *virtus* of Brigit and the primacy of his presentation of her deeds. A writer's emphases depended on his territorial affiliation. Whereas Cogitosus looked from Kildare to Rome, the writers of the *Vita Prima* (ca. 750) and *Bethu Brigte* (ca. 900 but from earlier sources) focused on Armagh, Patrick's church.[1] Both later writers came from farther north, in the territory that used to be part of Leinster but, by the seventh century, had fallen to ruling groups from Mide. Their Saint Brigit and their churches competed for customers with Cogitosus and Kildare; their job was to emphasize Brigit's connections to their own region and people while supporting the larger *paruchia* of Brigit.[2] Meanwhile, their ecclesiastical colleagues vied for souls with the cult-keepers of Patrick and other saints from stronger kingdoms than Brigit's own. Hagiographers from still other places and other centuries wrought their own strategies for saintly success.

Brigit's successors at Kildare eventually lost the larger contest for supremacy among Ireland's churches, but her hagiographers achieved their goals. They aimed to build a local tradition for Brigit and associate it with a network of Brigidine places, leaving others to exploit the cult for political patronage and profit. Saintly cult was the ecclesiastical equivalent of ancient territories; at once a monument to religious practice, a geographical reality, and a political symbol, its limits and meanings shifted constantly in relation to the physical environment. Local cult-keepers depended on Brigit's prestige to attract tribute and protection from their neighbors. Rulers of Kildare and kings of Leinster used the claims of hagiography to bolster their own claims to dominance over other religious communities and other political regions of Ireland. Collectively, the hagiographers' tactics established Brigit as one of the premier patrons of Ireland and set a precedent for the claims of other hagiographers on behalf of their own ecclesiastical and royal sponsors.

Cogitosus and his fellow hagiographers wrote Brigit's many lives for many different places, but men and women at all these places had to work at her cult every day. That flowering vine of ecclesiastical cooperation that Cogitosus so enthusiastically envisioned had to be tended in less ideal conditions than the hagiographer described. Neither Brigit's vowed followers nor the rest of the Irish population occupied exclusively ekphratic landscapes. The territories of Brigit were busy with practical uses and cluttered by gendered limits that shifted again during the eighth and ninth centuries. Churches might represent Rome architecturally and Jerusalem symbolically, but they remained built spaces on physical ground. Old issues of gendered access to the physical space of churches had arrived in Ireland with the rest of Christianity's baggage. The limits on women's use of Brigit's churches posed problems for the saint's many biographers as well as her ecclesiastical successors, male and female. Kildare, with its public architecture and female abbesses, remained an exceptional sanctuary upon legally partitioned landscapes whose properties and polities belonged officially to family men. Religious professionals of both sexes dedicated to Brigit shared allegiance to the woman saint but lived the religion in a hierarchy of administrative and sacral spaces, within larger territories fixed by kinship and political alliances. Abbesses, bishops, ordinary nuns, monks, priests, and laypeople all strove to reconcile the concepts of holiness and gender, to live out that reconciliation in daily religion, and to locate that reconciliation in a material environment.

The collision of cult imperatives, competition for management of Brigit's growing reputation, and the realities of living out Brigit's mission in a patriarchal society led eighth- and ninth-century writers to revise her Life in unpredictable ways. Rather than emphasizing Brigit's exceptional main church at Kildare, or promoting their own communities as alternatives for Brigit's cult, Brigidine hagiographers redefined her travels and landscapes. They resorted to the old-fashioned rhetoric of fluidly defined territories. They relocated more of her adventures to distant provinces. They turned away from Rome as the object of Kildare's imitation to focus on Armagh as Kildare's competitor for ecclesiastical authority. They ignored the visible history of Brigit's body and her basilica at Kildare.[3] Instead, the saint's intimacy with landscapes and her ability to cross boundaries and move effortlessly through borderlands guided these revised legends of Brigit. Her routes expanded. Her command over creatures and elements increased. Her primary goal became the shepherding and sheltering of fellow travelers, rather than arrival at a particular destination. Scenes of her interactions with the natural and supernatural environments became more prominent than descriptions of Brigit's stable architecture. Druids roamed the lively episodes of her vita, pagan warriors threatened the saint and her colleagues, columns of fire brightened the nighttime horizons, and God's creatures succumbed to magical illogic.

The authors of *Vita Prima* and *Bethu Brigte* crafted a double strategy: first, they punctuated their stories of Brigit's circuits around Ireland with miracles set outside churches; second, the hagiographers purposely invoked Brigit's sympathy with the natural environment, making sly allusions to discarded pagan practices and mythologies and equating her femininity with ancient powers over the landscape.[4] Whereas Cogitosus devised Brigit as an organizer of christianized territories, later hagiographers presented her as an intermediary between the historic pagan wilderness and the enclosed Christian society of forts, monasteries, and churches. Thus each generation of hagiographers, church builders, and their audiences renegotiated the meaning of Brigit's deeds to fit its surroundings.

Shared Space

The physical landscape of Ireland probably did not change much between Cogitosus's late seventh century and the end of the ninth century. The Scandinavians had arrived in 795 off the coast near Dublin. By 840, groups of Vikings were wintering in Ireland, and by 900 they had created a series of permanent settlements on the eastern and southwestern coasts. Nonetheless, the population of the island grew slowly, and the loci of political power shifted as they always had. People lived in the same places and farmed in the same ways, without much new technology or imported crops. Beginning in the tenth century, farmers in regions surrounding Dublin, Waterford, and other harbor settlements began to send their surplus wheat and barley to the lords of rudimentary urban markets rather than to rural chieftains and monastic settlements. Networks of traffic shifted course when the Scandinavians directed their ships from Irish coasts into the North Sea, as well as to Viking settlements in Britain and Europe.[5] Bits of jewelry and liturgical furniture rummaged from Irish churches turned up in graves of the Viking homelands; likewise, objects of Scandinavian manufacture moved inland from the Irish coast with soldiers and traders, just as Roman goods had once invaded. As a couple of modern archaeologists have put it, the tenth century saw a "great flood of silver" washing through Ireland from sources as far away as Byzantium. Much of it was neither plunder nor symbolic exotica, but coinage gained in international commerce. One hoard found at Kildare included thirty-four coins from England, buried around 991.[6]

Irish sacral sites, the paths of pilgrimage, and routes of doctrinal exchange remained basically the same, although new foundations sprang up and architectural fashions changed slightly.[7] Even in Dublin, where Vikings eventually established their largest settlement on the island, monasteries remained continuously in business throughout the ninth and tenth centuries. Missionaries and monastic founders had already built their major Christian settlements, which were not much disrupted after the first century of Scandinavian raids— at least, some historians argue, they suffered no more violence than in intertribal attacks of the previous decades.[8] Churchmen and churchwomen had buried all their saints in the earth or encased them in marvelous reliquaries, scratched crosses on all the ambiguously threatening markers of the pagan past, and rung their liturgical bells across the land to mark Christian conquest. They had created Christian itineraries and histories, commemorated in hagiography and visible in familiar landmarks around the island. Cogitosus's Brigit had long ago built a church, a territory, and a saintly reputation.

Already in Cogitosus's time, Kildare had become a busy monastery within an episcopal *civitas*. He had called Kildare an "episcopal and conventual see" governed jointly by an archbishop of bishops and abbess of abbesses. At the end of Cogitosus's account, after his description of rituals within the basilica, Cogitosus had listed the regular ritual events that took place within the greater bounds of Kildare: feasts, healings and presumably exorcisms, the gathering of crowds, and offerings of gifts and tribute. These well-attended dramas put Kildare on the ecclesiastical map. "A city," Cogitosus posited, "gets its name from the fact that many people congregate there." He was paraphrasing Isidore of Seville, but Isidore was only partly right.[9] Cities enjoyed their geographical prestige not just because of the number of people who lived there and visited but also because of the collective identity and status of their residents, and because residents and visitors alike accepted the symbolic significance of the place. In late antique Gaul and Britain, governmental officials and bishops had directed the spectacles that lent reputation to their cities. In Cogitosus's scheme, Kildare chose a woman saint for its impresario. It was Brigit's city, found and arranged by her. She herself had marked out its boundaries in a ritual more often performed by abbots and bishops, according to other Irish saints' lives.[10] Bishop Conláed kept her company in Kildare's sanctuary for all eternity, but he did not direct her pageants.

At Cogitosus's Kildare, where the hagiographer lived among *fratres* (monks) and *virgines* (nuns), both an abbess and a bishop presided. Cogitosus's description of rituals and the layout of Kildare's sanctuary suggest that they shared administration.[11] Until the late tenth century, there was also an abbot, who may have been a religious leader, a kind of community manager, or both, depending upon who filled the position.[12] Monastic annalists recorded the obits of Kildare's governing team fairly regularly from 639 until the arrival of the Normans in Leinster, listing 20 abbesses, at least 20 abbots (up to 936), and 26 bishops called occasionally bishop of Leinster, along with assorted scribes, anchorites, and scholars.[13] Although Kildare's abbess, bishop, and abbot did not take office jointly, the tenure of these many officials overlapped; sometimes bishops were abbots, too, and occasionally more than one bishop seem to have presided simultaneously—or, at least, resided—at Kildare. Some also held offices at other religious communities. The first reliable historical notice of an individual at Kildare mentions a bishop, Áed Dub mac Colmáin (d. 639), who was also an abbot. Cogitosus may have written at the request of Áed Dub, who was certainly in a position to sponsor a new church and a vita, given his royal connections. Leinster genealogists knew Áed Dub as the brother of the Uí Dúnlainge king of Leinster, Fáelán; and as uncle to Óengus and cousin to Brandub, both abbots of Kildare after Áed.[14]

The rulers of Kildare may have secured their jobs by evincing piety and ability, but their birth and gender were more crucial. By 650, it helped to be a member of the Uí Dúnlainge dynastic group, which supplied ecclesiastical officials at Kildare from Aéd Dub's generation to the twelfth century, at least. In fact, the great codex of royal genealogies, which recorded the many generations of Leinster's ruling elite, may have come from Kildare's scriptorium in the twelfth century.[15] Six men of a particular branch of Uí Dúnlainge, the Uí Dúnchada, served as bishop or abbot of Kildare over about a hundred years (798–885). At least one abbess—Muirenn, daughter of Cellach Uí Dúnchada (d. 831)—came of that family too. Uí Dúnchada men also ruled Leinster in the same century. When they took provincial power again in the tenth century, their kinsmen governed Kildare once more.[16] Meanwhile, when territorial control passed to other Leinster families, they took positions at Kildare. Between 885 and 968, one king and two other potential kings ruled Brigit's church.[17]

Kildare's other administrators were from various noble families within and beyond the province. Between the mid-ninth century and early eleventh century, a series of abbesses came from a local lesser tribe, the Fothairt, Brigit's own kin. Kildare's male administrators were not Fothairt, though, nor were they from the displaced tribe of Conláed, Brigit's first bishop.[18] It may be that different interest groups within Kildare, each supported by kin groups outside the monastery, negotiated power-sharing at Brigit's settlement in an arrangement parallel to secular tribal confederations.[19] Traditional laws governed the ownership of lands upon which the church was built and the community's revenues, as well as the relationship between Kildare's leadership and its tenants.[20] However, the politics of any given moment also influenced the sharing of power over ecclesiastical administration. Factions from noble families may purposely have negotiated governing roles for men and women of different backgrounds and regions in the province in order to protect the interests of subgroups within Kildare as well as kin groups outside the community. If so, the decreasing status of the Fothairt in relation to the Uí Dúnchada after 750 must have colored both the selection of abbesses and bishops and their relations. If an abbess came of a lesser family than the bishop, did she kowtow to him? Was she more submissive than, say, a kinswoman who came of the more prestigious dynasty of the bishop? Or did abbesses from less powerful kin groups welcome an abbot or bishop of higher status as a protector and ally, just as a noblewoman and her family would value her royal husband?[21]

Exactly how men and women who governed Kildare acted out their relative status remains a mystery. If Patrick's hagiographer, Tírechán is a trustworthy reporter, the bishops and abbots of Armagh were particularly interested in taking on women's communities as protected clients of their own administration. Several passages in Tírechán's *Itineraria* of Patrick described how he placed a particular holy woman in a locale, which was a hagiographic formula indicating Armagh's supervision of the community established in that same place.[22] Other clerics in Tírechán's text also practiced the *cura monialum*, the responsibility of ministering to religious women's communities. Tírechán wrote, for instance, that bishop Cethiacus used to celebrate Easter in Corcu Sai but Holy Monday at the *locum* of Comgella at Áth Dá Loarcc near Kells, and that "the monks of Cethiachus say that Comgella was a nun to Cethiachus."[23] Tírechán was suggesting that the nun was subordinate to or somehow dependent upon the bishop and, further, that the community of Áth Dá Loarcc was still a client church, but the words revealed no details. Elsewhere in the hagiographic canon, pleasant scenes of hospitality usually illustrated a similar relationship between a community of women and men who exercised the *cura*. In saints' lives, these men were not coresidents but bishops and abbots who visited women's places, which were either internally segregated from the larger monastery or discrete communities located elsewhere.

Men in the hagiographic tales accepted no women as leaders except a few aged, holy virgins who offered sage advice that men were free to refuse. Ecclesiastics in these episodes were subject to the wisdom of women but not their institutional authority. Some zealots even rejected all contact with abbesses, saintly or other. In the medieval vita of Íte, a seventh-century abbess and saint, a young novice demanded of his monastic seniors, "What reason is there for you, wise and great men, to visit that old lady?"[24] Although the elders scolded him and Íte herself later teased him for the remark, the monk was expressing a familiar tension. How could vowed women actively manage the ecclesiastical hierarchy? A female saint might, in rare instances, function as an *érlam*, the patron responsible for founding a place, determining the headship of its church, and protecting its inhabitants (*familia*) until the Last Judgment and beyond.[25] But in practice, the gender bias inherent in both Christian ideology and local custom inevitably limited the range of Kildare's female rulers. Virtue and wisdom were insufficient bases for authority over family property, political territory, and clerical space.

Kildare was a wealthy place; even if its founder had disdained material possessions, her colleagues and heirs did not. In one episode of a later medieval vita, Brigit's nuns tried to hide pious gifts of jewelry from her so that she would not distribute the baubles among the poor, and Bishop Conláed complained that she had given his episcopal vestments to vagrant lepers. Their reactions suggest that, saintly exceptions aside, the sons and daughters of kings would not have sought the community's leadership if it did not bring profits beyond the spiritual. But women could not be trusted to maintain such riches. In the twelfth century, the office of abbess was valuable enough to incite bloodshed at the highest levels. The king of Uí Fáeláin died at Kildare in 1127, trying to win Kildare for his daughter. A few years later, Diarmaid Mac Murchadha, king of Leinster, raped the abbess in order to discredit her and her family, and to promote his aggressive campaign for control of the province.[26]

Gender ideology, social status, and access to the community's wealth all informed the daily contact of Kildare's governing men and women in the early Middle Ages. Old, shared patterns of movement governed their interactions too. Bishops, abbesses, and abbots lived with or near other vowed women, monks, priests, and laypeople. Every day they had to decide how to move past each other, make way, visit among themselves, and line up in procession. For direction, they relied on both ritual tradition and personal politics. Did they dine together? The Irish vitae of other saints described happy occasions when nuns and monks feasted; Irish saints of both genders seem to have been fond of sharing a beer. Brigit herself was credited with singing, in a Middle Irish poem, that she "would like a great ale-feast for the King of kings and the folk of heaven drinking it for all eternity," going on to describe her urge to cook for the savior.[27] This commensality of spiritual kinship was crucial to the ideal of an orderly Christian settlement that mirrored conventional social life. But between feasts were long bouts of daily reality that women and men relished or resented, depending on status, gender, occasion, and physical environment, not to mention what there was to eat.

All the residents of early medieval Kildare hid from recorded history in their off-hours. The sources rarely reveal the mundane uses of monastic spaces. The seventh- and eighth-century penitentialists, in their long lists of rules for Christians, prohibited a monk and a nun traveling out of an ecclesiastical settlement together, but had little to say about paths and shelters within a monastic city. Cogitosus envisioned separate but equal access to church spaces for vowed men and women, with barriers between clerical and secular congregations. The annalists revealed that Kildare had a scriptorium and at least occasionally a workshop for masons. A comb maker labored in the town in 909 when the king of Leinster fell off a horse just outside his house.[28] Yet no other comb makers of Kildare achieved a place in written history. We have no references to female comb makers, scribes, or sculptors. In stories, women sewed for the clergy and made clothing for their entire communities, but whether Brigit's nuns did so we cannot say. In one hagiographic episode, Brigit liberated a slave whose owner desperately wanted to keep her because of her sewing skills; the woman ended up as a nun with Brigit.[29] However, most of the female characters in her vitae tended to cattle and their products. Some other early medieval saints' lives referred to monastic settlements with dedicated spaces for different kinds of labors. In addition to barns and sheds, the sixth-century monastery at Í (Iona) included private quarters (*tegoriolum*) where its abbot Columcille might read and write quietly.[30] But no mention of an abbess's house at Kildare appeared until 1132.[31]

Typically communities with enough means constructed separate shelters for scholars, visitors, and each gender of resident ecclesiastics. The largest settlements had distinct neighborhoods for subgroups. At Armagh the devotees of Brigit had a house or subenclosure within the larger city, supposedly founded by Patrick for his sister Lupait but no doubt of later date. Most likely it was added at the edge of the main community, just as the later nuns' church at Clonmacnoise sat about a half mile from the central enclosure.[32] While the eighth- and ninth-century vitae mentioned guesthouses at places where Brigit visited, they did not locate one at Kildare.[33] In 797, annalists referred to a separate house at Kildare for elders or scholars (*tech sruithe*) with its own abbess or administrator (*abatissa*). A *tech mor* (literally "big house") or communal hall appeared in the entry for 964. Still, without foundations or other rubble, it is hard to know who used these buildings and when they appeared or disappeared. Residents of Kildare revised their architecture constantly. Although annalists seemed to confirm Cogitosus's favorable estimation of the basilica in 762, when they referred to the *altair* and *crocaingel* (chancel?) of the church, in 1050 there was a *daimliacc* (stone church) at Kildare and in 1067 a *teampull*. These may have been the same main church, but more likely Kildare's great basilica had given way to the usual motley collection of church buildings.[34] The only datable medieval structure remaining (mostly) intact at Kildare today is the freestanding round tower; under it, archaeologists unearthed coins from around 1135, putting its construction in the mid–twelfth century.[35]

Variation among monastic settlements appeared mostly in wealth, size, and quality of structures rather than particular architectural elements. None of these structures, except the complex basilica, were unique to Kildare. Major monasteries in medieval Ireland consistently featured enclosing walls or ditches focused on a modest main church or burial shrine, accompanied by dwellings, outbuildings or storage tunnels, cemeteries for the Christian dead, and other sculptural markers of sacral space such as crosses, inscribed slabs, wells, and external shrines. At least two stone high crosses stood outside Kildare's churches at some point, and a few carved fragments, now kept in the modern church, probably came from grave slabs.[36] Some settlements also boasted more uniquely Irish monuments such as bullauns (bowl-shaped stones that collected healing waters) or *leaba* (literally beds, but meaning raised stone slabs used as burial markers).[37] Small huts rather than dormitories housed men and women. Both religious and domestic buildings were normally built of wood and so burned fairly regularly. Kildare went up in flames repeatedly. The *Annals of Ulster* mentioned fires in 710, 775, and 779, and again in 836 when Vikings set the blaze. *Dairthech* (oaken house) was a common term for church buildings at monasteries large and small, as were *teampall, oratorium,* or *eclais/ecclesia.* When builders used stone, they often said so, as when annalists called the structure at Armagh *damliac* and *oratorium lapideum*—stone church—although a *teampall* could be of stone, too.[38] Kildare's layout and its eleventh-century combination of churches were probably typical, then, of large religious settlements.[39]

It is crucial to remember, though, that of the handful of early medieval communities wealthy enough to build and rebuild extensively, only one was dedicated to and co-governed by a woman. Although women and men shared other religious settlements, only a handful of other places was founded and governed by women. None of these was as architecturally complex or durable as Kildare. None matched the wealth of Kildare and well-endowed settlements of men. And, although other female saints supposedly maintained and even expanded their monasteries, later medieval communities of Irish nuns were consistently poorer, smaller, and less conveniently located than men's monasteries. In fact, while estimates for the total number (not necessarily coeval) of ecclesiastical settlements in early medieval Ireland range from 145 to 2,000, references to only a dozen or more named women's communities still exist in the collective memory of antiquarians and onomasticians.[40]

Ireland's religious women may just be hard for modern observers to see. Religious settlements went through gendered life cycles, sometimes disappearing from the historical sources but not going out of business. Tantalizing references to nameless, unlocatable communities and vowesses dot the textual evidence. Place-names such as Ballynacallagh (*baile na caillech,* nuns' community) or local memories of an ancient women's foundation may or may not be trustworthy for the Ireland of 1,300 years ago. On the other hand, when a little convent of women ran out of resources, its inhabitants may have either moved out or moved aside while a group of men moved into the same sacral space, rebuilding and gaining new endowments to support their project. This does not mean necessarily that nuns or their spaces were lost. In a few places in England it seems clear that vowed women lingered on in discrete houses near newly male communities, sharing resources and rituals with monks. In other cases, vowesses simply lived in family homes. Owners of religious settlements apparently revised their layouts, altering enclosures and expanding shelters to suit the gender of inhabitants, rebuilding churches when necessary

or fashionable, and rewriting rules about access according to prevailing gender norms. They also moved entire communities and renamed existing settlements when women moved in or out.[41]

In general, probably far more communities included both religious men
and vowed women than modern historians used to believe. Whereas spatial
practices in mixed-gender communities varied considerably by period and
region, the architectural organization of Irish monastic settlements does not
seem to have changed much before the twelfth century and the introduction
of new Continental orders. Regardless of ideas about gender and religion, the
Irish tended simply to replace buildings or add small structures to existing
compounds rather than overhauling outdated settlements. Most churches remained relatively small and unsophisticated. Most domestic structures were
humble, damp, and probably uncomfortable. The level of architectural technology did not easily allow for meaningful gender segregation either within a
single ecclesiastical community or among the settlements of a given region.[42]
Irish farmers built for intervisibility, so that families of one farm might be able
to see at least one other homestead. Laws of clientage and property sharing, as
well as the demands of agriculture and herding, reinforced the need for individual communities to be accessible and within easy distance of each other.[43]
Only hermits sought seclusion and exile. Only reformers complained about
the easy association of vowed women and monks, as the Englishman Bede
kvetched about nuns and monks at Coldingham in England.[44]

Yet from as early as the eighth century, if not before, Irish writers realized
the doctrinal contradiction inherent in mixed-sex religious settlements. Hagiographers in the centuries after Cogitosus depicted gender relations among
vowed women and men as increasingly less cooperative. One well-known
eighth- or ninth-century retrospective posited three stages of clerical development: in the Patrician age of missionizing, clerics "did not spurn the administration and fellowship of women." Within half a century, men had begun to
disdain women's authority and segregate their monasteries. Finally, another
half century later, the best monks avoided women's temptations altogether and
took to the desert.[45] Typical of Christian teleology, things could only get worse
according to this scheme before they got better. Hagiographers and rule makers
of this period imagined the past as a state of purity when women could avoid
their sinful natures long enough to become saints, govern communities, and
behave properly in mixed-sex settlements. Their own times, however, brought
a more precarious state of broken vows. Hagiographers wrote about clueless
male saints who had slept sinlessly with virgins, only to be reprimanded by
more worldly colleagues.[46]

Early medieval authorities debated how best to respond to women's religious vocations and men's responsibility for directing women. In the eighth century, radical writers associated with the monastery of Tamlachta about 40 kilometers to the northeast of Kildare, criticized any but the most carefully choreographed contact between monks and laity, or men and women under vows. But the same writers frowned on abbots who refused the company of authentic holy women.[47] Hagiographers and rule makers also complained about sexual infractions committed by both nuns and monks, which most likely resulted from regular, permissible contact. Rule makers based their arguments on ideology, not on any realistic flaws in the architectural design of religious settlements. They urged increased supervision of religious men and women rather than prevention of contact or visibility. Only later in the medieval period, with the influx of new monastic orders and their straight-angled cloisters, did Irish theologians and builders seek inventive ways to build walls between women and men and to keep ordinary Christians out of the cloister altogether.

Still, men and women in religious settlements daily negotiated solutions to the common problems of shared space. The briefest brush of nun with monk or the most cursory contact between abbess and bishop carried profoundly gendered implications for access to space and its uses. Christians had long been taught to use gender as one of their primary vocabularies for discussing both religious perfection and ecclesiastical organization. Saint Patrick himself had brought gendered religious practice to Ireland. His stories of desperate women denied the celibate life by their fathers or masters posed an urgent problem for early organizers of Christian communities. The first Irish hagiographers, too, anticipated gender tensions in organized religious life. Tírechán depicted Patrick preaching one sort of Christianity to kings and landowners, to whom God might guarantee power and prestige, and another version of the creed to princesses. For young women, he cast the Son of God as a good marriage prospect for the afterlife.[48]

Cogitosus reconciled this gendered religious belief and practice with his enthusiastic arrangement of Kildare's orderly spaces. He also routinized women's rule over sacral and secular territories with his stories of Brigit's travel and building. Later vitae, by contrast, still depicted Brigit and other female saints demonstrating *virtus* in the company of all sorts of men but typically showed women to be ecclesiastical authorities only in settlements peopled primarily by other women. A couple of writers betrayed some melancholy about the ultimate resolution of gendered tension over monastic space. One commentator on an early ninth-century Irish martyrology repeated the prophecy of Saint Íte, who announced that no nuns would succeed her as abbess, for her settlement would eventually belong to men.[49] Another writer recounted the experience of the seventh-century Saint Munnu, who yielded his little monastery to a rather demanding nun while predicting that men would eventually take over the place again. The decline of gender cooperation theorized by Irish writers of the early Middle Ages thus justified a perceived parallel decline in women's occupation of religious space, as well as in the authority of abbesses beyond their own communities.

In the eighth and ninth centuries, leaders of Brigit's other communities had to manage the same daily contest for space as did the abbesses of Kildare, but without the unique advantages conferred by Brigit's main place. These women and men of other monasteries did not dwell in the shadow of Dún Ailinne, nor were they governed by princesses from Leinster's ancient dynasties. They did not worship in a Roman-style basilica, infused with the immanence of the saint, divided and ordered by chambers and tombs, and busy with the traffic of pilgrimage. They did not enjoy the wealth and prestige of Brigit's city, nor did their leaders exercise the singular influence of the abbess of Kildare. Increasingly, Kildare's abbess became the only woman with official, if largely symbolic, political power in Ireland. An interlinear gloss on one early medieval legal tract referred to the abbess (whoever she might have been at the time) as the only "woman who holds back the streams of war," suggesting that she negotiated important treaties—although annalists never mentioned an abbess actually gathering and pacifying factions as the abbots of Armagh and Clonmacnoise did.[50] Still, no other female could even hope to wield such public legal authority.

Households of vowesses and more modest monasteries and churches dedicated to Brigit benefited only indirectly from the influence of Kildare's abbess and Cogitosus's propaganda. They had to solve their own spatial problems and stake their own claims locally. Brigit's followers beyond Kildare had to use every canny strategy they could find to prove, by word and building if not by body and miracle, that the woman saint's influence pertained there.

Brigit after Kildare

Unlike Patrick, whose seventh-century hagiographers explicitly claimed lands and congregations in the voice of the saint, Brigit made no official demands on behalf of her many followers. She officially declared her dominion over political territory only once in the hagiographic literature in an episode identical in both eighth-century vitae. As a baby in Connacht, far from her native land, she had cried out distinctly, "This will be mine!" Thus she indicated her ecclesiastical representatives' putative dominance of that province and their rights to collect revenues in her name.[51] From the start, though, Brigit's hagiographers elaborated the natural claims to all Ireland of her abbatial and episcopal successors. Cogitosus had employed a variety of rhetorical strategies. In his introduction, he announced the islandwide authority of the abbess of Kildare over all communities of religious women in Ireland and all churches and religious settlements in the province of Leinster. His narrative also described a holy patroness whose powers clearly outshone those of any other Christian leader, male or female, and whose travels and miracles in *imitatio Christi* linked her historically to the savior himself. Finally, he located Brigit's body at Kildare and thus centralized custody of her influence.

Cogitosus's eighth-century successors shifted emphasis, however, honing only one of his tactics. They too identified Brigit with Jesus. In their tales she also multiplied provisions and healed lepers as the savior did. However, although these later writers mentioned settlements founded by Brigit, they did not discuss architecture. They recalled secondary relics but not the saint's body or tomb. In their stories of Brigit's travels, Brigit outshone but submitted to male religious officials, never competing directly for territory or space. She still demonstrated her superior holiness before crowds of Christians, but usually on the road, in the open, or in domestic settings of kitchens and farmyards. Instead of directing pilgrims to her church, these hagiographers argued for Brigit's control of landscapes outside of Leinster, her mastery of nature and its creatures, and her marvelous protection of fellow travelers.

The eighth-century hagiographers wrote in different political circumstances, in a cooler gender climate, and with more experience of hagiography than Cogitosus. *Vita Prima* (hereafter *VP*) and the *Bethu Brigte* (hereafter *BB*) were probably based on seventh-century sources shared by Cogitosus. Donatus of Fiesole, who also wrote about Brigit in the ninth century, identified Ultán moccu Conchobair (d. 660) and Ailerán the Wise (d. 665) as the first authors of Brigit's cult, but their works are long lost.[52] Both men came from territory north of Leinster. Ultán lived among the Síl nÁedo Sláine of the southern Uí Néill and framed his hagiographic politics accordingly. Similarly, Ailerán probably came from Uí Chairpre under southern Uí Néill domination, where he located some of the saint's adventures. Their stories of Brigit's travels together with selections from Cogitosus the Leinsterman provided sources for the writers of *VP* and *BB*. Both of these eighth-century vitae were produced by now-anonymous ecclesiastics probably living in the provincial borderlands just to the north of Kildare that had once belonged to Leinster dynasts.[53] *VP* repeated and enhanced Cogitosus's episodes in simpler Latin.[54] *BB* was a composite work based on stories from Cogitosus but also introduced a little new material. In addition, *BB*'s author wrote in both Latin and Irish.

Thus the three earliest extant lives of Brigit, composed over the space of 150 years, told overlapping versions, arranged in different itineraries, of Brigit's journeys and life two centuries (and more) earlier. Their common goal was glorification of Brigit, but their discrete purposes were promotion of local versions of her cult. None of the vitae yields very precise historical information, in modern terms, for Brigit's existence. Only Cogitosus's vita celebrated Kildare and located Brigit's dead body there in familiar architecture. *BB* placed the girlish Brigit at an assembly in Kildare earlier in her career; in one episode, Bishop Ibor announced to the gathering of twenty-seven saints that Brigit was a new Mary and that her settlement was "open to heaven and . . . will be the richest of all in the whole island." But that vita did not locate Brigit's death or burial at Kildare.[55] *VP* named Kildare only once in Latin translation as Cella Roboris.

All three hagiographers (or five, if we include Ailerán and Ultán as separate authors) agreed on the basic details of Brigit's saintly career, as did later versions of her life produced throughout the Middle Ages.[56] She was born on one of her possible birth dates in the north of the province of Leinster, a child of the tribe called the Fothairt (related to the modern town of Faughart where later tradition holds that Brigit was born). Her mother was called Broicsech. *VP* and *BB* revealed that Broicsech was a slave from another province bought and impregnated by Brigit's father, Dubthach, a free client (*vir nobilis*) of the king of Leinster.[57] Her parentage and birth were symbolic border crossings of status and tribal affiliation for the Brigit of *VP* and *BB*. While Brigit was still in the womb, her mother was sold to an Uí Néill poet, then to a druid from the north who was descended of a Munster man and a woman from Connacht. Indirectly, then, Brigit had connections by birth and household to all the provinces of Ireland.

Before infancy she was already on the move. Her pregnant mother once rode in a chariot with Brigit's father, Dubthach, past the house of a druid. Dubthach was resisting his legal wife's order to sell the pregnant slave. (This motif appears in secular tales of hero-kings, where a son of a ruler and his concubine or slave turns out to be the next king.)[58] Brigit somehow communicated her presence to the pagan prophet, for he demanded to know who was in the passing chariot. "Take good care of this woman," he advised Dubthach, "for the child she has conceived will be extraordinary." To the pregnant woman he announced, "You will give birth to an illustrious daughter who will shine in the world like the sun in the vault of heaven."[59] When the moment came, in fact, Brigit's mother gave birth while standing over the threshold of the druid's house, just after milking the cows, to a child whom she washed in the pure and nourishing new milk (another literary motif common in stories of heroes).[60] Thus at the moment she entered the world, Brigit connected the pagan past of druids and magic to the Christian future of saints and miracles. The first druid had announced the baby's mission, and the second druid confirmed it: he was watching the stars for portents, as druids always had, but he saw instead a column of fire rising from the house that sheltered the baby. Fire and flames signified direct spiritual connection to God, but to Irish audiences the fiery shaft also recalled the *lúan láith*—some sort of radiant halo--that shot from the heads of saga heroes.[61] Brigit was at once apostle, inspired by the burning tongues of wisdom, and mighty warrior of Christianity. Her holiness could not fit beneath a pagan roof. Fireballs arose skyward from Brigit at several points during her childhood. Each time, the panicked household believed the house was burning until they found the child, source of the flames, slumbering unharmed. Such signs of the holy were easy for pagans to translate, the hagiographer seemed to argue, just as mythological tropes were simply christianized. He told how Brigit would not eat food prepared in the druid's house but would only drink milk from a red-eared white cow, an animal that turned up elsewhere in Irish mythological literature as magical.[62]

The peripatetic Brigit of the two later vitae could not be contained by walls, roofs, or territorial boundaries. Both texts emphasized her time on the road rather than any permanent architecture built by her. Both also set her most significant wonders outside rather than in churches, houses, or forts. In hagiographic language, her travels signaled her ecclesiastical rule, as both readers of and characters in the vitae realized. In *BB*'s version of the episode where she claimed Connacht, the baby Brigit pronounced the words in the ecclesiastical language of Latin—although the story itself was in Irish—while lying spread-eagled in a formal position of prayer, the cross vigil. Both language and posture belonged to clerics, not laypeople, still less infants untrained in Latin. The cross vigil was meant to be performed in church rather than in the dirt outside the kitchen door. In both versions of the episode, Brigit's rejection of existing territorial boundaries and her claims to other people's private property got her and her household kicked out of Connacht by nervous neighbors.[63] The druid knew better than his fellow Connachtmen, for he realized that the bonds of slavery could not contain Brigit either. After moving the household to Munster, he manumitted Brigit's mother and converted to Christianity, but not before witnessing another of the girl's persuasive miracles. Brigit then returned to a Christian foster mother's house in her birthplace of Leinster, thus completing her first circuit of Ireland: from conception in Leinster north to Uí Néill territory, thence to Connacht and Munster with the druid, and back home again.

In all versions of her vita, Brigit spent her childhood in the pastures, dairy, and kitchen of her father, foster mother, or mother's owner. She herded animals, cooked bacon, and made butter. All these were typical female provisioning chores in well-supplied households. In such domestic settings the child-saint performed homely miracles from an early age. She multiplied scarce food for guests and donated household stores to the poor and even to hungry dogs. In one episode, surely meant to be comical, she gave away all of her father's possessions. According to both *VP* and *BB,* Dubthach was so annoyed with her holy thieving that he loaded Brigit in his chariot and drove off to the king's fort in order to sell her into slavery. He marched into the royal hall and complained to the king, paraphrasing the desert fathers, that "whatever she lays her hand on, she takes."[64] But while Dubthach was haggling with the king, Brigit sat in the chariot outside chatting with beggars. She cheerfully donated his sword, given him by the king, to the first indigent who asked, later telling her furious father: "I gave it to Christ." The king recognized her holiness or else was savvier than Dubthach—at any rate, he refused to enslave the girl.[65] Like the ignorant folk of Connacht who had rejected her claims to dominion, Dubthach could not grasp that, by mere virtue of her holiness, Brigit had a right to any property she wanted.

Eventually, after resisting marriage, Brigit was allowed to make a vow of chastity and take the veil, thus becoming a religious professional. *VP* and *BB* disagreed about who consecrated Brigit and where it occurred, but the story is the only one common in most details to all three early accounts. During the ritual of her vow, at the moment of veiling, Brigit manifested another fiery column. She also grasped a wooden pedestal or altar rail during the ceremony that afterward became living wood, fresh and green to the writer's day. The three versions differed about the species of wood, though; *BB* specified acacia, also used for the Ark of the Covenant.[66] The identity of the presiding bishop and the site of the veiling changed in each story, too, in details that carried far more political resonance than timber. Cogitosus credited Mac Caille, a bishop associated with a church at Cruachán of Brí Éile in the borderlands of ancient Leinster (modern county Offaly).[67] Tírechán, writing to exalt Patrick's jurisdiction but acknowledging Brigit's cult, had insisted that the event took place in a different church founded by Patrick in Mag Telach.[68] *VP* placed the affair in Patrician territory in Mide and gave the honor to Patrick's disciple, bishop Mel, although Mac Caille made a cameo in the episode. *BB* reconciled all these traditions by sending Brigit to Cruachán in search of Mel, where she met two virgins who directed her to Mag Telach; led by Mac Caille, she found Bishop Mel there. Mac Caille raised the veil, but angels took it from his hands and placed it on Brigit's head while Mel recited the prayers and blessings for consecration. As in the episode of babyhood dominion, these events took place in Latin within the mostly Irish-language vita, thus heightening the liturgical and miraculous significance of Brigit's vow. Latin phrases invoked biblical precedent, emphasizing these particular moments in Brigit's life and transhistorical events, but also raised the passage to the level of ritual each time it was read aloud to eager audiences.[69]

To make clear whose prestige was greatest, though, in this exalted gathering of prelates, virgins, and angels, the author of *BB* added an episode unique among medieval texts in Ireland or anywhere else. Bishop Mel was so "intoxicated with the grace of God" while chanting the liturgy of consecration that he accidentally read the ordination ceremony for bishops instead. Making the best of the situation, and ignoring centuries of ecclesiastical law and custom in the face of Brigit's *virtus,* the Patrician bishop announced, "This virgin alone in Ireland will hold the episcopal ordination."[70] Where as Saint Genovefa had acted like a bishop, Brigit actually was one, at least according to this lone hagiographer. Within the hagiographical episode, the saint herself did not acknowledge the unique event but instead accepted a donation of land nearby at Fid Éoin, still in Patrick's territory, where she performed three miracles before moving on.[71]

After the public drama of her vow, Brigit traveled from settlement to settlement, house to house around the provinces of Leinster, Munster, and Connacht. In both later versions of her vita, she also went north into Mide to meet Patrick and visit his churches there. She performed miracles en route, healing plenty of lepers and other patients, feeding hungry nuns and crowds of visiting clerics, halting bandits, preventing murders, and making peace. She took on female followers in districts both within and beyond Leinster, establishing communities of vowed women that mostly remained nameless in the vitae. Perhaps early medieval audiences read their own settlements into these passages. The landscapes of the later two vitae were more specific about territories and bishops than Cogitosus had been, though. *VP* generally included more incidental material and dialogue than the other two versions while *BB* added topographical detail. *VP* also finished with the story of how Brigit's successor, Darlugdach, wished to accompany her to heaven. (*BB* now lacks a proper beginning and ending.)

The two later vitae differed significantly from Cogitosus's text by relocating much of Brigit's miraculous activity and altering the political implications of her life. In these versions, the saint made several circuits of the island. She traveled again to every one of the five provinces and made prolonged sojourns to the north with Patrick and his colleagues. As the Celticist Kim McCone has pointed out, Brigit's journeys comprised three related maps of jurisdictional claims for Kildare: Northern Leinster and Mide, which was the territory of the southern Uí Néill; Munster and Connacht; and forays north sandwiched between visits to Kildare and the plain of Mag Life in northern Leinster.[72] In Cogitosus's day, the mid-seventh century, the kings of Leinster still had the faint prospect of governing central Ireland. But by 700 the kings of the southern Uí Néill, the most powerful dynastic confederation in Ireland, had pushed their borders south into Leinster territory. Brigit's tour of Mide and the borderlands carried political significance because by the time these two vitae were written, at least seventy-five years after Cogitosus had composed his vita, this area belonged spiritually to Patrick, patron of the Uí Néill. As McCone has argued, the common textual sources of *VP* and *BB* (the vitae by Ailerán and Ultán) were probably composed before the Uí Néill moved permanently south. In the eighth century when *VP*'s author wrote of Brigit's superior miracles before Patrick and his bishops, the writer was still asserting the limited authority of Brigit's cult-keepers within this territory already lost by Leinster. Brigit's miracles in these lands, as well as stories of her acquisitions of endowments and of communities belonging to other women, staked the continuing claim of her followers to ecclesiastical dominance up north when their political grasp was weakening.[73] In conjunction with Cogitosus's foundational text and the establishment of Brigit's cult center at Kildare, this was an effective claim for widespread *paruchia*. Hagiographers assumed that priests, monks, and nuns dedicated to Brigit would celebrate her feast day and pray for her intercession; that they would support Kildare's ecclesiastical position at councils and synods, and the political endeavors of Kildare and its allies throughout Ireland; and that they would gather revenues and donations and send a proportion of that wealth to Kildare.[74]

Hagiographers had more tools at hand than simple declarations of ecclesiastical hierarchy, however. The same issue faced daily by the abbess of Kildare, when she tried to exercise authority among men in her community, also troubled Brigit's hagiographers. How might a woman assert control over sacral spaces? These literate men had to make a case for Brigit's singular status among the founders of Ireland's churches to set precedent for Kildare's medieval abbesses among male ecclesiastical leaders. Mel's botched ordination laid the abbesses' claim to episcopal status. The motif of transterritorial travel betrayed another strategy for imposing Kildare's influence. However, Brigit's biographers (after Cogitosus) also employed a distinctly feminine vocabulary of sainthood to bolster their claims for the saint and thus for her vowed followers. Rather than arguing that Brigit could claim the same dominance of sacral space as a cleric, they argued that Brigit used this space differently but even more efficaciously than male saints and other ordained men.

The writers used two techniques to represent Brigit's special authority over sacral sites and consecrated spaces. First, they located many of her adult miracles outside the sheltering constraints of ecclesiastical architecture. Just as no house could contain the infant Brigit and no province prevent her dominion, no church or settlement could enclose and limit her adult wonderworking. This seems like an ironic development for a saint who first established her reputation for raising a basilica. But in the seventh or eighth century, before the trade in holy bones flourished across Europe, a patroness could leave only one body to consecrate a single basilica. Outside Kildare she worked in the open. Not one of her miracles occurred in an official Christian structure except for her veiling. Whereas Genovefa had entered other men's cities and worked miracles in other saints' churches, Brigit had to make a bid for authority in a different architectural context. She approached her holy colleagues in domestic space, traditionally belonging to women, or outside in public assembly places.

One of her crucial performances took place, according to *VP*, while she was literally on the move across the region of Tethbae. From her chariot, Brigit observed an entire household driving their cattle and lugging their possessions along the road. She offered her chariot to them and perched with her nuns at the roadside. Then she sanctified the spot with a miracle. "Dig under the sod," she ordered her nuns, "so that water may gush forth. For there are people coming along who have food but are thirsty since they have nothing to drink." At her order, the women effortlessly dug a well, even as Moses had once struck the desert sands and produced a fountain. A chieftain with his foot soldiers and horsemen came by, stopping to offer Brigit a pair of horses. Next came no less than Patrick with his faithful followers, carrying provisions but lacking water. The nuns offered them a drink. Oddly reminiscent of Cogitosus's orderly congregation, the entire social order processed to Brigit at that roadside site: a family of ordinary laypeople with their servants, a political leader with his warriors, and representatives of the ecclesiastical establishment. Every one of them partook of Brigit's charity at the well she had so marvelously created. Together, Patrick, Brigit, and company ate and drank together, rendering thanks and glorifying Brigit nowhere near a church.[75]

In other episodes of travel, Brigit's mobility caused tension with the men who exercised the *cura monialum* or administration of religious women. Once Patrick's bishops, Mel and Melchu, invited her on a visit to Patrick. En route another cleric with a slow-moving entourage, including cattle, carts, and baggage, asked to join them. When the bishops objected but Brigit agreed, they left Brigit behind with the unhurried priest. She lingered, too, to cure cripples and the diseased. Eventually she and her companions made it to Tailtiu, an ancient assembly site in Mide, where an episcopal synod was under way. Patrick was trying to resolve a dispute between another bishop and the woman who had accused him of fathering her son. At a loss over the ambiguous evidence, the council summoned Brigit. She made the sign of the cross over the new mother, which caused the woman's head to swell hideously; Brigit also blessed the baby, who fingered another depraved priest as his father. Again, the clerics responded with ritual thanks and glorification of Brigit as they accepted the confession of the baby's mother. The synod had chosen Tailtiu as a meeting place because of its historical resonances of territorial dominance. By her miracle, Brigit showed the episcopal deliberations made before her arrival to be meaningless. In legends, Irish kings had to render righteous judgments in order to evince the *fír flathemon* or "truth" of authentic lordship; bad judges lost their royal positions.[76] Brigit's judicial miracles proved her to be a just ruler and enabled her to capture Tailtiu and its Uí Néill territory.

Brigit followed her assertion of lordship by assuming ecclesiastical authority, too, thanks to another wonder. After the synod, everyone scattered to the houses of local people for the night. The assembly had been too big to shelter in any single church or hall. A countryman invited Brigit to bless his new house. She and her companions were just sitting down to dinner when she sensed that the host was a pagan. "We cannot eat your food unless you first get baptized," she informed the home owner. Another nun reminded her that the man had long resisted baptism at Patrick's hand. Nonetheless, he, along with his entire household, instantly agreed to convert. Brigit could not perform the ritual, though, because she was a woman; she never challenged institutional rules limiting women's participation in rituals. However, the accused and cleared bishop, Brón, fortuitously arrived to do the honors. The next day Patrick scolded Brigit not for arranging a baptism but for traveling without a priest. "From this day on," he insisted, "your charioteer is always to be a priest."

In the gendered logic of the eighth-century Christian establishment, Brigit did not baptize a man in church but wrought a miracle of conversion in domestic space. She could not act as a priest but took one as her servant.[77] In a later episode, Brigit ordered the charioteer to preach to her while driving them across Mag Life, which he did, but she chastised his impoliteness when he kept his face to the road and his back to her. She conducted several miracles to keep the chariot moving safely while he faced her and spoke.[78] Brigit's hagiographers purposefully invoked her ability to modify religious activity to suit nonreligious, unbuilt spaces belonging to laypeople, pagans, and women. In other stories of the same vita, Brigit turned domestic spaces into holy places with her protection by conducting cures, repelling thieves and murderers, and bringing cattle home to barns.[79]

Like many early saints, Brigit could sense and control distant events. Because she could see through the material world, she could also alter other people's perception of the physical landscape—but only to their benefit, of course. Once she so befuddled a local man that he got lost in his "own native place" and ended up where she wanted him, at her church.[80] Another time she brought to her door a famous recluse who had refused even to look upon the face of vowed women; he spent three days and nights preaching to Brigit's community.[81] When kings or bishops—including that alleged sinner, bishop Brón—strayed en route to visit Brigit, she made clear the way to her house that they might bring their gifts and enjoy her hospitality.[82] To all these wandering men Brigit revealed the refuge of Kildare.

In addition to constructing a new vocabulary of female sanctity, Brigit's hagiographers employed another canny strategy. They recounted stories of Brigit's interactions with other saints and clerics at significant points in her circuits of Ireland. In addition to the story of Patrick and Brón, another set piece involved Brigit nodding off during one of Patrick's lengthy sermons only to reveal upon waking that she had received a vision directly from God. She had seen plowmen sowing good seed and reaping new milk in a fruitful land; this, Patrick informed her, was a vision of himself and herself spreading the word of God. She had also glimpsed evil plowmen sowing weeds and water streaming from furrows; this, according to Patrick, was an apocalyptic vision of nonbelievers and evildoers.[83] Just as the paternity episode demonstrated Brigit's superior wisdom, so the dream episode proved her intimate link to God and established her as the missionary equal of Patrick. If Patrick played Joseph when interpreting her dream, Brigit was Pharaoh, ruler of the lands. At the same time, Patrick functioned as the typical witness and publicist of a private miracle, a figure prominent in Irish hagiography as the sidekick to visionary saints. For her part, Brigit not only interpreted visions for male clerics and helped them find their way across hostile territory but also clothed them in the vestments necessary for Christian ritual. She agreed, for example, to weave Patrick's own burial shroud after predicting his death and burial.[84] She was at once a typical woman, caring for her men's needs and ministering their deaths, and a visionary who could see even what Ireland's apostle could not. Without her, the vitae taught, bishops could not understand what they saw, go where they needed to go, make informed decisions about church law, perform the rites of their churches for the people of Ireland, or even have proper burials. It did not matter that priests and bishops controlled the consecrated spaces and formal liturgies of churches—they still needed the charisma of Brigit to practice effective religion.

Brigit's miracles and movements in Patrick's territory added weight to her distinctly feminine authority. She moved like a royal bride from her father's house to a new place beyond the guardianship of her Leinster kinsmen. She was responsible, as any good wife, for acting as liaison between her affiliates in the north and the south of Ireland, enforcing peace among them and protecting both. Already by the time these vitae were written, Kildare and Armagh had made a treaty limiting Kildare's jurisdiction to the churches and people of Leinster and officially subordinating Brigit's authority to that of Patrick. Inscribed in a text called the *Liber Angeli* (Book of the Angel) composed around 700—between Cogitosus's time and the writing of the two slightly later vitae of Brigit—this text laid out a compromise agreed to by churchmen and churchwomen of the two most powerful communities in Ireland:

> Between holy Patrick and Brigit, pillars of the Irish, there existed
> so great a friendship of charity that they were of one heart and one
> mind. Christ worked many miracles through him and her. The holy
> man, then, said to the Christian virgin: O my Brigit, your paruchia
> will be deemed to be in your province in your dominion, but in the
> eastern and western part it will be in my dominion.[85]

In other words, Kildare would order the churches of the province of Leinster only, while Armagh controlled the rest of Ireland. This was an Armagh author's version of the agreement. The *VP* and *BB* told a different version in which baby Brigit had announced her possession of Connacht and the adult saint had claimed the rest of the island. But in both accounts Brigit formally submitted to the clerical authority of Patrick as a good wife to her husband. *Bethu Brigte* put it plainly. Once, while Bishop Ibor recounted a dream to his fellow Leinster clerics, Brigit approached. Ibor had dreamed that the Virgin Mary had visited Ireland. He declared that "today a girl, for whom it has been prepared by God, will come to us like Mary." As the hagiographer wrote, "It happened thus." Brigit arrived.[86] Cogitosus had cast Brigit in imitation of Christ, but *BB* turned her into another mother of the savior, a title she retains today.[87]

The authors of the *VP* and *BB* thus established Brigit's reputation in relation to Patrician foundations and via her movement through open spaces and public places, but without reference to the fixed point of Kildare or to the wonder-working powers of her body there. The *BB* mentioned no durable objects associated with the saint that might have become valued relics, reverently kept upon altars in Brigidine churches. Instead, the eighth-century hagiographer described miracles accomplished with fungibles, mostly water. By raising a hand in blessing or touching a vessel, Brigit changed water to beer or warm milk. She sprinkled water upon lepers and blind men to heal them. Only *VP* mentioned a couple of potential relics, although without explicitly identifying them as objects of worship or their locations as pilgrimage destinations. In one story, a woman came to beg alms; when Brigit offered her a cloak or a cow, the maiden objected that robbers would steal such items. Brigit gave instead her a belt. Dipped in water, she told the woman, the girdle would heal people who would, in turn, provide her with food and clothing in thanks. The woman immediately tried out the wonder-working powers of the girdle on a sick child whose parents donated good clothes. Over the years, she healed many people and grew rich, buying land and giving donations to the poor. The author did not indicate whether she lived in a religious community, nor did he reveal what became of the girdle or even the recipient's name.[88] His tactic was utterly unlike the device used by Patrick's earliest hagiographers, who recited a litany of Patrician liturgical tools, books, and bodily parts left by the saint with the churches he founded west of the Shannon River.[89]

Similarly vague stories in the Brigidine vitae involved the donation of a silver chain to Brigit, which her nuns preserved as evidence of a miracle but without advertising any miraculous properties; a lump of silver received by a vowed woman named Kinna; a shrine containing liturgical vestments that Brigit once sent floating over the sea to Saint Sénán; and a rock that the saint mysteriously bored with her fingers for no obvious reason, although cup-marked boulders are common enough in Ireland. These were the sorts of objects that other churches kept as relics of their patrons but which Brigit's hagiographers did not locate except vaguely with personal names.[90] Likewise, in another episode Brigit reminisced about her miracles, telling another nun: "When I was a little girl, I made a stone altar as a child's game and the angel came and perforated the stone at the four corners and put four wooden legs under it," adding that she had told the woman so that she might "glorify God." The wooden-legged stone sounds much like a portable altar carried by traveling priests among dispersed settlements, but aside from setting the episode in Brigit's native Leinster the hagiographer gave no details about the altar.[91] In these vitae, Brigit made her living mark on the landscape itself rather leaving behind manufactured objects.

At Kildare, Brigit lay in the basilica whence she confirmed the access of religious women to the monastic city's consecrated spaces. But Brigit's female followers in other communities had no body on which to base their claims for the saint, thus less control over spaces and territories.[92] They argued implicitly, as the Roman authority Gregory the Great had argued more plainly, that saints had to work harder and perform better miracles in places that lacked their bodily relics in order to persuade witnesses of their ubiquitous *virtus*.[93] In seeking ways to publicize her prowess, Brigit's second and third hagiographers turned the lack of body parts from liability into an advantage. Hagiographers from these other communities argued that the land was infused with the saint's immanence. They cast Brigit as a mistress of the unbuilt environment who was joyful on the move, at ease with beasts, in charge of wells and ancient assembly places. (In doing so they unwittingly created a mold for Celtic sanctity that would spread to other cults and hagiographers in Ireland.) For hagiographers and their audiences, such characteristics enabled a bodiless but highly gendered Saint Brigit to protect the people who inhabited and roamed her territories. No devotees needed to visit her material remains. No bones or manufactured relics were necessary to sanctify her places or validate the ecclesiastical position of her vowed women. The history of her passing sufficed to establish her presence.

Yet this was not the same authority that Cogitosus had dreamt for Brigit and her abbesses. In the schemes of her northern hagiographers, Brigit's influence outside her own home and kin was less persuasive in church than in wild settings that had traditionally belonged to feminine powers.

How Saint Brigit Became a Goddess

The first generation of Irish hagiographers told a history of traffic, settlement, and building. Cogitosus had located Kildare at the crossroads of tribal migratory routes and the highways of Roman traders. The later vitae still touted connections between Brigidine communities and Rome but not via conventional roads. *Vita Prima* told a marvelous tale about Brigit's intimacy with events at the heart of Christendom. She once stood rapt in prayerful trance while her neighbors made a great din; upon questioning, she revealed that she had been listening to masses chanted in the tombs of Peter and Paul. Since no one else had the same privilege, she sent messengers to bring back the Roman liturgy and, when they arrived again in Ireland, she sent her men back to Rome again for more recent liturgical updates.[94] Neither she nor any other professed woman considered traveling abroad, though. Brigit did not need to see Rome or its architecture. It was enough to mimic the words and gestures of its priests.

The story of Brigit evolved as her cult spread and accumulated a history, and as Christian communities matured. The saint turned up as a character in the lives of other saints and in secular epics. Poets wrote hymns and prayers to her. In martyrologies, calendars, and litanies, her feast day appeared among days devoted to Mediterranean martyrs and Irish comrades. Her story compounded when other holy women called Brigit or Brig populated the same texts, cluttering the landscape with churches named after themselves, and confusing the literati who tried to sort out same-named saints. The *Comainmnigud naebúag,* or list of female saints with identical names kept in the twelfth-century Book of Leinster, included ten Brigits and fourteen Brigs, and these were just the famous women with that name.[95] Suddenly, after Cogitosus spread the saint's reputation, Brigits were multiplying like loaves and fishes. Each Brigit had places, and each place bore more girls called Brigit. Women all over Ireland lived in imitation of these Brigits.

Even if the architecture of religious settlements did not change much during the early Middle Ages, the gendering of religious spaces in Ireland also grew more complex with issues of property, status, kinship, and political authority. Elaborate laws developed to regulate the relation of a saint's original community to its ecclesiastical satellites, and to track the property and dues that supported these clientage relations.[96] The gender bias of formal laws worked to the disadvantage of Kildare's community, but the nobility of its managers was in its favor. The discomfort that came with a female patron who could neither officially rule nor preach showed in later versions of Brigit's vitae.

Some features of Brigit's hagiography remained fixed by gender, such as her affinity for the natural world and the domestic character of her miracles. Other characteristics of her cult were built into the genre of hagiography and could not change. Her biographers repeated the ancient testimony of witnesses to Brigit's wonder, used biblical motifs and themes, and borrowed from earlier Continental models of sanctity. But in the eighth and ninth centuries, hagiographers needed something more to justify Brigit's peculiar position as Ireland's first and only major extraterritorial female saint. Although they wrote from a land that refused women political or ecclesiastical authority, their traditional literature offered a full repertoire of political symbols cast in feminine terms. They used this old vocabulary to revise Brigit's cult to fit the constantly changing boundaries, territories, and dynasties of the provincial hierarchy. These proponents of cult quite sensibly culled arguments from existing political histories, in the process further embedding Brigit into the ancient landscapes of Leinster.

The hagiographers located Saint Brigit's story within a larger context of tribal histories and legendary rulers of the pagan past. To begin with, they made their hero look more like other traditional heroes.[97] Brigit's unusual birth on the threshold of a house, her connections with a prophesizing druid, her insistence on drinking only the milk of a red-and-white cow, and her cranial pyrotechnics all referred to tales about ancient Ireland and established Brigit as a native hero in the Irish tradition. One episode of *VP* explicitly invoked a famous episode from the familiar Ulster cycle of heroic tales. Brigit was reluctantly traveling by chariot with Bishop Mel to seek a doctor to cure her ferocious headaches. She fell from the chariot when crossing a ford and gashed her head on a rock; her blood, when mingled with water, restored voice to two mute women. When Brigit and Mel finally reached the doctor, he told them that a greater physician than he had already healed Brigit, and Mel admitted his mistake. The chariot accident recalled a different kind of tale altogether, though; in *Longes Macc nUislenn* (Exile of Uisliu's Sons), the heroine Deirdriu had been captured and kidnapped by her enemies and, instead of becoming the concubine of one of them, leapt from a chariot to dash her brains on a rock.[98] That heroine eluded her master with suicide, whereas Brigit tumbled out, picked herself up unharmed, and immediately healed some ailing witnesses to her miracle. Like Deirdriu, Brigit proved superior to her supposed master, Bishop Mel. Such literary references posited Brigit as the last of a long line of heroes marked for greatness from birth, whereas Patrick, by comparison, had been born a foreigner and brought as a slave to Ireland.

The hagiographers constructed a second, even stronger argument for Brigit's territorial dominance based on allusions to secular literature and the saint's gender. Brigit ruled religious landscapes and kingdoms with a specifically feminine power derived from historical mythologies. Whatever the cults that had compelled men and women before christianization, hagiographers and other writers had come to depict paganism as primitive and feminized, as opposed to the civilized, masculine character of Christian organization and episcopal territories. In Christian texts, pagans from the past were typically nature-oriented, practicing their rites al fresco like Caesar's druids. They were unpredictable and magical, as were the women of Irish sagas and proverbs. Finally, in stories of ancient pagan Ireland, political leaders were seduced and misled by its magicians and spirits who were, at least in this mythology, women as often as men.[99] "Save us," begged a prayer attributed to Patrick, "from the spells of women, smiths, and druids."[100]

Brigit's talents were similar to the tricks of spellbinding women from secular tales. Like druids, she could see across distances and through time to events past, present, and future.[101] Like queens of the otherworld, she could manipulate visible landscapes and move among realities. She could glamour travelers and animals according to her desires, leading them astray or home as she pleased. Her mastery over even the wildest of beasts had been well established by Cogitosus; the two later vitae repeated tales of fierce boars, elusive foxes, cattle and sheep that followed the saint's commands. Indeed, any Irish reader or hearer of Brigit's vitae knew that boars and cattle were important animals in the iconography of Celtic traditions in Ireland and elsewhere (for instance, the Bible), and turned up frequently as magical characters in the secular literature of the early medieval period.[102] Brigit also reigned over the natural features of the landscape and the weather. At her touch, the stripped beam of a church railing became a living tree. Rain did not fall upon her harvests nor storms threaten her sheep. In one section of the *BB*, she chanted this verse:

> Grant me a clear day
> for Thou are a dear friend, a kingly youth:
> for the sake of thy mother, loving Mary,
> ward off rain, ward off wind.

> My king will do it for me,
> rain will not fall till the night
> on account of Brigit today,
> who is going here to the herding.[103]

Landscape yielded to her. Dark and impenetrable woods gave up easy paths to those under her protection, while thieves lost their way in broad daylight. In one episode of the *VP*, her women companions were halted at a river with the Connachtmen and Uí Néill, both traditional enemies of the Leinstermen. The armies refused to help the women cross. So Brigit manipulated the waters. While the river roiled up above the unhelpful soldiers' heads, it remained calm for Brigit's nuns, reaching just to their knees so that they were able to wade across.[104] By comparison, in the seventh- or eighth-century cattle-rustling Ulster saga *Táin Bó Cúailnge*, the river Cronn purposely whipped its waters to prevent the passage of impious armies while heroes moved easily across peaceful landscapes.[105] Finally, Brigit also interpreted the skies as easily as druids read the stars; besides shooting fire from her skull, she informed a crowd of admirers that the thundercloud lowering over their heads signified Patrick's burial place. She even, in a famous episode, hung her cloak on a sunbeam.[106]

Her constant safe travel across the lands of Ireland, her ability to interpret and control the landscape and the skies, and her power to protect or destroy men on the move all pointed toward a mastery of nature and territory that even Patrick could not claim. True, the earliest vitae of Patrick put him on the plains before Tara (Temair) clearing the skies of darkness and halting druidic snows, and he also controlled the bounty of fish in rivers.[107] This was the kind of weather-making countermagic practiced by saints across Christendom.[108] Tírechán also claimed that Patrick's travels had produced architecture just as Brigit's Cogitosan journey yielded Kildare's basilica. In the seventh-century versions of his life, Patrick left a patchwork of small foundations scattered across the northern half of Ireland, which he staffed with his disciples and equipped with bells, gospels, and other liturgical furniture. His episcopal job was to perform Christian rituals that, as his Continental colleagues had long established, occurred only in properly built and consecrated spaces. He did not display any particular ease with the outdoors or familiarity with nature's creatures.

The writers of *VP* and *BB* also used Brigit's affinity with her territory to cast her as a protecting spirit of the Leinster people when invaded by their enemies, especially the troublesome Uí Néill. Long ago, the hagiographers proposed, heroines, warrior-women, and territorial goddesses from myths and king tales had actively defended the land.[109] In this new Christian era, Brigit and other saints took up the watch over Leinster. In one episode of her vitae, she granted to the king of Leinster a long life and victory in his "perennial feud with the Uí Néill" even though other stories showed Brigit on good terms with the southern Uí Néill and their bishops in Mide. Soon after, the king went to battle to prevent an invasion of his homeland and called on Brigit's support against the Uí Néill. His men clamored to heaven and were granted a vision of Brigit in the van of battle, staff in her right hand and the usual column of fire blazing skyward from her head—Clovis had seen just such a fiery apparition before his decisive meeting with the Alamanni. The Leinster king thereafter waged thirty successful campaigns in Ireland and nine more in Britain. More important, Brigit's supernatural shield remained effective after his death, for when the Leinstermen carried his lifeless body into another battle against the Uí Néill, they routed the invaders.[110] Whereas the pagan king Loegaire of Temair had refused baptism and been buried crouching toward Leinster, Brigit's Christian kings went boldly to war fortified by her flaming presence. Historical Leinster armies may have called upon Brigit herself to lead the van too, even if they saw her only as an icon upon a banner.[111]

Thus, like the territorial goddesses who had preceded her in literature and religion, Brigit ruled the land of her kin and protected its kings, at least according to her hagiographers. As Thomas Torma has pointed out, they must have known texts similar to *Baile in Scáil*, a densely symbolic ninth-century narrative in which a queenly figure of Sovereignty doles out the liquor of political authority to successive kings. No doubt Medb, the famous dominatrix of Ulster sagas, ruler of Connacht, and queen of seven feeble kings, was also a familiar figure.[112] Hagiographers dwelt among landmarks and even whole territories that had gained their names from queens and princesses touted in topographical legends. Rivers, fords, hills, lakes, and entire plains were called after royal women who had expired dramatically in or near them.[113] Brigit, chaste spiritual consort of Leinster kings, was also bound historically to Kildare and Dún Ailinne, but she continued to abide along the trails that she had followed around Ireland. She lived on in the monasteries and churches dedicated to her, in objects that had once belonged to her or just touched her body, in prayers to her, and in the written words of her vitae. Her political children could call her image into battle. Brigit's immanence infused the very ground beneath all of them, for the saint was manifest in her unbounded territory. This ideology of portable dominion proved invaluable to Brigit's cult-keepers and mythmakers. Political power had once resided in a sacral spot like Temair or Dún Ailinne, so that he who controlled the hill also ruled the territory. But when saints replaced legendary kings, and Christian churches and burial places revoked the power of inaugural sites and other old holy places, their dominion knew no limits.

By the eighth century, then, Brigit's hagiographers and other supporters of her *paruchia* had realized that the key to Brigit's widespread authority lay in her unique relation to the land and its creatures. They used all the available languages of landscape to establish that authority in their histories of the saint and her cult. Although they knew, from Cogitosus's vita or from their common Latin sources, and from visits to Kildare itself, that Brigit's body lay at the heart of Leinster, they also argued that her sanctity spread over the entire island. Churches and religious communities professing devotion to the saint only marked the most visible of her places. But the vast territory of the saint, unbound by the politics or history of a single dynasty or kingdom, also included unbuilt sacral sites identified only by older methods for locating divinity in the landscape.

Brigit had not always been a goddess, although there may well once have been a deity or several called Brig. Cogitosus had made perfectly feasible arguments for Brigit's authority without invoking literary conventions beyond the traditional Christian canon. However, as Irish religious communities became increasingly hierarchical and competitive, and as women faced growing limits on their authority over sacral spaces and clerical confederations, the writers of Brigit's cult developed new tactics for describing her authority. Hagiographers of the eighth and ninth centuries used traditional motifs of feminine territoriality to reconstruct Brigit. By 900, the nexus of symbols produced the goddess Brigit known in early medieval literature. According to Cormac mac Cuilennáin, a scholar, bishop, and king of Munster in that period, the very word "Brigit" had come to mean "goddess":

> Brigit .i. banfile ingen in Dagdae. Is_ insin Brigit b_ n-_xe .i. band_a
> no adratis filid. Ar ba rom_r 7 ba roán a frithgnam. Ideo eum
> deam uocant poetarum. Cuius sorores erant Brigit b_ legis 7 Brigit
> b_ Goibne ingena in Dagda, de quarum nominibus pene omnes
> Hibernenses dea Brigit uocabatur.

> Brigit, that is, the female poet, daughter of the [god] Dagdae. This is
> Brigit the female seer, or woman of insight, i.e. the goddess whom
> poets used to worship, for her cult was very great and very splendid.
> It is for this reason that they call her the goddess of poets by this
> title, and her sisters were Brigit the woman of leechcraft and Brigit
> the woman of smithcraft, i.e. goddesses, i.e. three daughters of the
> Dagdae are they. By their names the goddess Brigit was called by all
> the Irish.[114]

In Cormac's version, in fact, three goddesses were once called Brigit. Each had her own specialization in poetry, healing, or craft.[115] One of the Dagdae's daughters turned up again as Bríg in the ninth-century *Cath Maige Tuired* (Second Battle of Moytura), a story about an ancient fight between two supernatural tribes for control of Ireland. This Bríg was one of the Túatha Dé Danann (tribe of the goddess Danu), the supernatural clan that supposedly lived under the *síde* (sg. *síd*) or fairy mounds that still litter the island. In this legendary account and other, later histories, Brigit mediated between human and supernatural tribes. She also brokered contact between quick and dead by inventing keening, the characteristic Irish shrieking and weeping over corpses.[116]

Writers, preachers, and devotees understood the complexity of multiple Brigits and their layered cult histories. If the Irish could keep track of three divine Brigits, they were also perfectly capable of distinguishing goddesses from the many nuns called Brigit and Brig. And if Saint Brigit of Kildare behaved like a goddess, there was a good reason. Her body must still have lain at the heart of Leinster in the eighth and ninth centuries, when the authors of the second and third vitae acknowledged her specially gendered guardianship of Ireland. Later, men would carry her bones north. Meanwhile, devotees continued to construct churches in her name all around Ireland. Someone took the time to list eighty religious communities owing dues and allegiance to Kildare. Most of the churches seem to have been women's settlements located in Kildare or the adjoining counties of Laois and Offaly, but foundations from Wexford to Tyrone were on the list.[117] About three times as many settlements associated with Brigit turned up in the medieval documents, often amounting to nothing more than place-names: twenty-seven of those recorded were called simply Cell Brighde, Brigit's monastery, although which Brigit was not always clear.[118] These were just the communities visible and durable enough to merit notice.

Once Brigit became portable, Irish men also took her to Wales, Scotland, and Britain, although not all of her indigenous attributes translated into foreign languages. She became Saint Ffraid in Wales at Llansantffraid. In the ancient core of London and at Brideswell, she presided as Saint Bride. In Scotland, Bride guarded the Douglas clan through the centuries.[119] Brigit's cult spread to mainland Europe at least as early as the eighth century. Monks from Germany to Provence copied her vita for the benefit of their brothers. She reached Italy by 850 when Donatus, the Irish-born bishop of Fiesole, built a church for her in Piacenza and composed a versified version of her vita to celebrate. Donatus offers a glimpse of Irish itineraries abroad, for he also raised a hospice for Irish pilgrims en route to Rome.[120]

Still later, Brigit went to Spain and Sweden. A well near Husaby once belonged to Irish Brigit.[121] Her name was popular among parents of Swedish baby girls, including the mother and father of the famous fourteenth-century mystic, another Sancta Brigita. Everywhere Christians celebrated saints' feast days, Brigit took her place on the liturgical calendar with Martin, Genovefa, and Patrick. Europeans who could not speak Brigit's language composed new hymns and vitae to celebrate the Irish woman.[122] Every year on the first of February, churches full of women and men who had never seen Ireland listened to a version of her life. Some may have heard of Kildare's basilica, while others may have wondered at the saint's reputation for divinity—if they could understand the hagiographers' subtle manipulation of Irish literary motifs. Her domesticity and ease in unbuilt places must have resonated with the gender clichés of other cultures.

It is ironic but not coincidental that, as later hagiographers sought new ways to express Brigit's authority around Christendom, religious women in Ireland were becoming less mobile and less visible. Throughout the early Middle Ages, church leaders organized stable congregations, monasteries, and parishes. The walls and boundaries that had once excluded pagans now protected vowed women. Christian doctrine and Irish gender ideology insisted that nuns stay put. With the enduring exception of Brigit, women built only to delineate their own holy places, not as public acts of christianization. They traveled to visit each other, not to mark their dominions. They offered hospitality and advice to male colleagues, but did not march to meet them or contest with them in ecclesiastical establishment. Nor did they share rule.

Brigit's new persona as patroness of fields and farms made her a timeless symbol of feminine nature, but made her useless as a historical model for other vowed women. Like an ancient king's enclosure, the settlement at Kildare remained important as a sacral site because of its place in the past, not because of the active authority of its women outside their little piece of Leinster. The position of Kildare's abbess, whoever she was, remained exceptional among ecclesiastical leaders, but the role was largely symbolic. Brigit's cult spread, but Brigit herself went literally to ground, surfacing in legends of her ancient divinity and at unbuilt, local wells and springs. Other churches replaced Kildare, other vitae obscured the ekphratic phrases of Cogitosus. As the Middle Ages marched on, the hagiographic *logos* of Brigit reduced the tangible, visual power of her first place in the shadow of Dún Ailinne.

8

Relics

In 1161, someone in Paris whispered that the canons of Sainte-Geneviève had misplaced her head and that it had not been buried with the rest of her bones. The rumormonger may have been a monk from Saint-Denis or a canon at Nôtre Dame. Both the monastery north of town and the bishop's church on the Île de la Cité had been tussling with the community at Sainte-Geneviève over property and authority in Paris. Nonetheless, the accusation spread rapidly around the city and among the French bishops assembled there for a major council. The Genovefans panicked. A mob gathered. The bishops demanded that Saint Genovefa's tomb be busted open and the body examined.

What did the community of Sainte-Geneviève fear? Presumably, even if the saint lacked a head, she remained immanent at her sanctuary. For more than five centuries she had shielded the city against floods and invaders. Just forty years previously she had processed in her reliquary across the river to Nôtre Dame, where she healed Parisians stricken with a burning fever. Any of her bones might serve to channel her intercession, bringing relief and holding off disease or rising waters. Skulls were no more precious than any other body part; although reliquaries shaped like heads had become popular in the previous century, these ornate containers usually held collections of slivers from multiple bodies rather than a single intact skull. Almost as early Genovefa's lifetime, secondary relics—things that had touched or emanated from the saint—had proven as ritually efficacious as whole bodies of saints. Altars around France contained wisps of hair, bits of bloody cloak, or minuscule fragments of tooth and bone from any number of holy dead. Sainte-Geneviève had a treasury full of such relics to spare, including mementos of Peter and Paul.

The issue for the canons of Sainte-Geneviève, then, was not saintly presence manifested bodily. Instead, the legitimacy of their history and of Genovefa herself was at stake. If the spectacle of disinterment revealed a headless body, every other detail of Genovefa's past was also open to challenge. If the story of her burial beneath the church proved false, then Genovefa's discovery of Denis, her role in the conversion of France, and all her virtues and powers of protection were as flimsy as the wood of her first graveside oratory on the hill. Her miracles too would be false, like the magic of heathens and heretics. If she had no head, then she had no authentic history.

The monks of Saint-Denis should have been more sympathetic, for Genovefa had once authenticated their own patron's remains. What is more, they would suffer an identical crisis two and a half centuries later. In 1410 the canons of Nôtre Dame challenged the community of Saint-Denis before the Parlement of Paris to prove that they kept the genuine head of Denis. The canons from the island claimed to have it in their own treasury. The Parlement could not decide which provenance was more persuasive. It had been too long since Martin, followed by Genovefa, Germanus, and Gregory of Tours, among others, had shown how to legitimate a sacral site by examining its buried bodies. In the sixth or seventh century, the local bishop could have made a decision about authenticity and then reestablished the cult with a public ritual of elevation and translation, displaying the saint's remains to the public and reconsecrating the holy tomb. In the same period, a determined local congregation could have imposed a historically dubious cult upon an ambiguously marked tomb. If the early medieval crowd or their bishop had decreed a saint, then there was a saint. But by the end of the Middle Ages, neither French bishops nor their flocks could spontaneously create a saint, nor could they tell one body from another or find genuine charismats among the impostors. It was only a few years after the cranial crisis at Saint-Denis that the Burgundians would allow the English to burn the teenage Jeanne d'Arc as a witch. In 1410, the Parlement threw up its collective hands and asked the king to render a judgment. He decided in favor of the royal abbey where his ancestors lay. Saint-Denis had the right head.[1]

Back in 1161 the canons at Sainte-Geneviève need not have worried. They had their head too, as witnesses admitted when they opened the box of bones on January 10. Genovefa remained at the spot she had chosen. The nexus of gender, landscape, and architecture that had produced her cult was still operative, even though Paris and its churches had changed radically over the centuries.

Although not all of the assembled bishops were immediately persuaded—indeed, some said that the head belonged to "some other wretched old woman"—they too eventually accepted the truth. King Louis VII, an admirer of the Merovingians and the first monarch to keep his residence in Paris since Clovis, approved the verification.[2] The grumbling bishops retreated to their own churches, whence to continue the contest with Sainte-Geneviève on another day.[3] January 10 became another feast day of Genovefa celebrated in Parisian churches as the *revelatio reliquiarum* (revelation of the relics). Pilgrims resumed their ascent up the hill to Genovefa, and donations filled her attendants' coffers. Patterns of traffic between her spot on the left bank, Nôtre Dame on the island, and Saint-Denis in the northern suburbs flowed on. Genovefa's church flourished for a few centuries more.

Still, although the spectacle at her tomb reaffirmed Genovefa's integrity, the challenge suggested that her purpose and place in Paris had changed forever since the brief heyday of her popularity. The bishops' charge of headlessness had to have been, at the very least, imaginable to the Parisians. The threat to Genovefa's cult was not predictable but the result of developments in the history of Paris's churches and churchgoers. The story of her cult's origins had been viable only at an earlier moment in the city's religious history when Merovingian royalty had made Genovefa their patron. In the same way, Brigit's first vita revealed the ambitions of her earliest cult-keepers and the passage of pilgrims and royalty in seventh-century Leinster. But when Brigit left Kildare, the later vitae and the holy wells of Ireland told another story of her cult at a time when men and women built a different kind of Christianity than Brigit or her early medieval hagiographers had known.

Like those twelfth-century Parisians, we have cause to doubt the authenticity of Genovefa's Paris and Brigit's Kildare. We cannot open the saints' tombs to prove that they built religion at the brink of the Middle Ages. Even their devoted hagiographers could not claim much substantiating personal detail for their patronesses. The saints' bodies and churches are long gone. All we have are bits of memory collected like relics from texts and other ruins. Like ancient proselytizers and rebuilders, we can construe the *spolia* in order to reconstruct the *longues durées* of landscape, gender, and religion. But dry words and immovable stones, for all their suggestive powers, cannot fully relate the experience of conversion as lived by an individual. Christianization did not come at the decision of a preacher or king in a historical moment but from the repeated passages of many women and men from place to particular place, and the mutual influences of those passages and places. As *romanitas* dissolved into the foundations of medieval Europe, in Paris and in Kildare, two women helped build the places of christianization. As soon as they finished, other builders and users of religion reconsidered, moved on, and built again from the *spolia* of previous Christianities.

No Body, No Saint

Brigit never lost her head, but her mortal remains disappeared completely at the end of the Middle Ages. The body probably left Leinster after 800 when it was snatched by invading Norsemen or carried into refuge like Genovefa. No one ever noted Brigit's return to Kildare. Annalists mentioned that the remains of Bishop Conláed, once enshrined at her side, had been disinterred and re- placed in a portable reliquary, but they said no word about his partner.[4] Brigit may have come back after Vikings burned Kildare, but by the twelfth century she had left for good. Gerald of Wales reported that she resurfaced in Ulster in 1185 when the bodies of three saints—herself, Patrick, and Columcille—were "found" and translated together into one tomb at Dún Lethglaise (Downpat- rick), the traditional burial site of Patrick.[5] Inspiration for reburial probably came from the reforming bishops of Armagh in collusion with the new Anglo- Norman lord of Ulster, John de Courcy, all of whom aimed to promote Down- patrick's mother church of Armagh as the ecclesiastical umbilicus of Ireland. In traditional Irish fashion, Patrick's latest promoter took the saints of Kildare and Iona hostage in order to secure the cooperation of their followers and guar- antee his own saint's territorial supremacy. In 1293, the Irish archbishop of Armagh, Nicholas Mac Maol Íosa, countered with a rediscovery of the relics at Saul, a mile or so from Downpatrick, whence he had them removed to another new shrine.[6]

After her brief reappearance at Downpatrick near the end of the thirteenth century, however, Brigit finally vanished from the surface of Ireland. During the Tudor regime the shrine at Downpatrick was leveled and all three saints' remains strewn abroad. A bit of Brigit's toe or leather might once have been kept in the bronze shoe shrine now housed in the National Museum in Dublin. The empty shoe was a sixteenth-century copy of an earlier shrine, which had belonged in 1410 to a church at Loughrea in County Galway. Someone had also carried a few of Brigit's tokens to Glastonbury, where pilgrims viewed them in the nineteenth century; there was a necklace, a little bag, and some of her weav- ing implements.[7] A patch of her cloak, perhaps recovered from its place on the sunbeam, is still in Bruges, where it arrived in the eleventh century courtesy of an Anglo-Saxon noblewoman.[8] Statues of the saint popped up in churches across northern Europe. Brigit's head purportedly but improbably went south to Lisbon in the baggage of Irish crusaders. The skull was there in 1770 when

the Irish historian De Burgo stopped to see it. Local Catholics devoted to Brigit brought their cattle and sheep to Lumiar to be blessed by her once a year.[9]
Pilgrims may still visit her head, along with the skulls of many other holy men
and virgins in the church of the classic decapitee, John the Baptist, at Lumiar.[10]
But it may not be Brigit's head at all—the Bollandists of Brussels scientifically
determined that her head went either to Neustadt or to Cologne, where shrine-
keepers also claimed to have it.[11] Meanwhile, a fragment returned across the
ancient sea lanes to Ireland in 1929, although not to Kildare.[12] At Kildare itself,
nothing was left of physical Brigit and not much more of Brigit's landscape by
then. Even in the 1200s, Brigit's community was no longer the only monastery
in town or the most prosperous church in the province. It is possible that the
bishop or abbess continued to collect revenues from the eighty-eight communities listed as dependents of Kildare in the Book of Leinster, but it is just as
likely that the list referred to a previous, more prosperous period.[13] In 1152 the
division of Ireland into four archiepiscopal sees had put Kildare's bishop under
the authority of the archbishop of Dublin. Although Brigit's prelates continued
to style themselves occasionally "Bishop of Leinster," and although the first of
Kildare's Anglo-Norman bishops, Ralph of Bristol, rebuilt the cathedral in 1232,

FIGURE 8.1. Domnach Airgid (fourteenth through fifteenth century, Gospel-book
shrine, silver, courtesy of National Museum of Ireland). Central figure is Saint Brigit.

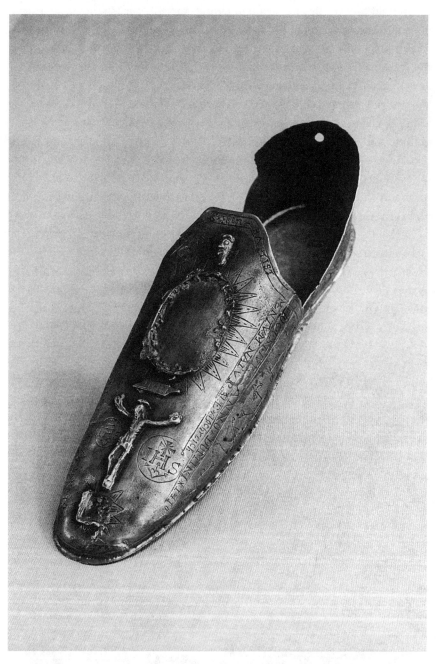

FIGURE 8.2. Shoe shrine of Saint Brigit, ca. 1410 (bronze, courtesy of National Museum of Ireland).

FIGURE 8.3. Saint Brigit, late medieval statue in Sint-Leonarduskerk, Zoutleeuw, Belgium (photograph by Colum Hourihane).

Kildare would never be so prominent as it had been in the couple of centuries after Brigit's life.

Instead of expanding Brigit's venerable community, Ralph and his successors supported new monasteries dedicated to other saints. It was probably during Ralph's episcopate that Augustinian canons replaced the monks of Brigit's church.[14] Franciscans and Carmelites built houses in the town during the second half of the same century, and a hospital followed by 1307.[15] Meanwhile, local kings and chiefs had yielded the region to the new lords of Kildare, beginning with the Welsh-Norman adventurer Richard Filtzgilbert de Clare. The medieval rulers of Leinster also preferred to patronize cathedral canons and mendicant orders rather than remnants of the pre-Norman Christian establishment. But even the bishops and canons of Kildare cathedral had to struggle for extra income in the century or two before the Henrician Dissolution of monasteries.[16]

Even though the women's community at Kildare had dwindled long before the monks disappeared, nuns vowed to Brigit may still have lived sporadically in the area until 1540. Despite the dispersal of nuns, Tudor inquisitors found that the convent still collectively owned lands and cottages in Kildare and, in 1605, eighty acres more in Knockinalliagh.[17] The last nun of Kildare to catch a scribe's eye turned up in court records in 1482 when she was accused of producing a child by the abbot of Monasterevin.[18] Brigit did not appear to defend the abbot's honor as she had protected Bishop Brón. Nor did she descend from her place in heaven to prevent the last Catholic bishop of Kildare from being ejected in 1560 after refusing to take the oath of supremacy in allegiance to Elizabeth I. Later, pilgrims still attended Brigit on her feast day, but they could no longer celebrate her with the ancient liturgy or kneel at her tomb.[19]

Kildare remained prominent on the religious landscape of northern Leinster, though, despite its saint's departure, its eventual neglect and dilapidation, and its revision in the late nineteenth century as a staid Church of Ireland house of worship. Back in the very early Middle Ages, when the Christians of early medieval Leinster had raised their eyes to Dún Ailinne on the hilltop above Kildare, they had seen an ageless capital of dynastic heroes. In the post-Dissolution centuries, when locals passed by the ruined church of Brigit, they recognized the landmarks of venerable Christianity and Irishness. As Brigit's territory became a landscape of English occupation, Anglican establishment, and cyclical rebellion, not to mention the barren setting for starvation and despair in the 1840s, Kildare's purpose became symbolic. Antiquarians and other scholars discovered that Kildare had been not only an important ecclesiastical foundation but also a site of ancient and mysterious powers.

More than any other structure, the little rectangular ruin behind Brigit's old church called the Fire-house inflamed the imaginations of tourists and antiquarians who considered Kildare. Gerald of Wales had written of its peculiarities in the later twelfth century when Kildare still flourished. "In Kildare, in Leinster, which the glorious Brigit has made famous," Gerald pointed out, "there are many miracles worthy of being remembered."

> And the first of them that occurs to one is the fire of Brigid which, they say, is inextinguishable. It is not that it is strictly speaking inextinguishable, but that the nuns and holy women have so carefully and diligently kept and fed it with enough material, that through all the years from the time of the virgin saint until now it has never been extinguished . . . although in the time of Brigit there were twenty servants of the Lord here, Brigit herself being the twentieth, only nineteen have ever been here after her death until now, and the number has never increased. They all, however, take their turns, one each night, in guarding the fire. When the twentieth night comes, the nineteenth nun puts the logs beside the fire and says: "Brigit, guard your fire. This is your night." And in this way the fire is left there, and in the morning the wood, as usual, has been burnt and the fire is still alight.[20]

The monks at Saigir, Kilmainham, and Inishmurray had reputedly kept eternal fires, too, but left no architectural evidence.[21] Perhaps it was the history of Kildare's other buildings, once so grand and now tumbled, that romanced its visitors. Or maybe the legend of the flame within, now extinguished, caught their melancholy attention. But the pull of the place was strong even to non-locals who could not possibly fully appreciate Leinster traditions of saints and sacred places. For instance, not long after the stripping of Ireland's altars in the mid–sixteenth century, Richard Stanyhurst, a Dublin-born scholar and contributor to Holinshed's *Chronicles*, had read Gerald's account and had traveled purposely to research the spot where the fire had once burned. He did not mention medieval refurbishments of the cathedral or the sculptural achievements of local tomb carvers of the earlier sixteenth century; he was interested solely in the empty stone structure behind the church.[22] "There was in Kildare an antient monument named the ffire house wherein Cambrensis saith, was there continuall fire kept day and night, and yet the ashes never increased," Stanyhurst recalled in his *De Rebus in Hibernia Gestis of* 1584. "I did see such a monument like a vault, which to this daie they call the ffire house."[23] Was Stanyhurst compelled by the holy mystery, the visible antiquity, or the unruly paganism of the place? The fire-house summed up, for this Catholic convert and descendant of Anglo-Norman conquerors, a dubious history of a primitive micro-Christianity.

In later generations, artists sketched the site, thus enshrining the fire-house and Kildare's ruins in the canon of Irish antiquities. Austin Cooper drew it in 1784 after several other gentleman artists had rendered it in the 1770s.[24] Mervyn Archdall, an antiquarian of the same generation as Cooper, published a short history of the flame with illustrations of the church, relating how the Archbishop Henry de Loudres of Dublin had put out the fire in 1220 but some-one had relit it to flicker until the Dissolution of Irish monasteries.[25] The poet Thomas Moore used Brigit's perpetual fire to symbolize Ireland's inextinguish-able spirit of independence in his *Irish Melodies* of 1832. The saint's flame was "the bright lamp, that shone in Kildare's holy fane, And burn'd through long ages of darkness and storm."[26] To romantics from Gerald to Moore, the fire signified simultaneously Brigit's sanctity and the intoxicating legends of pagan bonfires that had burned in a Celtic Ireland untainted by English, Viking, or even Christian invaders.

Around the time that Moore was rhapsodizing, the indomitable surveyor and scholar John O'Donovan was collecting legends at Kildare as part of his

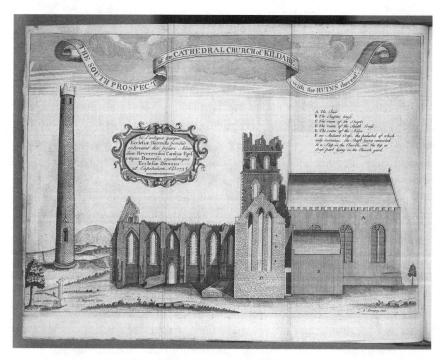

FIGURE 8.4. Kildare in 1764 (Austin Cooper, from *Whole Works of Sir James Ware Concerning Ireland*, courtesy of Henry E. Huntington Library).

mission to measure and map Ireland for the Ordnance Survey. He spoke Irish and read Latin. He had a thorough grounding in medieval texts; later, travels finished, he edited multiple volumes of medieval monastic chronicles called *Annala Ríoghachta Eireann,* or the Annals of the Four Masters.[27] He also had a keen eye for architectural and environmental relics of the past and a shrewd estimation of local traditions about them. He regularly wrote long letters to headquarters during his travels, describing what he found in elegant if unromantic phrases. He also complained about the weather, his fatigue, and his lack of proper research materials.

Nonetheless, in 1837 O'Donovan relentlessly visited every hillock, abandoned settlement, and fragment of anciently built space in the county of Kildare. He was especially keen to find Dún Ailinne and to view the ruins of Brigit's monastery. When local farmers told O'Donovan that the Hill of Allen, five miles north of the church of Kildare, was the site of famous battles and once the fortress of the hero Fionn MacCumhaill, he surveyed the site but dismissed the legends. In his letters, he wryly recounted the adventures of a visionary named Donnelly who was convinced that Fionn had buried his treasure deep within the hill. In 1835 Donnelly had blasted open the rocks and stood ready with his gun to shoot Fionn's enchanted dog, which guarded the wealth throughout eternity. But no dog had emerged, and no treasure had come to the surface. When O'Donovan spoke to him, Donnelly was still awaiting a second vision. At any rate, O'Donovan pointed out, although the hill boasted traces of fieldworks and offered excellent views, the medieval annals proved that the Hill of Allen was not the site of Leinster's oldest legends. Leinster's origins lay in an Iron Age fort at Knockaulin, a few miles away and much closer to the town of Kildare.[28] The fort there looked down upon the Curragh, the vast plain originally "formed into a common by that Saintess" Brigit when she built her church. O'Donovan rehearsed a tale about the trick Brigit had played on King Labraidh Long Ears in order to gain land from him. He also described the legendary fertility of the great plain of the Curragh, how its grasses were never depleted no matter how heavy the grazing, and how the plain had once served as a sports field for another king of Dún Ailinne. Antiquities littered the area: raths, stones marked with footprints, megaliths, the Black Pig's Dyke. This was the landscape of Kildare, church of Brigit.

But Kildare itself was disappointingly bare of signs of the legendary past. Nothing was left from Brigit's day, although townsfolk pretended to point out the sites of her house, her oak tree, and even the ancient fire-house where her nuns and, before them, devotees of a pagan deity had kept an eternal flame. O'Donovan checked the medieval sources and mocked the "insulse stories" about a spooky flame told by the gullible Gerald of Wales. (Gerald also claimed to have seen the original oak trunk.)[29] But even O'Donovan thought the ruins behind the cathedral might be genuinely ancient. He scrutinized earlier maps for indications of the fire-house. He proposed that Brigit herself had ordered it built in the fifth century, not as a reminder of ancient Celtic practice or the Vestal Virgins of Rome, as some had argued, but in pious imitation of the biblical tabernacle in Leviticus.

If legends endured in the fantasy of the fire-house, the architectural reality of Kildare was a cold hearth in 1871 when a committee for the restoration of the cathedral had observed, "The choir is the only part of the building still roofed and used for service . . . the rest of the church is in ruins." One architect asked, "What is there to restore? . . . Two dilapidated nave walls, one transept, and a portion of one side of a tower."[30] Nonetheless, the committee recommended incorporating the *spolia* into the neo-Gothic structure that stands at Kildare today. The archbishops of Canterbury, Armagh, and Dublin gathered near a recently planted young oak in September 1896 to commemorate the new edifice. No mention was made of attending nuns, although Daniel Delany, bishop of Kildare and Leighlin, had officially reestablished the Brigidine order at Tullow in 1807.[31] But most of an entire issue of the new *Journal of the Kildare Archaeological Society* celebrated the rededication of Kildare that year with articles about its colorful past. George Cowell concluded his article by observing that Kildare's saint had "a sentimental advantage over St. Patrick" deriving primarily from her gender and ethnicity. According to Cowell, Brigit's reputation was justified "not merely because she was a woman but because she was an Irish woman, one of pure Celtic descent, and the first woman who was prominently engaged in Church work in Ireland."[32]

When Kildare's fire went out and its nuns dispersed, the saint had lost her home in the territory she had once defined. When her body finally disappeared for good, she lost historical specificity, too. She was no longer the builder saint whose tracks mapped the route from Kildare to the heavenly Jerusalem. Instead, she was reduced to a ghost of ancient Ireland that haunted Kildare's ruined fire-house. The ruins were an epitaph for whatever historical continuity might have linked Brigit's Ireland to the modern island. To Catholics, Brigit gradually became the least important third of a triad of patrons, after Patrick and Columba. She was a guardian of all Irish souls and many places around Christendom, but protectress of no particular territory. Even at her official national shrine at her supposed birthplace of Faughart, statues of the other two patrons loomed over the stairway and guarded access to the virgin saint. To the Protestant establishment of the Church of Ireland, Saint Brigit was less important than her reconstructed cathedral, which symbolized Anglican resistance to organized Catholicism. As the dean of Kildare put it in a sermon of 1892,

Kildare "never belonged to the Church of Rome . . . it belonged from the time of St. Brigid to the present day, to the Church of Ireland, and to no other body."[33] He may not have meant the play on words, but the dean was celebrating a Kildare without the grounded, historical, embodied Brigit.

Over the long centuries, while observers from Stanyhurst to Mr. Cowell enthused over ruined antiquities and ancient flames, many devout Catholics sought Brigit elsewhere. Most of her churches and monasteries had disappeared after the eighteenth-century legislation forbidding the formal practice of Catholicism, but the saint reappeared in the oddest places. She particularly favored wells. From Kildare to Mayo, Brigit left her name on watering holes that were architecturally simple but thickly coded. Some springs had no mark but a single stone by a bubble in the ground. Other sites included combinations of monuments and markers: standing stones, bullauns (bowl-shaped stones), flagstones, trees adorned with clooties and other offerings, signposts, grave-yards, pools, and streams as well as the spring itself, with or without resident fish or eels. Pilgrims' uses of Brigit's wells were suitably intricate, too. One early nineteenth-century observer watched visitors to Tobhar Brighde (Brigit's well) in Roscommon who trudged "bareheaded and barefooted from ten to twenty miles for the purpose of crawling on their knees round these wells, and upright stones and oak trees westward as the sun travels, some three times, some six, some nine, and so on, in uneven numbers until their voluntary pen-ances were completely fulfilled."[34] The rituals of coming, going, and circling that suppliants had formerly acted out in the precincts of Kildare's basilica, they now performed in fields and on hills. The ritual journey was still complex, with sunwise circuits and symbolically ordered signposts, but its paths did not aim toward Kildare or any other Christian church. The customs of these days, called pattern (or patron) days, did not belong under a roof.[35]

Although Brigit may have presided over water sources much earlier than the nineteenth century, no one described the activities of pilgrims to her wells before then. Most of the holy wells outside Leinster had probably been dedi-cated initially to other saints. The springs drew Brigit's presence and acquired her name only during Penal times, after formal Catholic practice had dispersed behind the hedges and into the corners of the countryside. As monasteries shut their doors, not all saints' cults were strong enough to survive the lack of infrastructure. Yet at least ninety premodern sites named after or associated with Brigit endured until Edmund Hogan could collect them in his repertory of Irish place-names published in 1910. Of these, nine were wells; only one well was mentioned in a manuscript earlier than 1200.[36] Historical sources from the early modern period also mentioned a few enduring Brigidine locations, for instance, Tech Brigde, which the chieftain O'Donnell burned in 1596 when

raiding Galway town.[37] More recent gazetteers added a Brideswell here, a Tub-
berbreed there. No one knew how many water sources belonged to Brigit during the intervening centuries—probably many more than we can count now.
Brigit was able to leave her name on so many places precisely because her cult
had diffused into the unbuilt landscape long before, when the hagiographers
had relocated her to nature and de Courcy had shifted her bones to the north.
Like the Virgin Mary, she became familiar across an expansive geography precisely because she no longer had a favorite home. Only a few other national
saints survived the transition out of doors and beyond their native territories.
Saints Patrick and Brendan also acquired wells beyond their homelands. They
too were famous travelers around Ireland.[38]

The iconography of Brigit's canonical legend, rewritten repeatedly through
the later Middle Ages, eased the eventual relocation of her cult to open places.
In the hands of fourteenth- and fifteenth-century writers, Brigit became a saint
for farmwives and chaste girls. New introductions to the later hagiographic
texts, which derived from *Vita Prima* rather than Cogitosus, emphasized her
virginity and humility rather than her ecclesiastical authority. Her vita in the
fifteenth-century *Leabhar Breac* began by urging women to celibacy and warn-
ing them against false chastity. In the birthing episode, when Brigit fell to earth
upon the threshold, her mother still washed the baby Brigit in new milk, but
now, according to the hagiographer, the milk-bath symbolized "the merits of
Saint Brigit, to wit, with the brightness and sheen of her chastity." The details
of politics and travel and the subtle implications of Brigit's contests with male
ecclesiastics disappeared from these stories. Instead, late medieval writers included new material like the song Brigit sang as she worked in her father's
house. She tunefully invoked Jesus' blessing of her kitchen while she filled
hampers with miraculously abundant butter. In the same vita, Saint Brendan
came to visit her at Kildare and found her herding sheep in the rain; when
Brigit thoughtlessly hung her cloak on the sunbeam, Brendan did the same.
It was no longer uniquely Brigit's miracle. In fact, Brendan helped Brigit articulate the gendered difference among spiritualities when they discussed the
sunbeam incident. "Each of them confessed to the other," wrote the hagiographer. "Said Brenainn: 'Not usual is it for me to go over seven ridges without
giving my mind to God.' Said Brigit: 'Since I first gave my mind to God, I never
took it from Him at all.'" Perhaps Brigit was able to focus because she was
not distracted any longer by the ecclesiastical politics of Kildare, but Brendan
thought it was because she stayed at home with her sheep rather than traveling
constantly, as he did.

Brigit no longer commanded equal treatment by bishops and kings in later
stories of her life, though men remained respectful of her piety. When it came

time to build Kildare, according to the late fourteenth-century vita, Brigit did not choose and consecrate the site herself but instead went to fetch Bishop Ibar to perform the ritual marking out of her city. In the same episode, the local Uí Dúnlainge warlord passed by the church building site with cartloads full of peeled rods perfect for building a wattle-and-daub settlement but refused to donate them. Brigit had to resort to punitive miracles, paralyzing his horses until he finally yielded the building materials to her.[39] In fact, rather than the confident ruler of a mixed-sex community, as in her earlier vitae, Brigit became the most bashful of saints around men. "She never washed her hands, or her feet, or her head amongst men," enthused the latest hagiographer. "She never looked into a male person's face. She never spoke without blushing." Instead of preaching or miraculously redirecting wanderers through the wilderness, the Brigit of these later vitae desired "to feed the poor, to repel every hardship, to be gentle to every misery." Although the hagiographer credited her with founding churches, Brigit herself had become a carrier of spirituality rather than an aggressive preacher and builder of religion. "She was a vessel for keeping Christ's body," the hagiographer wrote, "she was a temple of God. Her heart and mind were a throne of rest for the Holy Spirit." Finally, rather than ordering the natural world in imitation of the Creator, she herself was now one of its more special creatures: "Her type among created things is the Dove among birds, the Vine among trees, the Sun above stars." The late medieval hagiographer never wondered where her relics lay.

Even while Brigit's later vitae diminished her travels, the texts did not introduce any new settings for her deeds. She moved, as she always had, among kitchens and sheep pastures. Homely wonders in domestic venues outweighed her public displays of *virtus* at open sites. Pilgrims learned from these household and farmyard miracles to imitate Brigit in the patterns of holy wells rather than to witness her vita at high masses in official liturgies. Hagiographic stories of Brigit's headache and the self-mutilation of her eyes, first recounted in the early vitae, inspired devotees to seek relief from headaches and eye disease in the saint's healing waters. Brigit's increase of dairy products and harvest miracles drew women suffering gynecological problems or difficult pregnancies to her wells.[40] Her cult produced healings and penances, miracles of fertility and abundance, but few episodes of political patronage and triumph.

The same gendered qualities that sent Brigit to the wells also pushed her into the social class of uneducated, unsophisticated Christian worshipers. For literate observers of the nineteenth and twentieth centuries, devotions at holy wells were for the peasants. Protestant and Catholic churchmen both derided the patterns as superstitious if not downright debauched and dangerous.[41] They disapproved of the seemingly casual, inexplicable postures and repetitions of

patterns, which signaled beliefs quite literally outside the ecclesiastical structure. Without Christian architecture to separate men and women, the sexes
mingled too intimately on pattern days. At Liscannor in the early nineteenth
century, Brigit had not yet acquired her fine glass phonebooth, but a mob of
pilgrims always arrived nonetheless on the evening before her annual feast day.
William Shaw Mason, a parochial surveyor and observer of Irish rural life, wrote
in 1819 that "numbers of people male and female assemble at St. Bridget's Well
and remain there the entire of the night. They first perform their rounds and
then spend a good part of the time in invoking this St. Bridget over the well,
repeating their prayers and adorations aloud and holding their conversations
with the saint etc. When this ceremony is over they amuse themselves until
morning by dancing and singing."[42] Pilgrims apparently violated boundaries
separating religious from secular celebration too. Non-Irish observers typically
noted the carousing, obscene dancing, and drunken quarrels at patterns, not
to mention women hiking their skirts up to crawl around on their knees, with
plenty of blood and mayhem resulting.[43]

Antiquarians such as O'Donovan linked the feast day frolics of the nineteenth century directly to the ancient popularity of the particular cult they
celebrated. The oldest saints remained present, he argued, where patterns remained strong; where cults lapsed, so did religious heritage. When he visited
Saint Conall's Well on Inis Caol off the coast of Donegal, he found it a "place of
amusement and drinking." He further noted, though, that "when the R.C. clergy
thought it proper to condemn the practice," it led to the "rapid decrease in the
fame of [Saint] Conall the Slender [Conall Caol]." On the other hand, if devotees
resisted interpretative and architectural revisions of cult sites, neither orthodox
policing nor modern engineering could prevent them reaching the sacred waters and using the wells as they pleased. O'Donovan told another story of a well
at Outeragh in Leitrim. When an impious farmer filled in the holy well in order
to stop pilgrimage traffic, the well resurfaced in the next townland over, where
people began to visit it on Brigit's day.[44] In O'Donovan's time some traditional
wells had already gone dry from unbelief and neglect. Plenty persisted, though,
and many "jumped" as did the Outeragh well. Local users decided where to find
their saints and when to visit. O'Donovan duly noted the wells on maps.

When traditional patterns lapsed and were no longer visible, revivalist visitors followed O'Donovan's directions to the wells.[45] Beginning in 1935, eager
young men from the Coimisiún Béaloideasa Éireann (Irish Folklore Commission), armed with ordnance survey maps and a handbook for collecting oral
tradition, spread out among native practitioners to seek antique stories about
odd behavior in the countryside. They learned that on Saint Brigit's Eve families left milk outside for the visiting saint.[46] Everywhere in Ireland, women

wove special Brigit's Crosses of straw, reeds, or rushes to hang in their kitchens and on their doors (available for purchase today in gift shops and airports). According to the collected folklore, Donegal wives used to cast the *brat Bríde* (Brigit's cloak) over calving cows to ease their pain. In Mayo cross-dressing boys bore a turnip-headed corn dolly called the *brídeog* (little Brigit) among the farms on Bridget's Eve.[47] Such customs supplied more than one modern interpreter with enough evidence to convict twentieth-century farmers of paganism.[48] To folklorists, this was the timelessly authentic Ireland. One government manual declared that "the social life of the country people—the historic Irish nation—is mirrored in what is known in Irish-speaking districts as seanchas [heritage]."[49] For Gaelic revivalists and patriots, Celticity lived on in the latently pagan routines of Brigit's pilgrims and transvestite farmboys. This simple tribe of peasants shared, in Yeats's words, "the vast and vague extravagance that lies at the bottom of the Celtic heart."[50]

Even the saints participated in this modern recovery of ancient Celticity. Tales of ancestors descended from gods and goddesses began to emerge from academic presses in the 1890s, borne into print by the Gaelic revival. Whole cycles of sagas and myths about the origins of Celtic Ireland appeared in pedantically annotated volumes of medieval literature. Brigit kept turning up in these legends of the peopling of Ireland, epics of royal bloodshed, and poetic invocations. Charles Plummer, who edited two major collections of Irish saints' lives in 1910 and 1922, made the same literary connection that hagiographers had hinted at in the eighth and ninth centuries—but for different reasons. Plummer lived and worked on an academic landscape shaped by a nineteenth-century interest in the origins of such things: religions, languages, cultures, races, species. In his preface to the Christian vitae he argued for Brigit's start as a goddess as ancient as the Vedic deities of India.[51] Even R. A. S. Macalister, a staunch advocate of Brigit's historical integrity as a missionary, related the saint and her cult to mythic Ireland. He argued in 1919 that young Brigit must have been a recent convert, for "no Christian lady would willingly bear a name so heathenish" as Brig or Brigit "while paganism was still a force." Macalister deduced that Brigit had been named after the goddess whose cult she had tended before becoming that Christian lady.[52]

Whether or not they believed Brigit to be a historical or a mythological figure, both Plummer and Macalister understood her as a link to the Celtic past also recoverable in pagan myths, folk memory, and the ruins of ancient landscapes, although not in the churches of Christendom. For these interpreters as well as a whole cadre of historians, linguists, and archaeologists, Brigit was a holy vessel—not for the Holy Spirit, as the *Leabhar Breac* hagiographer had piously claimed, but a receptacle in which Celticity might be transmitted from its non-Roman, pre-Christian source to a rebellious modern Ireland. Like the heroines of medieval epic, Deirdre and Queen Maeve, or the women of more recent legend, Grace O'Malley and Cathleen ni Houlihan, Brigit defended the twentieth-century Free State and nursed the Republic of Ireland. The unortho-dox patterns of pilgrimage carried out in her name at wells—circling counter-clockwise, crawling into tunnels, strange incantations of healing—confirmed her lost divinity but also the eternal resilience of Celticity. Her fire-house, the most visible remnant of her history, reminded tourists not of Saint Brigit but of a sacrality much older than Jesus Christ. Inevitably, the historical landscape of Ireland had become authentically formerly pagan once again. Priests and colonial administrators had simply littered it for centuries with superfluous architecture brought from Rome or London. But Temair, Cruachain, and Dún Ailinne still loomed on the hilltops, gaining more significance with each inex-plicable pattern day custom, each rediscovered poem about almost-forgotten kings, and each careful excavation into Irish soil.

Since then, neither written nor textual evidence has constrained the vital-ity of Brigit's cult. A variety of Christian and non-Christian groups continue to celebrate her mutable history as a story of enduring rituals on a static landscape, without anchoring her cult physically to Kildare at any particu-lar historical moment. Brigit's flame burns again, or still, in Kildare, as of Brigit's Day, 2006.[53] Celtic-inspired Christians from a variety of sectarian backgrounds have created congregations around the world based on models they believe were used first by the cryptopagan Christians of ancient Ireland. Scholars and modern worshipers have built new Brigits for themselves. If they believe Brigit to be a goddess of poetry and inspiration or a saintly pa-troness of milking and spinning, then of course she is. She is also a spirit within wells and a shy nun in a phone booth. Modern literati in search of Brigit's origins must be tolerant of the ways in which the saint has endured. Without serious research into the religious structures of a particular com-munity and its believers, none of us knows another one's Brigit. The nun in the phone booth is not the Brigit whose bones were once caressed by the fingertips of pilgrims. She is not the Brigit of the Gaelic revival, the *Leabhar Breac*, or ninth-century hagiography. She is not the Brigit who walked the landscapes of Cogitosus's Kildare.

The Returns of Genovefa

Genovefa's cult ended in nationalism too, but the saint remained in Paris almost until the present day. Whereas Brigit disappeared into the countryside during centuries of political turmoil and Catholic repression, Genovefa simply withdrew quietly behind the walls of her prosperous community, dwelling safely in her reliquary. She survived the birth of France, the expansion of Paris far beyond its ancient limits, and both the Reformation and Counterreformation of Christianity. She even suffered the move to a new church on the site of the Panthéon. But when her city became the modern capital of the republic, Genovefa finally succumbed to the combined forces of liberty, equality, and fraternity. Her rebuilt basilica outlasted the church at Kildare by more than four centuries, but her body and cult finally disappeared in the Revolution.

Genovefa's shrine occupied the historical heart of Paris long after its residents had forgotten their proud origins in Caesar's conquest. Although mostly confined to her sanctuary, the saint returned to Parisian streets whenever pilgrims processed to her shrine and asked her out. King Louis the Pious came to her hill in 826. By then, canons had formed a community at Sainte-Geneviève and had built a small hospice for guests.[54] Around that same time, someone recorded a series of miracles that occurred at her tomb. In one instance, a blind and mute man recovered both sight and speech while praying before her shrine, even as her canons were celebrating communion. A similar miracle brought speech and sight to a man who visited the saint at the precise moment when a priest read the Gospel aloud at Sunday mass. In fact, the happy pilgrim vowed to remain with the saint for the rest of his life. A blind child could see again after his mother lit a candle to Genovefa in the church. A neighbor woman got into trouble when she impudently labored on the feast of the Virgin Mary's birth. Adding insult to her misdeed, the woman pointed out that the Virgin had been a laboring woman, so why shouldn't she herself also work? Her wool-carding combs became stuck fast to her hands. Only prayer in Genovefa's church could unglue her. In yet another incident, the canons at Sainte-Geneviève found the body of one of their brothers, victim of an accidental fall, only after praying to Genovefa. In all these episodes, Genovefa no longer worked alone to protect her devotees. The keepers of Genovefa's shrine mediated these dramatic liturgical moments with prayer and the provision of props and settings. The saint's wondrous cures replicated the miracles of the Eucharist, the reading of Gospel, and the lighting of votive candles that clerics performed regularly. Genovefa had become a natural resource of the community and its church, managed by the canons and doled out to the needy in times of emergency.

In moments of crisis, though, Genovefa still wielded her unique powers of rescue outside the church walls. She prevailed over the elements and the enemies of Paris when properly invoked. "You have heard, brothers," wrote the teller of these tales, "of how holy virgins have triumphed over human evils and dangers; hear now of even more wondrous power over waters." When flood threatened the island in the Seine one spring, the bishop ordered general fasts. The churches of Saint Stephen and John the Baptist offered no refuge. Even the Virgin at Nôtre Dame fell under siege by the Seine. The bishop sent priests out to find a place to conduct services and beg God to forgive the city's sins. One clergyman rowed over to a nuns' community where the sisters preserved Genovefa's deathbed. Amazingly, the waters had spared the bed, although the flood rose as high as the monastery's windows. Crowds of onlookers, including the bishop himself, gathered to have a look as the waters began to recede. "Her body was absent, but her power present," declared the scribe.[55] After that demonstration, Genovefa's devotees brought the saint out of her sanctuary and into the streets whenever they needed to quell the Seine. It may well be, as one historian has suggested, that episodes from Genovefa's vitae—the cure of her mother's blindness with well water, the encounter with the river monsters, her command of the river during storms—inspired the Parisians to call upon Genovefa. Perhaps, though, these exempla simply justified the faithful's decision to approach Genovefa before Paris's other patrons.[56]

Simple geography also shaped the continuing relationship between Parisians and Genovefa. She presided high and dry from her hill on the left bank when the river inundated houses clustered on the island. Pilgrimage uphill to Sainte-Geneviève, prayerful invocation of the saint, and Genovefa's stately descent with her clerics to Nôtre Dame was all part of the ritual of recovery of territory from fickle Sequana. Likewise, when ergotism (called by the chronicler, *ignis sacra*, holy fire) struck the city in 1129, no relief arrived until Genovefa emerged from her church and went down into the city. Christ had turned a deaf ear while doctors applied all their skills and medicines to no avail. The bishop and canons of Nôtre Dame tried deploying their relics, but still the fever raged. Genovefa, out of respect for the Virgin Mother, meanwhile had refrained from intervening until invoked. When the bishop of Paris finally recalled how Genovefa had saved the city before—once from the Huns, once from flood— he ascended the hill to seek her aid. The bishop begged her canons to escort Genovefa to Nôtre Dame, where she might heal her patients in person. After much preparation, the canons agreed to a procession with relics across the river. Attended by raucous multitudes, the saint was borne by ordained men to Nôtre Dame. There Genovefa's intercession healed all but three victims of the holy fire. But afterward, when the canons made ready to return Genovefa to the hill, a mob tried to prevent them. The Parisians wanted to keep her permanently closer to hand. The canons had to sneak their relics back across the river after nightfall.[57]

FIGURE 8.5. Procession of canons of Genovefa (Bibliothèque Sainte-Geneviève, ms 1283, f. 21, fourteenth century, Bibliothèque Sainte-Geneviève). The historiated initial R contains a depiction of the procession of Genovefa's relics on November 26, 1130, when a burning fever (probably ergotism) afflicted hundreds of Parisians. After the bishop of Nôtre-Dame sought the saint's help at her shrine, her canons carried her remains to the bishop's church, where they miraculously cured the afflicted. The date became another annual feast day of Genovefa: Miracles of the Ardents.

The history of Genovefa and her church in postmedieval Paris has been skillfully told.[58] Maps of Paris carefully located the spires of Sainte-Geneviève atop her hill in the sixteenth, seventeenth, and eighteenth centuries. Genovefa's processions continued until 1725.[59] In collaboration with Denis and Marcel, she sheltered Parisians through centuries of civil war, religious upheaval, plagues, and famines. Her collegial relations with other saints—that is, the politics of ecclesiastical factions within Paris—were played out on the streets and in the churches of the city. In 1248, when King (and later saint) Louis brought the Crown of Thorns from Saint-Denis to Sainte-Chapelle and summoned the saints of Paris to the dedication of his glorious new church, neither Genovefa nor Marcel attended.[60] Genovefa remained the local caretaker of the royal house, to whom the Bourbons appealed when their sons were ill or their women in danger of death; each time the saint demonstrated her healing powers, the royal family thanked her canons with gracious gifts to her church. Genovefa's public face became increasingly elegant with each donation and

FIGURE 8.6. *Les ardents*, Gilles du Boys, 1594, painted on the statutes of the confraternity of the porters of the reliquary of Saint Genovefa (ms 1874, p. 3, Bibliothèque Sainte-Geneviève).

IN FESTO
S. GENOVEFÆ
DE MIRACULO ARDENTIUM.

FIGURE 8.7. Procession with relics of Genovefa (Vespers of Sainte-Geneviève, 1711, based on 1655 original, Bibliothèque Sainte-Geneviève ms 121, f. 15). The relics of Genovefa and Marcel are carried past the church of Sainte-Geneviève-des-Ardents on their way to Nôtre-Dame, followed by canons and abbot of Sainte-Geneviève, the archbishop of Paris, members of the Parlement, and other notables.

FIGURE 8.8. Church of Sainte-Geneviève, 1589 (map of Paris, Ortelius, *Theatrum Orbis Terrarum*, courtesy of Henry E. Huntington Library).

every newly wrought reliquary. Her relation with the Bourbons was so intimate, in fact, that she was eventually tried by republicans as a royalist collaborator and antirevolutionary. Still, even after they tossed her ashes into the Seine, she loyally returned to her sinful children during the restoration of the monarchy in the shape of minor relics recovered from other shrines and stashed in Nôtre Dame and Saint-Étienne-du-Mont. A miraculous pendant-reliquary in the Musée National du Moyen Age still guards her memory and supposedly a wisp of her mortal remains.[61] And in 2002, the French government declared a national celebration of the 1,500th anniversary of her death simultaneous with the observance of such varied events as the 600th anniversary of the conquest of the Canary Islands, the 500th anniversary of Francis Xavier's death, and the hundredth anniversary of the law requiring infant vaccinations.[62]

FIGURE 8.9. Pendant reliquary of Genovefa, gold with enamel, once containing fragments of the True Cross and of Saint Genovefa's remains, ca. 1370 (courtesy of Musée de Cluny).

Genovefa's tomb and church were destroyed and ultimately erased from the map of Paris. Her memory lives on in monuments, though, including the chapel and cenotaph within Saint-Étienne and the library named after her near the site of her original church.[63] In Nanterre, the well where she had cured her mother of blindness became a target of pilgrimage. On estates once owned by her canons in Paris, medieval churches may also have risen in her honor.[64] Congregations dedicated to her appeared mostly in the old diocese of Sens. Churches called after her still stand in Limbourg, Quebec, and Missouri, among other places. She can even claim a reference in the lines of a modern rock song about the Mississippi River.[65] But Geneviève never gained the widespread following that Brigit has found wherever Irish women ventured around the Catholic world, or the popularity that Saints Martin and Denis enjoyed at home in France as well as abroad.

The story of Genovefa told on her feast day did not change much over the years, despite revisions of her vita in the Carolingian period and a completely new vernacular version composed in the fourteenth century. However, each author emphasized a particular attribute of the saint: she was guardian of

FIGURE 8.10. Genovefa with sheep (ms 91, f. 120v, missal for the use of the Abbaye Sainte-Geneviève de Paris, 1488–1517, courtesy of Bibliothèque Sainte-Geneviève). This is the first known depiction of Genovefa as a shepherdess, which later became a favorite iconographical motif for the saint.

FIGURE 8.11. Genovefa at Arcis, Pierre Puvis de Chavannes, Panthéon (photograph by John Montano).

Paris, thaumaturge, virgin nun, or mothering nurturer. Portraits of Genovefa always suited discrete historical moments. In the early modern period, she usually appeared as a simple shepherdess or a gentle reader, often holding a candle to light her book while an angel and a demon hovered above. This formerly urban saint occasionally sat among sheep on a green hillside. In other images, she loomed over her city as a larger-than-life protectress. Traditionally, Genovefa appeared demurely youthful or even as a child before the bishops Lupus and Germanus. But in the nineteenth century, after Paris's several revolutions, Genovefa's age finally caught up with her on the interior walls of the Panthéon. In these works of Pierre Puvis de Chavannes, Genovefa became an old woman as wizened and serene as Mother Teresa (whom the portrait eerily resembles). A muscular Clovis strides through these murals too, sporting a flowing blond mustache and metal hat but lacking a shirt. Meanwhile, Geneviève's towering twentieth-century statue on the Pont de la Tournelle is an androgynous facsimile of the saint. Its sleek, erectile form shoots upward, reminding the devout that she once opened heaven to the Parisians.[66]

FIGURE 8.12. Genovefa on Île-Saint-Louis, Paul Landowski, 1924–28 (photograph by the author).

The Nexus of Gender, Landscape, and Conversion

Women and men carried Christianity from one place to another around the early medieval world. They took it from Rome to Arles, to Tours or Paris, on to the coast, thence to Sussex, Wales, and Kildare. They carried it back and forth across fields, cities, hills, and waters. Sometimes these wanderers brought spoken words of proselytization. Other times they toted complex artifacts, such as an illuminated Gospel or a relic. They transported simple tools, too, like the little metal stick that priests used to divide the Eucharistic host into portions, imperial coins, and precious vestments. Some travelers brought intangibles: the idea of a building, a style of behavior, or a way of looking at the world. Every day, women and men took Christianity over miles of sea and highway. Every day, others shifted the religion just a few steps at a time. Constantly in movement, Europeans chose whether to be Christian, how to be Christian, and how Christian to be. They decided where to go and what to do as Christians, and how to live in a Christian world with other Christians. They did this both consciously and without thinking about it. They did it at the same time that they were choosing how to be male or female, Celtic or Roman, Parisian or Fothairt, and any number of other roles and qualities.

No one chose, though, to be a saint. Saints were born. If fire shot out of a baby's head and bishops came seeking her charisma, then a saint was revealed to her public. She manifested her innate qualities by controlling and improving nature and its creatures, thus visibly convincing other Christians to revere her and seek her assistance. After she died, wonders continued at the tomb of an authentic saint, thus persuading pilgrims to maintain their relations with her and those who kept her shrine. Believers learned of her miracles by witnessing them, by reading or hearing stories, or simply by visiting the places where her miracles had happened and might occur again. Together, saint and devotees negotiated her cult, much as audiences and builders of architecture jointly made buildings. Some cults, like some buildings, lasted a very long time. Some fell slowly to ruins or just melted into the ground. Still other saints' cults provided the *spolia* from which Christians built new forms of worship and belief in later times.

Saint Brigit followed the same course as Saint Genovefa, but one saint did not inspire the other or provide a model for her hagiographers—so far as anyone knows. Their cults grew discretely, separated by at least a generation and by many miles. Nonetheless, each saint and her cult helps explain the other. Read together, the histories of these two saints allow us to plot the course of christianization across earliest medieval northern Europe. Preachers brought the same Christian doctrines via the same methods of proselytization to each saint's territory. Genovefa and Brigit appeared at the same point in the process of local christianization—after men had brought the Word but before their kinsmen and neighbors had delimited Christian territories with properly built capitals. Both women revised their landscapes with similar aims and the identical reward of saintly commemoration, using purposeful travel and strategic building to articulate religious change and ecclesiastical leadership when no other authoritative expressions were available to them qua women. They converted landscapes because they could not preach, teach, or otherwise conduct the rituals of Christianity. The medieval keepers of both cults exploited the visible, tangible results of these women's missions in order to define a unique style of sanctity focused on the enduring evidence of their two shrines.

Genovefa and Brigit had never traveled the same landscape. The physical and political environment of the Parisian basin and southern Ireland in the earliest Middle Ages required different kinds of territories, churches, and cults. Kinship, gender, and politics operated according to laws and customs specific to Ireland or Gaul. Yet, although material environment set discrete stages for christianization in different parts of Europe, Christian doctrine imposed the same gendered limits on religious leaders everywhere and thus propelled these holy women on their parallel journeys. *Romanitas* provided both method and goal for their christianizing projects. The nexus of landscape, religion, and gender continued to reshape both cults after the saints died. Sometimes gender trumped environmental conditions and cultural ideologies to become the dominant influence on the material development of these saints' cults, as when the Merovingians shifted interest to their episcopal patron, Saint Denis. Occasionally, though, religion mitigated gender inequalities and undermined indigenous political structures, as when the abbesses of Kildare ruled over men and their properties. At other moments, the physical landscape or gender politics restrained and contained religious women. Neither Genovefa nor Brigit dared the sea journeys of Patrick or Germanus. Instead, each was content to build a homely micro-Christendom.

Both Genovefa and Brigit traded in cultural exotica. Like merchants bearing trinkets or brides bringing fabulous dowries to new houses, they carried the goods of *romanitas* and Christianity across political boundaries to their neighbors and allies. Parisians adapted Genovefa's gifts to suit their ancient city and its architecture. Likewise, the people of Leinster modified Christianity and *romanitas* for Ireland's flexible kingdoms and legendary landscapes. Together, builders and users of Christian holy places mapped new religion onto familiar landscapes. Even after the saints had died, keepers of their cults preserved the memory of Genovefa and Brigit in their buildings, bodies, and histories so that generations of admirers might follow their paths to their territories. Throughout the medieval and early modern centuries, long after the original meanings of the saints' deeds had dwindled to mere literary formula and iconography, suppliants continued to seek the protection and care of Brigit and Genovefa at their tombs, in their relics, and in feast-day stories of the saints' accomplishments on earth. But as their churches crumbled, and as Christians chose new routes to other holy places in the daily traffic of religion, the two holy women settled deeper into the Christian landscapes that they had created. Eventually, all that Genovefa and Brigit had built became precious but enigmatic *spolia* of Europe's conversion to Christianity.

Notes

For a list of abbreviations, please see the bibliography.

INTRODUCTION

1. Hall, *Lived Religion in America*, vii–xiii.
2. Pluskowski and Patrick, "'How Do You Pray to God?'" 46.
3. Delogu, "The Papacy, Rome, and the Wider World," 197–220; Brown, *Rise of Western Christendom*, 218.

CHAPTER 1

1. *VGA* 13. Note that numbers following all classical texts cited in this book refer to sections, not page numbers.
2. The work of a number of cultural, historical, and theoretical geographers has become increasingly popular among historians, who have begun to agree with Edward Soja that the temporally ordered "historical narrative" must be "spatialized." For a brief history of critical geography, see Soja, *Postmodern Geographies*.
3. Kinney, "Rape or Restitution of the Past?" 53–62. Kinney, among other scholars more cautious than I, criticizes twentieth-century art historians such as Hans Peter L'Orange for imposing an archaeological view on historical audiences, resulting in a kind of historical double vision in which any monument has both a present programmatic meaning and an assemblage of connotations from the past. She argues ("Rape or Restitution") that audiences of architecture rarely understood precise meanings of *spolia* and, further, that the reuse of earlier art or architectural materials constituted a

suppression and fragmentation of collective memory rather than an active use of the past. From this, Kinney concludes that *spolia* are by nature both disruptive and ambiguous in meaning. I argue throughout this book that the documents of late antique and early medieval northern Europe demonstrate general—if often inaccurate—familiarities with local, imperial, and Christian pasts, as did architecture and its remains, and that Europeans were deliberately juxtaposing these in the process of christianization. Not all Europeans understood *spolia* in the same ways or with the same depth; that is precisely the basic argument of this book.

4. Guy Halsall, "Movers and Shakers," 277–91. For general trends in the recent historiography of barbarian invasions, see the other essays in the same volume; also James, *The Franks;* Patrick Geary, "Barbarians and Ethnicity," and Brent D. Shaw, "War and Violence," both in Bowersock, Brown, and Grabar, *Late Antiquity,* 107–29, 130–69; and for a dour view of barbarians, Ward-Perkins, *Fall of Rome.*

5. Shaw, "War and Violence," 138–40.

6. Julius Caesar, *De bello gallico* 6.3.4; but cf. variant "Lucotecia," Ptolemy, 2.8; Duval, *De Lutèce oppidum,* 18–22; Couperie, *Paris through the Ages,* I: "Formation of the site and prehistory"; Colbert de Beaulieu, *Les monnaies gauloises des "Parisii"*; but see also Lombard-Jourdan, *Aux origines de Paris,* 19–23, regarding the site of battle and location of *oppidum;* Sorel, "Le choix du site," 87–88.

7. Duval, *La vie quotidienne en Gaule,* 99.

8. Butler, "Late Roman Town Walls," 44; Woolf, "Urbanization and Its Discontents in Early Roman Gaul," 115–31.

9. Duval, *Lutèce oppidum,* 143–91.

10. On the symbolism of Roman cities: Rykwert, *The Idea of a Town,* 41–71; Woolf, *Becoming Roman,* 112–26; Zanker, "The City as Symbol," 25–41. On the growth of Roman Paris: Février et al., *Histoire de la France urbaine,* vol. 1, *La ville antique des origines au IXe siècle,* 274–75.

11. Duval, *Lutèce oppidum,* 105–11.

12. Didier Busson, *Paris,* 76–77, 161–62; Duval, Périn, and Picard, "Paris," 97–129.

13. Butler, "Late Roman Town Walls," 25–50; Couperie, *Paris through the Ages,* III: "The Late Empire"; Greenhalgh, *Survival of Roman Antiquities in the Middle Ages,* chap. 4, "Mediaeval Towns and Their Walls in Gaul and Italy."

14. Butler, "Late Roman Town Walls," 40.

15. Greenhalgh, "Mediaeval Towns and Their Walls in Gaul and Italy"; Fevrier, "Origin and Growth of the Cities of Southern Gaul," 1–28; Blagg, "Re-use of Monumental Masonry in Late Roman Defensive Walls," 134–35.

16. Ammianus Marcellinus, *Res gestae* 16. 1–5; Butler, "Late Roman Town Walls," 45; Julian, *Misopogon,* 340D–342D; Grenier, *Manuel d'archéologie gallo-romaine* 1:414–20. Ammianus called the Parisian island a "fort" rather than a city: *Res gestae* 15.11.3 ("Parisiorum *castellum,* Lutetiam *nomine*"), 20.4; but cf. Van Ossel, "L'antiquité tardive," 63–79 at 65 and n. 17. See also Duval, *Lutèce oppidum,* 296–98; *Lutèce: Paris de César à Clovis,* 362–68.

17. *MGH AA* 9:552–612; Harries, "Church and State in the *Notitia Galliarum,*" 26–43.

18. Mirot, *Manuel de géographie historique de la France*, I: *L'unité française*, 32 and carte II.

19. Bekker-Nielsen, *Geography of Power*, 21–22.

20. Braudel, *Identity of France*, 50–57.

21. Bekker-Nielsen, "Navigable River-Systems and Urban Development," 111–22.

22. Woolf, *Becoming Roman*, 129–30, 137.

23. For a full list of officers, including military personnel, ca. 400, see *Notitia dignitatum*; see also Loseby, "Gregory's Cities," 245–56.

24. Mathisen, *Roman Aristocrats in Barbarian Gaul*, 15, 168 n. 34; Gilliard, "Senators of Sixth-Century Gaul," 685–97.

25. Van Dam, *Leadership and Community*, esp. 16–56.

26. James, *The Franks*, 51–52; Fanning, "Emperors and Empires in Fifth-Century Gaul," 288–97; Gregory of Tours, *Historiae* 2.9; see also Elton, "Defence in Fifth-Century Gaul," 167–68.

27. Salvian of Marseilles, *De gubernatione Dei*, 6.

28. Gregory of Tours, *Historiae* 2.27; also Fanning, "Emperors and Empires in Fifth-Century Gaul," 288–97; also Geary on Aegidius and Syagrius, *Before France and Germany*, 81ff.

29. *Chronica Gallia* for 439, 441; Gildas, *De excidio Britanniae*, 20.

30. Sidonius Apollinaris, *Ep.* 7.1

31. Gauthier, "From the Ancient City to the Medieval Town," 47–66.

32. Harries, "Christianity and the City in Late Roman Gaul"; Loseby, "Gregory's Cities"; Harries, "Church and State in the *Notitia Galliarum*," 26–43.

33. Bouvier, *Histoire de l'église de l'ancien archidiocèse de Sens*, 1.

34. Duchesne, *Fastes épiscopaux*, 2:469; Bekker-Nielsen, *Geography of Power*, 18–19; see also Mathisen, "The 'Second Council of Arles,'" 511–54.

35. Mathisen, *Roman Aristocrats in Barbarian Gaul*, 90–115; Heinzelmann, "L'aristocratie et les évêches," 75–90. See also Eugippius, *Ep. ad Paschasium* 7.

36. Heinzelmann, "The 'Affair' of Hilary of Arles (445) and Gallo-Roman Identity," 239–51.

37. Chevallier, "La function politique I," 180–93.

38. Bekker-Nielsen, *Geography of Power*, 18–19; Roblin, *Terroir de Paris*, 92–96.

39. Kubischek, "Itinerarien"; Miller, *Itineraria Romana*; Caló Levi and Caló Levi, *Itineraria Picta*; Weber, *Tabula Peutingeriana*.

40. Muhlberger, "Looking Back from Mid-century," 35.

41. *MGH AA* 9:138; Muhlberger, "Looking Back from Mid-century," 28–37.

42. Salvian of Marseilles, *De gubernatione Dei* 6; Van Dam, "Pirenne Thesis and Fifth-Century Gaul," 327–28; Mathisen, *Roman Aristocrats in Barbarian Gaul*, 68–70.

43. Ausonius, *Ordo urbium nobelium* 10 (*Arelas*: "Gallula Roma Arelas"); 6 (*Treveris*: "Armipotens dudum celebrari Gallia estit / Trevericaeque urbis solium, quae proxima Rheno / pacis ut in mediae gremio secura quiescit, / imperii vires quod alit, quod vestit et armat").

44. Gildas, *De excidio Britanniae*; Jones, "Geographical-Psychological Frontiers in Sub-Roman Britain," 45–58.

45. Olster, "From Periphery to Center," 93–104.

46. Sidonius Apollinaris, *Ep.* 4.17.48; see also Mathisen, *Roman Aristocrats in Barbarian Gaul*, 125–31.

47. Sidonius Apollinaris, *Ep.* 5.5.

48. Woolf, *Becoming Roman*, 136–37.

49. Peytremann, "Les structures d'habitat rural," 1–28; Roymans, "The Sword or the Plough," 60–65.

50. Hiddink, "Rural Centres," 201–33; Dyson, *Roman Countryside*, esp. 55–73.

51. Geary, *Before France and Germany*, 108–9; Duby, *Early Growth of the European Economy*, 17–30.

52. Groenman–Van Waateringe, "Wasteland," 113–17.

53. Roymans, "The Sword or the Plough," 60–61. But see also Halsall, *Settlement and Social Organization*, 178–82, 249–51.

54. Ferdière, *Campagnes en Gaule romaine*, 1: 63–86.

55. Woolf, *Becoming Roman*, 206.

56. Ibid., 157–59; Roymans, "The Sword or the Plough," 102–3.

57. Percival, *Roman Villa*, 175–77.

58. McCormick, *Origins of the European Economy*, esp. 83–114.

59. Woolf, *Becoming Roman*, 148–57; Roblin, *Terroir de Paris*, 151–52.

60. Coulon, *Gallo-Romains* vol. 1, 101–4.

61. Sidonius Apollinaris, *Epp.* 2.2, 2.9, 8.4, *Carm.* 22; Fortunatus, *Carm.* 1.18–20, 3.12; cited in Percival, "Fifth-Century Villa," 158; also Percival, *Roman Villa*, 171.

62. Duval, *Lutèce oppidum*, 334–35: (H)OSPITA REPLRE LAGONA[M] CERVESA . . . COPO CONDITU(M) (H)ABES – EST – REPLE, DA!; 300–301.

63. Grenier, *Manuel d'archéologie gallo-romaine*, 2:602–3. For a photograph of the famous carved third-century Weinschiff kept by the Rhenische Landsmuseum, see *REMUS*, http://www.remus.museum/html/en/museum.php?id=1308.

64. Grenier, *Manuel d'archéologie gallo-romaine*, 2:1015–17.

65. Bourne, *Aspects of the Relationship between the Central and Gallic Empires*.

66. Constantius, *Vita S. Germani* 19, 24; Van Dam, *Leadership and Community*, 45–46.

67. Reece, "The Third Century," 27–38; Hopkins, "Taxes and Trade in the Roman Empire," 101–5. On the general trend, Ward-Perkins, *Fall of Rome*, 87–120.

68. Grenier, *Manuel d'archéologie gallo-romaine*, 2:546–55.

69. Derks, *Gods, Temples, and Religious Practices*, 143–44.

70. *VGA* 27.

71. Hallsall, "Social Identities," 147–49.

CHAPTER 2

1. *VGA* 1: *Nemetodorensis parochia . . . septem ferme milibus a Parisius urbe abest.*

2. Heinzelmann, *Vies anciennes*, 20, on variant spellings and debates over authenticity of place-name; Jullian, "Sainte Geneviève à Nanterre," 372–75; Grenier, *Manuel d'archéologie gallo-romaine*, 1:152–54. See also White, *Roman Britain:* "Nemeton Page"; Rivet and Smith, *Place-Names of Roman Britain*, 254.

3. Fortunatus, *De basilica S. Vin. Vern.* in *Misc., PL* 88:71B–C: "Nomine Ver-nemetis voluit vocitare vetustas,/ Quod quasi fanum ingens Gallica lingua refert"; Dowden, *European Paganism*, 134–36; Piggott, *The Druids*, 63; http://www.roman-britain.org/nemeton.htm; Cunliffe, *The Ancient Celts*, 197–98; The goddess Nemetona shared altars in England and Germany with Mars Loucetius and graced her own altar at Speyer, but she did not name these sites, she merely shared with them some sacred quality; see Woolf, *Becoming Roman*, 132–33.

4. Heinzelmann, *Vies anciennes*, 21–22; *Cath Maige Tuired*, 126–27.

5. Brunaux, *Celtic Gauls*, 2–9.

6. Woolf, *Becoming Roman*, 222–29.

7. Van Andringa, "Vase de Sains-du-Nord," 27–44.

8. Derks, *Gods, Temples, and Ritual Practices*, 122–24; Aldhouse-Green, *Symbol and Image*, 45–73.

9. *ThesCRA* 5:138; Aldhouse-Green, *Symbol and Image*, 42.

10. Bémont, "À propos d'un nouveau monument de Rosmerta," 23–44; Aldhouse-Green, *Symbol and Image*, 42–43; Brunaux, *Religions gauloises*, 72–73.

11. Derks, *Gods, Temples, and Ritual Practices*, 91–94, 119–30; Aldhouse-Green, *Celtic Goddesses*, 105–16.

12. Aldhouse-Green, *Celtic Goddesses*, 160–87; Caesar, *De bello Gallico* 6.17.

13. See Derks's thoughtful discussion in *Gods, Temples and Ritual Practices*, 119–30.

14. Caesarius, *Sermones* 53; Wood, "Early Merovingian Devotion in Town and Country," 61–76; Wood, "Pagan Religions and Superstitions East of the Rhine," 253–79.

15. See the essays in Scott and Webster, *Roman Imperialism and Provincial Art*, especially Scott, "Provincial Art and Roman Imperialism: An Overview," 1–8; Webster, "Art as Resistance and Negotiation," 24–51; and Rodgers, "Female Representation in Roman Art'" 69–93. See also Roymans, "The Sword or the Plough," 9–125; Derks, *Gods, Temples, and Ritual Practises*, 33–35.

16. Brunaux, *Celtic Gauls*, 76–78.

17. Van Andringa, *Religion en Gaule romaine*, 65–71.

18. Deyts, *Un peuple de pélerins*, esp. 13–16.

19. Fauduet, *Atlas des sanctuaires*, 102–4.

20. Van Andringa, *Religion en Gaule romaine*, 76–77; Rey-Vodoz, "La Suisse dans l'Éurope des sanctuaires gallo-romains," 7–17; Weber, "Les sanctuaires de tradition indigène en Allemagne romain," 17–24; Cabuy, "Temples et sanctuaires de tradition indigène en Belgique romaine," 24–33; Marion, "Occupations protohistoriques," 85–95.

21. Fauduet, *Atlas des sanctuaires*, 118–20.

22. Brunaux et al., *Gournay I*.

23. Cf. Germany, where similar pillars were erected in towns and in relation to other monuments: Woolf, "Representation as Cult," 117–34; Woolf, *Becoming Roman*, 236–37.

24. Barroul, "Les sanctuaires gallo-romains du Midi de la Gaule," 49–72; also Fauduet's catalogue of different sites and structures at fanums, *Atlas des sanctuaires*, esp. 119–30; Woolf *Becoming Roman*, 234–36; Blin, "Un sanctuaire de *vicus*," 91–117; Durand, "Un sanctuaire 'rural,'" 119–29.

25. Fauduet, *Atlas des sanctuaires*, 120–24.

26. Young, "Que restait-il de l'ancien paysage religieux," 241–50.

27. "Lauit illud in fonte qui erat in medio ciuitatis . . . et surrexit fons sub basilica eius et si qui infirmorum tetigerit, saluus factus est." *AASS* Oct. 7, col. 812–15, passage reprinted in Frézouls, *Villes antiques de la France*, 182–83; see also 230–31. Many thanks to Greg Woolf for this reference. See also http://www.exagonline.com/grand/site/eng/site.htm.

28. Kapps, *Escolives Sainte-Camille gallo-romain*; also Société Archéologique d'Escolives, http://membres.lycos.fr/archeoescolives/.

29. Eusebius, *Vita Constantini* 2.54–58; also 2.45, 4.25; Curran, "Moving Statues in Late Antique Rome," 46–58; Jerome, *Ep.* 107.2. On the closing of temples and destruction of idols: *Codex Theodosianus* 16.10.4 (a. 346), 16 (a. 399); 16.10.19.1 (a. 408). See also Saradi-Mendelovici, "Christian Attitudes toward Pagan Monuments," 47–61.

30. Scheid, "Épigraphie et sanctuaires guérisseurs en Gaule," 51–53; Tertullian, *De idolatria* 2; Tertullian, *De spectaculis* 8; Augustine, *Ep.* 46; Ambrose, *Ep.* 18.31.

31. Mansi, *Sacrorum conciliorum*, 3:766, cited in Curran, "Moving Statues in Late Antique Rome," 49.

32. Marjorian, *De aedificiis publicis*, novel 4, in Meyer and Mommsen, *Leges*, 161; Alchermes, "*Spolia* in Roman Cities of the Late Empire."

33. *Concilia Galliae*, 265; Roblin, "Fontaines sacrées," 235–51; Landes, *Dieux guérisseurs*, esp. essays by Rousselle and Caulier.

34. Scheid, "Épigraphie et sanctuaires guérisseurs en Gaule," 25–40.

35. Scheid, "Sanctuaires et thermes sous l'Empire," 205–16; Aldhouse-Green, *Pilgrims in Stone*; Deyts, *Un people de pèlerins*; Bourgeois, *Divona*; Chevallier, *Eaux thermales*.

36. Woolf, "Uses of Forgetfulness in Roman Gaul," 361–81.

37. Poulin, "Cinq premières vitae de sainte Geneviève," 134–37.

38. Gregory of Tours, *Historiae* 1:30.

39. Poulin, "Cinq premieres vitae de sainte Geneviève," 136; *Liber Mozarabicus*, 609; Roblin, *Terroir de Paris*, 179–81; Wood, "Constructing Cults in Early Medieval France," 155–57; Pearce, "Processes of Conversion in North-west Roman Gaul," 61–78.

40. Poulin, "Les Cinq permières vitae de sainte Geneviève,"135, re: *relatio*.

41. Lifshitz, "Apostolicity Theses in Gaul," 213–18. See also Picard, "Auxerre," 52–65; Vieillard-Troiekouroff, *Monuments religieux*, 59–65.

42. Thacker, "Loca Sanctorum," 1–43, esp. summary on 41.

43. Eusebius, *Ecclesiastical History* 5, preface.

44. Bammel, "Products of Fifth Century Scriptoria," 430–62. See Paulinus, *Ep.* 28.5 for what he learned from Rufinus's translation. For use of Jerome, Orosius, and Eusebius, see Gregory of Tours, *Historiae*, prefaces to Books 1 and 2, as well as 1.6, 1.41, 2.9.

45. Irenaeus, *Adversus haereses* 1:1 (*SC* 263); Tertullian, *Adversus Iudaeos* 7; Cyprian, *Ep.* 68.

46. Mansi, *Sacrorum conciliorum* 2:476–77.

47. Duval, *Inscriptions antiques*, vol. 1, no. 30.

48. Galvao-Sobrinho, "Funerary Epigraphy," 431–62; Harries, "Death and the Dead in the Late Roman West," 57.

49. Duval, *Inscriptions antiques,* vol. 1, no. 43; Vieillard-Troiekouroff, *Monuments religieux,* 215.

50. Dubois, "L'emplacement des premiers sanctuaires de Paris," esp. 28–32; Gregory of Tours, *GC,* 103; Vieillard-Troiekouroff, *Monuments religieux,* 215–16.

51. Harries, "Death and the Dead in the Late Roman West," 60–61.

52. Gregory of Tours, *GC* 103.

53. *Codex Theodosianus* 16.10.4, 9.

54. Vieillard-Troiekouroff, *Monuments religieux,* 202–4.

55. Dubois and Beaumont-Maillet, *Sainte Geneviève de Paris,* 34–35.

56. Picard, "L'évolution des lieux de sepulture," 311–20.

57. See the sixth-century life of Amator of Auxerre, *AASS,* May 1, 56; Gregory of Tours, *Historiae* 1.31; Loseby, "Bishops and Cathedrals," 144–55.

58. Wharton, *Refiguring the Postclassical City,* on Dura Europos, 15–63.

59. Mabire la Caille, "Topographie de Melun," 82–83.

60. Fleury et al., *Paris de Clovis à Dagobert,* 20–21.

61. For examples of Martin's habits and dress: Sulpicius Severus, *Ep. I ad Eusebium; Dialogi* 2.3, 2.5 *et pass.*

62. Sulpicius Severus, *VM* 10.

63. Ibid., 4; Stancliffe, *St. Martin and His Hagiographer,* esp. 149–59; Cooper, "Household and Empire," 91–108.

64. Sulpicius Severus, *VM* 12.

65. Ibid., 13.

66. Ibid., 14; Gen. 19; Deut. 9:9; 1 Sam. 7:6; Ezra 10:6.

67. Farmer, *Communities of Saint Martin,* 15–16.

68. Sulpicius Severus, *VM,* Fontaine's introduction, pp. 133–35.

69. Sulpicius Severus, *VM* 11; translations are by F. R. Hoare in Noble and Head, *Soldiers of Christ,* 1–29. The classic analysis of Martin and his cult is Stancliffe, *St. Martin and His Hagiographer.*

70. Young, "Paganisme, christianization," 16–24; Yasin, "Commemorating the Dead," chap. 1, "The Problem of Seeing Christian Tombs."

71. Pietri, " Les sépultres privilegiés en Gaule "133–42; Jones, "Geographical-Psychological Frontiers in Sub-Roman Britain," 45–58.

72. Picard, "Espace urbain," 209. See also van Egmond, *Conversing with the Saints,* esp. chaps. 2 and 3 (25–64).

73. Van Dam, *Leadership and Community,* 141–49; Constantius of Lyon, *Vita S. Germani,* introduction at 7–106.

74. Constantius of Lyon, *Vita S. Germani* 6, 10, 17; translations are by F. R. Hoare, in Noble and Head, *Soldiers of Christ,* 81, 84–85, 89.

75. *Codex Theodosianus* 16.10.10–11; Fauduet, *Atlas des sanctuaires,* 120–24. But see MacMullen, *Christianity and Paganism,* 20–21.

76. Rousselle, *Croire et guérir;* Duval, *Dieux de la Gaule,* 113–18.

77. Sulpicius Severus, *Dialogi* 3, 8.

78. Gregory I, *Dialogi* 2, 8.

79. Jonas of Bobbio, *Vita Columbani* 17: Luxeuil.

80. Young, "Que restait-il de l'ancien paysage religieux," 241–50.

CHAPTER 3

1. Thecla is probably the best-known victim. See Burrus, *Sex Lives of Saints*, 56–60.

2. Caesarius of Arles, *Sermones* 52, 53; *Concilium in Trullio* 28.

3. *VGA* 3: "Vulgi multitudo . . . in medio occurentium coetu."

4. Gregory of Tours called Nanterre a *vicus*; the hagiographer referred to it as *parochia*, an ecclesiastical district: *VGA* 1; Gregory of Tours, *Historiae* 10.28. See also Roblin, *Terroir de Paris*, 36, 126; also 155: in the sixth century, "un *vicus* . . . le terme est pratiquement à cette époque l'équivalent d'*ecclesia*"; Van Dam, *Leadership and Community*, 67.

5. Heinzelmann, *Translationsberichte*, 66–77; Heinzelmann, *Vies anciennes*, 46–48.

6. *VGA* 25: "Maxima pars populi"; 27: "occurrit ei multitudo populi"; 42: "universa turba"; 45, where the crowd consists of demoniacs: "inerguminorum multitudo"; 47: "eam . . . universi honoraverunt."

7. Jullian, "Saint Geneviève à Nanterre," 372–75; Heinzelmann, *Vies anciennes*, 47–48; Roblin, *Terroir de Paris*, 125–27.

8. Dubois, "Sainte Geneviève et son temps," 65–79.

9. *VGA* 8: "Illa, quæ retro sequitur, anteponatur . . ."

10. Ibid., 10.

11. Sulpicius Severus, *VM* 19.

12. Cf. Victricius of Rouen, *De laude sancorum* 6.

13. *VGA* 14: "Summi antestites Martinus et Anianus pro virtutum suarum admiratione valde laudati sunt . . . Porro Genouefa nonne dignum est honorari quæ idem orationibus suis predictum exercitum, ne Parisius circumvaret, procul abegit?"

14. Ibid., 15.

15. Dubois, "Sainte Geneviève et son temps," 65–79; Dubois and Beaumont-Maillet, *Sainte Geneviève de Paris*, 37.

16. *VGA* 16; Poulin, "Cinq premières vitae de sainte Geneviève," 138–39; *Shepherd of Hermas* 3, Similitude 9, chap. 15.

17. *VGA* 16; Gregory of Tours, *GM* 71; Fortunatus, *De basilica domni dionysi, Carminum epistolarum expositionum* 1.11; *Carminum spuriorum*, app. 6; both in *MGH AA* 4.1, 13–14 (IX) ; 383–84 (VI); *Gloriosae (Passio ss Dionysii, Rustici et Eleutherii), MGH AA* 4.2, 101–5; Poulin, "Cinq premières vitae de sainte Geneviève," 125–26, 134–37, 150–52.

18. Six miles according to the *Gloriosae*, 28; four miles or four leagues according to the vita of Genovefa, *VGA* 17; Heinzelmann, *Vies anciennes*, 159–61; de Montesquiou-Fezensac, "'In sexto lapide,'" 51–60; Crosby, *St. Denis*, 456 n. 25.

19. Poulin, "Cinq premières vitae de sainte Geneviève," 150; Hilduin, abbot of Saint-Denis, composed a vita of Denis at the request of Louis the Pious, *PL* 106, 14–50; see also the list of bishops of Paris contained in the ninth-century sacramentary in Duchesne, *Fastes épiscopaux*, 2:460–61.

20. Her name, like her legend, surely derived from the Gallo-Roman settlement of Catulliacus. *MGH AA* 4 :104; Vieillard-Troiekouroff et al., *Anciennes églises suburbaines de Paris*, 208–11.

21. *PL* 106, col. 50.

22. Heinzelmann, *Vies anciennes*, 43.

23. Roblin, *Terroir de Paris*, 121.

24. Lifshitz, "Martyr, the Tomb, and the Matron," 337.

25. The earliest recension of *VGA* 18, reads *virtus deerat*, suggesting she lacked the influence, but cf. sec. 40 of the same version, where the besieged Parisians *virtus pre inopia deerat*.

26. *VGA* 19–20. Joël Schmidt argues that Genovefa made her plea before a synod at Saint-Étienne: *Sainte Geneviève*, 152–55. This seems unlikely, given the general neglect of bishops in the vita as well as the restricted public roles of women in ecclesiastical venues. See also the *Gloriosae*, which describes the anonymous burial of Denis and his companions: "Where afterward Christians raised a basilica over the martyrs' bodies at great cost and with great care" ("Unde postmodum christiani basilicam super martyrum corpora mango sumptu cultuque eximio construxerunt"), sec. 31, p. 104; see also Beaujard, *Le culte des saints en Gaule*, 166.

27. See also Jerome's Life of Hilary, *PL* 23, col. 51: *terribilem valde et remotum locum*, although surrounded by fruit-bearing trees and at the site of a ruined temple.

28. Woolf, *Becoming Roman*, 106–12.

29. Rapp, *Holy Bishops in Late Antiquity*, 105–25.

30. *VGA* 18.

31. Thanks to Ann Marie Yasin for this interpretation. Dix, "Manufacture of Lime," 331–46.

32. Périn, "Saint-Denis," 210; Wyss et al., *Atlas historique de Saint-Denis*, 28–29.

33. Fleury and France-Lanord, *Trésors mérovingiens*, 39–64. On the often confusing jumble of graves at Gallo-Roman cemeteries, see Sidonius's story of his grandfather's grave: Sidonius Apollinaris, *Epp.* Bk. 3,12.1; also Effros, *Merovingian Mortuary Archaeology*, 175–82, where she cites the Sidonius episode.

34. Fleury and France-Lanord, *Trésors mérovingiens*, 53–64.

35. *VGA* 30.

36. Gregory of Tours, *Historiae* 9.6.

37. John Chrysostom, *Hom.* 26 *on Acts* 3–4; reported in Palladius, *Dial.* 5, 146–49; Taft, "Women at Church in Byzantium," 72–74.

38. Coates, "Venantius Fortunatus and the Image of Episcopal Authority," 1109–37.

39. Caillet, *L'Évergétisme monumental Chrétien*, 418–26.

40. Hiddink, "Rural Centres," 220; Sotinel, "Le personnel episcopal," 105–26, at 115–16; Pietri, "Evergétisme et richesses ecclésiastiques," 317–37; Thacker, "Loca Sanctorum," 28–31, 41.

41. Geary, *Before France and Germany*, 34–35.

42. *VGA* 27.

43. Sidonius Apollinaris, *Epp.* 7:5.3; 9.6.

44. Picard, *Province ecclesiastique de Sens*, 16.

45. *VGA* 47.

46. Victricius of Rouen, *De laude sanctorum*, 15.

47. Ibid., 25, 36.

48. Ibid., 37.

49. Ibid., 42; Poulin, "Cinq premières vitae," 142–43.

50. *VGA* 46–47.

51. Sulpicius Severus, *VM* 17; Poulin "Cinq premières vitae de sainte Geneviève," 127–32; Heinzelmann, *Vie anciennes*, 54–56.

52. Dubois, "Sainte Geneviève et son temps," 65–79. Cf. Constantius of Lyon, *Vita S. Germani* 32.

53. *VGA* 35: "Protinus duo monstra feruntur vario colore ab eodem loco egressa, do corum nidore duabus fere oris navigantes foededissimo flatu perculsi sunt."

54. By the ninth-century recension of the vita, the two smelly beasts had become two gigantic serpents: *VGC* 29: "De cuius arboris gremio gemini anguis, socii scilicet sceleris, uersicoloribus squamis, teterrimi odoris, inmense magnitudinis referuntur egressi." See Poulin, "Cinq premières vitae de sainte Geneviève," 78.

55. LeGoff, "Ecclesiastical Culture and Folklore in the Middle Ages," interprets Marcel's dragon as symbolic of the saint's control over the physical environment and thus as a foundation legend, 167–73 at 173: "May we not look upon this text as evidence of an early example of medieval construction, after a hesitant clearing of land and installation of rudimentary drainage, under the aegis of a bishop-entrepreneur who was also a spiritual pastor and political leader?" Genovefa's story chronologically preceded all the hagiographic episodes cited by LeGoff.

56. Sluhovsky, *Patroness of Paris*, 36–49.

57. *VGA* 29.

58. Ibid., 50.

59. Ibid., 32.

60. Ibid., 30.

61. Moreira, "Augustine's Three Visions," 1–14. Augustine's theology of vision appears in *De Genesi ad litteram*, *CSEL* 28.

62. Wierschowski, *Die regionale Mobilität in Gallien*, chap. 8, "Die mobilität des Frauen."

63. McNamara, *Sisters in Arms*, 85–97.

64. *VGA* 46.

65. Ibid., 50.

66. Ibid., 28.

67. Ibid., 26.

68. Wyss et al., *Saint Denis*, "The Tomb of Saint Denis."

69. *VGA* 56.

CHAPTER 4

1. Fanning, "Clovis Augustus and Merovingian *Imitatio Imperii*," 321–35.

2. Grabar, *Martyrium*, 1:234–40, 360–61; Wharton, *Refiguring the Post-Classical City*, 85–94; Vieillard-Troiekouroff, *Monuments religieux*, 206–7.

3. Dubois and Beaumont-Maillet, *Sainte Geneviève de Paris*, 64–67.

4. Geary, *Before France and Germany*, 98–99; Fanning, "Clovis Augustus and Merovingian *Imitatio Imperii*," 321–35; Daly, "Clovis," 619–64.

5. Wickham, *Early Medieval Italy*, 65.

6. *VGA* 26.

7. Remigius's two letters to Clovis are in Grundlach, *Epistulae Austrasicae*, 407–9; Avitus's letter to Clovis in *MGH AA* 6:2, 75–76; see also Daly, "Clovis," 637–41; Van Ossel, "L'antiquité tardive," 63–79.

8. Périn, "Paris mérovingien," 500.

9. Viellard-Troiekouroff, "Chapiteaux de marbre," 105.

10. *VGA* 56.

11. Gauthier, "From the Ancient City to the Medieval Town," 56–57; compare Lavoye, where three main graves of the fifth century were laid on the site of a former villa: Joffroy, *Cimetière de Lavoye*; Geary, *Before France and Germany*, 104.

12. Stevens, "Transitional Neighborhoods and Suburban Frontiers," 187–200; see also Cleary, *Extra-mural Areas of Romano-British Towns*, 165–72, also cited in Stevens, 188 n. 5.

13. In Cassiodorus, *Variae, Ep.* 3.9, 10. See also Brenk, "Spolia from Constantine to Charlemagne," 103–9.

14. Gauthier, "From the Ancient City to the Medieval Towns," 55, 61; Gregory of Tours, *Historiae* 5.17. See also Salvian, *De gubernatione Dei* 6; Wickham, *Early Medieval Italy*, 79 n. 60.

15. *Codex Theodosianus* 15.1; Alchermes, "*Spolia* in Roman Cities of the Late Empire."

16. Gauthier, "Paysage urbain en Gaule," 57; Brogiolo, "Ideas of the Town," 99–126.

17. Loseby, "Gregory's Cities," 239–84.

18. Veilliard-Troiekouroff, *Monuments religieux*, 207; Veilliard-Troiekouroff et al., *Anciennes églises suburbaines de Paris*, 166–68; Périn, "Paris: Églises des Saints-Apôtres ou Saint-Pierre," 159–64, esp. map of burials bottom of 161; Krüger, *Königsgrabkirchen*, 40–54.

19. Van Ossel, "L'antiquité tardive," 65–67.

20. *VGA* 54–55; Heinzelmann, *Vies anciennes*, 102.

21. Cooper, "The Martyr, the *Matrona*, and the Bishop," 297–317; Lifshitz, "The Martyr, the Tomb, and the Matron," 311–41.

22. Bonnet, "Les églises en bois," 217–36.

23. Lebeuf, *Histoire de la ville et de tout le diocese de Paris*, 1:229; Vielliard-Troiekouroff et al., *Anciennes églises suburbaines de Paris*, 168 n. 3.

24. Prudentius, d. ca. 409, and Ceraunus, d. 614.

25. Gregory of Tours, *Historiae* 2.36–37.

26. " . . . Apud urbem Turonicam obiit, tempore Injuriosi episcopi: quae Parisios cum magno psallentio deportata, in sacrario basilicae S. Petri, ad latus Chlodovechi regis sepulta est . . . Nam basilicam illam ipsa construxerat in qua et Genovefa beatissima est sepulta." *Hist.* 4.1; also 2.43, 3.10, 3.18, 5.18, 5.49; *GC* 89. See also Vieillard-Troiekouroff, *Monuments religieux*, 206–8.

27. Mackie, *Early Christian Chapels*, 163–68.

28. Gregory of Tours, *GM* 37; Crook, *Architectural Setting of the Cult of the Saints*, 49–52.

29. Sidonius Apollinaris, *Epp.* 2, 10.

30. *VGA* 56: "Cui est porticus adplicata triplex, nec non et patriarcharum prophetarumque et martyrum adque confessorum veram vetusti temporis fidem, que sun tradita libris storiarum, pictura refret." Grabar and Vieillard-Troieckouroff place the images inside the portico rather than the church itself, and Grabar assumes they were mosaics: Grabar, *Martyrium*, 2:125; Vieillard-Troieckouroff et al., *Anciennes églises suburbaines de Paris*, 171. See also Mackie, *Early Christian Chapels*, 149–51.

31. Périn, "Paris: Église des Saints-Apôtres," 159–64.

32. Pluskowski and Patrick, "'How Do You Pray to God?'" 49–50.

33. Geary, *Before France and Germany*, 131. See also Gregory of Tours, *De passione et virtutibus S. Juliani* 4–5, in *MGH SRM* 1.

34. Gregory of Tours, *Historiae* 2.17.

35. *Libellus de ecclesiis Claromontanis* 13, in *MGH SRM* 7 :461; Prévot, "De la tombe sainte au sanctuaire," 209–16.

36. McNamara, "Chaste Marriage and Clerical Celibacy," 22–33. Venantius also mentioned Placidina, wife of Leontius II, a bishop in Bordeaux, who decorated a church to Martin there: *Carmina* 1.6. See also Muschiol, "Men, Women and Liturgical Practice," 201.

37. Pimpaud et al., *Paris: A Roman City*, http://www.culture.gouv.fr/culture/arcnat/paris/en/index.html.

38. Gregory of Tours, *Historiae* 3.18, 4.1; *Liber historiae Francorum* 23, 24, 27; Périn, "Paris: Église des Saints-Apôtres," 162.

39. Paul the Deacon, writing in the eighth century, would treat Lombard queens in the same way; see his references to Gundiperga and her mother who also built memorial churches, Paul the Deacon, *Historia Langobardorum* 4.47 in *MGH SRLI.*

40. *Vita S. Chrothildis*, 341–48, at sec. 14; trans. McNamara, *Sainted Women*, 50.

41. The most exalted women she met were a tribune's wife and a young woman named Cilinia, who had a retinue of serving women: *VGA* 28–29.

42. Gregory of Tours, *Historiae* 2.43; *Vita S. Chrothildis* 10–11.

43. *Vita S. Chrothildis* 11; McNamara, *Sainted Women*, 45.

44. *Vita S. Chrothildis* 8.

45. Ibid., 12.

46. Roblin, *Terroir de Paris*, 154–76.

47. Viellard-Troiekouroff, *Monuments religieux*, 201–6; Dubois, "Sainte Geneviève et son temps," 65–79.

48. Périn, "Paris: Église des Saints-Apôtres," 160; cf. Vieillard-Troiekouroff et al., *Anciennes églises suburbaines de Paris*, 183–85.

49. Vieillard-Troiekouroff et al., *Anciennes églises suburbaines de Paris*, 182–83; Fossard et al, *Recueil général des monuments sculptés*, 1:183–92, and accompanying plates; Busson, *Paris.*

50. *Vita S. Eligii*, 634–741, sec. 32.

51. Périn, "Paris: Église des Saints-Apôtres," 162.

52. Sluhovsky, *Patroness of Paris*, 1–28, 206–9.

53. Périn, "Paris: Église des Saints-Apôtres," 159–60.

54. *Concilia Galliae*, 204, 218, 274.

55. Périn, "Paris: Église des Saints-Apôtres," 160; Périn, "Tombe de Clovis," 363–78; but see Vieillard-Troiekouroff, *Monuments religieux*, 206.

56. Gregory of Tours, *Historiae* 5.18, 5.49; *Liber historiae Francorum* 4.1; Périn, "Tombe de Clovis," 363–78.

57. *VGC* 42.

58. *Concilia Galliae*, 148, 280–82.

59. Gregory of Tours, *GC* 89.

60. *Translatio Germani episcopi Parisiaci vetustissima* in *MGH SRM* 7:425.3: "in monasterio beati Petri hospitio".

61. *Vita S. Crothildis* 11, 13; see also later references to churches named after the apostle, *Liber historiae Francorum* 17; Odorannus, *PL* 142:801ff.; see also *Vita S. Balthildis* 18 in *MGH SRM* 2:482–508.

62. Fortunatus, *Carmina*, 2.10; Constantius, *Vita Germani episcopi Parisiaci* in *MGH SRM* 7:342. See also *Liber historiae Francorum* 26.

63. Gregory of Tours, *Historiae* 6.27, 34; Vieillard-Troiekouroff, *Monuments religieux*, 206.

64. Gregory of Tours, *Historiae* 5,18, 6.46, 8.10; Vieillard-Troiekouroff et al., *Les anciennes églises suburbaines de Paris*, 93; Vieillard-Troiekouroff, *Monuments religieux*, 211–14.

65. *Liber historiae Francorum*, 26; Gregory of Tours, *Historiae* 4.21.

66. Gregory of Tours, *Historiae* 9.42.

67. Crosby, *Royal Abbey of Saint-Denis*, 24–27; Fleury and France-Lanord, *Trésors mérovingiens*, 81–101 and passim.

68. Gregory of Tours, *GM* 63.

69. Ibid., 50.

70. Crook, *Architectural Setting of the Cult of the Saints*, 12–13.

71. Augustine, *De cura pro mortuis gerenda*, 16.

72. Gregory of Tours, *GM* 38.

73. Gregory of Tours, *Historiae* 5.32.

74. Rosenwein, *Negotiating Space*, 37–41.

75. Gregory of Tours, *Historiae* 6.32.

76. Ibid., 33.

77. Ibid., 58.

78. Ibid., 33.

79. *Vita S. Eligii* 1.32.

80. Ibid., 1.30.

81. Gregory of Tours, *GM* 71.

82. Sluhovsky, *Patroness of Paris*, 3–4.

83. Victricius of Rouen, *De laude sanctorum* 1, 6.

84. Ibid., 17; Poulin, "Cinq premières vitae de sainte Geneviève," 143; Thacker, "Peculiaris patronus noster," 1–24.

85. Crosby put it: Genovefa, "although extremely popular, as a woman could hardly have been accepted as a patron of the Salian Franks." Crosby, *Royal Abbey of Saint-Denis*, 458 n. 42.

86. Monin, *Histoire de la ville de Saint-Denis*, 5–8; Atsma and Vezin, *Chartae Latinae antiquiores*, 6–7. See also Ganz and Goffart, "Charters Earlier Than 800," 906–32.

87. Dagobert's charters in Atsma and Vezin, *Chartae Latinae antiquiores*, 10–11, 22; see Levillain, "Etudes sur l'abbaye de Saint-Denis," 7–65; Crosby, *Royal Abbey of Saint-Denis*, 6–12.

88. *Gesta Dagoberti* 17–20.

89. Crosby, *Royal Abbey of Saint-Denis*, 29–50.

90. *Gesta Dagoberti* 17.

91. Lombard-Jourdan, "Légende de la consécration par le Christ," 237–69.

92. Suger, *De consecrationae ecclesiae*; Crosby, *Royal Abbey of Saint-Denis*, from a doctoral dissertation of 1937.

93. At Auxerre, for instance, advocates of Saint Germanus produced new vitae of the saint as well as a diocesan history based on the papal Liber pontificalis. See Egmond, *Conversing with the Saints*, especially references on p. 1, n. 1.

94. For the later vitae and miracles, see below, chapter 8; also Poulin, "Cinq premières vitae de sainte Geneviève," esp. 154, 162–63, 166–67, 173.

95. Charters: Lasteryrie du Saillant, *Cartulaire général de Paris*, 21, 39, 59; Giard, "Étude sur l'histoire de l'abbaye de Sainte-Geneviève," 41–126.

CHAPTER 5

1. Doherty, "Monastic Town in Early Medieval Ireland," 45–75.

2. Charles-Edwards, *After Rome*, 118–19.

3. Thomas, "Early Medieval Munster," 9–16.

4. Bieler, *St. Patrick and the Coming of Christianity*, 1–3; Kelly, *Early Irish Farming*, 319; Bateson, "Roman Material from Ireland," 21–92; Bateson, "Further Finds of Roman Material," 171–80; Thomas, "Imported Late-Roman Mediterranean Pottery," 245–55; Charles-Edwards, *Early Christian Ireland*, 145–58.

5. Thomas, "Imported Late-Roman Mediterranean Pottery," 251–52; Edwards, *Archaeology of Early Medieval Ireland*, 96–98.

6. Carver, introduction to *The Cross Goes North*, 4–5; Waddell, "Irish Sea in Prehistory," 10; for dissemination of foreign burial styles and goods, Raftery, "Iron Age Burials in Ireland," 173–204, at 200; Wooding, *Communication and Commerce*, 22–26.

7. Rynne, "La Tène and Roman Finds," 231–43; Bateson, "Roman Material from Ireland," 72–73.

8. Edwards, *Archaeology of Early Medieval Ireland*, 1–5; Robinson, "Romans and Ireland Again," 19–31.

9. Mac an Bhaird, "Ptolemy Revisited," 1–20; Freeman, "Greek and Roman Views of Ireland," 11–13; Raftery, *Pagan Celtic Ireland*, 200–219. But see also Wooding, *Communications and Commerce*, 22–23: "Direct links between Ireland and Gaul are unlikely in the fifth century and earlier."

10. Wooding, *Communication and Commerce*, 22–23, 41–42; Raftery, "Iron-Age Ireland," 178–80.

11. Edwards, *Archaeology of Early Medieval Ireland*, 68–73.

12. On comparative acculturation in southern and northern Britain, see Higham, "Roman and Native in England North of the Tees," 153–74.

13. Carson and O'Kelly, "Catalogue of the Roman Coins from Newgrange," 33–55; Raftery, *Pagan Celtic Ireland*, 180, 210.

14. Raftery, "Iron Age Studies in Ireland," 156–58.

15. Mytum, *Origins of Early Christian Ireland*, esp. 49–52; Carver, *The Cross Goes North*, 4–5.

16. Raftery, *Pagan Celtic Ireland*, 182–85; Lynn, "Some 'Early' Ring-Forts and Crannogs," 147–58; Watts, *Christians and Pagans in Roman Britain*, 209–14; Swift, *Ogham Stones and the Earliest Irish Christians*, 1–26, esp. 19–20.

17. Raftery, "Conundrum of Irish Iron Age Pottery," 147–156; see also Edwards, *Archaeology of Early Medieval Ireland*, 68–75; Collis, "Across the Great Divide," 3.

18. Richards, "Irish Settlements in South-west Wales," 133–62; Thomas, *Celtic Britain*, 114–16; Ó Cathasaigh, "Déisi and Dyfed," 1–33; Thomas, "Early Medieval Munster," 9–16; Alcock, "Was There an Irish Sea Culture-Province in the Dark Ages?" 55–65; Miller, "Date-Guessing and Dyfed," 33–61; Mytum, *Origins of Early Christian Ireland*, 23–36; Charles-Edwards, *Early Christian Ireland*, 155–76.

19. "Rome taught the Britons to carve stone," according to R. G. Collingwood, writing in the 1930s, "to paint wall-plaster, to decorate floors in mosaic." In his proudly imperialist estimation, British efforts rose barely "above the level of dull, mechanical limitation to that of even third-rate artistic achievement." Collingwood and Myres, *Roman Britain and the Anglo-Saxon Settlements*, 249–50.

20. Bateman, "Public Buildings in Roman London," 47–57; Marsden, "London in the 3rd and 4th Centuries," 99–108; Guest, "Manning the Defences"; Watson, "'Dark Earth' and Urban Decline in Late Roman London," 100–106; Fulford, "Epilogue," 107–12; *Notitia dignitatum*, 11: "In Britanniis: Praepositus thesaurorum Augustensium"; Whittaker, *Frontiers of the Roman Empire*, 152–53; Ottaway, *Archaeology in British Towns*, 101–3. On living near and around towns rather than within walls: Bullough, "Social and Economic Structure and Topography," 351–99.

21. Tertullian, *Adversus Iudaeos* 7; Origen, *Hom.* 4, *PG* 12, 698; see also Thomas, *Christianity in Roman Britain*, 43; Watts, *Christians and Pagans in Roman Britain*, 8–11.

22. *Concilia Galliae*, 148: Conc. Arelatense, p. 15; Athanasius, *Ep. ad Jovianum* 2; Athanasius, *Apologia contra Arianos*, 1; Sulpicius Severus, *Historia sacra* 2.41, in Schaff, *Nicene and Post-Nicene Fathers* 11.

23. Jerome, *Commentariorum in Jeremiam prophetam* 6, in *PL* 24; Constantius, *Vita S. Germani*, 12–27; De Paor, *Saint Patrick's World*, 18–19.

24. Jones, "Early Christian Archaeology in Europe," 319–34; Brooks, "Review of the Evidence for the Continuity in British Towns," 77–102; Thomas, *Christianity in Roman Britain*, 170–80; Jones, "St. Paul in the Bail, Lincoln," 325–47.

25. Sparey-Green, "Cemetery of a Romano-British Christian Community," 61–76; Sparey-Green, "Where Are the Christians?" 93–107, esp. 97; Knight, "Basilicas and

Barrows," 119–26; Thomas, *Christianity in Roman Britain*, 202–27; Guy, "Roman Circular Lead Tanks in Britain," 271–76.

26. Cunliffe, *Fishbourne*.

27. Constantius, *Vita S. Germani*, 14, 16; Gildas, *De excid. Brit.*, 10.2; Rodwell, "Role of the Church in the Development of Roman and Early Anglo-Saxon London," 91–99; Niblett, "Roman Verulamium," 97–100; Thomas, *Christianity in Roman Britain*, 69, 180; Sharpe, "Martyrs and Local Saints in Late Antique Britain," 75–154; Sharpe, "Late Antique Passion of St. Alban," 30–37; Dark, *Civitas to Kingdom*, 258–66; Niblett, "St Albans in the Post-Roman Period," 166–77.

28. Blair, *Church in Anglo-Saxon Society*, 183–91.

29. Dark, *Civitas to Kingdom*, 36–39; Frend, "Failure of Christianity in Roman Britain"; Frend, "Roman Britain, a Failed Promise"; Biddle, "Archaeology, Architecture, and the Cult of Saints in Anglo-Saxon England," 1–31.

30. Thomas, *Christianity in Roman Britain*, 170–74. Farther from towns, nothing but the rectangular shape of foundations raised from previous ruins hints at fourth-century religious buildings; in one case, the builders may have ritually exposed pagan votive objects first: Watts, *Christians and Pagans in Roman Britain*, 209–14.

31. Bowden, "A New Urban Élite?" 9–11.

32. Gildas, *De excid. Brit.*, 3.66; Bateman, "Public Buildings in Roman London," 47–57; Evans, "From the End of Roman Britain to the 'Celtic West,'" 91–104; White, *Roman Britain*.

33. Prosper Aquitanus, *Chronicon*, PL 51, col. 595; Mytum, *Origins of Early Christian Ireland*, 36–43; Dumville, "St. Patrick and Fifth-Century Irish Chronology," in Dumville, *Saint Patrick*, 51–57; Thomas, "Palladius and Patrick," 13–37; Ó Cróinín, "New Light on Palladius," 28–34.

34. Ó Cróinín, *Early Medieval Ireland*, 22–23; De Paor, *Saint Patrick's World*, 41; Charles-Edwards, *Early Christian Ireland*, 234.

35. Dumville, "Auxilius, Iserninus, Secundinus, and Benignus," in Dumville, *Saint Patrick* 89–105; De Paor, *Saint Patrick's World*, 40–43; Flanagan, "Christian Impact on Early Ireland," 25–51. See also the maps in Thomas, "Palladius and Patrick," 34–35.

36. Smyth, *Celtic Leinster*, 9.

37. Bitel, *Isle of the Saints*, 48–56.

38. Thomas, "Palladius and Patrick," 15; Columbanus, *Opera*.

39. *Synodus episcoporum*, edited and translated by Bieler as "First Synod of Saint Patrick," *Patrician Texts*, 54–59. See Charles-Edwards, *Early Christian Ireland*, 245–47.

40. Ó Cróinín, "New Light on Palladius"; see relevant years in *AU*.

41. Charles-Edwards, "Social Background to Irish *Peregrinatio*," 55; on exile and ethnic consciousness, see also Bourke, "*Peregrinatio Columbae*," 79–88.

42. Patrick, *Conf.* 43.

43. De Paor, *Saint Patrick's World*, 88.

44. Patrick, *Conf.* 1; Snyder, *Age of Tyrants*, 78–79.

45. Patrick, *Conf.* 9–10; Mohrmann, *Latin of Saint Patrick*; Nagy, *Conversing with Angels and Ancients*, esp. 25–39.

46. Patrick, *Conf.* 1.; *Ep.* 10.

47. Muirchú, [*Life of Patrick*] 6–8.

48. Patrick, *Conf.* 16.

49. Ibid., 19.

50. Ibid., 29; Nagy, *Conversing with Ancients and Angels*, 44–45.

51. Patrick, *Conf.* 28, 33, 37.

52. Ibid., 40–41.

53. Augustine, *Conf.* 8.2.

54. Patrick, *Conf.* 16, 23; *Ep.* 3.

55. Swift, "Patrick, Skerries and the Earliest Evidence," 61–78.

56. Bieler, *Patrician Texts*, 116–21, 138–39, 164–65; Charles-Edwards, *Early Christian Ireland*, 233–40.

57. Pender, "Guide to Irish Genealogical Collections"; *CGH*, 24–86; Charles-Edwards, *Early Irish and Welsh Kinship*, 117–25.

58. Mac Shamhráin, *Church and Polity in Pre-Norman Ireland*, 10, 44–47; Byrne, *Irish Kings and High-Kings*, 130–56.

59. Such histories of prehistoric pioneers eventually helped the medieval Irish place their ancestors into the grand narrative of the earth's peopling told in Bible and Latin chronologies, which had passed them by. See Scowcroft, "Leabhar Gabhála, I," 81–142.

60. Corthals, "Rhymeless 'Leinster Poems,'" 79–100; Bhreathnach, "Genealogies of Leinster," 250–67. See also O'Rahilly, *Early Irish History and Mythology*, 92–101; *CGH*, 18–22 (118a6–57), 334–35 (311a1–61).

61. Smyth, *Celtic Leinster*; *Orgain Denna Ríg*; *Fled Dúin na nGéd*; see also Carney, "Three Old Irish Accentual Poems," 23–80.

62. *CGH*, 18–19 (118a18–20); see also Ó Cuív, "Some Items from Irish Tradition," 179–83.

63. O'Rahilly, *Early Irish History and Mythology*, 101–17, and 13, where he identifies it with Ptolemy's *Dunon*; Mac an Bhaird, "Ptolemy Revisited," 1–20.

64. O'Rahilly, *Early Irish History and Mythology*, 101–17; *FM*, 4658–77.

65. Grabowsi, "Historical Overview of Dún Ailinne," 32–36; Wailes, "Excavations at Dún Ailinne," 14:5–11; 15:507–17; Wailes, "Excavations at Dún Ailinne, Co. Kildare," 79–90.

66. Mount, "Environmental Siting," 117–28.

67. Cooney, "Reading a Landscape Manuscript," 1–49, esp. 15–16.

68. See the discussion of distribution of ringforts in Leinster and, more generally, principles of settlement in Ireland in the premedieval and early medieval periods in Stout, *Irish Ringfort*, esp. 14–21, 57–59.

69. Aalen et al., *Atlas of the Irish Rural Landscape*, 42.

70. Waterman, *Excavations at Navan Fort*; Mallory and Lynn, "Recent Excavations and Speculations on the Navan Complex," 532–41.

71. Lynn, "Knockaulin (Dún Ailinne) and Navan," 51–56; Raftery, *Pagan Celtic Ireland*, 71–74.

72. Eogan, *Excavations at Knowth*; Herity, "Survey of the Royal Site of Cruachain in Connacht: I," 121–42; Herity, "Survey of the Royal Site of Cruachain in Connacht: II," 125–38.

73. Mallory and Lynn, "Recent Excavations and Speculations on the Navan Complex," 540–41; Raftery, *Pagan Celtic Ireland*, 71; Lynn, "Iron Age Mound in Navan Fort," 33–57; Robertson, "Navan Forty Metre Structure," 25–32.

74. *CGH*, 20 (118a29); "Hail Brigit," 6; Grabowski, "Historical Overview of Dún Ailinne," 33; Smyth, *Celtic Leinster*, 18; Ó Corráin, "Creating the Past," 1–32.

75. Koch and Carey, *Celtic Heroic Age*, 41–42. See also Carney, "Three Old Irish Accentual Poems," 69–70, where he discusses pre-Christian loanwords from Latin, including *trebun (tribunus), legión (legio), míl (miles)*.

76. Ó Corráin, "Creating the Past," 22–23; Baumgarten, "Geographical Orientation of Ireland in Isidore and Orosius," 189–203.

77. *CGH*, 22–23 (118b2–17).

78. Roberston, "Navan Forty Metre Structure," 30.

79. *AU* 727; Aitchison, *Armagh and the Royal Centres*, 59–61.

80. *CGH*, 8 (116c15–17).

81. Koch and Carey, *Celtic Heroic Age*, 45.

82. Lucas, "Sacred Trees of Ireland," 16–54; Watson, "The King, the Poet, and the Sacred Tree," 165–81.

83. Kelleher, "Early Irish History and Pseudo-History," 113–27.

84. Charles-Edwards, *Early Christian Ireland*, 235–37, 550.

85. Smyth, *Celtic Leinster*, 19–20; Ó Riain, "Towards a Methodology in Early Irish Hagiography," esp. 157–58.

86. Aitchison, *Armagh and the Royal Centres*, esp. introduction, 1–49, and 189–91.

87. Ibid., 204–6.

88. *Félire Óengusso*, 24–27 (ll. 165–212), modified translation.

89. Trans. Ní Dhonnchadha, *Field Day Anthology*, 4:70–72.

90. MacCana, "Aspects of the Theme of King and Goddess," 7 (1955–56): 76–114, 356–413; 8 (1958–59): 59–65; Jaski, *Early Irish Kingship and Succession*, 57–72.

91. Bitel, *Land of Women*, 206–16.

92. Bitel, *Isle of the Saints*, 42–57.

93. Bieler, *Irish Penitentials*, 54–59. The synod's decrees also referred to a bishop "staying" in "several churches," which could mean all sorts of things—that a bishop lived in the same building or enclosure where Christians worshiped, that he moved from one church to another, or that he traveled from one community to another, staying with whoever might take him in.

94. Bieler, *Patrician Texts*, 158–61, River Dub; Cross, *Motif-Index*, D2151, F930–933.

95. Bieler, *Patrician Texts*, 152–55.

96. Harbison, *Pre-Christian Ireland*, 42–86; McMann, "Forms of Power," 525–44; Bradley, *Archaeology of Natural Places*, 147–61.

97. O'Brien, "Pagan and Christian Burial in Ireland," 130–37.

98. Fry, *Burial in Medieval Ireland*, 40–43; Thomas, "Early Medieval Munster," 9–16; Swift, *Ogham Stones and the Earliest Irish Christians*.

99. *Celtic Inscribed Stones Project*, Colbinstown: COLIN/2, http://www.ucl.ac.uk/ archaeology/cisp/database/.

100. Carey, "Saint Patrick, the Druids, and the End of the World," 43 n. 5.

101. Tírechán, *Collectanea* 8.2, in Bieler, *Patrician Texts*, 130; Swift, "Patrick, Skerries and the Earliest Evidence," 65, 75.

102. Bieler, *Patrician Texts*, 132–33.

103. Ibid., 142–45.

104. Raftery, *Pagan Celtic Ireland*, 188–96.

105. Fry, *Burial in Medieval Ireland*, 43–47.

106. Bieler, *Patrician Texts*, 114–15; 154–57: "Puto enim ideo eum reliquit quia Deus eum saluare noluit."

107. Ibid., 136–37.

108. Cogitosus, *Vita S. Brig.*, 22. For another incident of pagan oaths, see Bieler, *Patrician Texts*, 102, l. 17, *signa crudelitatis* glossed *diberca*. Church leaders forbade Christians to make such vows; see Bieler, *Irish Penitentials*, 160, sec. 4: "uel uotiui mali siue crudelis." See also McCone, *Pagan Past and Christian Present*, 220–23.

109. Bieler, *Patrician Texts*, 84–87.

110. Ibid., 92–93.

111. Or in 558: *AU* 558, 560. See also Binchy, "The Fair of Tailtiu and the Feast of Tara," 134–37.

112. Binchy, "The Fair of Tailtiu and the Feast of Tara," 152–53, 158–59.

113. Caulfield, "Neolithic Settlement of North Connaught," 195–215; Cooney, "Reading a Landscape Manuscript," 10–15.

114. Clinton, "Settlement Patterns in the Early Historic Kingdom of Leinster," 295–96.

115. Dooley, "Plague and Its Consequences in Ireland," 215–28.

116. Aalen et al., *Atlas of the Irish Rural Landscape*, 40–49; Mitchell and Ryan, *Reading the Irish Landscape*, 246–96; Stout, "Early Christian Ireland," 81–109.

117. Meyer, *Instructions of King Cormac*, 17–18.

118. *Bretha Comaithcesa* in Binchy, *CIH*, 64–79, quotation at 64. For background on farm property and its ownership, see Kelly, *Early Irish Farming*, chap. 12: "Land-tenure," 398–431 on ownership, and 431–437 on trespass and other violations.

119. Kelly, *Guide to Early Irish Law*, 273; Kelly, *Early Irish Farming*, 372–78; Ó Corráin, "Some Legal References to Fences and Fencing in Early Historic Ireland."

120. Binchy, *CIH*, 41; Kelly, *Early Irish Farming*, 376–77.

121. Later commentators on the tract, dissatisfied with ambiguous boundaries, specified the legal signifiers: *clarbla, ailbla, findbla, noesbla, bla mucniaghe, 7 gnobla, bla imfogla, 7 linnbla, rodarcbla, bla neasbaige, bla reime*: a flat mark impossible for any *seanchaid* (antiquarian) to determine; a stone mark; a tree mark recognizable by a living or fallen tree; a deer mark, an area frequented by deer or cows, as well as mounds, streams, rivers, roads, ditches, and proper fences: Binchy, *CIH*, 201.

122. Binchy, *CIH*, 205–13.

123. Kelly, *Guide to Early Irish Law*, 17–26.

124. Binchy, "An Archaic Legal Poem," 156–59.

125. Binchy, *CIH*, 442, 459–60, 532–33.

126. Mytum, *Origins of Early Christian Ireland*, 60–75, esp. 74.

127. Smyth, *Celtic Leinster*, 32–33.

128. Charles-Edwards, *Early Irish and Welsh Kinship*, 61–73; Ó Cróinín, *Early Irish History and Chronology*, 162–64; Bitel, *Isle of the Saints*, 97–101; Ó Corráin, "The Early Irish Churches," 327–41.

129. Bitel, *Land of Women*, 113–17, and sources cited there.

130. Binchy, *CIH*, 378–89, 422; Binchy, "Distraint in Irish Law," 22–71; Kelly, *Guide to Early Irish Law*, 178–79.

131. Binchy, *CIH*, 502–4; Kelly, *Guide to Early Irish Law*, 70.

132. *CGH*, 13; Ó Cróinín, *Early Medieval Ireland*, 63–64.

133. Binchy, *CIH*, 505.

134. Williams, "Excavations at Ballyutoag, County Antrim," 37–49; Patterson, *Cattle-Lords and Clansmen*, 78–79 and passim.

135. Binchy, *CIH*, 47–48.

136. Dillon, "Stories from the Law-Tracts," 47–48, 57–58.

137. *Book of Leinster* 1, 29–89; Stokes, "Prose Tales in the *Rennes Dindsenchas*," 44–47; Aldhouse-Green, *Celtic Goddesses*, 82–83; MacCana, "Aspects of the Theme of King and Goddess," 7 (1955–56): 76–114, 356–413; 8 (1958–59), 59–65.

138. Herbert, "Celtic Heroine?" 13–22.

139. Nash, "Remapping the Body/Land," 227–50.

CHAPTER 6

1. Much of this chapter first appeared in slightly different form as "Ekphrasis at Kildare: The Imaginative Architecture of a Seventh-Century Hagiographer," *Speculum* 79 (2004): 605–27.

2. Bieler, *Irish Penitentials*, 54.

3. James and Webb, "'To Understand Ultimate Things and Enter Secret Places,'" 1–17; Webb, "Aesthetics of Sacred Space," 59–74; Nelson, "To Say and to See," 148–68.

4. Cogitosus, *Vita S. Brig.*; Connolly and Picard, "Cogitosus' Life of St. Brigit," intro. Chapter numbers of the translation are close but not identical to those of the Latin editions. Connolly and Picard's translation contains thirty-one chapters written about Brigit's lifetime, thirty-two plus prologue and epilogue in the entire vita.

5. Cogitosus, *Vita S. Brig.* 39; Connolly and Picard, "Cogitosus' Life of St. Brigit," sec. 32.

6. Cogitosus, *Vita S. Brig.* 1, 40.

7. Ibid. Among the many to speculate on Cogitosus's identity, which remains, nonetheless, a mystery: Sharpe, "*Vitae Sanctae Brigitae*," 83–89; Esposito, "On the Earliest Latin Life of St. Brigit of Kildare," 322.

8. Picard, "Structural Patterns in Early Hiberno-Latin Hagiography," 67–82. See also Bray, "Body of Brigit"; Connolly and Picard, "Cogitosus' Life of St. Brigit," 5–9; Sellner, "Brigit of Kildare," 402–19.

9. Bede, *Historia Ecclesiastica* 3.7: "Venit in provinciam de Hibernia pontifex quidam, nomine Agilberctus, natione quidem Gallus, sed tunc legendarum gratia Scripturarum in Hibernia non parvo tempore demoratus . . . rediit Galliam et accepto

episcopatu Parisiacae civitatis ibidem senex ac plenus dierum obiit"; Charles-Edwards, *Early Christian Ireland*, 8–9.

10. Picard, "Structural Patterns in Early Hiberno-Latin Hagiography," 67–82; Berschin, "Radegundis and Brigit," 72–76.

11. Cogitosus, *Vita S. Brig.* 3.

12. McCone, "Bríd Chill Dara," 30–92; Charles-Edwards, *Early Christian Ireland*, 421–29; Neuman de Vegvar, "*Romanitas* and Realpolitik," 53–170; Cummian, *Letter De Controversia Paschali*, esp. 7–32. Many thanks to Carol Neuman de Vegvar for graciously allowing me to see her article before its publication.

13. Bede, *Historia Ecclesiastica* 2.19; Charles-Edwards, *Early Christian Ireland*, 429–38; see also Charles-Edwards, "Penitential of Theodore," esp. 160–61. Cogitosus clearly depicted Brigit speaking before assemblies but not necessarily taking part in synods; *Vita Prima* placed Brigit in clerical meetings, thus establishing the responsibility of Kildare's leaders to do the same: 23 (sec. 39), 34–35 (sec. 71).

14. Cogitosus, *Vita S. Brig.* 4, 6, 8, 9.

15. Ibid., 13, 14, 15.

16. Ibid., 20, 23.

17. Ibid., 19; also 8, 14, 27, 30, 33.

18. Ibid., 7, 9, 18, 19, 23, 24.

19. Ibid., 8, 31.

20. Ibid., 11, 13.

21. Ibid., 12, 14, 15.

22. Ibid., 18, 22.

23. Ibid., 19, 33.

24. Ibid., 33.

25. Ibid., 29; see also 6–8, 10–15; *VP*, 23–24 (sec. 40). Cf. Tírechán's claims about the four similarities of Patrick and Moses: Bieler, *Patrician Texts*, 164–65.

26. Cogitosus, *Vita S. Brig.* 28.

27. Ibid., 24; Connolly and Picard, "Cogitosus' Life of St. Brigit," 20 (sec. 22).

28. Cogitosus, *Vita S. Brig.* 34.

29. Ibid.

30. O'Loughlin, "Tombs of the Saints," 2–3.

31. Cogitosus, *Vita S. Brig.* 39; Neuman de Vegvar, "*Romanitas* and Realpolitik," 163–65.

32. Edwards, *Archaeology of Early Medieval Ireland*; Stout, "Early Christian Ireland," 81–109; Swan, "Ecclesiastical Settlement in Ireland," 50–56.

33. Ó Carragáin, "Architectural Setting of the Cult of Relics," 130–76; Edwards, "Celtic Saints and Early Medieval Archaeology," 238–43.

34. See Adomnán, *Life of Columba*, 504, where Adomnán mentions a church at Iona with an exedra divided from the main nave by a wall and door; 410, for a church door locked with keys; 454, for dressed timber used in expanding the church; 528, for lamps in the church.

35. Bieler, *Patrician Texts*, 146, 150–51, 158–59, 186–87; Doherty, "Basilica in Early Ireland," 309.

36. Bieler, *Patrician Texts*, 62; Wasserschleben, *Die irische Kanonensammlung*, 58, 279. See also Charles-Edwards, *Early Christian Ireland*, 378.

37. Herren, *Hisperica Famina*, 108–9. The poem also mentions square chapels fashioned of sacred oaks: "Ultrum alma scindis securibus robora, uti eo quadrigona demsis scemicare oratoria tabulatis," 68.

38. Doherty, "Basilica in Early Ireland," 312–13; Flanagan, "Christian Impact on Early Ireland," 25–42.

39. Cogitosus, *Vita S. Brig.* 33.

40. Irish canonists, writing about seventy-five years after Cogitosus, assumed three precincts within an ecclesiastical settlement, labeled sanctus, sanctior, and sanctissimus. Only clerics could enter the inner sanctuary: Wasserschleben, *Die irische Kanonensammlung*, 175.

41. Frank, *Memory of the Eyes*, 29–34, 104–114; Hahn, "Seeing and Believing," 1079–1106, esp. 1105

42. Cogitosus, *Vita S. Brig.* 37.

43. Webb, "Aesthetics of Sacred Space," 66–68.

44. Neuman de Vegvar, "*Romanitas* and Realpolitik," 165–67; Ó Carragáin, "Architectural Setting of the Cult of Relics," 139–40.

45. Ward-Perkins, *From Classical Antiquity to the Middle Ages*; Davis, *Book of the Pontiffs*, 22–23, 38–39 and passim.

46. Cramp, "Jarrow Church," 220–28; Cramp, "Monkwearmouth," 230–37. See also Rodwell, "Role of the Church in the Development of Roman and Early Anglo-Saxon London," 91–99.

47. Cf. St. Ninian's Isle, where wooden transennae separated altar area from nave: Thomas, *Early Christian Archaeology of North Britain*, 160, cited in Neuman de Vegvar, "*Romanitas* and Realpolitik."

48. Gregory of Tours, *Historiae* 2.14.

49. Bradley, "Archaeology, Topography, and Building Fabric," 29.

50. *BB* 6, 24.

51. Duval, *Auprès des saints corps et âme*; Reynaud, "Les morts dans les cités épsi-copales," 23–30; Treffort, "Du *cimiterium christianorum* au cimetière paroissial," 55–63; Sapin, "Architecture and Funerary Space in the Early Middle Ages," 39–60.

52. Gregory of Tours, *Historiae* 2.15–17.

53. Webb, "Aesthetics of Sacred Space," 72–73; Kinney, "Church Basilica," 124–25.

54. Le Blant, *Inscriptions chrétiennes*, vol. 1: nos. 170, 176, trans. Van Dam, *Saints and Their Miracles in Late Antique Gaul*, 312, 314. See also Gregory of Tours, *Historiae* 2.14.

55. Van Dam, *Saints and Their Miracles*, 314; Venantius Fortunatus, *Carmina*, 2.14, 10.6; see also Harries, "Christianity and the City," 88–89.

56. Campbell, "Debt of the Early English Church to Ireland," 332–46; Grimmer, "Saxon Bishop and Celtic King," 1–9.

57. Aldhelm, *Carmina* 3, see n. 32 there; trans. Lapidge and Rosier, *Aldhelm, The Poetic Works*, 47–49.

58. Aldhelm, *Carmina* 3, ll. 47–58: "Classibus et geminis psalmorum concrepet oda . . . Fratres concordi laudemus voce Tonantem / Cantibus et crebris conclamet turba sororum. . . . Unusquisque novum comat cum voce sacellum / Et lector lectrixve volumina sacra revolvant." See also Lapidge and Rosier, *Aldhelm*, 236 n. 24.

59. Lapidge and Rosier, *Aldhelm*, 35–36.

60. Duggan, "Was Art Really the 'Book of the Illiterate'?" 227–51.

61. Bradley, "Archaeology, Topography, and Building Fabric," 29, and references on 44 n. 11; *Martillenus* in Le Blant, *Inscriptions chrétiennes*, vol. 1: no. 179, trans. Van Dam, *Saints and Their Cults*, 315: "there is reserved for him a crown of righteousness." See also crowns, Hahn, "Seeing and Believing," 1096 n. 125; also, on light, 1084; Pietri, "Les sépultres privilegiés en Gaule," 133–42. See also the ninth-century decor at Saint Peter's, with its crowns hanging on either side of the altar described in the continuation of the *Liber pontificalis*, PL 128, 525.

62. Kinney, "Church Basilica," 128–29, 132–34; Hahn, "Seeing and Believing," 1092.

63. Bradley, "Archaeology, Topography, and Building Fabric," 29.

64. Gilchrist, *Gender and Material Culture*, 133–38.

65. Brown, *Cult of the Saints*, 87–88; Hahn, "Seeing and Believing," 1099–1103.

66. Bailey, "Seventh-Century Work at Ripon and Hexham," 9–18.

67. Bieler, *Patrician Texts*, 120.

68. Hahn, "Seeing and Believing," 1097; Pietri, "L'inhumation privilegié en Gaule," 133–42.

69. Bertelli, "Visual Images of the Town in Late Antiquity and the Early Middle Ages," 127–46.

70. Such events took place at different points in liturgical time, as in the Easter rituals performed over four days and all around the Holy Sepulcher in Jerusalem. The monks of other Irish monasteries probably moved around their compounds from one small church to another during their liturgies. O'Loughlin, "Tombs of the Saints," 1–14; van Uytfanghe, "La Bible dans les Vies de saints mérovingiennes," 103–12.

71. On annual audiences for vitae: Aldhelm, *De virginitate*, 119; Schulenburg, *Forgetful of Their Sex*, 25–27.

72. For debate on this point, see Roberta Gilchrist's reconstruction of the layout in *Gender and Material Culture*, 135, mentioned by Neuman de Vegvar, "*Romanitas* and Realpolitik," 155–156. For Neuman de Vegvar's own suggestion, 159 and figure 10.4.

73. Bieler, *Patrician Texts*, 70.

74. Cummian, *Letter De Controversia Paschali*, 92–95.

75. Bieler, *Patrician Texts*, 186; Charles-Edwards, *Early Christian Ireland*, 435. See also Bourke, *Patrick*, esp. 15–23.

76. Cogitosus, *Vita S. Brig.* 31. Perhaps, as Charles-Edwards has argued for Armagh, this was Kildare's claim to the pallium; *Early Christian Ireland*, 432 n. 70.

77. Verkerk, "Pilgrimage *ad Limina Apostolorum* in Rome," 9–26; Ó Cróinín, "Cummianus Longus and the Iconography of Christ," 268–79.

78. Charles-Edwards, *Early Christian Ireland*, 271–77, 416–38; see also Armagh's contesting claim voiced in the *Liber Angeli*: Bieler, *Patrician Texts*, 188–90.

79. Frank, *Memory of the Eyes*, esp. 29–34, 114–33. It was no coincidence that Brigit healed the blind, as Dorothy Bray has pointed out.

80. Bertelli, "Visual Images of the Town in Late Antiquity and the Early Middle Ages," 127–46.

81. Connolly and Picard, "Cogitosus' Life of St. Brigit," 6; Num. 35.

82. Howlett, "Vita I Sanctae Brigitae."

83. Van Dam, *Saints and Their Miracles*, 316; Bailey, "Seventh-Century Work at Ripon and Hexham," 16–17.

84. Davis, *Book of the Pontiffs*, 22–23, 38–39, et pass.

85. O'Loughlin, " Exegetical Purpose of Adomnán's *De Locis Sanctis*," 37–54; O'Loughlin, "View from Iona," 98–122.

86. Bieler, *Patrician Texts*, 84.

87. Bitel, "Body of a Saint," 209–28.

88. Bradley, "Archaeology, Topography, and Building Fabric," 29–36; Gerald of Wales, *Topographia Hiberniae* in O'Meara, *History and Topography of Ireland*, 81–82.

89. Cogitosus, *Vita S. Brig.* 2; Connolly and Picard, "Cogitosus' Life of St. Brigit," 11.

CHAPTER 7

1. For translation and commentary on *VP*, see Connolly, "*Vita Prima Sanctae Brigitae.*" For dates and origins of both texts, see McCone, "Brigit in the Seventh Century"; Sharpe, "*Vitae Sanctae Brigidae*," 81–106; Esposito, "On the Early Latin Lives of St. Brigid of Kildare," 120–65; Ó Briain, "Brigitana," 112–37.

2. McCone, "Brigit in the Seventh Century," 122.

3. Some material from this chapter appeared originally as Bitel, "Body of a Saint."

4. McKenna, "Apotheosis and Evanescence," 74–108.

5. Hudson, "Changing Economy of the Irish Sea Province," 39–66; Mitchell and Ryan, *Reading the Irish Landscape*, 297–98.

6. Mitchell and Ryan, *Reading the Irish Landscape*, 299; Bradley, "Archaeology, Topography, and Building Fabric," 36.

7. Ó Carragáin, "Architectural Setting of the Cult of Relics," 130–76.

8. Lucas, "Plundering and Burning of Churches in Ireland," 172–229; but see also Smyth, "Effect of Scandinavian Raiders," 1–38.

9. Isidore, *Etymologiae*, xv, ii.1.

10. Cogitosus, *Vita S. Brig.*, 39: "quae Sancta certo limite designauit Brigida."

11. Ibid., 37, 38.

12. Doherty, "Some Aspects of Hagiography," 300–328; Etchingham, *Church Organization in Ireland*.

13. *AU* for years 639, 640, 696, 698, 748, 752, 787, 798, 804, 823, 829, 830, 865, 870, 885, 886, 905, 922, 955, 967; also a *secnab* or vice-abbot at 845.

14. Meyer, *Fianaighecht*, ix; Smyth, *Celtic Leinster*, 66; Etchingham, "Kildare before the Normans," 9.

15. Smyth, *Celtic Leinster*, 103.

16. Ó Corráin, "Early Irish Churches," 327–38; Etchingham, "Kildare before the Normans," 10–11.

17. *AU*, 885; *FM*, 923, 968; Gwynn and Hadcock, *Medieval Religious Houses*, 83.

18. Etchingham, "Kildare before the Normans," 16–20; Mac Shamhráin, *Church and Polity in Pre-Norman Ireland*, 181; Bhreathnach, "Genealogies of Leinster," 264–65; McCone, "Brigit in the Seventh Century."

19. Ó Corráin, "Early Irish Churches," 337.

20. *Córus Béscnai*, in *CIH*, 1820–21; Charles-Edwards, "*Érlam*," 267–90.

21. Mac Shamhráin, *Church and Polity in Pre-Norman Ireland*, 133–37.

22. Bieler, *Patrician Texts*, 148, 150, 152, 156–58 (secs. 31.2, 34.2, 37.2, 43.3); Charles-Edwards, *Early Christian Ireland*, 223–26.

23. Bieler, *Patrician Texts*, 144–46 (sec. 27).

24. Plummer, *Vitae*, sec. 31; Sharpe suggests an early original, which Kenney puts in the seventh century (unlikely): Sharpe, *Medieval Irish Saints' Lives*, 394–95; Kenney, *Sources*, 389–90. For more examples of relations among male and female monastics and clerics, see Bitel, *Land of Women*, 183–87.

25. Charles-Edwards, "*Érlam*," esp. 290.

26. *AU*, 1127, 1132.

27. Greene, "St. Brigid's Alefeast," 150–53; retrans. Máirín Ní Dhonnchadha in *Field Day Anthology*, vol. 4, *Irish Women's Writing and Traditions*, 73–74.

28. *Fragmentary Annals*, 166, cited in Bradley, "Archaeology, Topography, and Building Fabric," 35.

29. *VP*, 74.

30. Adomnán, *Life of Columba*, 358–60, 494; MacDonald, "Aspects of the Monastery and Monastic Life," 271–302.

31. *AU*, 1132.

32. Gwynn and Hadcock, *Medieval Religious Houses*, 312–13.

33. *VP*, 52.

34. Ó Carragáin, "Architectural Setting of the Cult of Relics," 150–52.

35. Bradley, "Archaeology, Topography, and Building Fabric," 33.

36. Ibid., 35.

37. Bitel, *Isle of the Saints*, 66–74.

38. Manning, "References to Church Buildings in the Annals," esp. 38–39.

39. Swan, "Ecclesiastical Settlement in Ireland," 50–56.

40. Bitel, *Land of Women*, 169–75; Hall, *Women and the Church in Medieval Ireland*, esp. chaps. 2 and 3; Swan, "Ecclesiastical Settlement in Ireland"; Gwynn and Hadcock, *Medieval Religious Houses*, 307–26; Hughes, *Early Christian Ireland*, 234–35.

41. Foot, *Veiled Women*. See especially Foot's argument that the seeming decreases in religious women and women's communities are due more to historical methods than to an actual decrease in numbers of religious women; *Veiled Women*, 1:1–34.

42. Bitel, *Land of Women*, 195–98.

43. Stout, "Early Christian Ireland," 94–101.

44. Bede, *Historia ecclesiastica* 4.25; Yorke, "Bonifacian Mission and Female Religious in Wessex," 145–72; Boniface, *Ep.* 14.

45. Heist, *Vitae*, 81–83.

46. Ibid., 392–93.

47. Gwynn and Purton, "Monastery of Tallaght," 140, 144.

48. Bieler, *Patrician Texts*, 142–44.

49. *Félire Óengusso*, 44; "Life of Munnu," in Heist, *Vitae*, 201.

50. *CIH*, 2294; see also Binchy, "Bretha Crólige," 26.

51. *VP*, 47.

52. Kenney, *Sources*, 361–62 (151.i).

53. McCone, "Brigit in the Seventh Century," 114–15; Picard, "Structural Patterns in Early Hiberno-Latin Hagiography," 81; Connolly, "*Vita Prima Sanctae Brigitae*," 7.

54. Sharpe, "*Vitae Sanctae Brigidae*"; Connolly, "*Vita Prima Sanctae Brigitae*," 7.

55. *BB*, 11.

56. *AASS* Feb. 1, 141–155; Kenney, *Sources*, 361–62 (151.i); Young, "Donatus Bishop of Fiesole," 13–26.

57. *CGH*, 3.

58. Cross, *Motif-Index*, 387: L.10, L.110.

59. *VP*, 2.

60. Cross, *Motif-Index*, 163: D.1515.3.

61. For explanation and references, see *Dictionary of the Irish Language*, 443, col. 224 under 2 *lúan*.

62. *VP*, 11; *BB*, 5; Cross, *Motif-Index*, 64: B.182.2.0.3; Hamp, "Imbolc/Oimelc," 106–13; Torma, "This Woman Alone," esp. chap. 4 (225–66): "Feasts and Abundance," for a discussion of milk, purity, and white, red-eared cows.

63. *VP*, 11.

64. *VP*, 14; Connolly, "*Vita Prima Sanctae Brigitae*," 18.

65. Ibid.; *BB*, 12–13.

66. *Set[h]im:* Grosjean; *BB*, 48 n. 177; Exod 25:10.

67. Cogitosus, 1; *BB*, 47, n. 164–65.

68. Bieler, *Patrician Texts*, 136–37.

69. Judith Bishop, "Language and Authority."

70. *BB*, 17–19.

71. *BB*, 48, n. 186–87.

72. McCone, "Brigit in the Seventh Century," 107–45.

73. *VP*, 42, 44, 57.

74. Charles-Edwards, *Early Christian Ireland*, 252–55; Ó Corráin, "Early Irish Churches," 327–41.

75. *VP*, 21.

76. As described in the *speculum principum* text, *Audacht Morainn*, ca. 700; see *Audacht Morainn*, 6–7. For the possibly cognate figure called Brig *ambue* who seems to have been a legal expert: *CIH*, 1654; McCone, *Pagan Past and Christian Present*, 162–63.

77. *VP*, 40.

78. Ibid., 50.

79. Ibid., 45–46.

80. Ibid., 47.

81. Ibid., 72.

82. Ibid., 84, 85.

83. Ibid., 55.

84. Ibid., 58.

85. Bieler, *Patrician Texts*, 190–191.

86. *BB*, 11; see also p. 42, n. 83 on the earliest reference to Brigit as "Mary of the Gael": Rawl. B 502, 125b.

87. Mooney, "*Imitatio Christi* or *Imitatio Mariae?*" 52–77.

88. *VP*, 44.

89. Bieler, *Patrician Texts*, 122.

90. *VP*, 48, 112, 113, 116. Some of these were mentioned by Catherine McKenna in her November 2004 lecture to a UCLA audience, "Bride's Head Revisited." McKenna also pointed out that the vision of Brigit mentioned in *VP* 88 could have been a painted icon.

91. *VP*, 87.

92. Lacan, "Mirror Stage as Formative of the Function of the I," 1–7; see also Kay and Rubin, *Framing Medieval Bodies*, 2.

93. Gregory the Great, *Dialogi*, 2.38; Thacker, "Loca Sanctorum," 18–20.

94. *VP*, 90.

95. *Book of Leinster*, vol. 6, 1673.

96. The pertinent legal text is *Córus Béscnai*, *CIH*, 520–36, 903–5, 1812–21. See also Charles-Edwards, "Church and Settlement," 167–75; Kelly, *Guide to Early Irish Law*, 29–36.

97. McCone, *Pagan Past and Christian Present*, 182–83.

98. *VP*, 29; "Longes mac nUisnig," in Best and O'Brien, *Book of Leinster*, 5:1170.

99. On "pagan" as "female," see Bitel, *Land of Women*, 204–22, and references there.

100. *Vita Tripartita*, 1:50–51.

101. *Táin Bó Cúailnge: Recension I*, 613–15, 642–45; *BB*, 3.

102. Lucas, *Cattle in Ancient Ireland*; Dunn, *Cattle-Raids and Courtships*; Raftery, *Pagan Celtic Ireland*, 168–77; *Audacht Morainn*, 12; *Triads of Ireland*, 8, 12, 30; *Scéla Mucce Meic Dathó*, 7; Kelly, *Early Irish Farming*, 281–82.

103. *BB*, 46.

104. *VP*, 95. See also the holy virgin mentioned by Tírechán, who crossed the River Suck: Bieler, *Patrician Texts*, 146.

105. O'Rahilly, *Táin Bó Cúailnge: Recension I*, ll. 198, 1160.

106. *VP*, 58, 91.

107. Bieler, *Patrician Texts*, 90, 94, 158–60.

108. Flint, *Rise of Magic in Early Medieval Europe*, 185–90; Bitel, *Isle of the Saints*, 31–32.

109. Byrne, *Irish Kings and High-Kings*, 155–56.

110. Gregory of Tours, *Historiae*, 2.37; *VP*, 88, 89. See also the *Bóroma* cycle of tales about the perennial feud between Leinster and the kings of Tara, in which Brigit played a large part: Stokes, "The Borama," *RC* 13 (1892): 32–124, 299; Buttimer, "The Bórama."

111. Suggested by McKenna, "Bride's Head Revisited."

112. Torma, "This Woman Alone," chap. 2 (29–43): "Brigit and Gender," esp. Conclusion; *Baile in Scáil, CELT,* http://www.ucc.ie/celt/published/G105001/index.html.

113. Bitel, "Landscape, Gender, and Ethnogenesis in Pre-Norman Invasion Ireland," 171–91. Contra McCone, "Brigit in the Seventh Century," 110–11 and passim; there is no evidence beyond the names themselves to support a pre-Christian association of these sites with Bríg/Brigit.

114. Meyer, *Sanas Cormaic*, 15; McCone, *Pagan Past and Christian Present*, 162.

115. Meanwhile, another goddess figure named Bríg *briugu* (hospitaller) turned up in legal legends beginning in the eighth century, as did a female judge called Bríg *ambue* (foreigner). Both appeared in stories about women rendering legal decisions in a system that traditionally disenfranchised all women; *ambue* may also indicate an outlaw or warrior-woman: *CIH*, 377.26, 380.14–15, 1654.12; Kelly, *Guide to Early Irish Law*, 358; McCone, *Pagan Past and Christian Present*, 162.

116. *Cath Maige Tuired*, 56–57.

117. *Book of Leinster*, 6: 1580–81.

118. Hogan, *Onomasticon*, mostly under "C."

119. Bowen, "Cult of St. Brigit," 33–47; Ó Riain, "The Irish Element in Welsh Hagiographical Tradition," 291–303, at 292; Young, "St. Brigit in a Medieval Welsh Poem," 279; Breeze, "Shrine of St. Brigit at Olite, Spain," 85–96; Milne, *St. Bride's Church London.*

120. Young, "Donatus Bishop of Fiesole," 13–26.

121. Schmid, "Culte en Suède de Sainte Brigide l'Irlandaise," 108–15.

122. Kenney, *Sources*, 362 (151.iv), 363 (155).

CHAPTER 8

1. Crosby, *Royal Abbey of Saint-Denis*, 6; Delaborde, "Procès du chef de Saint-Denis en 1410," 297–409.

2. Clark, "'The Recollection of the Past Is the Promise of the Future,'" 92–113.

3. *AASS* Jan. 3, 152–53; Sluhovsky, *Patroness of Paris*, 20–21.

4. *AU* 800: "*Positio reliquiarum* Conlaid h-i scrin oir & argait." Cf. the entry for the following year: "*Positio reliquiarum* Ronaen *filii* Berich *in arca auri & argenti*."

5. *AASS* Feb. 1, 110–11; *Book of Fenagh*, 252–63; also cited in Fry, *Burial in Medieval Ireland*, 177.

6. Gerald of Wales, *Topographia*, 3.18; Gerald of Wales, *Expugnatio*, 2.35; *Annals of Loch Cé*, in *CELT* (http://celt.ucc.ie/published/G100010A/index.html) and *Annals of the Four Masters* in *CELT* (http://www.ucc.ie/celt/published/T100005C/index.html) under 1293; Martin, "John, Lord of Ireland," 135.

7. Murphy, "Kildare," 292. See also Pollard, *In Search of St. Brigid*, 9–10.

8. McClintock, "Mantle of St. Brigid at Bruges," 32–40.

9. Murphy, "Kildare," 291; Burke, *Hibernia Dominicana*, 857–58.

10. McKenna, "Bride's Head Revisited." Thanks to McKenna for the gracious gift of a vivid postcard featuring the head reliquary.

11. *AASS* Feb. I, 112. Hogan claimed to have seen her finger at Cologne; *Onomasticon* under *colofonida*.

12. Leycock, "St. Brigid's Parish, Killester," http://www.killester.dublindiocese.ie/relic.htm.

13. *CGH*, 112–18, 210–12.

14. Gwynn and Hadcock, *Medieval Religious Houses*, 320; Archdall, *Monasticon hibernicum*, 323.

15. Bradley, "Archaeology, Topography, and Building Fabric," 36; Gwynn and Hadcock, *Medieval Religious Houses*, 252.

16. Devlitt, "See Lands of Kildare," 358–65; *Calendar of Documents, Relating to Ireland*, vol. 1, no. 1519; Gillespie, "St. Brigid's Cathedral in the Age of Reform," 48–61.

17. Archdall, *Monasticon hibernicum*, 802; Hall, *Women and the Church in Medieval Ireland*, 152–53.

18. Gwynn and Hadcock, *Medieval Religious Houses*, 83, 320.

19. Gillespie, "St. Brigid's Cathedral in the Age of Reform," esp. 50–51.

20. Gerald of Wales, trans. O'Meara, *History and Topography*, 81–82.

21. Hughes and Hamlin, *Celtic Monasticism*, 30.

22. Rae, "Architecture and Sculpture," 775.

23. Stanyhurst, *De rebus in Hibernia*, quoted in Holinshed, *Chronicles*, 2:29.

24. Cowell, "St. Brigid and the Cathedral Church of Kildare," 245; Harbison, "Some Views of St. Brigid's Cathedral, Kildare," 83–95.

25. Archdall, *Monasticon hibernicum*, 2:232.

26. Moore, "Erin! Oh Erin!" *Works*, 3:71–72.

27. *FM* in *CELT*, http://www.ucc.ie/celt/published/T100005A/index.html.

28. O'Donovan, *Letters*, vol. 16, no. 32; Smyth, *Celtic Leinster*, 48–49.

29. Cowell, "St. Brigid and the Cathedral Church of Kildare," 247; O'Donovan, *Letters*, vol. 16, nos. 128, 188–97.

30. Kildare Cathedral, *Kildare Cathedral Restoration; Irish Builder* 17, no. 379 (1875): 277; Wilkinson, "St. Brigid's Cathedral, Kildare," 103, 105.

31. O'Riordan, *The Brigidine Sisters*, http://www.brigidine.org.au/about/early.asp.

32. Cowell, "St. Brigid and the Cathedral Church of Kildare," 236.

33. *Kildare Observer*, August 13, 1892; Wilkinson, "St. Brigid's Cathedral, Kildare," 111.

34. Rev. Charles O Conor of Bellanagare, "Third Letter to Columbanus," quoted in Hardy, *Holy Wells of Ireland*; also cited in Logan, *Holy Wells of Ireland*, 114, and Harbison, *Pilgrimage in Ireland*, 231.

35. Larkin, "Devotional Revolution in Ireland," 625–52.

36. Hogan, *Onomasticon*, passim.

37. *FM* for 1596.

38. Harbison, *Pilgrimage in Ireland*, esp. 233.

39. Stokes, *Lives of Saints from the Book of Lismore*, 63.

40. Ó Catháin, *Festival of Brigit*, 1–26; Logan, *Holy Wells of Ireland*, 82.

41. Logan, *Holy Wells of Ireland*, 78–84.

42. Ibid., 45, quoting Shaw Mason, *Statistical Account, or Parochial Survey of Ireland*.

43. Logan, *Holy Wells of Ireland*, 133–40, 150–51.

44. Ibid., 67.

45. O'Donovan, quoted in ibid., 151; Brenneman and Brenneman, *Crossing the Circle*, 4–5.

46. Ó Cathasaigh, "Cult of Brigid," 75–94.

47. Ó Catháin, *Festival of Brigit*, 1–11.

48. MacNeill, *Festival of Lughnasa*, passim; and Ó Cathasaigh, "Cult of Brigid."

49. Ó Giolláin, *Locating Irish Folklore*, 134.

50. Yeats, *Celtic Twilight*, repr., http://www.gutenberg.org/files/10459/10459.txt; also cited in Ó Giolláin, *Locating Irish Folklore*, 106.

51. Plummer, *Vitae*, vol. 1: cxxxvi, cxli, cxlix, clxvi, clxx, clxxvii.

52. Macalister, "Temair Breg," 340.

53. *Solas Bhríde*, http://www.solasbhride.ie/flame-of-brigid.htm.

54. *AASS* Jan. 3, 148: "in tecto monasterii."

55. *AASS* Jan. 3, 148.

56. *Fragmentum de miraculis Sanctae Genovefae*, 135–38; Sluhovsky, *Patroness of Paris*, 32–46, discusses these texts as well as Genovefa's water iconography.

57. *AASS* Jan. 3, 152.

58. Sluhovsky, *Patroness of Paris*, esp. chaps. 2 and 3 on ritual processions and sacralization of space.

59. Kaplan, "Religion, Subsistence, and Social Control," esp. 144–46.

60. LeGoff, "Ecclesiastical Culture and Folklore," 161, 331 n. 8.

61. Cl. 23314, described at http://www.musee-moyenage.fr/pages/page_id18493_u1l2.htm.

62. *Célébrations nationale 2001*, http://www.culture.gouv.fr/culture/actualites/celebrations2002/manifstgenevieve.htm.

63. Bibliothèque Sainte-Geneviève, http://www-bsg.univ-paris1.fr/home.htm.

64. Roblin, *Terroir de Paris*, 183.

65. Farrar, "Tear-Stained Eye": "Saint Genevieve can hold back the water / But saints don't bother with a tear stained eye."

66. Sluhovsky, *Patroness of Paris*, 206–9.

Bibliography

ABBREVIATIONS

AASS: Bollandus, Johannes, et al., eds. *Acta sanctorum quotquot toto orbe col-*
untu: Vel à catholicis scriptoribus celebrantur, quae ex Latinis & Graecis . . .
Antwerp: apvd Ioannem Mevrsivm, 1643–. http://acta.chadwyck.co.uk.
AU: Annals of Ulster. The Annals of Ulster (to A.D. 1131). Ed. Seán Mac Airt
and Gearóid Mac Niocaill. Dublin: Dublin Institute for Advanced
Studies, 1983.
BB: Bethu Brigte. Ed. and trans. Donnchadh Ó hAodha. Dublin: Dublin Insti-
tute for Advanced Studies, 1978.
BHL: Bollandists. *Bibliotheca hagiographica latina antiquae et mediae aetatis*.
Brussels: Socii Bollandiani, 1898–1901.
CCSL: Corpus Christianorum: Series Latina. Turnholt: Typographia Brepols,
1953–.
CELT: Corpus of Electronic Texts: The Online Resource for Irish History, Lit-
erature and Politics. Cork: National University of Ireland, Cork, 1997–.
http://www.ucc.ie/celt/.
CGH: Corpus Genealogiarum Hiberniae. Ed. M. A. O'Brien. Dublin: Dublin
Institute for Advanced Studies, 1962.
CIH: Corpus Iuris Hibernici. 6 vols. Ed. Daniel Binchy. Baile Átha Cliath:
Institiúid Ard-Léinn Bhaile Átha Cliath, 1978.
Cogitosus, *Vita S. Brig.*: Vita II, *AASS* Feb. 1, 135–41. Trans. Connolly and
Picard, "Cogitosus's Life of St. Brigit."
Connolly, Sean and J. M. Picard, trans. "Cogitosus's Life of St. Brigit." *JRSAI*
117 (1987): 5–27.
CSEL: Commission for Editing the Corpus of the Latin Church Fathers (CSEL).
Vienna, 1864–. http://www.oeaw.ac.at/kvk/.

EC: *Études celtiques.*

Ep.: *Epistola.*

Epp.: *Epistolae.*

FM: *Annals of the Four Masters.* Ó Cléirigh, Míchél, et al. *Annala Rioghachta Eireann.* Ed. and trans. John O'Donovan as *Annals of the Kingdom of Ireland by the Four Masters, from the earliest period to the year 1616.* 7 vols. 2nd ed. Dublin: Hodges, Figgis, and Co., 1856. http://www.ucc.ie/celt/published/T100005A/index.html.

Gregory of Tours, GC: *Liber in Gloria confessorum. MGH SRM* 1:744–820.

Gregory of Tours, GM: *Liber in Gloria martyrum. MGH SRM* 1:484–561.

Gregory of Tours, VP: *Liber vitae patrum. MGH SRM* 1:661–744.

JCKAS: *Journal of the Co. Kildare Archaeological Society.*

JRSAI: *Journal of the Royal Society of Antiquaries of Ireland.*

MGH: *Monumenta Germaniae Historica inde A.C. 500 usque ad 1500.* Hannover and Berlin, 1826–.

MGH AA: *Auctores antiquissimi.*

MGH Epp. Sel.: *Epistolae selectae.*

MGH Gest. Pont. Rom.: *Gesta pontificum Romanorum.*

MGH SRM: *Scriptores rerum Merovingicarum.*

PL: *Patrologiae cursus completus. Series Latina.* 221 vols. Ed. J.-P. Migne. Paris, 1844–92. http://pld.chadwyck.com/.

PRIA: *Proceedings of the Royal Irish Academy.*

RC: *Revue Celtique.*

SC: *Sources chrétiennes.* Paris: Éditions du Cerf, 1941–.

Sulpicius Severus, VM: Severus, Sulpicius. *Vita S. Martini. SC* 133.

ThesCRA: *Thesaurus Cultus et Rituum Antiquorum. Lexicon antiker Kulte und Riten.* Vol. 5: *Personnel of cult. Kultinstrumente.* Ed. T. Hölscher, I. Krauskopf. Los Angeles: Getty, 2005.

VGA: *Vita Genovefae virginis Parisiensis.* Ed. Bruno Krusch. *MGH SRM* 3 (1896): 204–38, 85–686.

VGB: *Etude critique sur le texte de la Vie latine de saint Geneviève de Paris.* Ed. Charles Alfred Kohler. Paris: F. Vieweg, 1881. N.B. This edition also contains redaction *VGD*.

VGC: Künstle, K. "Eine wichtige hagiographische Handschrift." *Römische Quartalschrift* 22, no. 1 (1908): 17–29.

VP: *Vita Prima S. Brigidae: AASS* Feb. 1, 118–35.

OTHER PRIMARY SOURCES

Adomnán. *Adomnán's Life of Columba.* Ed. and trans. A. O. Anderson and M. O. Anderson. New York: T. Nelson, 1961.

Aldhelm. *Carmina. MGH AA* 15. In *Aldhlem, The Poetic Works.* Trans. Michael Lapidge and James L. Rosier. Dover, NH: D. S. Brewer, 1985.

———. *De virginitate.* In *Aldhelm, The Prose Works.* Trans. Michael Lapidge and Michael Herren. Totowa, NJ: Rowman & Littlefield, 1979.

Ambrose. *Epistolae. PL* 16:875–1286.

Ammianus Marcellinus. *Rerum gestarum libri.* Ed. and trans. John C. Rolfe. Loeb Classical Library. Cambridge, MA: Harvard University Press, 1935–39.

Athanasius. *Apologia contra Arianos*. Ed. and trans. William Bright as *The Orations of St. Athanasius: against the Arians*. Oxford: Clarendon Press, 1873.

———. *Epistola ad Jovianum 1*. In J. P. Migne, ed. *Patrologia cursus sompletus . . . Series Graeca*. Paris: Migne, 1857–66. Vol. 6: 813–22.

Atsma, Hartmut, and Jean Vezin, eds. *Chartae Latinae antiquiores: Facsimile-Edition of the Latin Charters Prior to the Ninth Century*, 13: *France* I. Zurich: Graf, 1981.

Audacht Morainn. Ed. and trans. Fergus Kelly. Dublin: Dublin Institute for Advanced Studies, 1976.

Augustine. *Confessio*. CSEL 33.

———. *De cura pro mortuis gerenda*. PL 40.

———. *Epistolae*. PL 33.

Ausonius, Decimus Magnus. *Ordo urbium nobelium*. Intratext Digital Library. [Rome?]: Èulogos, 2007. http://www.intratext.com/IXT/LAT0574/_IDX018.HTM.

Baile in Scáil. Ed. Kuno Meyer. *Zeitschrift für Celtische Philologie* 3 (1901): 457–66. Online at http://www.ucc.ie/celt/published/G105001/index.html.

Bede. *Historia ecclesiastica* in *Opera historica*. Ed. and trans. J. E. King. Loeb Classical Library. Cambridge, MA: Harvard University Press, 1930.

Bethu Brigte. Ed. and trans. Donncha Ó hAodha. Dublin: Dublin Institute for Advanced Studies, 1978.

Bieler, Ludwig, ed. *The Irish Penitentials*. With appendix by D. A. Binchy. Dublin: Dublin Institute for Advanced Studies, 1975. Originally published 1963.

———, ed. and trans. *The Patrician Texts in the Book of Armagh*. Scriptores Latini Hiberni 10. Dublin: Dublin Institute for Advanced Studies, 1979.

Binchy, D. A., ed. and trans. "Bretha Crólige." *Ériu* 12 (1938): 1–77.

Boniface, Saint. *Epistolae*. Ed. Michael Tangl as *Die Briefe des heiligen Bonifatius und Lullus*, MGH Epp. Sel. 1. Berlin, 1916.

Book of Fenagh in Irish and English. Ed. William Hennessy, trans. D. H. Kelly. Dublin: Alexander Thom, 1875.

Book of Leinster, formerly Lebar na Núachongbála. 6 vols. Vols. 1–5. Ed. R. I. Best, Osbern Bergin, and M. A. O'Brien. Vol. 6 ed. Anne O'Sullivan. Dublin: Dublin Institute for Advanced Studies, 1954–83.

Bourke, Angela, et al., eds. *Field Day Anthology of Irish Writing: Irish Women's Writing and Traditions*. Vol. 4. Washington Square, NY: New York University Press, 2002.

Caesar, Julius. *C. Iulii Caesari commentariorum De bello Gallico*. In *Ibiblio: the Public's Library and Digital Archive*. Chapel Hill, NC: University of Northern Carolina Chapel Hill, 199?–: http://www.ibiblio.org/caesar/.

Caesarius of Arles. *Sermones*: CCSL 103–4.

Calendar of Documents, Relating to Ireland: Preserved in Her Majesty's Public Record Office, London, 1171–[1307]. Ed. H. S. Sweetman. Great Britain: Public Record Office. London: Longman, 1875–86. 5 vols.

Cath Maige Tuired: The Second Battle of Mag Tuired. Ed. Elizabeth A. Gray. Dublin: Irish Texts Society, 1982.

Chronica Gallia. MGH AA 9.

Codex Theodosianus. Ed. Theodor Mommsen and Paul Krueger. Repr., Hildesheim: Weidmann, 1990.

Columbanus, Saint. *Opera*. Ed. G. S. M. Walker as *Sancti Columbani Opera*. Scriptores Latini Hiberniae 2. Dublin: Dublin Institute for Advanced Studies, 1957.

Concilia Galliae. *CCSL* 148, 148A.

Concilium in Trullio. In Schaff, *Seven Ecumenical Councils*, "The Canons of the Council in Trullo."

Constantius of Lyon. *Vita S. Germani*. Ed. and trans. René Borius. *SC* 112. Also trans. F. R. Hoare in *Soldiers of Christ: Saints and Saints' Lives from Late Antiquity and the Early Middle Ages*, ed. Thomas F. X. Noble and Thomas Head, 75–106. University Park: Pennsylvania State University Press, 1995.

Cummian, Saint. *Cummian's Letter De Controversia Paschali and the De Ratione Conputandi*. Ed. Dáibhi Ó Cróinín and Maura Walsh. Toronto: Pontifical Institute of Mediaeval Studies, 1988.

Cyprian of Carthage. *Epistolae*. *PL* 4: 191–438.

Davis, Raymond. *The Book of the Pontiffs: The Ancient Biographies of the First Ninety Roman Bishops to 175 AD*. Liverpool: Liverpool University Press, 1989.

Duchesne, Louis. *Fastes épiscopaux de l'ancienne Gaule*. 2 vols. Paris: A. Fontemoing, 1900–1915.

Duval, Paul-Marie, ed. *Les inscriptions antiques de Paris*. 2 vols. Paris: Imprimerie Nationale, 1960.

Eugippius. *Epistola ad Paschasium*. *MGH Auct. Antiq*. 1, 1–3.

Eusebius of Caesarea. *The Ecclesiastical History*. Ed. and trans. Kirsopp Lake. Cambridge, Mass.: Harvard Univ. Press; London: Heinemann, 1926.

———. *Vita Constantini*. Trans. Averil Cameron and Stuart G. Hall as *Eusebius' Life of Constantine*. Oxford: Oxford University Press, 1999.

Félire Óengusso Céili Dé. Ed. and trans. Whitley Stokes. London: Harrison and Sons, 1905.

Fled Dúin na nGéd. Ed. Ruth Lehmann. Mediaeval and Modern Irish Series 21. Dublin: Dublin Institute for Advanced Studies, 1964.

Fortunatus, Venantius Honorius Clementianus. *Carmina*. *MGH AA* 4.1.

———. *Miscellanea*. *PL* 88.

———. *Vita S. Radegundis regina*. *MGH SRM* 2:358–95.

———. *Vita Sancti Germani*. *MGH SRM* 7:372–418.

Fragmentary Annals of Ireland. Ed. and trans. Joan Newlon Radner. Dublin: Dublin Institute for Advanced Studies, 1978.

Fragmentum de miraculis Sanctae Genovefae. In J. N. de Wailly, L. V. Delisle, and C.M.G.B. Jourdain, eds., *Recueil de Historiens des Gaules et de la France*, vol. 23, 135–38. Paris: Imprimerie Nationale, 1894.

Gerald of Wales. *Expugnatio Hibernica*. Ed. and trans. A. B. Scott and F. X. Martin as *Expugnatio Hibernica: The Conquest of Ireland*. Dublin: Royal Irish Academy, 1978.

———. *Topographia Hiberniae*. Trans. John J. O'Meara as *The History and Topography of Ireland*. Atlantic Highlands, NJ: Humanities Press, 1982.

Gesta Dagoberti. *MGH SRM* 2:399–425.

Gildas. *Liber querulus de excidio Britanniae*. Ed. and trans. Michael Winterbottom as *The Ruin of Britain*. London: Phillimore, 1978.

Gloriosae (Passio ss. Dionysii, Rustici et Eleutherii). *MGH AA* 4:2:101–5.

Greene, David, ed. and trans. "St. Brigid's Alefeast." *Celtica* 2 (1952): 150–53. Retranslated by Máirín Ní Dhonnchadha in *Field Day Anthology,* vol. 4, *Irish Women's Writing and Traditions,* ed. Angela Bourke et al., 73–74. Washington Square, NY: New York University Press, 2002.

Gregory of Tours. *Historiae. MGH SRM* 1:31–450. Trans. L. Thorpe, *Gregory of Tours: The History of the Franks.* Harmondsworth: Penguin Classics, 1974.

Gregory the Great. *Dialogi. PL* 77:13–128.

Grundlach, W., ed. *Epistulae Austrasicae.* In Henri M. Rochais, ed., *Liber Scintillarum. CCSL* 117. Brepols: Turnhout, 1957.

Gwynn, E. J., and W. J. Purton, eds. "The Monastery of Tallaght." *PRIA* 29 C (1911): 115–79.

Hardy, Philip Dixon. *The holy wells of Ireland, containing an account of those various places of pilgrimage and penance which are still annually visited by thousands of the Roman Catholic peasantry.* Dublin: P. D. Hardy, etc., 1836.

Heist, W. W., ed. *Vitae sanctorum Hiberniae: Ex codice olim Salmanticensi nunc Bruxellensi.* Brussels: Société des Bollandistes, 1965.

Herren, Michael, ed. and trans. *Hisperica Famina: I. The A-Text.* Toronto: Pontifical Institute of Mediaeval Studies, 1974.

Hilduin, Abbot of Saint-Denis. *Vita S. Dionysii. PL* 106: 14–50.

Holinshed, Raphael. *Chronicles of England, Scotlande, and Irelande. The Second Volume of Chronicles: Conteining the description, conquest, inhabitation, and troublesome estate of Ireland.* London, 1586.

Irenaeus, Bishop of Lyon. *Adversus haereses. Contre les Hérésies. SC* 32, 100, 152, 153, 210, 211, 263, 264, 293, 294.

Isidore. *Etymologiae.* Ed. W. M. Lindsay. Oxford: Clarendon Press, 1911.

Jerome. *Commentarius in Hieremiam prophetam. CCSL* 74.

———. *Epistolae. CSEL* 546.

———. *Vita S. Hilarionis. PL* 23:29–54.

Jonas of Bobbio. *Vita Columbani. MGH SRM* 4:505–17.

Julian. *Misopogon.* Ed. and trans. Wilmer Cave Wright in *The Works of the Emperor Julian.* 3 vols. Loeb Classical Library. Cambridge, MA: Harvard University Press, 1962–90.

Koch, John T. and John Carey, eds. *The Celtic Heroic Age: Literary Sources for Ancient Celtic Europe and Early Ireland and Wales.* 4th ed. With John Carey. Aberystwyth: Celtic Studies Publications, 2003. Originally published 1994.

Kreuger, Paul and Theodor Mommsen, eds. *Codex Theodosianus.* 2 vols. Repr. Hildesheim: Weidmann, 1990.

Lasteyrie du Saillant, Robert Charles. *Cartulaire général de Paris; ou Recueil de documents relatifs à l'histoire et à la topographie de Paris.* Paris: Imprimerie Nationale, 1887–.

Le Blant, E., ed. *Inscriptions chrétiennes de la Gaule antérieures au VIIIe siècle.* 2 vols. Paris: L'Imprimerie Impériale, 1856–65.

Libellus de ecclesiis Claronmontanis. MGH SRM 7.

Liber historiae Francorum. MGH SRM 2: 238–338.

Le Liber Mozarabicus Sacramentorum et les manuscrits mozarabes. Ed. Anthony Ward et al. Rome: C.L.V. Edizioni Liturgiche, 1995.

Liber Pontificalis: MGH Gest. Pont. Rom. Trans. Davis, *Book of the Pontiffs.*

Mansi, Giovan Domenico, ed. *Sacrorum conciliorum nova et amplissima collectio: in qua praeter ea quae Phil. Labbeus et Gabr. Cossartius . . . et novissime Nicolaus Coleti in lucem edidere ea omnia insuper suis in locis optime disposita exhibentu.* 54 vols. Paris: H. Welter, 1901–1927.

Meyer, Kuno, ed. and trans. *Fianaigecht: being a collection of hitherto inedited Irish poems and tales relating to Finn and his Fiana, with an English translation.* Dublin: School of Celtic Studies, Dublin Institute for Advanced Studies, 1993.

———, ed. and trans. "Hail Brigit: An Old-Irish Poem on the Hill of Alenn." Halle: M. Niemeyer, 1912.

———, ed. and trans. *The Instructions of King Cormac Mac Airt.* Todd Lecture Series 15. Dublin: Hodges, Figgis and Co., 1909.

———, ed. and trans. *Sanas Cormaic.* Halle: Niemeyer; Dublin: Hodges, Figgis and Co., 1913.

Muirchú. [*Life of Patrick.*] In Bieler, *Patrician Texts,* 62–123.

Notitia dignitatum, accedunt notitia urbis Constantinopolitanae et Laterculi Provinciarum. Ed. Otto Seeck. Berlin: Weidmann, 1876.

Notitia Galliarum. In Seeck, *Notitia dignitatum,* 261–74.

O'Donovan, John. *Letters containing information relative to the antiquities of the counties of [Ireland]. Collected during the progress of the Ordnance survey in 183– Reproduced under the direction of Rev. Michael O'Flanagan.* [42 vols. in] 10 vols. Bray: [s.n.], 1927–1934.

Ó Riain, Pádraig, ed. *Corpus Genealogiarum sanctorum Hiberniae.* Dublin: Dublin Institute for Advanced Studies, 1985.

Orgain Denna Ríg. Ed. David Greene in *Fingal Rónáin and Other Stories.* Mediaeval and Modern Irish Stories 16. Dublin: Dublin Institute for Advanced Studies, 1955.

Patrick [Patricius]. *Confessio.* Ed. and trans. Ludwig Bieler as *Libri epistolarum Sancti Patricii episcopi.* Dublin: Royal Irish Academy, 1993.

Paulinus of Nola. *Epistolae. CSEL* 29.

Plummer, Charles, ed. *Vitae sanctorum Hiberniae partim hactenus ineditae, ad fidem codicum manuscriptorum.* 2 vols. Oxford: Clarendon Press, 1910.

Prosper Aquitanus. *Chronicon. MGH AA* 9: 341–449.

Salvian of Marseilles. *De gubernatione Dei. SC* 220.

Scéla Mucce Meic Dathó. Ed. Rudolf Thurneysen. Dublin: Dublin Institute for Advanced Studies, 1935. Reprinted in 1951.

Schaff, Phillip, ed. *Nicene and Post-Nicene Fathers.* Second series. Peabody: Hendrickson, 1995.

———. *The Seven Ecumenical Councils.* Christian Classics Ethereal Library. http://www.ccel.org/ccel/schaff/npnf214.html.

Severus, Sulpicius. *Dialogi. CSEL* 1:152–216.

———. *Epistolae. CSEL* 1:138–51.

———. *Historia Sacra. CSEL* 1:1–105.

Shepherd of Hermas. In J. B. Lightfoot, trans.; J. R. Harmer, ed. *Apostolic Fathers.* Repr. Kessinger Publishing: [n.p.] 2003: 159–246.

Sidonius Apollinaris. *Carmina.* Ed. and trans. W. B. Anderson. *Poems and Letters.* Loeb Classical Library. Cambridge, MA: Harvard University Press, 1936.

———. *Epistolae.* Ed. and trans. W. B. Anderson. *Poems and Letters.* Loeb Classical Library. Cambridge, MA: Harvard University Press, 1936.

Stanyhurst, Richard. *De rebus in Hibernia gestis. Accessit hibernicarum rerum appendix, ex Silvestro Giraldo Cambrensi collecta.* Antwerp: apud Christophorum Platinum, 1584.

Stokes, Whitley, ed. and trans. "The Borama." *RC* 13 (1892): 32–124, 299.

———, ed. and trans. *Lives of Saints from the Book of Lismore.* Oxford: Clarendon Press, 1890.

———, ed. and trans. "The Prose Tales in the *Rennes Dindsenchas.*" *RC* 16 (1895): 31–83, 136–67, 269–312.

Suger, Abbot. *De consecrationae ecclesiae Sancti Dionysii.* Ed., trans., and annotated Erwin Panofsky, *Abbot Suger on the Abbey Church of St.-Denis and Its Art Treasures.* Princeton, NJ: Princeton University Press, 1946.

Táin Bó Cúailnge: Recension I. Ed. and trans. Cecile O'Rahilly. Dublin: Dublin Institute for Advanced Studies, 1976.

Tertullian. *Adversus Iudaeos. CCSL* 2.

———. *De idolatria.* Ed. and trans. J. H. Waszink and J. C. M. van Winden. Leiden: Brill, 1987.

———. *De spectaculis. CSEL* 20: 1–29.

Tírechán. [*Itinerary of Patrick.*] In Bieler, *Patrician Texts,* 123–67.

Triads of Ireland. Ed. Kuno Meyer. Dublin: Hodges, Figgis and Co., 1906.

Victricius of Rouen. *De laude sanctorum. CC* 64:69–93. Trans. Gillian Clark, "Victricius of Rouen: Praising the Saints." *Journal of Early Christian Studies* 7 (Fall 1999): 365–99.

Vita S. Amatoris. AASS May 1:50–60.

Vita S. Balthildis. MGH SRM 2:482–508.

Vita S. Chrothildis. MGH SRM 2:341–48.

Vita S. Eligii. MGH SRM 2:634–742.

Vita Tripartita. Ed. and trans. Whitley Stokes as *The tripartite life of Patrick, with other documents relating to that Saint.* 2 vols. London: Printed for HMSO, by Eyre and Spottiswoode, 1887.

Wasserschleben, H., ed. *Die irische Kanonensammlung.* Leipzig: Bernard Tauchnitz, 1885.

Weber, Ekkehard, ed. *Tabula Peutingeriana: Codex Vindobonensis 324: vollst. Faks.-Ausg. im Originalformat.* Graz: Akadem. Druck- u. Verlagsanst., 1976.

SECONDARY SOURCES

Aalen, F. H. A., Kevin Whelan, and Matthew Stout, eds. *Atlas of the Irish Rural Land-scape.* Cork: Cork University Press, 1997.

Aitchison, N. B. *Armagh and the Royal Centres in Early Medieval Ireland.* Rochester, NY: Published for Cuithne Press by Boydell and Brewer, 1994.

Alchermes, Joseph. "*Spolia* in Roman Cities of the Late Empire: Legislative Rationales and Architectural Reuse." *Dumbarton Oaks Papers* 48 (1994): 167–78.

Alcock, L. "Was There an Irish Sea Culture-Province in the Dark Ages?" In D. Moore, ed., *The Irish Sea Province in Archaeology and History*, 55–65. Cardiff: Cambrian Archaeological Association, 1970.

Aldhouse-Green, Miranda J. *Celtic Goddesses: Warriors, Virgins and Mothers*. London: British Museum Press, 1995.

———. *Pilgrims in Stone: Stone Images from the Gallo-Roman Sanctuary of Fontes Sequanae*. BAR International Series 754. Oxford: Archaeopress, 1999. Distributed by Hadrian Books.

———. *Symbol and Image in Celtic Religious Art*. New York: Routledge, 1989.

Archdall, Mervyn. *Monasticon hibernicum: or, An history of the abbeys, priories and other religious houses in Ireland*. Dublin: Printed for L. White, 1786.

Bailey, Richard N. "Seventh-Century Work at Ripon and Hexham." In Tim Tatton-Brown and Julian Munby, eds., *The Archaeology of Cathedrals*, 9–18. Oxford: Oxford University Committee for Archaeology, 1996.

Bammel, C. P. Hammond. "Products of Fifth-Century Scriptoria Preserving Conventions Used by Rufinus of Aquileia." *Journal of Theological Studies* 30 (1979): 430–62.

Barruol, Guy. "Les sanctuaires gallo-romains du Midi de la Gaule." In Goudineau et al., *Sanctuaires de tradition indigène*, 49–72.

Barry, Terry, ed. *A History of Settlement in Ireland*. New York: Routledge, 2000.

Bateman, N. C. W. "Public Buildings in Roman London: Some Contrasts." In Watson, *Roman London*, 47–57.

Bateson, J. D. "Further Finds of Roman Material from Ireland." *PRIA* 76 C (1976): 171–80.

———. "Roman Material from Ireland: A Reconsideration." *PRIA* 73 C (1973): 21–97.

Baumgarten, Rolf. "The Geographical Orientation of Ireland in Isidore and Orosius." *Peritia* 3 (1984): 189–203.

Beaujard, Brigitte. *Le culte des saints en Gaule: Les premiers temps. D'Hilaire de Poitiers à la fin du VIe siècle*. Paris: Éditions Cerf, 2000.

Bekker-Nielsen, Tønnes. *The Geography of Power: Studies in the Urbanization of Roman North-West Europe*. BAR International Series 477. Oxford: BAR, 1989.

———. "Navigable River-Systems and Urban Development." In J-F. Bergier, ed., *Montagnes, fleuves, forêts dans l'histoire: Barrières ou lignes de convergence?* 111–22. St. Katharinen: Scripta Mercaturae, 1989.

Bémont, C. "À propos d'un nouveau monument de Rosmerta." *Gallia* 27 (1969): 23–44.

Berschin, Walter. "Radegundis and Brigit." In Carey et al., *Irish Hagiography*, 72–76.

Bertelli, Carlo. "Visual Images of the Town in Late Antiquity and the Early Middle Ages." In Brogiolo and Ward-Perkins, *The Idea and Ideal of the Town*, 127–46.

Bhreathnach, Edel. "The Genealogies of Leinster as a Source for Local Cults." In Carey et al., *Irish Hagiography*, 250–67.

Biddle, Martin. "Archaeology, Architecture, and the Cult of Saints in Anglo-Saxon England." In L. A. S. Butler and R. K. Morris, eds., *The Anglo-Saxon Church: Papers on History, Architecture and Archaeology in Honour of Dr. H. M. Taylor*, 1–31. CBA Research Report 60. London: Council for British Archaeology, 1986.

Bieler, Ludwig. *St. Patrick and the Coming of Christianity*. A History of Irish Catholicism 1. Dublin: Gill, 1967.

Binchy, D. A. "An Archaic Legal Poem." *Celtica* 9 (1971): 152–68.

———. "Distraint in Irish Law." *Celtica* 10 (1973): 22–71.

———. "The Fair of Tailtiu and the Feast of Tara." *Ériu* 18 (1958): 133–38.

Bishop, Judith. "Language and Authority in the *Bethu Brigte*." Twenty-Sixth Annual University of California Celtic Studies Conference. UCLA: Los Angeles, March 4–7, 2004.

Bitel, Lisa M. "Body of a Saint, Story of a Goddess: Origins of the Brigidine Tradition." *Textual Practice* 16 (2002): 209–28.

———. "Ekphrasis at Kildare: The Imaginative Architecture of a Seventh-Century Hagiographer." *Speculum* 79 (2004): 605–27.

———. *Isle of the Saints: Monastic Settlement and Christian Community in Early Ireland*. Ithaca, NY: Cornell University Press, 1990.

———. *Land of Women: Tales of Sex and Gender from Early Ireland*. Ithaca, NY: Cornell University Press, 1996.

———. "Landscape, Gender, and Ethnogenesis in Pre-Norman Invasion Ireland." In *Inventing Medieval Landscapes: Senses of Place in Western Europe*, ed. John Howe and Michael Wolf, 171–91. Gainesville: University Press of Florida, 2002.

Blagg, T. F. C. "Architectural Patronage in the Western Provinces of the Roman Empire in the Third Century." In King and Henig, *Roman West*, 167–88.

———. "The Re-use of Monumental Masonry in Late Roman Defensive Walls." In Maloney and Hobley, *Roman Urban Defences in the West*, 130–35.

Blair, John. *The Church in Anglo-Saxon Society*. New York: Oxford University Press, 2005.

Blin, Olivier. "Un sanctuaire de *vicus*: Jouars-Ponchartrain (Yvelines)." In Van Andringa, *Archéologie des sanctuaires en Gaule romaine*, 91–117.

Bonnet, Charles. "Les églises en bois du haut Moyen-Âge d'après les recherches archéologiques." In Gauthier and Galinié, *Grégoire de Tours*, 217–36.

Bourgeois, Claude. *Divona*. Vol. 1, *Divinités et ex-voto du culte gallo-romain de l'eau*. Paris: de Boccard, 1991.

Bourke, Cormac. *Patrick: The Archeology of a Saint*. Belfast: HMSO, 1993.

———. "*Peregrinatio Columbae*." In Mac Shamhráin, *Island of St. Patrick*, 79–88.

Bourne, Richard John. *Aspects of the Relationship between the Central and Gallic Empires in the Mid to Late Third Century AD with Special Reference to Coinage Studies*. BAR International Series 963. Oxford: Archaeopress, 2001. Distributed by Hadrian Books.

Bouvier, Henri, Abbé. *Histoire de l'église de l'ancien archdiocèse de Sens*. 3 vols. Paris: A Picard et Fils, 1906–11.

Bowden, William. "A New Urban Élite? Church Builders and Church Building in Late-Antique Epirus." In L. Lavan, ed., *Recent Research in Late-Antique Urbanism*, 57–68. *Journal of Roman Archaeology*. Supplemental Series 42. Portsmouth, RI: Journal of Roman Archaeology, 2001.

Bowen, E. G. "The Cult of St. Brigit." *Studia Celtica* 8–9 (1973–74): 33–47.

Bowersock, G. W., Peter Brown, and Oleg Grabar, eds. *Late Antiquity: A Guide to the Postclassical World*. Cambridge, MA: Belknap Press of Harvard University Press, 1999.

Bradley, John. "Archaeology, Topography, and Building Fabric: The Cathedral and Town of Medieval Kildare." *JCKAS* 29 (2000–2001): 27–47.

Bradley, Richard. *An Archaeology of Natural Places.* New York: Routledge, 2000.

Braudel, Fernand. *The Identity of France.* New York: Harper and Row, 1988.

Bray, Dorothy. "The Body of Brigit." Paper presented at CSANA Annual Meeting. South Bend, IN: Notre Dame, May 9–12, 2002.

Bray, Dorothy. "The Image of St. Brigit in the Early Irish Church." *EC* 24 (1987): 209–15.

Breeze, Andrew. "The Shrine of St. Brigit at Olite, Spain." *Cambridge Medieval Celtic Studies* 16 (1988): 85–95.

Brenk, Beat. "Spolia from Constantine to Charlemagne: Aesthetics versus Ideology." *Dumbarton Oaks Papers* 41 (1987): 103–9.

Brenneman, Walter L., Jr., and Mary G. Brenneman. *Crossing the Circle and the Holy Wells of Ireland.* Charlottesville: University Press of Virginia, 1995.

Brogiolo, G. P. "Ideas of the Town in Italy during the Transition from Antiquity to the Middle Ages." In Brogiolo and Ward-Perkins, *The Idea and Ideal of the Town,* 99–126.

Brogiolo, G. P., and B. Ward-Perkins, eds. *The Idea and Ideal of the Town between Late Antiquity and the Early Middle Ages.* Leiden: Brill, 1999.

Brooks, Dodie A. "A Review of the Evidence for the Continuity in British Towns in the 5th and 6th Centuries." *Oxford Journal of Archaeology* 5 (1986): 77–102.

Brown, Peter. *The Cult of the Saints: Its Rise and Function in Latin Christianity.* Chicago: University of Chicago Press, 1981.

———. *The Rise of Western Christendom.* Cambridge, MA: Blackwell, 1996.

Brubaker, Leslie, and Julia M. H. Smith, eds. *Gender in the Early Medieval World: East and West, 300–900.* New York: Cambridge University Press, 2004.

Brunaux, J-L. *The Celtic Gauls: Gods, Rites and Sanctuaries.* Trans. Daphne Nash. London: Seaby, 1988.

———. *Les religions gauloises (Ve–Ier siècles av. J.–C.): Nouvelles approches sur les rituels celtiques de la Gaule indépendante.* Paris: Éditions Errance, 2000.

Brunaux, J-L., P. Méniel, and F. Poplin, eds. *Gournay I: Les fouilles sur le sanctuaire et l'oppidum (1975–1984).* Amiens: Revue Archéologique de Picardie, 1985.

Bullough, Donald A. "Social and Economic Structure and Topography in the Early Medieval City." In *Topografia urbana e vita cittadina nell'alto Medioevo in Occidente, 26 aprile–1 maggio, 1973,* 1:351–99. Settimane de Studie del Centro di Studi sull'Alto Medioevo 21. Spoleto: Presso la sede del Centro, 1974.

Burke, Thomas. *Hibernia Dominicana. Sive Historica Provinciae Hiberniae Ordinis Praedicatorum.* Kilkenny: Ex Typographia Metternechiana sub signo Gryphi, 1762.

Burrus, Virginia. *The Sex Lives of Saints: An Erotics of Ancient Hagiography.* Philadelphia: University of Pennsylvania Press, 2004.

Busson, Didier. *Paris,* vol. 75 of *Carte archéologique de la Gaule.* Paris: Académie des Inscriptions et Belles-Lettres, 1998.

Butler, R. M. "Late Roman Town Walls in Gaul." *Archeological Journal* 116 (1959): 25–50.

Buttimer, Cornelius. "The Bórama: Literature, History and Political Propaganda in Early Medieval Leinster." Ph.D. diss., Harvard University, 1983.

Byrne, J. F. *Irish Kings and High-Kings*. 2nd ed. Portland, OR: Four Courts Press, 2001.

Cabuy, Yves. "Temples et sanctuaires de tradition indigène en Belgique romaine." In Goudineau et al., *Sanctuaires de tradition indigène*, 24–33.

Caillet, Jean-Pierre. *L'Évergétisme monumental Chrétien en Italie et à ses marges*. Collection de l'École française de Rome 175 (1993): 418–26.

Caló Levi, Annalina, and Mario Attilio Caló Levi. *Itineraria Picta. Contributo allo studio della Tabula Peutingeria*. Rome: L'erma di Bretschneider, 1967.

Campbell, James. "The Debt of the Early English Church to Ireland." In *Irland und die Christenheit: Bibelstudien und Mission*, ed. Próinséas Ní Chatháin and Michael Richter, 332–46. Stuttgart: Klett-Cotta, 1987.

Carey, John. "Saint Patrick, the Druids, and the End of the World." *History of Religions* 36 (1996): 42–53.

Carey, John, Máire Herbert, and Pádraig Ó Riain, eds. *Studies in Irish Hagiography: Saints and Scholars*. Portland, OR: Four Courts Press, 2001.

Carney, James. "Three Old Irish Accentual Poems." *Ériu* 22 (1971): 23–80.

Carson, R. A. G., and Claire O'Kelly. "A Catalogue of the Roman Coins from Newgrange, Co. Meath and Notes on the Coins and Related Finds." *PRIA* 77 C (1977): 33–55.

Carver, Martin, ed. *The Cross Goes North: Processes of Conversion in Northern Europe, A.D. 300–1300*. Rochester, NY: Boydell and Brewer, 2003.

Caulfield, Seamus. "The Neolithic Settlement of North Connaught." In Terrence Reeves-Smyth and Fred Harmond, eds., *Landscape Archeology in Ireland*, 195–215. BAR British Series 116. Oxford: BAR, 1983.

Champion, T. C., and J. R. Collis, eds. *The Iron Age in Britain and Ireland: Recent Trends*. Sheffield: J. R. Collis Publications, Department of Archaeology and Prehistory, University of Sheffield, 1996.

Charles-Edwards, Thomas, ed. *After Rome*. New York: Oxford University Press, 2003.

———. "Church and Settlement." In Proinséas Ní Chatháin and Michael Richter, eds., *Ireland and Europe: The Early Church/Irland und Europa: Die Kirche im Frühmittelalter*, 167–75. Stuttgart: Klett-Cotta, 1984.

———. *Early Christian Ireland*. New York: Cambridge University Press, 2000.

———. *Early Irish and Welsh Kinship*. New York: Oxford University Press, 1993.

———. "*Érlam*: The Patron-Saint of an Irish Church." In Thacker and Sharpe, *Local Saints*, 267–90.

———. "The Penitential of Theodore and the *Iudicia Theodori*." In Michael Lapidge, ed., *Archbishop Theodore: Commemorative Studies in His Life and Influence*, 141–74. New York: Cambridge University Press, 1995.

———. "The Social Background to Irish *Peregrinatio*." *Celtica* 11 (1976): 43–59.

Chevallier, R., ed. *Les eaux thermales et les cultes des eaux en Gaule et dans les provinces voisines.*: Actes du colloque, 28–30 septembre 1990, Aix-en-Bains. Caesarodunum 26. Tours: Centre de recherches A. Piganiol, 1992.

———. "La function politique I: Les monument à la gloire de Rome." In Robert Bedon, Raymond Chevallier, and Pierre, Pinon, eds., *Architecture et urbanisme en Gaule romaine*, 1:180–93. Paries: Éditions Errance, 1988.

Clark, William W. "'The Recollection of the Past Is the Promise of the Future.' Continuity and Contextuality: Saint-Denis, Merovingians, Capetians, and Paris." In

Virginia Chieffo Raguin, Kathryn Bush, and Peter Draper, eds., *Artistic Integration in Gothic Buildings*, 92–113. Toronto: University of Toronto Press, 1995.

Cleary, S. E. *Extra-mural Areas of Romano-British Towns*. BAR British Series 169. Oxford: BAR, 1987.

Clinton, Mark. "Settlement Patterns in the Early Historic Kingdom of Leinster (Seventh–Mid Twelfth Centuries)." In Smyth, *Seanchas*, 275–98.

Coates, Simon. "Venantius Fortunatus and the Image of Episcopal Authority in Late Antique and Early Merovingian Gaul." *English Historical Review* 115 (2000): 1109–37.

Colbert de Beaulieu, J-B. *Les monnaies gauloises des "Parisii."* Paris: Imprimerie Nationale, 1970.

Collingwood, R. G., and J. N. L. Myres. *Roman Britain and the English Settlements.* Oxford: Clarendon Press, 1936.

Collis, J. R. "Across the Great Divide," in Champion and Collis, *The Iron Age in Britain and Ireland*, 1–4.

Connolly, Sean. "*Vita Prima Sanctae Brigitae*: Background and Historical Value." *JRSAI* 119 (1989): 5–49.

Cooney, Gabriel. "Reading a Landscape Manuscript: A Review of Progress in Prehistoric Settlement Studies in Ireland." In Barry, *History of Settlement in Ireland*, 1–49.

Cooper, Kate. "Household and Empire: The Materfamilias as *Miles Christi* in the Anonymous *Handbook for Gregoria*." In Mulder-Bakker and Wogan-Browne, *Household, Women, and Christianities*, 91–108.

———. "The Martyr, the *Matrona*, and the Bishop: The Matron Lucina and the Politics of Martyr Cult in Fifth- and Sixth-Century Rome." *Early Medieval Europe* 8 (1999): 297–317.

Corthals, Johann. "The Rhymeless 'Leinster Poems': Diplomatic Texts." *Celtica* 24 (1993): 79–100.

Cosgrove, Art., ed. *A New History of Ireland*. Vol. 2, *Medieval Ireland, 1169–1534*. New York: Oxford University Press, 1987.

Coulon, Gérard. *Les Gallo-Romains.* Vol. 1, *Les villes, les campagnes, et les échanges.* Paris: Armand Colin, 1990.

Couperie, Pierre. *Paris through the Ages: An Illustrated Historical Atlas of Urbanism and Architecture.* Trans. Marilyn Low. New York: G. Braziller, 1971.

Cowell, George Young. "St. Brigid and the Cathedral Church of Kildare." *JCKAS* 2 (1897): 234–52.

Cramp, Rosemary J. "Jarrow Church." *Archeological Journal* 133 (1976): 220–28.

———. "Monkwearmouth." *Archeological Journal* 133 (1976): 230–37.

Crook, John. *The Architectural Setting of the Cult of the Saints in the Early Christian West, c. 300–1200.* New York: Oxford University Press, 2000.

———. "The Enshrinement of Local Saints in Francia and England." In Thacker and Sharpe, *Local Saints*, 189–224.

Crosby, Sumner McK. *The Royal Abbey of Saint-Denis: From Its Beginnings to the Death of Suger, 475–1151.* Edited and compiled by Pamela Z. Blum. New Haven, CT: Yale University Press, 1987.

Cross, Tom Peete. *Motif-Index of Early Irish Literature*. Indiana University Publications, Folklore Series 7. Bloomington: Indiana University Press, 1952.

Cunliffe, Barry W. *The Ancient Celts*. New York: Oxford University Press, 1997.

———. *Fishbourne: A Roman Palace and Its Garden*. London: Thames and Hudson, 1971.

Curran, J. "Moving Statues in Late Antique Rome: Problems of Perspective." *Art History* 17 (1994): 46–58.

Daly, William M. "Clovis: How Barbaric, How Pagan?" *Speculum* 69 (1994): 619–64.

Dark, K. R. *Civitas to Kingdom: British Political Continuity, 300–800*. New York: Leicester University Press, 1994.

Delaborde, H-F. "Le Procès du chef de Saint-Denis en 1410." *Mémoires de la Société de l'Histoire de Paris et de l'Île-de-France* 11 (1884): 297–409.

Delogu, Paolo. "The Papacy, Rome, and the Wider World in the Seventh and Eighth Centuries." In Julia M. H. Smith, ed., *Early Medieval Rome and the Christian West: Essays in Honour of Donald A. Bullough*, 197–220. Leiden: Brill, 2000.

De Paor, Liam. *Saint Patrick's World: The Christian Culture of Ireland's Apostolic Age*. Notre Dame, IN: University of Notre Dame Press, 1993.

Derks, Ton. *Gods, Temples and Ritual Practices: The Transformation of Religious Ideas and Values in Roman Gaul*. Amsterdam: Amsterdam University Press, 1998.

Devlitt, Matthew. "The See Lands of Kildare." *JCKAS* 9 (1918–21): 358–65.

Deyts, Simone. *Un peuple de pèlerins: Offrandes de pierre et de bronze des Sources de la Seine*. Revue Archéologique de l'Est et du Centre-Est, Supplement 13. Dijon: Revue Archéologique de l'Est et du Centre-Est, 1994.

Dictionary of the Irish Language: Based Mainly on Old and Middle Irish Materials. Compact edition. Dublin: Royal Irish Academy, 1983.

Dillon, Myles. "Stories from the Law-Tracts." *Ériu* 11 (1932): 42–65.

Dix, Brian. "The Manufacture of Lime and Its Uses in the Western Provinces." *Oxford Archaeological Journal* 1 (1982): 331–46.

Doherty, Charles. "The Basilica in Early Ireland." *Peritia* 3 (1984): 303–15.

———. "The Monastic Town in Early Medieval Ireland." In H. B. Clarke and A. Simms, eds., *The Comparative History of Urban Origins in Non-Roman Europe: Ireland, Wales, Denmark, Germany, Poland, and Russian from the Ninth to the Thirteenth Centuries*, 1:45–75. BAR International Series 255. Oxford: BAR, 1985.

———. "Some Aspects of Hagiography as a Source for Irish Economic History." *Peritia* 1 (1982): 300–328.

Dooley, Ann. "The Plague and Its Consequences in Ireland." In Lester K. Little, ed., *Plague and the End of Antiquity: The Pandemic of 541–750*, 215–28. Cambridge: Cambridge University Press, 2007.

Dowden, Ken. *European Paganism: The Realities of Cult from Antiquity to the Middle Ages*. New York: Routledge, 2000.

Drinkwater, John, and Hugh Elton, eds. *Fifth-Century Gaul: A Crisis of Identity?* New York: Cambridge University Press, 1992.

Dubois, Jacques. "L'emplacement des premiers sanctuaires de Paris." *Journal des Savants* [n.n.] (1968): 5–44.

———. "Sainte Geneviève et son temps." *Journal des Savants* [n.n.] (1983): 65–79.

Dubois, Jacques, and Laure Beaumont-Maillet. *Sainte Geneviève de Paris: La vie, le culte, l'art.* Paris: Beauchesne, 1982.

Duby, Georges. *The Early Growth of the European Economy: Warriors and Peasants from the Seventh to the Twelfth Centuries.* Trans. H. B. Clarke. Ithaca, NY: Cornell University Press, 1974.

Duggan, Lawrence G. "Was Art Really the 'Book of the Illiterate'?" *Word and Image* 5 (1989): 227–51.

Dumville, David N., ed. *Saint Patrick, A.D. 493–1993.* Rochester, NY: Boydell Press, 1993.

Dunn, Vincent A. *Cattle-Raids and Courtships: Medieval Narrative Genres in a Traditional Context.* New York: Garland, 1989.

Durand, Marc. "Un sanctuaire 'rural': Le temple gallo-romain de la forêt d'Halatte." In Van Andringa, *Religion en Gaule romaine,* 119–29.

Duval, Noël, ed. *Naissance des arts chrétiens: Atlas des monuments paléochrétiens de la France.* Paris: Imprimerie National Éditions, 1991.

———, gen. ed. *Les premiers monuments chrétiens de la France,* Vol. 3: *Ouest, Nord et Est.* Paris: Picard: Ministère de la culture et de la francophonie, Direction du patrimoine, Sous-direction de l'archéologie, 1998.

Duval, Noël, P. Périn, and J-Ch. Picard. "Paris." In J-Ch. Picard, ed., *Province Ecclésiastique de Sens (Lugdunensis Senonia),* 97–129. In Gauthier and Picard, *Topographie chrétienne.* Vol. 8.

Duval, Paul-Marie. *De Lutèce oppidum à Paris capitale de la France.* Paris: Hachette, 1993.

———. *Les dieux de la Gaule.* Paris: Payot, 1993.

———. *Paris antique: Des origines au troisième siècle.* Paris: Hermann, 1961.

———. *La vie quotidienne en Gaule pendant la paix romaine (Ier-IIIe siècles après J.-C.).* Paris: Hachette, 1952.

Duval, Yvette. *Auprès des saints corps et âme: L'inhumation "ad sanctos" dans la chrétienté d'Orient et d'Occident du IIIe au VIIe siècle.* Paris: Études Augustiniennes, 1988.

Dyson, Stephen L. *The Roman Countryside.* London: Duckworth, 2003.

Edwards, Nancy. *The Archaeology of Early Medieval Ireland.* London: B. T. Batsford, 1990.

———. "Celtic Saints and Early Medieval Archaeology." In Thacker and Sharpe, *Local Saints,* 225–66.

Effros, Bonnie. *Merovingian Mortuary Archaeology and the Making of the Early Middle Ages.* Berkeley: University of California Press, 2003.

Egmond, Wolfert S. van. *Conversing with the Saints: Communication in Pre-Carolingian Hagiography from Auxerre.* Turnhout: Brepols, 2006.

Elton, H. "Defence in Fifth-Century Gaul." In Drinkwater and Elton, *Fifth-Century Gaul,* 167–76.

Eogan, George. *Excavations at Knowth.* Dublin: Royal Irish Academy, 1984–97.

Esposito, Mario. "On the Earliest Latin Life of St. Brigit of Kildare." *PRIA* 30 C (1912): 307–26.

———. "On the Early Lives of St. Brigid of Kildare." *Hermathena* 24 (1935): 120–65.

Etchingham, Colmán. *Church Organisation in Ireland: AD 650 to 1000.* Maynooth: Laigin Publications, 1999.

——. "Kildare before the Normans: An Episcopal and Conventual See." *JCKAS* 19 (2000–2001): 7–26.

Evans, Jeremy. "From the End of Roman Britain to the 'Celtic West.'" *Oxford Journal of Archaeology* 9 (1990): 91–104.

Fanning, Stephen. "Clovis Augustus and Merovingian *Imitatio Imperii.*" In Mitchell and Wood, *World of Gregory of Tours*, 321–35.

——. "Emperors and Empires in Fifth-Century Gaul." In Drinkwater and Elton, *Fifth-Century Gaul*, 288–97.

Farmer, Sharon A. *Communities of Saint Martin: Legend and Ritual in Medieval Tours.* Ithaca, NY: Cornell University Press, 1991.

Farrar, Brett. "Tear-Stained Eye." *Trace.* Warner Bros. Records, 1995.

Fauduet, Isabelle, ed. *Atlas des sanctuaires romano-celtiques de Gaule I: Les fanums.* Paris: Éditions Errance, 1993.

Fentress, Elizabeth et al., eds. *Romanization and the City: Creation, Dynamics and Failures.* Proceedings of a conference held at the American Academy in Rome to celebrate the fiftieth anniversary of the excavations at Cosa, May 14–16, 1998. Portsmouth, RI: Journal of Roman Archaeology, 2000.

Ferdière, Alain. *Les campagnes en Gaule romaine.* 2 vols. Paris: Éditions Errance, 1988.

Février, Paul-Albert. "The Origin and Growth of the Cities of Southern Gaul to the Third Century A.D.: An Assessment of the Most Recent Archaeological Discoveries." *Journal of Roman Studies* 63 (1973): 1–28.

Février, Paul-Albert, Michel Fixot, Christian Goudineau, and Venceslas Kruta, eds. *Histoire de la France urbaine.* Vol. 1, *Le ville antique des origines au IXe siècle.* Paris: Seuil, 1980.

Flanagan, Deirdre. "The Christian Impact on Early Ireland: Place-Names Evidence." In Proinséas Ní Chatháin and Michael Richter, eds. *Ireland and Europe: The Early Church/Irland und Europa: Die Kirche im Frühmittelalter*, 25–51. Stuttgart: Klett-Cotta, 1984.

Fleury, Michel, and Albert France-Lanord. *Les trésors mérovingiens de la Basilique de Saint-Denis.* Woippy, France: Gérard Klopp, 1998.

Fleury, Michel, Guy-Michel Leproux, and Deny Sandron, eds. *Paris de Clovis à Dagobert.* Paris: Centre Culturel du Panthéon, 1996.

Flint, Valerie I. J. *The Rise of Magic in Early Medieval Europe.* Princeton, NJ: Princeton University Press, 1991.

Foot, Sarah. *Veiled Women.* 2 vols. Aldershot: Ashgate, 2000.

Fossard, Denise, Élisabeth Chatel, and M. Vieillard. *Recueil général des monuments sculptés en France pendant le haut Moyen Âge (IVe–Xe siècles).* Vol. 1, *Paris et son département.* Paris: Bibliothèque Nationale, 1978.

Frank, Georgia. *The Memory of the Eyes: Pilgrims to Living Saints in Christian Late Antiquity.* Berkeley: University of California Press, 2000.

Freeman, Philip M. "Greek and Roman Views of Ireland: A Checklist." *Emania* 13 (1995): 11–13.

Frend, William H. C. "Roman Britain, a Failed Promise." In Carver, *The Cross Goes North*, 79–91.

Frézouls, Edmond, ed. *Les villes antiques de la France*. Vol. 1. *Belgique 1: Amiens, Beauvais, Grand, Metz*. Strasbourg: AECR, 1982.

Fry, Susan Leigh. *Burial in Medieval Ireland 900–1500: A Review of the Written Sources*. Portland, OR: Four Courts Press, 1999.

Fulford, Michael. "Epilogue: A View of Roman London from the Hinterland." In Watson, *Roman London*, 107–12.

Galinié, Henri, and Elisabeth Zadora-Rio, eds. *Archéologie du cimetière chrétien:* Actes du 2e colloque ARCHEA. Orléans, 29 septembre–1 octobre, 1994. Tours: FERACF/La Simarre, 1996.

Galvao-Sobrinho, Carlos R. "Funerary Epigraphy and the Spread of Christianity in the West." *Athenaeum* 83 (1995): 431–62.

Ganz, David, and Walter Goffart. "Charters Earlier Than 800 from French Collections." *Speculum* 65 (1990): 906–32.

Gauthier, Nancy. "From the Ancient City to the Medieval Town: Continuity and Change in the Early Middle Ages." In Mitchell and Wood, *World of Gregory of Tours*, 47–66.

———. "Le paysage urbain en Gaule au Ve siècle." In Gauthier and Galinié, *Grégoire de Tours et l'espace gaulois*, 49–63.

Gauthier, Nancy, and Henri Galinié, eds. *Grégoire de Tours et l'espace gaulois:* Actes du congrès international, Tours, 3–5 novembre 1994. Tours: Revue Archéologique du Centre de la France, 1997.

Gauthier, Nancy, and J.-Ch. Picard, eds. *Topographie chrétienne des cités de la Gaule, des origines au milieu du VIIIe siècle*. 14 vols. Paris: de Boccard, 1986–2006.

Geary, Patrick J. *Before France and Germany: The Creation and Transformation of the Merovingian World*. New York: Oxford University Press, 1988.

———. *Living with the Dead in the Middle Ages*. Ithaca, NY: Cornell University Press, 1994.

Giard, René. "Étude sur l'histoire de l'abbaye de Sainte-Geneviève de Paris jusqu'à la fin du XIII siècle." *Mémoires de la Société de l'Histoire de Paris et de l'Île-de-France* 30 (1903): 41–126.

Gilchrist, Roberta. *Gender and Material Culture: The Archaeology of Religious Women*. New York: Routledge, 1994.

Gillespie, Raymond. "St. Brigid's Cathedral in the Age of Reform, 1500–1700." *JCKAS* 19 (2000–2001): 48–61.

———, ed. *St. Brigid's Cathedral Kildare: A History*. Maynooth: Kildare Archaeological Society, 2001.

Gilliard, F. "The Senators of Sixth-Century Gaul." *Speculum* 54 (1979): 685–97.

Goudineau, Christian, Isabelle Fauduet, and Gérard Coulon, eds. *Les Sanctuaires de tradition indigène en Gaule romaine*. Actes du colloque d'Argentomagus (Argenton-sur-Creuse/Saint-Marcel, Indre), 8, 9 et 10 octobre 1992. Paris: Éditions Errance; [Argenton-sur-Creuse]: Musée d'Argentomagus, 1994.

Grabar, André. *Martyrium: Recherches sur le culte des reliques et l'art chrétien antique*. 2 vols. [Paris]: Collège de France, 1943–46.

Grabowski, Kathryn. "The Historical Overview of Dún Ailinne." *Emania* 7 (1990): 32–36.

Greenhalgh, Michael. *The Survival of Roman Antiquities in the Middle Ages.* London: Duckworth, 1989. Republished by the author at http://rubens.anu.edu.au/.

Grenier, Albert. *Manuel d'archéologie gallo-romaine.* 2 vols. Repr., Paris: Picard Éditeur, 1985–.

Grimmer, Martin. "Saxon Bishop and Celtic King: Interactions between Aldhelm of Wessex and Geraint of Dumnonia." *Heroic Age* 4 (2001): 1–9.

Groenman–Van Waateringe, Willy. "Wasteland: Buffer in the Medieval Economy." In M. Colardelle, ed., *L'homme et la nature au Moyen Age: Paléoenvironnement des so- ciétés occidentales.* Actes du Ve Congrès international d'archéologie médiévale tenu à Grenoble (France), 6–9 octobre 1992, 113–17. Paris: Éditions Errance, 1996.

Guérout, J. "Le palais de la Cité à Paris, des origines à 1417." In *Mémoires de la Fédéra- tion des sociétés historiques et archéologiques de Paris et de l'Île-de-France,* 1:57–212. Paris: Fédération des Sociétés Historiques et Archéologiques de Paris et de l'Île-de-France, 1949.

Guest, Peter. "Manning the Defences: The Development of Romano-British Urban Boundaries." In Miranda J. Aldhouse-Green and Peter Webster, eds., *Artefacts and Archaeology: Aspects of the Celtic and Roman World,* 76–89. Cardiff: University of Wales Press, 2002.

Guy, C. J. "Roman Circular Lead Tanks in Britain." *Britannia* 12 (1981): 271–76.

Gwynn, A., and R. N. Hadcock. *Medieval Religious Houses: Ireland. With an Appendix to Early Sites.* Harlow: Longman, 1970.

Hahn, Cynthia. "Seeing and Believing: The Construction of Sanctity in Early-Medieval Saints' Shrines." *Speculum* 72 (1997): 1079–1106.

Hall, David D., ed. *Lived Religion in America: Toward a History of Practice.* Princeton, NJ: Princeton University Press, 1997.

Hall, Dianne. *Women and the Church in Medieval Ireland c. 1140–1540.* Portland, OR: Four Courts Press, 2003.

Halsall, Guy. *Settlement and Social Organization: The Merovingian Region of Metz.* New York: Cambridge University Press, 1995.

———. "Social Change around A.D. 600: An Austrasian Perspective." In Martin Carver, ed., *The Age of Sutton Hoo: The Seventh Century in Northwestern Europe,* 265–78. Rochester, NY: Boydell Press, 1992.

———. "Social Identities and Social Relationships in Merovingian Gaul." In Wood, *Franks and Alamanni,* 141–65.

Hamp, Eric P. "Imbolc/Oimelc." *Studia Celtica* 14 (1979–80): 106–13.

Harbison, Peter. *Pilgrimage in Ireland: The Monuments and the People.* Syracuse, NY: Syracuse University Press, 1992.

———. *Pre-Christian Ireland. From the First Settlers to the Early Celts.* London: Thames and Hudson, 1988.

———. "Some Views of St. Brigid's Cathedral, Kildare." *JCKAS* 19 (2000–2001): 83–95.

Harries, Jill. "Christianity and the City in Late Roman Gaul." In John Rich, ed., *The City in Late Antiquity,* 77–98. Routledge: London, 1996.

Harries, Jill. "Church and State in the *Notitia Galliarum.*" *Journal of Roman Studies*
   68 (1978): 25–43.
———. "Death and the Dead in the Late Roman West." In Stephen Bassett, ed., *Death
   in Towns: Urban Responses to the Dying and the Dead, 100–1600,* 56–67. Leicester:
   Leicester University Press, 1992.
Heinzelmann, Martin. "The 'Affair' of Hilary of Arles (445) and Gallo-Roman Identity
   in the Fifth Century." In Drinkwater and Elton, *Fifth-Century Gaul,* 239–51.
———. "L'aristocratie et les évêches entre Loire et Rhin jusqu'à la fin du VIIe siècle."
   Revue d'Histoire de l'Église de France 168 (1976): 75–90.
———. *Translationsberichte und andere Quellen des Reliquienkultes.* Typologie des
   Sources du Moyen Âge Occidental 33. Turnhout: Brepols, 1979.
Heinzelmann, Martin, and Joseph-Claude Poulin. *Les vies anciennes de Sainte Geneviève
   de Paris: Études critiques.* Paris: H. Champion, 1986.
Herbert, Máire. "Celtic Heroine? The Archaeology of the Deirdre Story." In Toni
   O'Brien Johnson and David Cairns, eds., *Gender in Irish Writing,* 13–22. Philadel-
   phia: Open University Press, 1991.
Herity, Michael. "A Survey of the Royal Site of Cruachain in Connacht: I. Introduction,
   the Monuments and Topography." *JRSAI* 113 (1983): 121–42.
———. "A Survey of the Royal Site of Cruachain in Connacht: II. Prehistoric Monu-
   ments." *JRSAI* 114 (1984): 125–38.
Hiddink, H. A. "Rural Centres in the Roman Settlement System of Northern Gallia
   Belgica and Germania Inferior." In Nico Roymans and F. Theuws, eds., *Images of
   the Past: Studies on Ancient Societies in North-Western Europe,* 201–33. Amsterdam:
   Instituut voor Pre- en Protohistorisches Archeologie, 1991.
Higham, N. J. "Roman and Native in England North of the Tees: Acculturation and
   Its Limitations." In John C. Barrett, Andrew P. Fitzpatrick, and Lesley Macinnes,
   eds., *Barbarians and Romans in North-west Europe: From the Later Republic to Late
   Antiquity,* 153–74. BAR International Series 471. Oxford: BAR, 1989.
Hogan, Edmund. *Onomasticon goedelicum locorum et tribuum Hiberniae et Scotiae; An
   Index, with Identifications to the Gaelic Names of Places and Tribes.* Dublin: Hodges,
   Figgis and Co., 1910. Reprint, Portland, OR: Four Courts Press, 1993.
Hopkins, Keith. "Taxes and Trade in the Roman Empire (200 B.C.–A.D. 400)." *Journal
   of Roman Studies* 70 (1980): 101–25.
Howlett, David. 'Vita I Sanctae Brigitae'. *Chronicon: An Electronic History Journal* 1
   (1997). University College Cork, Department of History: http://www.ucc.ie/
   chronicon/howfra.htm/.
Hudson, Benjamin. "The Changing Economy of the Irish Sea Province: A.D. 900–
   1300." In Smith, *Britain and Ireland,* 39–66.
Hughes, Kathleen. *Early Christian Ireland: An Introduction to the Sources.* Ithaca, NY:
   Cornell University Press, 1972.
Hughes, Kathleen, and Ann Hamlin. *Celtic Monasticism: The Modern Traveller to the
   Early Irish Church.* New York: Seabury Press, 1981.
James, Edward. *The Franks.* New York: Blackwell, 1988.
James, Liz, and Ruth Webb. "'To Understand Ultimate Things and Enter Secret
   Places': Ekphrasis and Art in Byzantium." *Art History* 14 (1991): 1–17.

Jaski, Bart. *Early Irish Kingship and Succession*. Portland, OR: Four Courts Press, 2000.

Joffroy, René. *Le cimetière de Lavoye: Nécropole mérovingienne*. Paris: A. & J. Picard, 1974.

Jones, Michael E. "Geographical-Psychological Frontiers in Sub-Roman Britain." In Mathisen and Sivan, *Shifting Frontiers in Late Antiquity*, 45–58.

Jones, Michael J. "Early Christian Archaeology in Europe: Some Recent Research." In N. J. Higham, ed., *Archaeology of the Roman Empire: A Tribute to the Life and Works of Professor Barri Jones*, 319–24. BAR International Series 940. Oxford: Archaeopress, 1994.

———. "St. Paul in the Bail, Lincoln: Britain in Europe?" In Kenneth Painter, ed., *Churches Built in Ancient Times: Recent Studies in Early Christian Archaeology*, 325–47. London: Society of Antiquaries of London; Accordia Research Centre, University of London, 1994.

Jullian, Camille. "Saint Geneviève à Nanterre." In *Mélanges offerts à M. Gustave Schlumberger, II. Numismatique et sigillographie archéologie*, 372–75. Paris: P. Geunther, 1924.

Kaplan, Steven L. "Religion, Subsistence, and Social Control: The Uses of Saint Genevieve," *Eighteenth-Century Studies* 13 (1979–80): 142–68.

Kapps, Raymond. *Escolives Sainte-Camille gallo-romain: Le site, le monument à arcades*. *Revue archéologique de l'Est et du Centre-Est*, Supplement 1. Dijon: Revue Archéologique de l'Est et du Centre-Est, 1974.

Kay, Sarah, and Miri Rubin, eds. *Framing Medieval Bodies*. Manchester: Manchester University Press, 1994.

Kelleher, John V. "Early Irish History and Pseudo-History." *Studia Hibernica* 3 (1963): 113–27.

Kelly, Fergus. *Early Irish Farming: A Study Based Mainly on the Law-Texts of the 7th and 8th Centuries A.D.* Rev. ed. Dublin: Dublin Institute for Advanced Studies, 1997.

———. *A Guide to Early Irish Law*. Dublin: Dublin Institute for Advanced Studies, 1988.

Kenney, J. F. *The Sources for the Early History of Ireland. I: Ecclesiastical*. Repr. Shannon, Ireland: Irish University Press, 1968.

Kildare Cathedral. *Kildare Cathedral Restoration*. [Inc. Report by George E. Street]. Dublin: Forster, 1871.

King, Anthony, and Martin Henig, eds. *The Roman West in the Third Century: Contributions from Archeology and History*. BAR International Series 109, vol. 1. Oxford: BAR, 1981

Kinney, Dale. "The Church Basilica." *Acta ad archaeologiam et artium historiam pertinentia* 15, n.s., 1 (2001): 115–35.

———. "Rape or Restitution of the Past? Interpreting *Spolia*." In Susan C. Scott, ed., *The Art of Interpreting*, 52–67. Papers in Art History from the Pennsylvania State University 9. University Park: Department of Art History, Pennsylvania State University, 1995.

Knight, Jeremy. "Basilicas and Barrows: Christian Origins in Wales and Western Britain." In Carver, *The Cross Goes North*, 119–26.

Krüger, Karl Heinrich. *Königsgrabkirchen der Franken, Angelsachsen und Langobarden bis zur Mitte des 8. Jahrhunderts: Ein historischer Katalog*. Munich: W. Fink, 1971.

Kubischek, W. "Itinerarien." In Hans Gärtner, ed. *Paulys Realencyclopädie der classischen Altertumswissenschaft, neue Bearbeitung begonnen von Georg Wissowa*, 2308–66. München: A. Druckenmüller, 1980.

Lacan, Jacques. "The Mirror Stage as Formative of the Function of the I." In *Écrits. A Selection*. Trans. Alan Sheridan. New York: Norton, 1977.

Landes, Christian, ed. *Dieux guérisseurs en Gaule romaine*. Lattes: Musée Archéologique Henri Prades, 1992.

Larkin, Emmet. "The Devotional Revolution in Ireland." *American Historical Review* 77 (1972): 625–52.

Lebeuf, Abbé. *Histoire de la ville et de tout le diocèse de Paris*. 5 vols. Paris: Féchoz et Letouzey, 1883.

LeGoff, Jacques. "Ecclesiastical Culture and Folklore in the Middle Ages: Saint Marcellus of Paris and the Dragon." In *Time, Work and Culture in the Middle Ages*, 159–88. Trans. Arthur Goldhammer. Chicago: University of Chicago Press, 1980.

Levillain, L. "Études sur l'abbaye de Saint-Denis à l'époque mérovingienne IV, Les documents d'histoire économique." *Bibliothèque de l'École des Chartes* 91 (1930): 5–65.

Lifshitz, Felice. "Apostolicity Theses in Gaul: The *Histories* of Gregory and the 'Hagiography' of Bayeux." In Mitchell and Wood, *World of Gregory of Tours*, 211–28.

———. "The Martyr, the Tomb, and the Matron: Constructing the (Masculine) 'Past' as a Female Power Base." In P. Geary, G. Althoff, and J. Fried, eds., *Medieval Concepts of the Past: Ritual, Memory, Historiography*, 311–41. Washington, DC: German Historical Institute; New York: Cambridge University Press, 2002.

Logan, Patrick. *The Holy Wells of Ireland*. Gerrards Cross, Buckinghamshire: Smythe, 1980.

Lombard-Jourdan, Anne. *Aux origines de Paris: Le genèse de la rive droite jusqu'en 1223*. Paris: Éditions du Centre National de la Recherche Scientifique, 1985.

———. "La légende de la consécration par le Christ de la basilique mérovingienne de Saint-Denis et de la guérison du lépreux." *Bulletin Monumental* 143 (1985): 237–69.

Lorren, Claude, and Patrick Périn, eds. *L'habitat rural du haut Moyen Age: France, Pays-Bas, Danemark et Grande Bretagne*. Actes des XIVe Journées internationales d'archéologie mérovingienne, Guiry-en-Vexin et Paris, 4–8 février 1993. Mémoires publiés par l'Association Française d'Archéologie Mérovingienne 6. Rouen: Association Française d'Archéologie, Musée des Antiquités de la Seine-Maritime, 1995.

Loseby, S. T. "Bishops and Cathedrals: Order and Diversity in the Fifth-Century Urban Landscape of Southern Gaul." In Drinkwater and Elton, *Fifth-Century Gaul*, 144–55.

———. "Gregory's Cities: Urban Functions in Sixth-Century Gaul." In Wood, *Franks and Alamanni*, 239–70.

Lucas, A. T. *Cattle in Ancient Ireland*. Studies in Irish Archaeology and History. Kilkenny: Boethius Press, 1989.

———. "The Plundering and Burning of Churches in Ireland: 7th to 16th Centuries." In Etienne Rynne, ed., *North Munster Studies: Essays in Commemoration of Monsignor Michael Molony*, 172–229. Limerick: Thomond Archaeological Society, 1967.

————. "The Sacred Trees of Ireland." *Journal of the Cork Historical and Archaeological Society* 68 (1963): 16–54.

Lutèce: Paris de César à Clovis: [exposition] Musée Carnavalet et Musée National des Thermes et de l'Hôtel de Cluny, 3 mai 1984–printemps 1985. Paris: Société des Amis du Musée Carnavelet, 1984.

Lynn, C. J. "The Iron Age Mound in Navan Fort: A Physical Realization of Celtic Religious Beliefs?" *Emania* 10 (1992): 33–57.

————. "Knockaulin (Dún Ailinne) and Navan: Some Architectural Comparisons." *Emania* 8 (1991): 51–56.

————. "Some 'Early' Ring-Forts and Crannogs." *Journal of Irish Archaeology* 1 (1983): 147–58.

Mabire la Caille, Claire. "La topographie de Melun." In Yves Gallet, ed., *Art et architecture à Melun au Moyen Âge.* Actes du colloque de l'histoire de l'art et de l'archéologie tenu à Melun les 28 et 29 novembre 1998, 81–100. Paris: Picard, 2000.

Macalister, R. A. S. "Temair Breg: A Study of the Remains and Traditions of Tara." *PRIA* 10 (1919): 231–399.

Mac an Bhaird, Alan. "Ptolemy Revisited." *Ainm* 5 (1993): 1–20.

MacCana, Proinsias. "Aspects of the Theme of King and Goddess in Irish Literature." *Études Celtiques* 7 (1955–56): 76–114; 356–413; 8 (1958–59): 59–65.

MacDonald, Aidan. "Aspects of the Monastery and Monastic Life in Adomnán's *Life of Columba*." *Peritia* 3 (1984): 271–302.

Mackie, Gillian. *Early Christian Chapels in the West: Decoration, Function and Patronage.* Toronto: University of Toronto Press, 2003.

MacMullen, Ramsay. *Christianity and Paganism in the Fourth to Eighth Centuries.* New Haven, CT: Yale University Press, 1997.

MacNeill, Máire. *The Festival of Lughnasa: A Study of the Survival of the Celtic Festival of the Beginning of Harvest.* London: Oxford University Press, 1962.

Mac Shamhráin, Ailbhe Seamus. *Church and Polity in Pre-Norman Ireland: The Case of Glendalough.* Maynooth: An Sagart, 1996.

————, ed. *The Island of St. Patrick: Church and Ruling Dynasties in Fingal and Meath, 400–1148.* Portland, OR: Four Courts Press, 2004.

Mallory, J. P., and C. J. Lynn. "Recent Excavations and Speculations on the Navan Complex." *Antiquity* 76 (2002): 532–41.

Maloney, John, and Brian Hobley, eds. *Roman Urban Defences in the West: a Review of Current Research on Urban Defences in the Roman Empire with Special Reference to the Northern Provinces, Based on Papers Presented to the Conference on Roman Urban Defences, Held at the Museum of London on 21–23 March 1980.* London: Council for British Archaeology, 1983.

Manning, Conleth. "References to Church Buildings in the Annals." In Smyth, *Seanchas*, 37–52.

Marion, Stéphane. "Les occupations protohistoriques du sanctuaire de La Bauve à Meaux (Seine-et-Marne)." In O. Buchsenschutz et al., eds., *L'Âge du Fer en Île-de-France.* Actes de XXVIe colloque de l'Association française pour l'étude de l'âge du fer, Paris and Saint-Denis, 9–12 mai 2002, 85–95. Paris: INRAP, 2005.

Marsden, Peter. "London in the 3rd and 4th Centuries." In Francis Grew and Brian Hobley, eds., *Roman Urban Topography in Britain and the Western Empire:* Proceedings of the third conference on urban archaeology organized jointly by the CBA and the Department of Urban Archaeology of the Museum of London, 99–108. London: Council for British Archaeology, 1985.

Martin, F. X. "John, Lord of Ireland, 1185–1216." In Cosgrove, *New History of Ireland* 2: 127–55.

Mason, William Shaw. *A Statistical Account, or Parochial Survey of Ireland.* Dublin: Printed for J. Cumming and N. Mahon, 1814.

Mathisen, Ralph W. *Roman Aristocrats in Barbarian Gaul: Strategies for Survival in an Age of Transition.* Austin: University of Texas Press, 1993.

———. "The 'Second Council of Arles' and the Spirit of Compilation and Codification in Late Roman Gaul." *Journal of Early Christian Studies* 5 (1997): 511–54.

Mathisen, Ralph W., and H. Sivan, eds. *Shifting Frontiers in Late Antiquity.* Brookfield, VT: Variorum, 1996.

McClintock, H. F. "The 'Mantle of St. Brigid' at Bruges." *JRSAI* 6 (1936): 32–40.

McCone, Kim. "Bríd Chill Dara." *Leachtaí Cholm Cille* 12 (1981): 30–91.

———. "Brigit in the Seventh Century: A Saint with Three Lives?" *Peritia* 1 (1982): 107–45.

———. *Pagan Past and Christian Present in Early Irish Literature.* Maynooth: An Sagart, 1990.

McCormick, Michael. *Origins of the European Economy: Communications and Commerce AD 300–900.* Cambridge: Cambridge University Press, 2001.

McKenna, Catherine. "Apotheosis and Evanescence: The Fortunes of Saint Brigit in the Nineteenth and Twentieth Centuries." In Joseph Falaky Nagy, ed., *The Individual in Celtic Literatures,* 74–108. CSANA Yearbook 1. Portland, OR: Four Courts Press, 2001.

———. "Bride's Head Revisited." Paper presented to Center for Medieval and Renaissance Studies, UCLA, November 19, 2004.

McMann, Jean. "Forms of Power: Dimensions of an Irish Megalithic Landscape." *Antiquity* 68 (1994): 511–44.

McNamara, Jo Ann. "Chaste Marriage and Clerical Celibacy." In Vern Bullough and James Brundage, eds., *Sexual Practices and the Medieval Church,* 22–33. Buffalo: Prometheus Books, 1982.

———. *Sisters in Arms: Catholic Nuns through Two Millennia.* Cambridge, MA: Harvard University Press, 1996.

McNamara, Jo Ann, John E. Halborg, and E. Gordon Whatley, eds. and trans. *Sainted Women of the Dark Ages.* Chapel Hill, NC: Duke University Press, 1999.

Miller, Konrad. *Itineraria Romana. Römische reisewege an der hand der tabula Peutengeriana.* Stuttgart: Strecker und Schröder, 1916.

Miller, M. "Date-Guessing and Dyfed." *Studia Celtica* 12–13 (1977–87): 33–61.

Milne, Gustav. *St. Bride's Church, London: Archaeological Research 1952–60 and 1992–5.* English Heritage Archaeological Report 11. London: English Heritage, 1997.

Mirot, Léon. *Manuel de géographie historique de la France. I: L'unité française.* Paris: Picard, 1947.

Mitchell, Frank, and Michael Ryan. *Reading the Irish Landscape*. Dublin: Town House, 1997.

Mitchell, Kathleen, and Ian Wood, eds. *The World of Gregory of Tours*. Boston: Brill, 2002.

Mohrmann, Christine. *The Latin of Saint Patrick: Four Lectures*. Dublin: Dublin Institute for Advanced Studies, 1961.

Montesquiou-Fezensac, Blaise de. "In sexto lapide: l'ancien autel de Saint-Denis et son inscription." *Cahiers Archéologiques* 7 (1954): 51–60.

Mooney, Catherine M. "*Imitatio Christi* or *Imitatio Mariae*? Clare of Assisi and Her Interpreters." In Catherine Mooney, ed., *Gendered Voices: Medieval Saints and Their Interpreters*, 52–77. Philadelphia: University of Pennsylvania Press, 1999.

Moore, Thomas. *The Works of Thomas Moore: Comprehending his melodies, ballads, etc. never before published without the accompanying music*. Vol. 3, *Irish Melodies*. Paris: A. & W. Galignani, 1832.

Moreira, Isabel. "Augustine's Three Visions and Three Heavens in Some Early Medieval Florilegia." *Vivarium* 34 (1996): 1–14.

Mount, Charles. "The Environmental Siting of Early Bronze Age Burials in County Kildare." *JCKAS* 18 (1994–95): 117–28.

Muhlberger, S. "Looking Back from Mid-century: The Gallic Chronicler of 452 and the Crisis of Honorius' Reign." In Drinkwater and Elton, *Fifth-Century Gaul*, 28–37.

Mulder-Bakker, Anneke, and Jocelyn Wogan Browne, eds. *Household, Women, and Christianities in Late Antiquity and the Middle Ages*. Medieval Women: Texts and Contexts. Turnhout: Brepols, 2005.

Murphy, Denis. "Kildare: Its History and Antiquities." *JCKAS* 2 (1898): 289–303.

Muschiol, Gisela. "Men, Women and Liturgical Practice in the Early Medieval West." In Brubaker and Smith, *Gender in the Early Medieval World*, 198–216.

Mytum, Harold. *The Origins of Early Christian Ireland*. New York: Routledge, 1992.

Nagy, Joseph F. *Conversing with Angels and Ancients: Literary Myths of Medieval Ireland*. Ithaca, NY: Cornell University Press, 1997.

Nash, Catherine. "Remapping the Body/Land: New Cartographies of Identity, Gender, and Landscape in Ireland." In Alison Blunt and Gillian Rose, eds., *Writing Women and Space: Colonial and Postcolonial Geographies*, 227–50. New York: Guilford Press, 1994.

Nelson, Robert S. "To Say and to See: Ekphrasis and Vision in Byzantium." In Robert S. Nelson, ed., *Visuality before and beyond the Renaissance: Seeing as Others Saw*, 143–68. New York: Cambridge University Press, 2000.

Neuman de Vegvar, Carol. "*Romanitas* and Realpolitik in Cogitosus' Description of the Church of St. Brigit, Kildare." In Carver, *The Cross Goes North*, 153–70.

Ní Bhrolcháin, Muireann. "The Manuscript Tradition of the Banshenchas." *Ériu* 33 (1982): 109–35.

Niblett, Rosalind. "A New Plan of Roman Verulamium." *Hertfordshire Archaeology* 9 (1987): 21–28.

———. *Roman Verulamium*. St. Albans: St. Albans Museum, 2000.

———. "St. Albans in the Post-Roman Period." In R. Niblett and I. Thompson, eds., *Alban's Buried Towns: An Assessment of St. Albans' Archaeology up to A.D. 1600*, 166–77. Oxford: Oxbow Books in association with English Heritage, 2005.

———. *Verulamium: The Roman City of St. Albans*. Stroud: Tempus, 2001.

Noble, Thomas F. X., ed. *From Roman Provinces to Medieval Kingdoms.* New York: Routledge, 2006.

Noble, Thomas F. X., and Thomas Head, eds. *Soldiers of Christ: Saints and Saints' Lives from Late Antiquity and the Early Middle Ages.* University Park: Pennsylvania State University Press, 1995.

Ó Briain, Felim. "Brigitana." *Zeitschrift für Celtische Philologie* 36 (1977): 112–137.

O'Brien, Elizabeth. "Pagan and Christian Burial in Ireland during the First Millennium A.D.: Continuity and Change." In Nancy Edwards and Alan Lane, eds., *The Early Church in Wales and the West: Recent Work in Early Christian Archaeology, History and Place Names*, 130–37. Oxbow Monograph 16. Oxford: Oxbow, 1992.

Ó Carragáin, Tomás. "The Architectural Setting of the Cult of Relics in Early Medieval Ireland." *JRSAI* 133 (2003): 130–76.

Ó Catháin, Séamas. *The Festival of Brigit: Celtic Goddess and Holy Woman.* Blackrock, Co. Dublin: DBA Publications, 1995.

Ó Cathasaigh, Donal. "The Cult of Brigid: A Study of Pagan-Christian Syncretism in Ireland." In James J. Preston, ed., *Mother Worship: Theme and Variations*, 75–94. Chapel Hill: University of North Carolina Press, 1982.

Ó Cathasaigh, Tomás. "The Déisi and Dyfed." *Éigse* 20 (1984): 1–33.

Ó Corráin, Donnchadh. "Creating the Past: The Early Irish Genealogical Tradition." Caroll Lecture 1992. *Chronicon* 1, no. 2 (1997): 1–32.

———. "The Early Irish Churches: Some Aspects of Organization." In Ó Corráin, *Irish Antiquity*, 327–41.

———, ed. *Irish Antiquity: Essays and Studies Presented to Professor M. J. O'Kelly.* 1981; Blackrock, Co. Dublin; Portland, OR: Four Courts Press, 1994.

———. "Some Legal References to Fences and Fencing in Early Historic Ireland." In T. Reeves-Smyth and F. Hamond, eds., *Landscape Archaeology in Ireland*, 247–51. BAR British Series 116. Oxford: BAR, 1983.

Ó Corráin, Donnchadh, L. Breatnach, and K. McCone, eds. *Sages, Saints and Storytellers: Celtic Studies in Honour of Professor James Carney.* Maynooth: An Sagart, 1989.

Ó Cróinín, Dáibhí. "Cummianus Longus and the Iconography of Christ and the Apostles in Early Irish Literature." In Ó Corráin et al., *Sages, Saints*, 268–79.

———. *Early Irish History and Chronology.* Portland, OR: Four Courts Press, 2003.

———. *Early Medieval Ireland, 400–1200.* Longman History of Ireland. London and New York: Longman, 1995.

———. "New Light on Palladius." *Peritia* 5 (1986): 276–83.

———, ed. *New History of Ireland.* Vol. 1: *Prehistoric and Early Ireland.* Oxford: Oxford University Press, 2005.

Ó Cuív, Brían. "Some Items from Irish Tradition." *Éigse* 11 (1964/66): 167–87.

Ó Giolláin, Diarmuid. *Locating Irish Folklore: Tradition, Modernity, Identity.* Sterling, VA: Stylus, 2000.

Ó hAodha, Donncha. "The Lament of the Old Woman of Beare." In Ó Corráin et al., *Sages, Saints*, 308–31.

O'Loughlin, Thomas. "The Exegetical Purpose of Adomnán's *De Locis Sanctis*." *Cambridge Medieval Celtic Studies* 24 (1992): 37–53.

———. "The Tombs of the Saints: Their Significance for Adomnán." In Carey et al., *Studies in Irish Hagiography,* 15–30.

———. "The View from Iona: Adomnán's Mental Maps." *Peritia* 10 (1996): 98–122.

Olster, David. "From Periphery to Center: The Transformation of Late Roman Self-Definition in the Seventh Century." In Mathisen and Sivan, *Shifting Frontiers in Late Antiquity,* 93–100.

O'Rahilly, Thomas. *Early Irish History and Mythology.* Dublin: Dublin Institute for Advanced Studies, 1946.

Ó Riain, Pádraig. "The Irish Element in Welsh Hagiographical Tradition." In Ó Corráin, *Irish Antiquity,* 291–303.

———. "Towards a Methodology in Early Irish Hagiography." *Peritia* 1 (1982): 146–59.

Ottaway, Patrick. *Archaeology in British Towns: From the Emperor Claudius to the Black Death.* New York: Routledge, 1992.

Patterson, Nerys Thomas. *Cattle-Lords and Clansmen: The Social Structure of Early Ireland.* Notre Dame, IN: University of Notre Dame Press, 1994.

Pearce, Susan M. "Processes of Conversion in North-west Roman Gaul." In Carver, *The Cross Goes North,* 61–78.

Pender, Séamus. "Guide to Irish Genealogical Collections." *Analecta Hibernica.* 7. Dublin: Stationery Office, 1935.

Percival, John. "The Fifth-Century Villa: New Life or Death Postponed?" In Drinkwater and Elton, *Fifth-Century Gaul,* 156–64.

———. *The Roman Villa: An Historical Introduction.* London: Batsford, 1976.

Périn, Patrick. "Paris: Églises des Saints-Apôtres ou Saint-Pierre." In Duval, *Premiers monuments chrétiens,* 159–64.

———. "Paris mérovingien, *sedes regia.*" *Klio* 71 (1989): 487–506.

———. "Saint-Denis: Église Saint-Denis." In Duval, *Premiers monuments chrétiens,* 209–18.

———. "La tombe de Clovis." In *Media in Francia. Recueil de mélanges offerts à Karl-Ferdinand Werner à l'occasion de son 65e anniversaire par ses amis et collègues français,* 363–78. Mauleivrier: Hérault-Editions, 1989.

Peytremann, Édith. "Les structures d'habitat rural du haut Moyen Âge en France (Ve–Xe s.)" In Lorren and Périn, *L'habitat rural,* 1–28.

Picard, Jean-Charles. "Auxerre." In Picard, *Province ecclésiastique de Sens,* 52–65.

———. "Espace urbain et sépultures épiscopales." *Revue d'histoire de l'église de France* 62 (1976): 205–22.

———. "L'évolution des lieux de sepulture au haut moyen âge." In *Évêques, saints et cités en Italie et en Gaule: Études d'archéologie et d'histoire.* Collection de l'École Française de Rome 242 (1998): 311–20.

Picard, Jean-Charles, ed. *Province Ecclésiastique de Sens (Ludunensis Senonia).* In Gauthier and Picard, *Topographie chrétienne.* Vol 8.

Picard, J.-M. "Structural Patterns in Early Hiberno-Latin Hagiography." *Peritia* 4 (1985): 67–82.

Pietri, C. "Evergétisme et richesses ecclésiastiques dans l'Italie du IVe à la fin du Ve siècle." *Ktema* 3 (1978): 317–37.

Pietri, L. "'Loca Sancta': La Géographie de la saintété dans l'hagiographie gauloise (IVe–VIe s.)." In Sofia Boesch Gajano and Lucetta Scaraffia, eds., *Luoghi Sacri e Spazi della Santità*, 23–35. Torino: Rosenberg and Sellier, 1990.

———. "Les sépultres privilegiés en Gaule d'après les sources litteraires." In Y. Duval and J.-Ch. Picard, eds., *L'inhumation privilegiée du IVe au VIIIe siècle en Occident: Actes du colloque tenu à Creteil les 16–18 mai 1984*, 133–42. Paris: de Boccard, 1986.

Piggott, Stuart. *The Druids*. New York: Thames and Hudson, 1985.

Pilet, C. *La nécropole de Frénouville*. 2 vols. BAR International Series 83. Oxford: BAR, 1980.

Pluskowski, Aleks, and Philippa Patrick. "'How Do You Pray to God?': Fragmentation and Variety in Early Medieval Christianity." In Carver, *The Cross Goes North*, 29–57.

Pollard, Mary E. *In Search of St. Brigid, Foundress of Kildare*. [Kildare: Saint Brigid's Cathedral,] 1988.

Poulin, Josephe-Claude. "Les cinq premières vitae de sainte Geneviève. Analyse formelle, comparaison, essai de datation." *Journal des Savants* (1983): 81–150. Repr. in Heinzelmann and Poulin, *Vies Anciennes*, 113–89.

Prévot, Françoise. "De la tombe sainte au sanctuaire: L'example de trois basiliques de Clermont d'après Grégoire de Tours." In Gauthier and Galinié, *Grégoire de Tours*, 209–16.

Rae, E. C. "Architecture and Sculpture, 1169–1603." In Cosgrove, *New History of Ireland* 2: 737–80.

Raftery, Barry. "The Conundrum of Irish Iron Age Pottery." In B. Raftery, ed., with Vincent Megaw and Val Rigby. *Sites and Sights of the Iron Age: Essays on Fieldwork and Museum Research Presented to Ian Mathieson Stead*, 147–56. Oxbow Monograph 56. Oxford: Oxbow, 1995.

———. "Iron Age Burials in Ireland." In Ó Corráin, *Irish Antiquity*, 173–204.

———. "Iron-Age Ireland," in Ó Cróinín, *New History of Ireland* 1:134–81.

———. "Iron Age Studies in Ireland: Some Recent Developments." In Champion and Collis, *Iron Age*, 155–61.

———. *Pagan Celtic Ireland: The Enigma of the Irish Iron Age*. New York: Thames and Hudson, 1994.

Rapp, Claudia. *Holy Bishops in Late Antiquity: The Nature of Christian Leadership in an Age of Transition*. Berkeley: University of California Press, 2005.

Reece, R. "The Third Century: Crisis or Change?" In King and Henig, *Roman West*, 27–38.

Reynaud, Jean François. "Les morts dans les cités épiscopales de Gaule du IVe au XIe siècle." In Galinié and Zadora-Rio, *Archéologie du cimetière chrétien*, 23–30.

Rey-Vodoz, Véronique. "La Suisse dans l'Europe des sanctuaires gallo-romains." In Goudineau et al., *Sanctuaires de tradition indigène*, 7–16.

Richards, Melville. "The Irish Settlements in South-west Wales." *JRSAI* 90 (1960): 133–62.

Rivet, A. L. F. and Colin Smith. *The Place-Names of Roman Britain*. Princeton, NJ: Princeton University Press, 1979.

Robertson, David A. "The Navan Forty Metre Structure: Some Observations Regarding the Social Context of an Iron Age Monument." *Emania* 10 (1992): 25–32.

Robinson, D. J. "The Romans and Ireland Again: Some Thoughts on Tacitus' *Agricola*, Chapter 24." *Journal of the Chester Archaeological Society* 75 (2000): 19–31.

Roblin, Michel. "Fontaines sacrées et nécropoles antiques, deux sites fréquents d'églises paroissiales rurales dans les sept anciens diocèses de l'Oise." *Revue d'Histoire de l'Église de France* 62 (1976): 235–51.

———. *Le Terroir de Paris aux époques gallo-romaine et franque: Peuplement et défrichement dans la Civitas des Parisii (Seine, Seine-et-Oise)*. Paris: Picard, 1971.

Rodgers, René. "Female Representation in Roman Art: Feminising the Provincial 'Other.'" In Scott and Webster, *Roman Imperialism and Provincial Art*, 69–93.

Rodwell, Warwick. "The Role of the Church in the Development of Roman and Early Anglo-Saxon London." In Martin Carver, ed., *In Search of Cult: Archaeological Investigations in Honour of Philip Rahtz*, 91–99. Rochester, NY: Boydell Press, 1993.

Rosenwein, Barbara. *Negotiating Space: Power, Restraint, and Privileges of Immunity in Early Medieval Europe*. Ithaca, NY: Cornell University Press, 1999.

Rousselle, Aline. *Croire et guérir: La foi en Gaule dans l'Antiquité tardive*. Paris: Fayard, 1990.

Roymans, Nico. "The Sword or the Plough: Regional Dynamics in the Romanisation of Belgic Gaul and the Rhineland Area." In N. Roymans, ed., *From the Sword to the Plough: Three Studies on the Earliest Romanisation of Northern Gaul*, 9–125. Amsterdam: Amsterdam University Press, 1996.

Rykwert, Joseph. *The Idea of a Town: The Anthropology of Urban Form in Rome, Italy and the Ancient World*. Princeton, NJ: Princeton University Press, 1976.

Rynne, Etienne. "The La Tène and Roman Finds from Lambay, County Dublin: A Reassessment." *PRIA* 76 C (1976): 231–43.

Sapin, Christian. "Architecture and Funerary Space in the Early Middle Ages." In Kelly M. Wickham-Crowley and Bailey K. Young, eds., *Spaces of the Living and the Dead: An Archaeological Dialogue*, 39–60. Oxford: Oxbow, 1999.

Saradi-Mendelovici, Helen. "Christian Attitudes toward Pagan Monuments in Late Antiquity and Their Legacy in Later Byzantine Centuries." *Dumbarton Oaks Papers* 44 (1990): 47–61.

Scheid, John. "Épigraphie et sanctuaires guérisseurs en Gaule." *Mélanges de l'École française de Rome: Antiquité* 104 (1992): 25–40.

———. "Sanctuaires et thermes sous l'Empire." In *Les thermes romains:* Actes de la table ronde organisée par l'École française de Rome: Rome, 11–12 novembre, 1988, 205–16. Collection de École Française de Rome 142. Rome: L'Ecole, Palais Farnèse, 1991.

Schmid, Toni. "Le culte en Suède de Sainte Brigide l'Irlandaise." *Analecta Bollandiana* 108 (19898): 108–15.

Schmidt, Joël. *Sainte Geneviève et la fin de la Gaule romaine*. Pairs: Perrin, 1990.

Schulenberg, Jane Tibbetts. *Forgetful of Their Sex: Female Sanctity and Society, ca. 500–1100*. Chicago: University of Chicago Press, 1998.

Scott, Sarah. "Provincial Art and Roman Imperialism: An Overview." In Scott and Webster, eds., *Roman Imperialism and Provincial Art*, 1–8.

Scott, Sarah, and Jane Webster, eds. *Roman Imperialism and Provincial Art*. New York: Cambridge University Press, 2003.

Scowcroft, R. Mark. "Leabhar Gabhála, I: The Growth of the Text." *Ériu* 38 (1987): 81–142.

Sellner, Edward. "Brigit of Kildare: A Study in the Liminality of Women's Spiritual Power." *Cross Currents* 39 (1989–90): 402–19.

Sharpe, Richard. "The Late Antique Passion of St. Alban." In Martin Henig and Phillip Lindley, eds., *Alban and St. Albans: Roman Medieval Architecture, Art and Archaeology*, 30–37. British Archaeological Association Conference Transactions 24. Leeds: British Archaeological Association and Maney Publishing, 2001.

———. "Martyrs and Local Saints in Late Antique Britain." In Thacker and Sharpe, *Local Saints*, 75–154.

———. *Medieval Irish Saints' Lives: An Introduction to the Vitae Sanctorum Hiberniae.* New York: Oxford University Press, 1991.

———. "'*Vitae Sanctae Brigidae*': The Oldest Texts." *Peritia* 1 (1982): 81–106.

Sluhovsky, Moshe. *Patroness of Paris: Rituals of Devotion in Early Modern France.* New York: Brill, 1998.

Smith, Brendan, ed. *Britain and Ireland 900–1300: Insular Responses to Medieval European Changes.* Cambridge: Cambridge University Press, 1999.

Smyth, A. P. *Celtic Leinster: Towards an Historical Geography of Early Irish Civilization, A.D. 500–1600.* Blackrock, Co. Dublin: Irish Academic Press, 1982.

———. "The Effect of Scandinavian Raiders on the English and Irish Churches: A Preliminary Reassessment." In Smith, *Britain and Ireland 900–1300*, 1–38.

———, ed. *Seanchas: Studies in Early and Medieval Irish Archaeology, History and Literature in Honour of Francis J. Byrne.* Dublin: Four Courts Press, 2000.

Snyder, Christopher A. *An Age of Tyrants: Britain and the Britons, A.D. 400–600.* University Park: Pennsylvania State University Press, 1998.

Soja, Edward, W. *Postmodern Geographies: The Reassertion of Space in Critical Social Theory.* New York: Verso, 1989.

Sorel, Phillipe. "Le choix du site." In *Lutèce: Paris de César à Clovis*, 87–88.

Sotinel, Claire. "Le personnel épiscopal: Enquête sur la puissance de l'évêque dans la cité." In Eric Rebillard and Claire Sotinel, eds., *L'Évêque dans la cité du IVe au Ve siècle: Image et autorité: Actes de la table ronde organisée par l'Istituto Patristico Augustinianum et l'École française de Rome: Rome, 1er et 2 décembre 1995*, 105–26. Rome: École Française de Rome, 1998.

Sparey-Green, Christopher. "The Cemetery of a Romano-British Christian Community at Poundbury, Dorchester, Dorset." In Susan M. Pearce, ed., *The Early Church in Western Britain and Ireland*, 61–76. BAR British Series 102. Oxford: Oxbow, 1982.

———. "Where Are the Christians? Late Roman Cemeteries in Britain." In Carver, *The Cross Goes North*, 93–107.

Stancliffe, Clare. *St. Martin and His Hagiographer: History and Miracle in Sulpicius Severus.* New York: Oxford University Press, 1983.

Stevens, Susan T. "Transitional Neighborhoods and Suburban Frontiers in Late- and Post-Roman Carthage." In Mathisen and Sivan, *Shifting Frontiers*, 187–200.

Stout, Matthew. "Early Christian Ireland: Settlement and Environment." In Barry, *History of Settlement in Ireland*, 81–109.

———. *The Irish Ringfort.* Dublin: Four Courts Press, in association with the Group for the Study of Irish Historic Settlement, 1997.

Swan, Leo. "Ecclesiastical Settlement in Ireland in the Early Medieval Period." In M. Fixot and E. Zadora-Rio, eds., *L'environnement des églises et la topographie religieuse des campagnes médiévales: Actes du IIIe Congrès international et d'archéologie médiévale: Aix-en-Provence, 28–30 septembre, 1989*, 50–56. Paris: Éditions de la Maison des Sciences de l'Homme, 1994.

Swift, Catherine. *Ogham Stones and the Earliest Irish Christians*. Maynooth: Cardinal Press, 1997.

———. "Patrick, Skerries and the Earliest Evidence for Local Church Organization in Ireland." In Mac Shamhráin, *Island of St. Patrick*, 61–78.

Taft, Robert F. "Women at Church in Byzantium: Where, When—and Why?" *Dumbarton Oaks Papers* 52 (1998): 27–87.

Thacker, Alan. "Loca Sanctorum." In Thacker and Sharpe, *Local Saints*, 1–43.

———. "Peculiaris patronus noster: The Saint as Patron of the State in the Early Middle Ages." In J. R. Maddicott and D. M. Palliser, eds., *The Medieval State: Essays Presented to James Campbell*, 1–24. Rio Grande, OH: Hambledon Press, 2001.

Thacker, Alan, and Richard Sharpe, eds. *Local Saints and Local Churches in the Early Medieval West*. New York: Oxford University Press, 2002.

Thesaurus cultus et rituum antiquorum (ThesCRA). 5 vols. Los Angeles, CA: J. Paul Getty Museum, 2004.

Thomas, Charles. *Celtic Britain*. London: Thames and Hudson, 1986.

———. *Christianity in Roman Britain to A.D. 500*. Berkeley: University of California Press, 1981.

———. "Early Medieval Munster: Thoughts upon Its Primary Christian Phrase." In Michael A. Monk and John Sheehan, eds., *Early Medieval Munster: Archaeology, History, and Society*, 9–16. Cork: Cork University Press, 1998.

———. "Imported Late-Roman Mediterranean Pottery in Ireland and Western Britain: Chronologies and Implications." *PRIA* 76 C (1976): 245–65.

———. "Palladius and Patrick." In Mac Shamhráin, *Island of St. Patrick*, 13–37.

Torma, Thomas. "This Woman Alone: Approaches to the Earliest Vitae of Brigit of Kildare." Ph.D. diss., University of Edinburgh, 2001.

Treffort, Cécile. "Du *cimiterium christianorum* au cimetière paroissal: Évolution des espaces funéraires en Gaule du VIe au Xe siècle." In Galinié and Zadora-Rio, *Archéologie du cimetière chrétien*, 55–63.

Van Andringa, William. ed. *Archéologie des sanctuaires en Gaule romaine*. Saint-Étienne: Publications de l'Université de Saint-Étienne, 2000.

———. *La religion en Gaule romaine: Piété et politique (1er-IIIe siècle apr. J.-C.)*. Paris: Éditions Errance, 2002.

———. "Le vase de Sains-du-Nord et le culte de l'*imago* dans les sanctuaires gallo-romains." In Van Andringa, *Archéologie des sanctuaires en Gaule romaine*, 27–43.

Van Dam, Raymond. *Leadership and Community in Late Antique Gaul*. Berkeley: University of California Press, 1985.

———. "The Pirenne Thesis and Fifth-Century Gaul." In Drinkwater and Elton, *Fifth-Century Gaul*, 321–33.

———. *Saints and Their Miracles in Late Antique Gaul*. Princeton, NJ: Princeton University Press, 1993.

Van Houts, Elisabeth. *Memory and Gender in Medieval Europe, 900–1200.* Toronto: Toronto University Press, 1999.

Van Ossel, Paul. "L'antiquité tardive (IVe–Ve s.) dans l'Île-de-France: Acquis et incertitudes." In Lorren and Périn, *L'habitat rural,* 63–79.

Van Uytfanghe, Marc. "La Bible dans les Vies de saints mérovingiennes." *Revue d'Histoire de l'Église de France* 62 (1976): 103–12.

Verkerk, Dorothy Hoogland. "Pilgrimage *ad Limina Apostolorum* in Rome: Irish Crosses and Early Christian Sarcophagi." In Colum Hourihane, ed., *From Ireland Coming: Irish Art from the Early Christian to the Late Gothic Period and Its European Context,* 9–26. Princeton, NJ: Index of Christian Art, Department of Art and Archeology, Princeton University in association with Princeton University Press, 2001.

Vieillard-Troïekoff, May. "Les chapiteaux de marbre du Haut Moyen-Âge à Saint-Denis." *Gesta* 15 (1976): 105–12.

———. *Les monuments religieux de la Gaule d'après les oeuvres de Grégoire de Tours.* Paris: H. Champion, 1976.

———. "Les anciennes églises suburbaines de Paris." *Mémoires.* Vol. 11: 17–279. Paris: Fédération des Sociétés historiques et archéologiques de Paris et de l'Ile-de-France, 1960.

Waddell, John. "The Irish Sea in Prehistory." *Journal of Irish Archaeology* 6 (1991–92): 29–40.

Wailes, Bernard. "Excavations at Dún Ailinne, Co. Kildare." *JRSAI* 100 (1970): 79–90.

———. "Excavations at Dún Ailinne, Near Kilcullen." *JCKAS* 14 (1970): 507–17; 15 (1971): 5–11.

Ward-Perkins, Bryan. *From Classical Antiquity to the Middle Ages: Urban Public Building in Northern and Central Italy, A.D. 300–850.* New York: Oxford University Press, 1984.

———. *The Fall of Rome and the End of Civilization.* Oxford: Oxford University Press, 2005.

Waterman, D. *Excavations at Navan Fort 1961–71.* Completed by C. J. Lynn. Belfast: Stationery Office, 1997.

Watson, Alden. "The King, the Poet and the Sacred Tree." *EC* 18 (1981): 165–81.

Watson, Bruce. "'Dark Earth' and Urban Decline in Late Roman London." In Watson, *Roman London,* 100–106.

———, ed. *Roman London: Recent Archaeological Work Including Papers Given at a Seminar Held at the Museum of London on 16 November, 1996.* Journal of Roman Archaeology Supplementary Series 24. Portsmouth, RI: Journal of Roman Archaeology, 1998.

Watts, Dorothy. *Christians and Pagans in Roman Britain.* New York: Routledge, 1991.

Webb, Ruth. "The Aesthetics of Sacred Space: Narrative, Metaphor, and Motion in Ekphraseis of Church Buildings." *Dumbarton Oaks Papers* 53 (1999): 59–74.

Weber, Gerhard. "Les sanctuaires de tradition indigène en Allemagne romain." In Goudineau, Fauduet and Coulon, *Sanctuaires de tradition indigène,* 17–23.

Webster, Jane. "Art as Resistance and Negotiation." In Scott and Webster, *Roman Imperialism and Provincial Art,* 24–51.

Wharton, Anabel Jane. *Refiguring the Postclassical City: Dura Europus, Jerashi, Jerusalem and Ravenna.* Cambridge: Cambridge University Press, 1995.

Whittaker, C. W. *Frontiers of the Roman Empire: A Social and Economic Study.* Baltimore: Johns Hopkins University Press, 1994.

Wickham, Chris. *Early Medieval Italy: Central Power and Local Society, 400–1000.* 1981; Ann Arbor: University of Michigan Press, 1989.

Wierschowski, Lothar. *Die regionale Mobilität in Gallien nach den Inschriften des 1. bis 3. Jahrhunderts n. Chr.: Quantitative Studien zur Sozial- und Wirtschaftsgeschichte der westlichen Provinzen des römischen Reiches.* Historia Einzelschriften 91. Stuttgart: Franz Steiner Verlag, 1995.

Wightman, Edith M. "The Towns of Gaul with Special Reference to the North-East." In M. W. Barley, ed., *European Towns, Their Archaeology and Early History.* New York: Published for the Council for British Archeology by Academic Press, 1977.

Wilkinson, Adrian. "St. Brigid's Cathedral, Kildare, and the Challenge of Disestablishment." *JCKAS* 19 (2000–2001): 96–115.

Williams, B. B. "Excavations at Ballyutoag, County Antrim." *Ulster Journal of Archaeology* 47 (1984): 37–49.

Wolfram, Herwig. *Das Reich und die Germanen: Zwischen Antike un Mittelalter.* Berlin: Seidler, 1990. Translated by T. Dunlap and published as *The Roman Empire and Its Germanic Peoples.* Berkeley: University of California Press, 1997.

Wood, I. N. "Constructing Cults in Early Medieval France: Local Saints and Local Churches in Burgundy and the Auvergne, 400–1000." In Thacker and Sharpe, *Local Saints,* 155–87.

———. "Early Merovingian Devotion in Town and Country." *Studies in Church History* 16 (1979): 61–76.

———, ed. *Franks and Alamanni in the Merovingian Period: An Ethnographic Perspective.* Rochester, NY: Boydell Press; San Marino: Center for Interdisciplinary Research on Social Stress, 1998.

———. "Pagan Religions and Superstitions East of the Rhine." In G. Ausenda, ed., *After Empire: Towards an Ethnology of Europe's Barbarians,* 253–79. Rochester, NY: Boydell Press; San Marino (R.S.M.): Center for Interdisciplinary Research on Social Stress, 1995.

Wooding, Jonathan M. *Communication and Commerce along the Western Sealanes, A.D. 400–800.* BAR International Series 654. Oxford: Tempus Reparatum, 1996.

Woolf, Greg. *Becoming Roman: The Origins of Provincial Civilization in Gaul.* New York: Cambridge University Press, 1998.

———. "Pagan Religions and Superstitions East of the Rhine." In G. Ausenda, ed., *After Empire: Towards an Ethnology of Europe's Barbarians,* 253–79. Rochester, NY: Boydell Press; San Marino (R.S.M.): Center for Interdisciplinary Research on Social Stress, 1995.

———. "Representation as Cult: The Case of the Jupiter Columns." In W. Spickermann, H. Cancik, and J. Rüpke, eds., *Religion in den germanischen Provinzen Roms,* 117–34. Tübingen: Mohr Sieback, 2001.

———. "Urbanization and Its Discontents in Early Roman Gaul." In Fentress, *Romanization and the City,* 115–31.

Woolf, Greg. "The Uses of Forgetfulness in Roman Gaul." In H-J. Gehrke and A. Möller, eds., *Vergangenheit und Lebenswelt. Soziale Kommunikation, Traditionsbuildung und historisches Bewußtsein,* 361–81. Tübingen: Narr, 1996.

Wyss, Michaël and Nicole Meyer Rodrigues, eds. *Atlas historique de Saint-Denis: Des origins au XVIII siècle.* Paris: Éditions de la Maison des Sciences de l'Homme, 1996.

———. *Saint Denis: A Town in the Middle Ages.* "The Tomb of Saint Denis." http://www. saint-denis.culture.fr/en/1_2a1_ville.htm.

Yasin, Ann Marie. "Commemorating the Dead—Constructing the Community: Church Space, Funerary Monuments and Saints' Cults in Late Antiquity," Ph.D. diss., University of Chicago, 2002.

Yeats, William Butler. *The Celtic Twilight.* Repr. London: A. H. Bullen, 1902. http:// www.gutenberg.org/files/10459/10459.txt.

Yorke, Barbara. "The Bonifacian Mission and Female Religious in Wessex." *Early Medieval Europe* 7 (1998): 145–72.

Young, Bailey, K. "Paganisme, christianisation et rites funéraires mérovingiens." *Archéologie Médiévale* 7 (1977): 5–81.

———. "Que restait-il de l'ancien paysage religieux à l'époque de Grégoire de Tours?" In Gauthier and Galinié, *Grégoire de Tours,* 241–50.

Young, Simon. "Donatus Bishop of Fiesole (829–76) and the Cult of St. Brigit in Italy." *Cambrian Medieval Celtic Studies* 35 (1998): 13–26.

———. "St. Brigit in a Medieval Welsh Poem." *Peritia* 15 (2002): 279.

Zanker, Paul. "The City as Symbol: Rome and the Creation of an Urban Image." In Fentress, *Romanization and the City,* 25–41.

ELECTRONIC SOURCES

Bibliothèque Sainte-Geneviève. http://www.bsg.univ-paris1.fr/home.htm.

Clement, Mark, and AMGR. *REMUS.* Wellin: Cyberlab, 2005. http://www.remus. museum/html/en/index.php.

Célébrations nationale 2001. "Sainte Geneviève." Ministère de la Culture at la Communication. Actualités. Événements. http://www.culture.gouv.fr/culture/actualites/ celebrations2002/manifstgenevieve.htm.

Celtic Inscribed Stones Project. Ed. Mark Handley, Kris Lockyear, et al. London: University College London Department of Archaeology, 2000–. http://www.ucl. ac.uk/archaeology/cisp/database/.

Leycock, Dermot. "St. Brigid's Parish, Killester, Dublin, Ireland." St. Brigid's Parish, Killester, Parish Archives. http://www.killester.dublindiocese.ie/relic.htm.

Musée National du Moyen Âge. Thermes et hôtel de Cluny: Collections. http://www. musee-moyenage.fr.

O'Riordan, Sr. Mary, CSB. "Early History of the Congregation." *The Brigidine Sisters.* History. http://www.brigidine.org.au/about/early.asp.

Pimpaud, Alban-Brice, et al. *Paris: A Roman City.* Paris: Ministère de la Culture et de la Communication, 2003. http://www.culture.gouv.fr/culture/arcnat/paris/en/ index.html.

Site archéologique de Grand (Vosges). http://www.exagonline.com/grand/site/eng/
site.htm.

Société Archéologique d'Escolives. http://membres.lycos.fr/archeoescolives.

*Solas Bhríde: Christian Community Centre for Celtic Spirituality in the Spirit of Brigid of
Kildare*. http://www.solasbhride.ie/flame-of-brigid.htm.

VROMA: A Virtual Community for Teaching and Learning Classics. http://www.
vroma.org.

White, Kevan W. *Roman Britain*. http://www.roman-britain.org/places._sin.htm#
civitates.

Index